Electoral Systems and Democracy

A *Journal of Democracy* Book

•

BOOKS IN THE SERIES

Edited by Larry Diamond and Marc F. Plattner

Assessing the Quality of Democracy (2005)
(Edited by Larry Diamond and Leonardo Morlino)

World Religions and Democracy (2005)
(with Philip J. Costopoulos)

Islam and Democracy in the Middle East (2003)
(with Daniel Brumberg)

Emerging Market Democracies: East Asia & Latin America (2002)
(Edited by Laurence Whitehead)

Democracy after Communism (2002)

Political Parties and Democracy (2001)
(Edited by Larry Diamond and Richard Gunther)

The Global Divergence of Democracies (2001)

Globalization, Power, and Democracy (2000)
(Edited by Marc F. Plattner and Aleksander Smolar)

The Democratic Invention (2000)
(Edited by Marc F. Plattner and João Carlos Espada)

Democratization in Africa (1999)

Democracy in East Asia (1998)

Consolidating the Third Wave Democracies (1997)
(with Yun-han Chu and Hung-mao Tien)

Civil-Military Relations and Democracy (1996)

The Global Resurgence of Democracy, 2nd ed. (1996)

Economic Reform and Democracy (1995)

Nationalism, Ethnic Conflict, and Democracy (1994)

Capitalism, Socialism, and Democracy Revisited (1993)

Published under the auspices of
the International Forum for Democratic Studies

Electoral Systems and Democracy

*Edited by Larry Diamond and
Marc F. Plattner*

The Johns Hopkins University Press

Baltimore

9 8 7 6 5 4 3 2 1

Chapters in this volume appeared in the following issues of the *Journal of Democracy:*
chapter 6, Winter 1991; chapters 7–9, Summer 1991; chapter 10, January 1993; chapter
11, April 1995; chapters 12–13, October 1995; chapter 14, April 2000; chapter 15, January
2001; chapter 16, October 2001; chapters 3, 5, April 2002; chapter 1, October 2003;
chapter 4, April 2004; chapters 2, 17–19, April 2006. For all reproduction rights, please
contact the Johns Hopkins University Press.

The Johns Hopkins University Press
2715 North Charles Street
Baltimore, Maryland 21218-4363
www.press.jhu.edu

Library of Congress Cataloging-in-Publication Data

Electoral systems and democracy / edited by Larry Diamond and Marc F. Plattner.
    p. cm. — (A journal of democracy book)
Includes bibliographical references and index.
    ISBN 0-8018-8474-8 (hardcover : alk. paper) — ISBN 0-8018-8475-6 (pbk. :
alk. paper)
    1. Representative government and representation—Case studies. 2. Democ-
racy—Case studies. 3. Elections—Case studies. I. Diamond, Larry Jay. II. Plattner,
Marc F., 1945– III. Series.

JF1051.E54 2006
320.6'3—dc22

                                                                2006016498

A catalog record for this book is available from the British Library.

CONTENTS

Acknowledgments   vii

Introduction, *Larry Diamond and Marc F. Plattner*   ix

I. Electoral Systems and Institutional Design

1. A Primer for Decision Makers,
   Donald L. Horowitz   3

2. A Global Snapshot,
   Richard W. Soudriette and Andrew Ellis   16

3. Dealing with Divided Societies,
   Benjamin Reilly   27

4. The Case for Power Sharing,
   Arend Lijphart   42

5. The Impact of Federalism,
   R. Kent Weaver   56

II. Is Proportional Representation Best?

6. Constitutional Choices for New Democracies,
   Arend Lijphart   73

7. The Problem with PR,
   Guy Lardeyret   86

8. PR and Democratic Statecraft,
   Quentin L. Quade   92

9. Double-Checking the Evidence,
   Arend Lijphart   98

10. The Primacy of the Particular,
    Ken Gladdish   105

III. Country and Regional Experiences

11. Constitutional Engineering in Southern Africa,
    Andrew Reynolds   121

12. Comment: Elections in Agrarian Societies,
    Joel D. Barkan   135

13. Rejoinder: The Case for Proportionality,
    Andrew Reynolds   146

14. Electoral Reform and Stability in Uruguay,
Jeffrey Cason   154

15. Devaluing the Vote in Latin America,
Richard Snyder and David Samuels   168

16. Why Direct Election Failed in Israel,
Emanuele Ottolenghi   182

17. The Politics of Reform in Japan and Taiwan,
Jih-wen Lin   196

18. The Curious Case of Afghanistan,
Andrew Reynolds   210

19. Iraq's Year of Voting Dangerously,
Adeed Dawisha and Larry Diamond   224

Index   239

ACKNOWLEDGMENTS

Electoral Systems and Democracy is the eighteenth volume in the *Journal of Democracy* book series, which was launched in 1993. During our long partnership with the John Hopkins University Press, we have published books focusing on democracy in every region of the world. Other *Journal of Democracy* books have addressed democracy's relation to many key thematic issues, including world religions, economic reform, civil-military relations, political parties, and nationalism. This newest book focuses on electoral systems, an essential democratic institution that can have a major impact on the functioning and consolidation of democracy. The chapters in this volume have been grouped into three sections: The first considers the variety of electoral systems worldwide and their advantages and drawbacks; the second focuses more precisely on the debate over the strengths and weaknesses of proportional representation (PR); and the third consists of a series of case studies that illuminate the consequences of differing electoral systems in Southern Africa, Latin America, Israel, Japan, Taiwan, Afghanistan, and Iraq.

Unlike some other *Journal of Democracy* books, this one is not drawn from papers prepared for a major conference on the topic. The *Journal* has always had a strong interest in institutional questions in general, and in electoral systems in particular. Our articles on this subject, including several of those included here, date all the way back to 1991, and we have continued to grapple with it ever since. Most recently, in the April 2006 issue, the *Journal* featured a cluster of four essays on electoral systems, and these too are included in the present volume. Thus this book has been some sixteen years in the making, and it encompasses not only the latest thinking on the topic, but also a number of now classic essays by some of the world's most eminent political scientists. Sadly, two of the senior scholars whose contributions appear in these pages, Ken Gladdish and Quentin L. Quade, have since passed away.

As the essays collected here span so long a time frame, they have benefited from the editorial contributions of a host of staff members and interns who have worked at the *Journal* over the years. Foremost among them has been our long-time executive editor Phil Costopoulos, who, except for a brief hiatus, has been with the *Journal* since its founding. Other members of the current editorial team, including Anja Håvedal (who is about to depart for a position in Afghanistan), Sumi Shane, and Zerxes Spencer, all had a hand in editing some of these essays when they first appeared in the *Journal*, and they were joined by our managing editor Sarah Bloxham and new assistant editor Eric Kramon in proofreading this volume. This is Sarah's first *Journal of Democracy* book, and she has done a superb job of handling its production, displaying a remarkable ability to maintain her calm demeanor even as publishing deadlines rapidly approach.

Finally, we are pleased to recognize once again those who have been steadfast in encouraging and supporting our work. The Lynde and Harry Bradley Foundation has continued to provide invaluable financial assistance. The board of directors of the National Endowment for Democracy and its president, Carl Gershman, have always given us their full backing. Our long and fruitful relationship with the Johns Hopkins University Press extends both to its journals division, where we work closely with Carol Hamblen and Bill Breichner, and to its book division, where we continue to benefit from the advice and expertise of executive editor Henry Tom, the guiding spirit behind the *Journal of Democracy* book series.

INTRODUCTION

Larry Diamond and Marc F. Plattner

Among the many factors that shape the character and viability of democracy around the world, electoral-system design holds a special fascination for democratic scholars and practitioners. Most of the facilitating factors for democratic development change only slowly, and not entirely by design. It may take many years (at least) to build a democratic political culture, an active and pluralistic civil society, and the administrative infrastructure of an effective state. And generating a relatively developed economy, with a sizeable middle class and only moderate levels of inequality, is a challenge that for many poor countries today must be measured in decades. Yet the institutional architecture of a country's political system can be changed relatively quickly. With some amendments to the constitution or the writing of a new one, a country may go from being unitary to federal or presidential to parliamentary. Often, the electoral system may be changed by legislation alone, even without a constitutional amendment. Among the many structural and historical variables that affect democracy, few are more open to rapid and intentionally designed change than the electoral system.

Adding to the fascination is the powerful accumulation of theory and evidence indicating that the design of the electoral system does matter quite a lot for the nature of the party system and the character of politics and public policy. Particularly in combination with a few other key variables, such as the structure of the executive (presidential or parliamentary) and the vertical distribution of power (unitary or federal), the electoral system can shape the coherence of party control of government, the stability of elected governments, the breadth and legitimacy of representation, the capacity of the system to manage conflict, the extent of public participation, and the overall responsiveness of the system. These dimensions of democratic character and quality, in turn, may well determine whether democracy survives or fails. A badly designed electoral system may polarize electoral politics or may fragment the parliament so severely that nothing can be accomplished. In either scenario, it may unwittingly empower extremist political forces whose commitment to democracy is ambiguous at best. Alternatively, if the electoral system tries to correct too decisively for the danger of fragmentation by manufacturing a majority, it may leave important social and political groups excluded or underrepresented, trading one problem for another that may be even more debilitating. Thus, while some theorists strongly recommend a particular type of electoral system as generally best for all countries, others warn that the challenge of appropriate design very much depends on the particular country context and on which danger (for example, the lack of a decisive majority or the exclusion of important minorities) represents the most serious threat to democracy.

In the opening essay of this collection, one of the leading theorists of democratic institutional design, Donald L. Horowitz, emphasizes how powerful the electoral system can be in shaping the character of a democracy and how vexing the choices can be. There are myriad ways that voter preferences can be aggregated in order to determine which parties get how many seats in parliament. "Every electoral system has biases," Horowitz warns, and no system merely passively translates "individual wishes into a collective choice." System designers—and the broader publics in whose interest they are acting—must therefore be aware of these biases and make conscious choices between competing values and imperatives.

Horowitz identifies six possible aims of an electoral system, some of which directly conflict with one another. First is the increasingly common normative goal of *proportionality*—trying to achieve a distribution of seats among parties in parliament that matches as closely as possible the relative party shares of the vote. It is in this respect that observers most often speak of "fairness." Yet, Horowitz stresses, fairness in this sense "is only one among several goals, and it may not be the most important goal." The most proportional outcomes are produced by one or another form of proportional representation (PR), and generally the fewer and larger the districts (up to the maximum point of the single nationwide district, as in Israel and the Netherlands), the more proportional the results. A second goal, however, is *accountability of elected representatives to constituents*, and the larger the districts, the weaker the direct ties between representatives and any kind of clear territorial constituency. Moreover, as Horowitz notes, PR (especially when using national lists) often "reposes great power in party leaders" to determine the rank order of the candidates on the list, further undermining accountability to voters. Horowitz's third goal is *durable governments*, ones that can persist in office for the elected term of parliament (if there is a parliamentary system). This goal, too, may come in conflict with proportionality, as the more purely proportional an electoral system is, the more fragmented the parliament (into multiple parties) and thus the more difficult it is to forge and sustain a ruling coalition.

A fourth goal is *facilitating the victory of the "Condorcet winner"* (the one candidate who would win every paired contest). This objective is poorly served by PR, but well advanced by the alternative vote (AV), which requires voters to rank the candidates in single-member districts, and which then redistributes the second (and if necessary, third and then lower-order preferences) of the weakest candidates until one candidate receives a majority. By giving politicians incentives to craft wider appeals beyond their political (e.g., ethnic or ideological) base, AV favors moderates. Thus, as Horowitz has written elsewhere, and as Ben Reilly discusses at length in his contribution to this volume, AV has intriguing possibilities for serving a fifth objective, *promoting interethnic (or interreligious) conciliation*. It can do so by inducing candidates and parties to moderate their appeals and reach out for the second-place preferences of other parties and ethnic groups. This kind of "vote pooling" logic can only work if there are a large number of districts in which no one party or group has a majority, and in any case, AV is a majoritarian system which can yield quite disproportional outcomes. Other mechanisms, such as the Lebanese system of ethnically reserved seats (but with all voters voting for all seats), can similarly or even more powerfully induce crossethnic alliances, but with other drawbacks. The sixth (related) goal is *minority officeholding*, which can be served not only by PR but also by more explicit and extreme devices, though at the cost of "providing incentives for candidates to take extreme positions in order to heighten" their appeal to their identity base.

These are difficult choices, encompassing powerful normative and political considerations, and yet the consequences of adopting a particular electoral system are not always straightforward, immediate, and predictable. The legacy of preexisting cleavages and incentives persists, at least for a while. Thus, Horowitz warns, "the full effects of a new system can only be gauged after two or three elections, when politicians and voters have adapted to its incentives."

As Richard Soudriette and Andrew Ellis show in Chapter 2, more than a few countries have changed their electoral systems in recent years. About one in eight have changed the basic nature of the system, and many others have made adjustments within the same system. Apparently, when they choose or redesign an electoral system, more and more countries are concerned these days with fairness and inclusiveness, including the representation of women and minorities. The most common type of major shift is from a majoritarian rule, such as the single-member-district, "first-past-the-post" (FPTP) system like that in the U.K. or the United States, either to PR or to a mixed system combining some single-member districts with some seats filled by PR lists. As they show in Table 2 (p. 21), since 1993 a dozen countries have made precisely that shift, while three have shifted from PR to a mixed system. Party-list PR is still used by more countries than any other type of system (over a third of countries that hold competitive elections employ it). But the mixed system is growing in appeal, in part because it provides for some degree of proportionality while tempering PR's tendency to party fragmentation, and in part because it enables countries to get some of the fairness and inclusion of PR along with some of the direct accountability to territorial constituencies that comes most naturally with single-member districts. Mixed systems vary considerably, however, particularly in terms of whether they follow a truly mixed logic or instead distribute seats to parties using the proportional rule. Most mixed systems are truly mixed or "parallel systems," in that one block of seats (in many countries it is half or sixty percent) is filled strictly through FPTP and the other through PR. A few countries, however, including Italy, New Zealand, Mexico, and Bolivia, have more or less emulated the German "mixed-member proportional" model. Under this system, the party list vote determines proportionally the overall share of seats for each party (subject to whatever threshold may be imposed, such as the 5 percent minimum in Germany). On top of seats it has won in the individual districts, each party then wins a quota of seats from its PR lists sufficient to give it a national allocation of seats proportional to its vote. Soudriette and Ellis provide in Table 1 a comprehensive inventory of the all the electoral systems used in all the world's countries, including for directly elected presidents, most of whom are chosen by the two-round, run-off system when no candidate receives a majority of the vote in the first round.

In chapter 3, the Australian political scientist, Ben Reilly, builds on the seminal work of Donald Horowitz to examine the utility of preferential electoral systems as a tool of ethnic conflict management. Like Horowitz, Reilly's concern is to examine to what extent electoral systems can "encourage cooperation and accommodation among rival groups, and therefore work to reduce the salience of ethnicity." Like Horowitz as well, Reilly favors vote-pooling mechanisms, which "make politicians reciprocally dependent on votes from groups other than their own." Such systems give an advantage to moderate candidates who reach across the divides of party and ethnicity to appeal for the second and lower-order preferences of the voters, and who thereby exhibit a "capacity to represent groups other than their own." In Reilly's terminology, these are "centripetal systems" in that they press parties and candidates toward the accommodating center. Both Horowitz and Reilly are drawn to the alternative vote as a potentially powerful mechanism in this regard. Each author also recognizes the value of the single transferable vote (STV), in which voters rank a larger number of candidates in multimember districts. STV functions like a proportional system. Thus, candidates do not need to win a majority of the vote, but rather a minimum quota (which, as Horowitz notes, would be one-fifth plus one in a four-seat district). The advantage of STV is that it is a fairer, more proportional system than AV, better able to represent minorities. The disadvantage, Horowitz stresses, is that the low threshold for election in a district "provides few incentives to interparty agreements to transfer votes," and thus generates "weaker incentives to compromise" than AV, under which a candidate must ultimately gather enough lower-order preferences to win a majority of votes in the district.

Weighing the experiences with preferential voting in Estonia, Australia, Fiji, and Papua New Guinea, Reilly concludes that these vote-pooling systems can foster ethnic accommodation and political movement toward the center. There are several conditions that must hold, however, for these effects to materialize. First, there must exist among both political leaders and the general electorate a "core group of moderates" ready to respond to the incentives generated by preferential voting. Second, because it takes time before political leaders and supporters grasp and adapt to the new incentives, system continuity is important; once a new electoral system is put in place, it has to be allowed to operate consistently through several elections. And third, groups must be structured and distributed across electoral districts so that there is real competition and uncertainty, and thus the need for different groups to pool votes in a number of different districts. If, as in Fiji, districts "are drawn in such a way as to become the exclusive preserve of one ethnic group or the other," then the crossethnic logic of preferential voting will never take hold.

The vote-pooling model of using the electoral system to encourage crossethnic alliances and appeals stands in pointed contrast to Arend Lijphart's consociational or "power-sharing" model of democracy in divided societies. The logic of this system, as Lijphart reprises it in chapter 4 of this volume, is to accept ethnic divisions as a given and then devise mechanisms to enable ethnic political parties to share power and resources in proportion to their votes and their numbers in the population. The two foundations of the model, Lijphart stresses, are power sharing—"the participation of representatives of all significant communal groups in political decision making, especially at the executive level"—and group autonomy, which gives different groups (either on a territorial or cultural basis) control over their own social practices, education, use of language, and so on. Proportional representation is the cardinal mechanism for fostering power sharing but in the full consociational version, there are three other mechanisms: 1) a grand coalition of all or virtually all the parties, who divide up ministries and other executive roles in rough proportion to their political strength in parliament and society; 2) a mutual veto over key government policies (which must therefore be reached by consensus); and 3) group autonomy through federalism or nonterritorial means.[1] Horowitz and others criticize the consociational model for putting so much faith in the willingness and ability of leaders to reach accommodation after elections have entrenched and polarized ethnic solidarities, instead of seeking to bridge divisions and forge conciliation in advance, through preelectoral coalitions.[2] In this essay, Lijphart dismisses critics of his consociationalism, including Horowitz, as having no realistic alternative to the power-sharing model. The alternative vote, he cautions, is a majoritarian system that can leave ethnic minorities severely underrepresented. Using the example of contemporary Iraq, Lijphart warns that any electoral system that does not ensure the fair and full representation of each group risks the group's alienation and rejection of the system; thus he strongly favors PR.

Power sharing, Lijphart insists, is not a "one-size-fits-all" model, but rather can be adapted in a variety of ways to different country circumstances. Still, he feels some institutional designs are generally right for all divided societies (indeed, for all countries). The best electoral system, he insists, is a fully proportional one (either PR or the German-style mixed-member proportional system), using closed or nearly closed party lists; this encourages the formation of strong, coherent parties. Some break on pure proportionality can be warranted, through the creation of multimember districts that are not too large in size or through the establishment of a modest electoral threshold. Lijphart particularly likes two-tiered PR systems such as the Danish one, where the majority of seats are elected from moderate-sized multimember districts, and then a smaller number of compensatory seats are allocated to ensure greater overall national proportionality between the parties' shares of votes and parliamentary seats. As in his voluminous other writings, Lijphart urges here that PR be joined to a parliamentary system of government, which facilitates coalition formation with broad power sharing and avoids the zero-sum character of presidential elections. Moreover, he urges that in parliamentary systems, the president should be a purely ceremonial head of state, and selected by parliament (ideally through some requirement for broad consensus) and not by direct vote of the people. Where groups are territorially concentrated, federalism is "an excellent way" to provide for their autonomy. In this respect, he recommends a weak upper house of parliament and a system of relatively small and homogeneous units to ensure autonomy and avoid domination by a few big states.

The role of electoral rules under federalism forms the concern of R. Kent Weaver's analysis in chapter 5. How, Weaver asks, do federalism and the electoral system interact with one another? Are federal systems somehow distinctive in what they require from an electoral system? Not very distinctive, he concludes: "Federalism is compatible with a variety of electoral rules at both the national and territorial levels." And thus federal systems vary widely in the number and character of parties that predominate. Some federal systems use PR and some the single-member-district plurality (or first-past-the-post) system. One, Australia, uses AV for the lower house and STV for the upper. Most use the same electoral system for subnational legislatures that they do for the national one. Where there are strong and distinct subnational identities, majoritarian electoral systems like FPTP tend to produce much more homogeneous territorial concentrations of party strength. Thus, in marked contrast to PR, FPTP electoral rules "appear significantly more likely to create a high risk of territorial exclusion from the governing-party caucus at the national level in parliamentary systems." This, in turn, may feed a region's sense of political alienation. Majoritarian electoral rules may keep small secessionist parties from winning many seats, but once such "antisystem" parties reach a critical plurality of 35 percent or more, FPTP may in fact strengthen them. These mixed implications leave Weaver unconvinced that there is any one best type of electoral system for governing democratic federations.

The Debate Over Proportional Representation

For several decades now, debates about institutional design in democracies have heavily revolved around the fundamental choice between majoritarian and power-sharing logics, and thus between FPTP and PR. In 1991, the *Journal of Democracy* published a seminal piece by Arend Lijphart arguing for the general superiority of proportional representation, especially in new democracies and deeply divided societies. Lijphart's bold essay inspired a vigorous debate between him and several critics of PR. In Section II we reproduce these articles, which continue to be widely cited. In chapter 6, Lijphart rejects majoritarian democracy in favor of the consensus model, which "tries to limit, divide, separate, and share power," and features multiple parties, coalition governments, and more equal executive-legislative power relations. By virtually ensuring a multiparty system, proportional representation (combined with parliamentarism) is a key device for structuring democracy in this consensual way. But in addition to ensuring minority representation and so better managing ethnic conflict, PR is preferable, Lijphart maintains, because it is intrinsically more democratic. Moreover, his data from the Western democracies suggest that parliamentary-PR systems have a higher quality of democracy, including higher rates of voter turnout, without the diminished governability and economic performance that many critics allege to be the "cost" of PR systems. Moderate PR systems, like those in Germany and Sweden, that give rise to a moderate number of parliamentary parties seem to offer the best combination of power sharing and governability for new democracies.

Lijphart's arguments are disputed from several perspectives. As our focus here is on electoral systems, we do not include the debate on parliamentary versus presidential government, but it is nevertheless worth noting here Donald Horowitz's argument that presidentialism can be a tool of ethnic conflict management by providing a transethnic symbol for the country and by generating incentives to ethnic moderation and compromise to the extent that vote-pooling rules are utilized. (These include the preferential vote and Nigeria's requirement that a presidential candidate must win at least 25 percent of the vote in at least two-thirds of the states to be elected on the first ballot).[3]

In chapters 7 and 8 Guy Lardeyret and Quentin Quade vigorously challenge Lijphart's case for PR and argue strongly for the advantages of majoritarian democracy. Indeed, Lardeyret favors the most majoritarian system possible, which (as Lijphart indicates) is not presidential but rather parliamentary government combined with the single-member-district plurality method of election—the Westminster system. Because such plurality elections for the legislature tend to give rise to a two-party or two-party-dominant system, they create strong parliamentary governments, fusing executive and legislative power, and free of the need for coalitions. Lardeyret believes the greatest danger lies in the fragmentation associated with parliamentary-PR systems, like the Fourth Republic that faltered in his native France. Quentin Quade also cites this example, as well as pre-Mussolini Italy and Weimar Germany, to show how PR can foster not conciliation and compromise but fragmentation, extremism, and governmental paralysis. Like most critics of the consensus model, Quade focuses attention on the intrinsically greater fragility of coalition government.

Precisely because it gives such wide scope to the representation of "minorities," and thereby encourages polarization and party fragmentation, PR, Lardeyret maintains, "is dangerous for countries faced with ethnic or cultural divisions." By contrast, "Parties in plurality systems tend to be moderate because most votes are to be gained among the undecided voters of the center." Ethnic moderation will be greatest when members of the same ethnic group must compete against one another in single-member districts, along crosscutting political and ideological lines of cleavage. Lardeyret prefers plurality electoral systems not only for the stronger, more stable and decisive governments they produce. He (like Quade) also believes that plurality electoral systems are "more democratic as well as more efficient," because, unlike PR, they lock out extremist parties, marginalize small parties, and give the choice of who will govern to the voters, rather than to elites of numerous parties negotiating in secret after the election, sometimes for weeks or even months. Quade writes: "Plurality voting encourages the competing parties to adopt a majority-forming attitude . . . to be moderate, to seek conciliation . . . in short, to do *before* the election, in the public view, the very tasks that Lijphart applauds PR systems for doing *after* the election."

The institutional choice of PR (with parliamentary government) or plurality elections (whether in a presidential or parliamentary system) involves more than the empirical and analytical debate between Lijphart and his critics. At play here as well is a tension between competing values. There is a certain intrinsic contradiction in democracies between representativeness and governability. PR systems risk some sacrifice in decisive governance and clear alternation of majorities in order to maximize representativeness. Opponents of PR put a higher priority on governability than on directly representing in the legislature the many divisions in society.[4] To be fair however, few prominent students of democracy would advocate the kind of extreme PR—with virtually no minimum threshold of the vote necessary for entry into parliament—that existed for some time in Italy and Israel. In fact, during the 1990s Italy switched to a much more majoritarian electoral system, while Israel has gradually raised its electoral threshold to 2 percent (in its most recent, March 2006 elections). As Lijphart emphasizes, there are many types and degrees of PR, and moderate PR, with thresholds like the 5 percent minimum in Germany, tend to give rise to only a moderate number of parties. In responding to Lardeyret and Quade in Chapter 9, Lijphart not only defends his comparative analysis of the performance of PR and majoritarian systems. He also reiterates the normative case for PR—"that disproportional election results are inherently unfair and undemocratic"—noting that none of Britain's postwar governing parties carried a majority of the vote (a fact that has held true for all of India's one-party governments as well).

Is there, then, one type of electoral system that is right for all countries and historical moments? In his reflection on the debate over PR, in chapter 10, Ken Gladdish insists not. There is in practice a wide range of electoral-system formulas. Each one, Gladdish stresses, has costs as well as advantages, and the type of system that will best serve democracy in a given country depends on the nature of its social cleavages and patterns of political mobilization. How a country resolves the tension between representativeness and governability is a value choice that must be informed by the country's own particular history and culture. PR not only facilitates legislative fragmentation, and thus heightens the difficulty of forming and maintaining governments, it may also produce bizarre coalitions of expedience that cannot govern coherently or minority cabinets that cannot govern with any confidence. Further, it has ambiguous consequences for representation, since party-list systems with large multi-member districts (or in the extreme, as in Israel and the Netherlands, no districts at all) sacrifice direct linkage between voters and representatives. This lack of accountability of MPs to specific geographical constituencies became a major issue in the debate over a permanent electoral system for South Africa.[5] Yet, particularly when there are more than two significant parties, as in Britain and India, plurality systems may give rise to severely disproportional results (the Labor and Conservative parties in Britain have repeatedly won thumping majorities in parliament with barely 40 percent of the vote, and often less). Moreover, Gladdish notes, plurality systems also tend to breed voter apathy in districts (often the vast majority) where the contest for the seat is a foregone conclusion. Crafting an electoral system thus involves hard choices that cannot be made theoretically or in the abstract, but must be done on the basis "of practicality and aptness relative to national circumstance."

Learning from Country and Regional Experience

If Gladdish is right that the best type of electoral system for a country depends on its social cleavages and political and historical realities, then we need to pay particular attention to the wide variation in country and regional experiences with electoral systems. This we do in Section III. We begin this review with a debate between two leading political science scholars of Africa, Andrew Reynolds and Joel Barkan, on whether PR is the best electoral system for African democracies. Reynolds (who wrote his Ph.D. dissertation under Arend Lijphart) argues enthusiastically for the combination of PR and parliamentary rule in the African context, echoing Lijphart's concern with promoting broad inclusion and power sharing and avoiding zero-sum politics. Reviewing the political experience of Malawi, Zambia, Namibia, and South Africa in the early 1990s, following the wave of transitions to democracy, he shows that none of Lardeyret's criticisms of PR hold up very well in southern Africa. Rather than foster extremism by including fringe parties in parliament, PR tends "to coopt extremists, giving them an incentive to press their case with ballots rather than bullets." This was a particularly striking consequence of the low electoral threshold that allowed white reactionary and black militant parties, as well as small liberal parties, to enter parliament in South Africa. Rather than promoting ethnically exclusive parties, PR has enabled South African parties to assemble distinctly multiracial lists of candidates, to a degree that would simply have been impossible under FPTP. Of course, given the electoral dominance of the African National Congress (ANC), it is easy to use the South African experience to rebut Lardeyret's warnings about the instability and weakness of governments under PR and the undue leverage of extremist parties. What worries Reynolds, however, is the PR system's failure to enable voters to hold representatives accountable (or even to know who their representatives are) when districts are as large as they are in South Africa. This is one reason why he strongly recommends PR in small to medium-sized districts (of, say, 5 to 12 members), and with open lists so that voters can choose individual candidates from the parties.

For ethnic conflict management, there is an even more compelling reason to favor PR in Africa, Reynolds argues. Like Weaver, he is concerned about the polarizing consequences under FPTP of electoral outcomes that leave individual parties totally dominant in particular regions. A classic example is the first multiparty elections in Malawi in

1994, where the three regionally based parties each won 75 to 100 percent of the seats in their territorial strongholds, despite the presence of significant opposition. In each case, the majoritarian character of FPTP left minority sentiment in each region virtually unrepresented, whereas with PR each region would have had some political presence of parties that were dominant in the other regions. Such a geographic mixing of representation helps to promote ethnic inclusion and cooperation within parties as well as between them, and thus to inhibit polarization. In addition, Reynolds finds that PR has produced a more diverse and representative South African parliament, in terms of race, ethnicity, and gender, than would likely have been achieved under FPTP.

These arguments leave Joel Barkan unmoved. In chapter 12, Barkan argues that FPTP—with its single-member districts and the close, organic ties that they forge between legislators and territorial constituencies—much better fits the circumstances and needs of a still predominantly rural Africa. In these countries, most people expect their representatives to help deliver on their basic needs for clean water, schools, roads, and health care, and voters evaluate parties and representatives "in terms of their potential for, or past record of, constituency service." PR, with its multimember (and often very large multimember) districts, is intrinsically inferior in this regard, to the point where (as in Namibia) members of parliament may "rarely make an appearance in rural areas." Indeed, this alarming representational gap prompted the ANC to assign its MPs arbitrarily to "represent" designated areas (with dubious results). Moreover, Barkan maintains, PR does not yield notably fairer (more proportional) outcomes in agrarian Africa. Rather, his analysis of specific elections suggests that in rural Africa, where people cluster territorially by ethnicity, FPTP produces allocations of seats to parties that are about as proportional as under PR, especially when all districts contain the same number of voters.

In rebutting Barkan, Reynolds makes two essential points in chapter 13. First, when one compares PR and FPTP systematically in Africa (rather than focusing on anomalous individual cases like Malawi), the claim to equal fairness collapses. Both within Southern Africa and in Africa as a whole, PR electoral systems yield significantly more proportional outcomes; "when it comes to translating seats into votes, PR is not just marginally superior [to FPTP] but substantially so." Second, irrespective of overall proportionality, one must worry about the geographic patterning of party strength. One key to ethnic conflict management and democratic consolidation in Africa, Reynolds reiterates, is to avoid the emergence of one-party states at the subnational (regional) level and to ensure a critical mass of competitive seats. Even where FPTP produces similar outcomes nationally, it does so by making particular parties nearly invulnerable within their areas of ethnic strength. Reynolds wants to use PR in moderate-sized multimember districts to generate crosscutting cleavages, so that a party from one ethnic base will still have an incentive to campaign in the "other" areas, and opposition parties subnationally will be kept in the electoral game, rather than permanently frozen out and alienated from the democratic process. In these respects, Reynolds uses a variation of Lijphart's method (PR) to achieve one of Horowitz's goals (inducing political parties to appeal across ethnic lines). As he has done in other published work, Reynolds recommends for South Africa the Scandinavian model of a two-tiered PR system, in which the disproportionality that may creep in from having relatively small multimember districts can be corrected with a second distribution of seats that brings each party's share of parliamentary seats into balance with its share of the national vote.

In chapter 14, the first of two essays focusing on Latin America, Jeffrey Cason assesses the impact of electoral reform on democratic stability in Uruguay. Uruguay has had over the decades one of the world's most unique and dysfunctional electoral systems, the "double simultaneous vote" (DSV). A form of proportional representation, DSV allows multiple party factions to contest for votes in the general election. In parliamentary elections, this has fostered a breathtaking fragmentation of party lists (in 1994, there were 641 lists from the three main parties, in a country of barely two million voters), because there has been no cost to the party for such fragmentation. Parties get a proportion of seats in parliament equivalent to the total vote share for all their factions (and factions in turn get a share of their party's seats equal to their share of the party vote). The result has been extremely weak, divided parties and severe clientelism. In presidential elections, the effects were even more perverse, as the winner of the presidential election was the candidate with the most votes from the party that received overall for its multiple candidates more votes than other party. This meant that presidents could be (and were) elected with less than a quarter of the vote personally, and without even being the most popular candidate. Inevitably, "These relatively thin mandates called into question the legitimacy of the eventual presidential winner."

Alarmed by the rise of the Left, the two established Uruguayan parties engineered a constitutional reform in 1996 to require a single presidential candidate for each party, chosen in a party primary, as well as a second-round runoff election in the event that no presidential candidate won a majority on the first round. Although the reform only slightly modified and rationalized the DSV system for the parliamentary elections (forbidding party factions to combine their votes for different lists after the election to win seats), it did have an immediate and striking effect on the next presidential election in 1999. In particular, the new majority rule for presidential election forced the Left alliance to move toward the political center and focused the second round of the presidential election much more on policy proposals. This "made the

Left appear less threatening" and made Uruguayan democracy less "risk-prone." Even the modest rationalization of DSV in parliamentary elections reduced the number of parliamentary lists and gave parties an incentive to unify. And by requiring broader coalitions for electoral success, the reforms made it easier for elected leaders to govern.

In chapter 15, Richard Snyder and David Samuels examine a distinctive feature of Latin American electoral systems, their exceptionally high levels of malapportionment—the "wide discrepancy between the share of legislative seats and the share of population held by electoral districts." Federal systems (of which there are several in Latin America, including Mexico and Brazil) often deliberately overrepresent some national units in the upper chamber of a parliament as part of the power-sharing federal "bargain." What is unique about many Latin American democracies, however, Snyder and Samuels show, is the degree of malapportionment of *lower chamber* seats—on average, this distortion is twice as severe in Latin American democracies as in the advanced industrial democracies. Moreover, they show, the overrepresentation of some districts and underrepresentation of others are by no means random with respect to social and political cleavages. Where malapportionment occurs in Latin America, it invariably gives national legislatures "a distinct rural and conservative bias." This unfairness, which is "often hidden from public view," not only handicaps urban and leftist constituencies in the battle over policies and resources, but also yields several other predictable consequences across countries and over time. It tends to widen rifts between presidents, who are elected from the entire country with all votes weighted equally, and assemblies that are disproportionately beholden to conservative and clientelistic rural bosses. It leaves presidents vulnerable to pressure from these rural interests, including the need to channel undue patronage to them (and thereby neglect wider and more substantively compelling urban needs). And it may compel national leaders to tolerate authoritarian enclaves in the countryside, because the presidents need the legislative support of these overrepresented rural bosses.

Snyder and Samuels review three possible innovations to address the problem. Judicial oversight of reapportionment, they argue, is less promising than in the United States because Latin American judiciaries are often much less independent and capable than North American ones. Based on the success of Mexico's independent Federal Electoral Institute (IFE, created in 1996), they see more promise in the creation of a "neutral, nonpartisan electoral commission that is legally obligated to reduce lower-chamber malapportionment." A third possible avenue is change in the electoral law itself, so that correcting malapportionment becomes part of a wider package of reforms to improve the quality of democracy. Of course, one possible reform is to do away with electoral districts altogether in favor of a single nationwide list (as in Peru), but this involves big costs in parliamentary accountability to the citizens.

Instead, they recommend a mixed electoral system, with enough seats allocated through PR (operating in a nationwide district) to temper any effects of malapportionment among single-member districts.

Political scientists are naturally drawn to the promise of electoral reform, but as Emanuele Ottolenghi warns in chapter 16, the cure can be worse than the original illness. Disgusted with the political paralysis and extortion that increasingly plagued the coalition-formation process in Israel's highly fragmented party system in the 1980s and early 1990s, and unable to achieve a dramatic alteration in an electoral system that fostered fragmentation, reformers pressed for a radical change in the very nature of parliamentary government. Under the plan that was eventually adopted in 1992, the prime minister was no longer to emerge from parliamentary bargaining (which gave small religious parties in between Labor and Likud extravagant power to make demands), but was to be directly elected by the people, in a separate ballot simultaneous with the traditional vote Israelis cast for a party list in their highly proportional system. This change, reformers confidently predicted, would not only give the directly elected prime minister the moral authority to form a government more quickly and to govern more decisively, it would also give him more seats, as he would sweep like-minded representatives into parliament on his "coattails."

In reality, as Ottolenghi shows, precisely the reverse occurred. Freed from having to use their parliamentary vote to signal their choice for prime minister, Israeli voters engaged in ticket splitting with a vengeance. While prime ministerial candidates were able to win majorities on the first ballot, the two major parties, Labor and Likud, hemorrhaged votes to smaller, more ideological, or single-issue parties, and the parliament became still more fragmented (going from 10 parties in 1992 to 15 in 1999). As a result, forming and maintaining majority coalitions became even more difficult, and "the executive remained hamstrung in its ability to forge ahead with coherent policies on controversial issues." So unsatisfying and indeed counterproductive were the consequences of the reform that the entire innovation was reversed in 2001 in favor of the traditional parliamentary system (but now with the valuable innovation of the "constructive vote of no confidence").[6] The lesson, Ottolenghi underscores, is that such constitutional innovation cannot be a substitute for fundamental electoral reform. The latter provides the only sure means of reducing parliamentary fragmentation, thereby strengthening the capacity of a prime minister to form and sustain coalitions and thus to govern effectively.

As in Israel, so in Japan and Taiwan citizens and civic groups became increasingly frustrated with features of their electoral system that seemed to foster the most unsavory aspects of politics. Here the culprit was the system of the single nontransferable vote (SNTV), a rare system used mainly in those two countries (and for a briefer period in Korea). Under

SNTV, candidates contend for seats in multimember districts, but the voter is allowed only a single vote, and "excess" votes may not be transferred to a party's other candidates in these districts. The top vote getters are elected by the plurality rule with whatever number of votes they receive. The system thus places an intense premium on party organization, which enables parties to properly estimate and distribute their voter support in a district. If a party nominates too many candidates, its vote may be spread too thinly, costing it seats. Yet if it nominates too few, it can also suffer. Money and organization become vitally important (to the point where political parties in Taiwan have even been known to instruct their voters to support different party candidates based on their birthdays, so that everyone born in January through March supports the party's first candidate in the district, those born April to June vote for the second candidate, and so on). Rarely does such coordination work flawlessly. A perverse feature of SNTV is that candidates of the same party are forced to compete against one another as well as against the opposition party candidates. Consequently, parties are highly factionalized and election campaigns are complex and hugely expensive, inducing politicians either to unleash huge flows of patronage to the district or to fashion extreme appeals to the ideological faithful.

In chapter 17, Jih-wen Lin explains how long-sought electoral reform from SNTV to mixed but more majoritarian systems was finally achieved in Japan (1994) and then Taiwan (2005). In each case, the public became disillusioned with the corruption and inefficiency of the political system, but this broad disaffection was not sufficient to force change. Rather, Lin shows, change could only happen when three factors converged. First, "public disappointment eroded the governing party's electoral strength and finally deprived the party of its dominant status," unfreezing a political situation that had seen insecure members of the ruling party blocking any reform. Second, a critical mass of influential politicians discovered that they had a personal interest in reform. Specifically, ruling party legislators whose electoral success was owed "to personal image rather than particularistic connections" realized that their fortunes could be better served by FPTP. Third, electoral reform had to become part of a larger, log-rolling deal in order to attract the support of a majority of legislators (especially from smaller parties threatened by the switch to a more majoritarian system). Although these conditions are derived from the political experience of Japan and Taiwan in switching from SNTV, they would seem to have relevance to other countries seeking electoral reform, and to explain why reform is so difficult to achieve: Even if society can be rallied behind the cause, legislators do not like to abandon the system that put them in parliament. Yet Lin's study underscores why electoral reform can matter. In the four elections following Japan's change to a more majoritarian electoral system, the party system has shown striking signs of consolidation toward a two-party system, and a similar trend is likely to unfold even more rapidly in Taiwan. While the legacy of patron-client networks still remains potent in Japan, Lin predicts that "as the two-party system takes shape, the mode of campaigning will likely come to focus more on policy issues and debate."

Ironically, just as Taiwan was abandoning SNTV, Afghanistan was adopting it for its 2005 legislative elections. Andrew Reynolds explains this "curious case" in chapter 18. As it happened, international experts like Reynolds himself had recommended that Afghanistan use closed-list PR in multimember districts based on the country's 34 historic provinces. This would give voters a fairly simple and accessible choice (identifiable by a symbol for each list) and would foster more proportional outcomes. Yet while there was a consensus against resurrecting the old FPTP system (inherited from British colonial rule but not used in 40 years), there was resistance to PR among Afghans who did not like or trust political parties, and from President Hamid Karzai himself (already elected the previous year), who wanted to allow Afghans to vote for individual candidates. International experts anticipated most of the problems that resulted from the use of SNTV. While the system apparently produced a fairly proportional outcome in ethnic terms, it yielded a chaotic party situation, with 33 political parties or groups in the assembly, most lacking any real coherence or a critical mass of assembly members. With the incentives to personal campaigning, powerful individuals were elected, including a substantial number of warlords, criminal gang leaders, religious fundamentalists, and drug traffickers. And given the large size of many of the districts, most candidates were elected with only small percentages of the vote. Voters were apparently confused by the profusion of candidates and the long list of names on the ballot, leading to a low voter turnout and a high incidence of spoiled ballots. Though President Karzai thought the system would work to his benefit, it instead weakened him, as experts had warned, leaving him with support from less than a third of the assembly. The result is a fragmented legislature hostile to Karzai, featuring "clientelism and shifting alliances" and mortgaged to "men with tainted pasts." Moreover, if other country experiences are any guide, the system will be difficult to change. Yet Reynolds warns, "If SNTV is used in subsequent elections, the fragmentation and parochialism of the legislature will increase, and politics in general will remain detached from the masses."

As Adeed Dawisha and Larry Diamond indicate in chapter 19, international experts on electoral systems fared little better in Iraq, where (more or less as in Afghanistan) they had recommended a system of party-list PR in multimember districts, based on the country's 18 provinces. The alternatives to PR were discarded one by one because of their substantive or technical unsuitability. FPTP was too majoritarian, and in any case drawing single-member districts was not possible in Iraq's fragile transitional circumstances. AV was infeasible for the same reason, and probably too complicated for first-time voters. STV was also ruled out for its complexity, and SNTV for its known perversities (as articulated above). By contrast, PR fit with the powersharing logic of emergent political practice and institutional design in Iraq, appealed to party leaders who wanted to consolidate their control, and lent itself well to the implementation of a 25 percent quota for female representation, as established in the interim constitution. Yet the question remained of how PR should be structured in Iraq. While several Iraqi and international officials had advanced proposals in 2004 for a two-tiered system on the Scandinavian model, with provincial lists and a compensatory adjustment from national lists to achieve greater overall proportionality, the UN electoral mission chose, for its simplicity and ease of administration, PR within a single nationwide district.

The difference between the two types of PR—district-based and national-list—may seem subtle but in fact carried huge consequences. The district-based system offered some hope of empowering local actors and identities, and thereby putting a break on the polarization of politics around national ethnic and sectarian identities. Then too, it might have generated ties between elected representatives and geographical constituencies, "making for greater local accountability." In the absence of any districts, or even any awareness of who the candidates were, "the January 2005 parliamentary elections became almost purely a national-identity referendum, untempered by any local component or flavor." In addition, the lack of any minimum floor of representation for geographical areas contributed to the Sunni boycott of the elections. Each of these developments distorted and polarized the political landscape in lasting ways. Thus, although for the December 2005 election Iraq implemented essentially the two-tiered, district-based PR system that had been recommended back in 2004, the polarization of party politics around ethnic and sectarian identities had by then become deeply entrenched. During the campaign "each alliance focused its energy on cementing support among its own base, while doggedly obstructing intrusions by other alliances into its home areas." Violence intensified, Iraqis again voted overwhelmingly along ethnic and religious lines, and the only secular, nonethnic list was crushed. As Dawisha and Diamond recount it, the Iraqi case tells a sobering tale of the limits of electoral-system engineering, once ethnic polarization and violence take hold.

The Afghan and Iraqi cases no doubt appear discouraging to electoral-system experts who believe each country might have fared better in its transition if their advice had been taken. Yet the broad trajectory of electoral systems in the world is much more hopeful. Over the last few decades, knowledge about the consequences of different electoral systems has accumulated and been disseminated. In general, the direction of change is away from the extremes of purely majoritarian and purely proportional systems, toward either mixed systems or proportional ones with at least some modest inducement to party aggregation. Preferential systems have yet to be tried on a large scale, but where they have been employed, their results have been, on the whole, promising. The more successful models, such as the German mixed-member proportional system and the Scandinavian two-tiered PR, have been gaining adherents, and the most dysfunctional systems, such as SNTV and the block vote (a hyper-majoritarian system based on multimember districts) have been losing out. Gradually, a kind of process of natural selection is unfolding, as democracies experiment and adapt, discarding what does not work, or at least what is not suitable for particular societies. Over time, we can expect to see more changes, in which countries seek to find a better balance between inclusion and governability, and between proportionality and accountability. There will no doubt be many more painful false starts and lost opportunities, but democracies in general are moving toward fairer, more rational, and more viable electoral systems.

NOTES

1. The early articulations of the model are Arend Lijphart, "Consociational Democracy," *World Politics* 21(January 1969): 207–25, and *Democracy in Plural Societies: A Comparative Exploration* (New Haven: Yale University Press, 1977). A more generic and comprehensive consideration of the model can be found in Arend Lijphart, *Patterns of Democracy: Government Forms and Performance in 36 Countries* (New Haven: Yale University Press, 1999).

2. Among the places where Donald Horowitz has critiqued the consociational model are *Ethnic Groups in Conflict* (Berkeley: University of California Press, 1985), 568–76; *A Democratic South Africa? Constitutional Engineering in a Divided Society* (Berkeley: University of California Press, 1991), 137–45, 167–71; and "Constitutional Design: Proposals versus Process," in Andrew Reynolds, ed., *The Architecture of Democracy: Constitutional Design, Conflict Management, and Democracy* (Oxford: Oxford University Press, 2002), 20–23.

3. Donald L. Horowitz, "Comparing Democratic Systems," *Journal of Democracy* 1 (Fall 1990): 73–79. The larger debate over parliamentary versus presidential government is reproduced in Larry Diamond and Marc F. Plattner, eds., *The Global Resurgence of Democracy*, 2nd ed. (Baltimore: Johns Hopkins University Press, 1996), 124–61.

4. Larry Diamond, "Three Paradoxes of Democracy," *Journal of Democracy* 1 (July 1990): 48–60.

5. Vincent Maphai, "The New South Africa: A Season for Power-Sharing," *Journal of Democracy* 7 (January 1996): 67–81.

6. This prohibits a vote of no confidence from bringing down a government unless it also puts forward an alternative coalition with a majority of votes to form a new government. The provision thus diminishes speculative efforts to bring down a government in order simply to get bargaining leverage over the formation of a new one.

I

Electoral Systems
and Institutional Design

1

A PRIMER FOR DECISION MAKERS

Donald L. Horowitz

Donald L. Horowitz *is James B. Duke Professor of Law and Political Science at Duke University and author, most recently, of* The Deadly Ethnic Riot *(2001). This essay is based on a paper written for the electoral-studies group at IKMAS, the Institute for Malaysian and International Studies at Universiti Kebangsaan Malaysia. The essay originally appeared in the October 2003 issue of the* Journal of Democracy.

To evaluate an electoral system or to choose a new one, it is necessary to ask first what one wants the electoral system to do. No electoral system simply reflects voter preferences or the existing pattern of cleavages in a society or the prevailing political party configuration. Every electoral system shapes and reshapes these features of the environment, and each does so in different ways. Here, I want to set out several possible purposes of electoral systems that can be found in the literature on the subject and then make some observations about those purposes and the electoral systems that further them.

First, however, I need to underscore a point just made about a common assumption—that the best electoral system is the one that straightforwardly and most accurately reflects the preferences of voters. The nature of an electoral system is to aggregate preferences and to convert them into electoral results, and no system can do this as a passive translation of individual wishes into a collective choice. Moreover, every electoral system has biases built into its mechanisms of decision, and these then feed back into the structure of choices confronting voters, constraining and changing choices that they might have made under other systems. Consequently, not only is there imperfect reflection of voter preferences in the first instance, but voter preferences themselves are shaped by the electoral system. Preferences do not and cannot exist independently of it.

The fact that each electoral system contains a different array of biases from every other electoral system means that those who decide among such systems can choose, in effect, to prefer one set of biases over another. And to prefer one over another is to make a policy choice. Hence one can speak of the goals of the system, even though the choice of bias is not always consciously made. It follows from this that there are as many potential goals of electoral-system choice as there are combinations of biases and systems. Any enumeration of goals is, therefore, a function of objectives that people living in a given society might wish to achieve and those they might wish to avoid, when matched against the propensity of particular electoral systems to produce results in one direction or another. Many such lists of goals, in other words, could be drawn up, and all such lists have an element of arbitrariness to them.

One last preliminary caveat. When we speak of goals to be achieved, there should be no illusion that the electoral system can, by itself, achieve them. Electoral systems shape and constrain the way in which politicians and constituents behave, but they are only one small part of the forces affecting the total constellation of behavior, even of political behavior. Miracles do not follow from changes of electoral systems. No one should expect more than incremental changes in behavioral patterns once the configuration of electoral incentives is altered. But sometimes increments of change can be surpassingly important.

Six Goals

Six aims of an electoral system come readily to mind. Some of these are mutually compatible, but some others are mutually incompatible, which is why it is so important to be clear about what one is choosing. (The choice, of course, must also be geared to the preexisting features of the political environment, since the functioning of electoral systems varies with the context.) Here are the six possible goals: 1) proportionality of seats to votes; 2) accountability to constituents; 3) durable governments; 4) victory of the "Condorcet winner"; 5) interethnic and interreligious conciliation; and 6) minority officeholding. I shall discuss each of these in turn.

1) Proportionality of seats to votes. Increasingly, scholars and decisionmakers are inclined to judge electoral systems by their ability or inability to produce proportional results. A political party that gains 20 percent of the total vote, it is argued, should win 20 percent of the total seats, rather than a few or no seats, which it may receive if elections are held on a constituency basis and its support is thinly spread rather than regionally concentrated. A party with 50 percent of the vote should, on this view, win only 50 percent of the seats rather than the 60 or 65 percent it may receive under electoral systems that often provide an inadvertent seat bonus to the largest party.

There are several ways to produce more or less proportional results, including list-system proportional representation (or PR, with its two

main variants, national lists and constituency lists) and the single transferable vote (STV). Some such systems can be married to other purposes
beside proportionality, particularly if combined with other systems in a
hybrid electoral arrangement, but PR is often inimical to some of the
other goals of electoral-system choice, as I shall suggest later. Fairness
of outcome, in the sense of proportionality of seats to votes, is only one
among several goals, and it may not be the most important goal. Because
it is easily measurable, however, proportionality tends to preempt other
goals. Discussions of proportionality should never be held in a vacuum.

It is also true that deviations from proportionality can be limited in
non-PR systems by attending to some of the sources of nonproportional
outcomes that do not derive from the electoral system as such. Among
those sources, malapportionment of constituencies (so that it takes two
or three times as many voters to elect one representative as it does to
elect another) is a very serious cause of disproportional results. Likewise, in PR systems, disproportional results favoring large parties can
be produced if competing lists are run in multimember constituencies,
each of which elects a small number of legislators.

2) Accountability to constituents. Elections to representative bodies
assume some degree of accountability of legislators to those who elect
them. It is generally thought that electoral systems which limit the power
of central party leaders to choose candidates produce more responsive
representatives. National list-system PR usually reposes great power in
party leaders to decide which candidates will have favorable positions
on the parties' lists and thus have better chances of being elected. When
central party leaders have such power, the sovereignty of the voter to
choose the candidates, rather than just to choose among candidates, is
thought to be impaired.

On this score, constituency-based systems, such as first-past-the-post
or even constituency-list PR (with small constituencies of perhaps three
or four seats), are said to be preferable. But there are other ways to
mitigate the domination of the process by central party leaders under
list PR. One way is to allow voters to alter the order of candidates on the
list, by voting for candidate 6 over candidate 3 on the list, for example.
This is called open-list PR, but it can have some perverse consequences,
especially in multiethnic societies.

3) Durable governments. Obviously, an electoral system cannot
represent the idiosyncratic opinions of every voter. Nevertheless, some
systems make it possible for many shades of opinion to be represented,
sometimes so many that the legislature ends up being fragmented, with
no party having anywhere near 50 percent of the seats. In such cases,
coalitions are, of course, necessary. Where the legislature is deeply
fragmented, it may be difficult to put together durable coalitions. Other
electoral systems may force parties to aggregate the diverse opinions in
a society for the sake of electoral success. Where this happens and diverse

opinions are represented within parties rather than across parties, the reduction in the number of parties makes it more likely that durable governments can be formed. And durable governments are thought to be desirable because they promote policy consistency and responsibility and, even more importantly, may avoid the instability that can result during interregna or from the creation of fragile, unpredictable coalitions.

4) *Victory of the Condorcet winner.* The Condorcet winner is the candidate who would receive a majority of the vote in a paired or head-to-head contest with each and every other candidate. The Condorcet winner is obviously the more popular candidate, whose victory, it is thought, ought to be preferred. But there are obstacles to this outcome. Since often there are more than two candidates, it is possible for some systems to produce results that disfavor the Condorcet winner. Sometimes first-past-the-post does this. Take a three-way contest in which candidates receive the following votes: X, 45 percent; Y, 40 percent; Z, 15 percent. Under first-past-the-post, candidate X wins. But if candidate Y faced only candidate X head-to-head, Y might be the candidate preferred by a majority of voters; and Y might also defeat Z in a paired contest. Electoral systems that can disfavor the Condorcet winner are sometimes thought to be wanting. But, of course, they may have other virtues.

There are systems that do a good job at picking the Condorcet winner. Both the alternative vote and the Coombs rule (discussed below) are good at eliciting second preferences that are suppressed by first-past-the-post systems. But both may have other disadvantages. Again, with electoral systems, it is always a question of knowing what one wants and choosing among alternatives, all of which will have some undesirable features.

5) *Interethnic and interreligious conciliation.* Electoral systems that produce proportional results or accountability to constituents or durable governments may or may not foster interethnic conciliation. One way to think about electoral systems and interethnic conciliation is to ask whether a given system provides politicians with electoral inducements for moderate behavior, that is, for compromises with members of other ethnic groups for the sake of electoral success. Some systems can do this. An electoral system originally devised in Lebanon—with ethnically reserved seats, multiseat constituencies, and common-roll elections—gives politicians very good reasons to cooperate across group lines, for they cannot be elected on the votes of their own group alone. They must pool votes (that is, exchange support) with candidates of other groups running in different reserved seats in the same constituency. Similarly, systems that require candidates to achieve a regional distribution of votes, in addition to a national plurality, may foster conciliatory behavior if territory is a proxy for ethnicity because groups are regionally concentrated. Nigeria pioneered this approach in its presi-

dential elections, and now Indonesia has gone in the same direction for its own presidential balloting.

On the other hand, electoral systems that allow politicians to be elected without behaving moderately may make postelectoral conciliation more difficult. Coalitions that are created after elections merely to form a government of 50 percent plus one of the seats in parliament may prove to be fragile when divisive ethnic issues arise. So, for interethnic conciliation, the question is how the electoral system affects the preelectoral calculations of parties and politicians.

6) Minority officeholding. Some writers, policy makers, and ethnic-group activists think that group proportionality ought to be a goal of electoral systems. The (debatable) assumption is that if group A comprises 10 percent of the population, it ought to comprise 10 percent of members of the legislature. Many electoral systems produce results that underrepresent members of minority groups in legislatures, if by *represent* we mean produce a share of electoral victors that is proportionate to the minority share of the population. In first-past-the-post elections, for example, if minorities are geographically well distributed, winning candidates may be drawn largely from the majority population. The goal of minority officeholding can thus be seen as an instance of the same phenomenon that gives rise to attempts to achieve proportionality between votes and seats, except that proportionality in that respect is *party* proportionality rather than *group* proportionality.

In some countries, notably the United States, serious efforts have been made to increase the minority share of legislators. In the context of plurality elections, the Voting Rights Act has been interpreted to require the redrawing of constituency boundaries in the direction of greater homogeneity, so as to facilitate the election of minority representatives where minorities constitute more than half of an electorate. There have been few suggestions that the electoral system itself be changed for this purpose. Some minority advocates, however, have urged consideration of the cumulative vote, an electoral system that allows voters in a multimember constituency to cast some or all of their votes for a single candidate, thereby maximizing the chance that a minority candidate could, on the basis of such cumulation, achieve victory over other candidates whose support was more widely but less intensely distributed. By providing incentives for candidates to take extreme positions in order to heighten their ability to attract all of the votes of a particular subset of voters, however, the cumulative vote could open the way to polarized politics.[1]

As this possibility shows, there may be a trade-off among the goals of group officeholding and interethnic conciliation. Similarly, proportionate minority officeholding does not guarantee that minority interests will receive attention in the legislative process. Indeed, minority officeholding may come at the expense of minority representation in this larger sense, for the creation of more homogeneous constituencies means not only more minority-dominated constituencies but also, correlatively, more constituencies in which majority-group voters dominate and in which majority-group candidates do not need to worry about minority support or minority interests.[2]

Choosing Among Goals

Many decision makers try to design the electoral system to maximize more than one goal. Germany, for example, has a constituency-based system, but with a proportional overlay, so that legislators have reasons to respond to their constituents but parties also receive an overall number of seats that is more or less proportional to the votes they have won nationally. There is an increasing trend toward adopting hybrid systems to achieve multiple goals, as New Zealand, Italy, and Japan all have done.

Some hybrid systems operate as the German one does, with plurality elections but a guarantee of proportional representation in the legislature based on the overall distribution of votes, while others utilize completely separate constituency elections and list-system PR elections. Japan is in the latter category. Each party gains its proportional share of list-PR seats plus as many plurality seats as it wins in single-member contests. Because there are more plurality than proportional seats and the apportionment of seats is done separately, the incentives of the Japanese system, unlike the German, resemble those of first-past-the-post systems. The proportional feature, however, makes it more difficult for any single party to secure a parliamentary majority.[3]

Despite the propensity toward hybrid systems, there are also strong cultural continuities in electoral arrangements. The United Kingdom, the United States, Canada, India, many Anglophone African countries, and Malaysia all use the first-past-the-post system, which is regarded as a system common in the English-speaking world. By contrast, continental Europe tends to use list PR, and so do Francophone countries in Africa. Some very poor decisions can be made on the basis of cultural affinity. Benin, a former French colony, opted, like France, for a presidential system, with a runoff election if no candidate receives a majority on the first ballot. By choosing the runoff system, Benin turned a relatively benign tripolar ethnic conflict into a much more serious bipolar conflict. Deliberate choice, not cultural affinity, ought to be the basis of decisions about electoral systems.

As postcolonial countries rethink their electoral arrangements, they often depart from their inherited electoral systems. There is some evidence of adoption of systems from outside zones of cultural or colonial affinity, but generally their choices stay close to those of the former metropole. When English-speaking countries, such as Ireland or Australia, choose proportional representation, they tend not to choose list-system PR. Instead, they tend to opt for the single transferable vote, sometimes called the Anglo-Saxon version of PR. And in other cases when they depart from first-past-the-post, they stay with single-member constituency systems, such as the alternative vote (AV), which has been used in Australia, Papua New Guinea, and Fiji.

New electoral systems have effects on party formation, party behavior, and party systems. It is a serious mistake to take the preexisting party configuration and project it unchanged into the future if a new electoral system is adopted. When mixed-member proportional representation was adopted in New Zealand, it became much harder to form a government after the first election, and a single right-wing party gained power in the governing coalition that it could never have had under the former first-past-the-post system. When the alternative vote was adopted in Fiji, two multiethnic coalitions were formed, embracing almost all parties, and one was able to form the government. In both cases, the new system altered the strength of preexisting parties and changed their alignments. Any new system could be expected to have comparably strong effects elsewhere, but the full effects of a new system can only be gauged after two or three elections, when politicians and voters have adapted to its incentives.

Conventionally, it is thought that first-past-the-post elections promote a party system with relatively few parties (sometimes only two). Under first-past-the-post, a party with as little as 48 percent of the vote is virtually guaranteed to receive more than 50 percent of the seats. (Even 40 percent of the vote gives a party a fair chance at a majority of seats.) Because of this seat bonus, first-past-the-post typically makes the formation of governments easier than it might be under some other systems and also makes governments more durable. Those who value stability and value consistency in policy making often prefer first-past-the-post. But, of course, first-past-the-post does not have these effects everywhere. In India, Malaysia, and Canada, first-past-the-post has been compatible with multiparty systems, because the structure of social cleavages makes it impossible to compress all the main tendencies into two or three parties. Still, plurality systems do provide inducements for the aggregation or amalgamation of divergent interests into a few parties.

List-system proportional representation, on the other hand, is said to facilitate the representation of social cleavages. Minority opinions that are unrepresented in plurality-winner systems may find expression where parties with 5 or 10 percent of the vote nationwide are accorded 5 or 10 percent of the seats. Where, however, there are multiple social cleavages, adoption of a highly proportional list system creates incentives for fragmentation rather than amalgamation of political tendencies. If many social groups are organized into separate parties, each of which can gain a small fraction of the total seats, the likelihood is that political differences will be magnified rather than compressed. Governments may be formed only with difficulty, their composition may be unpredictable, and their durability may be doubtful. Giovanni Sartori has called this situation "polarized pluralism," a situation fostered by PR and conducive to immobilism. Parties cultivate only their own supporters, and compromise is hard to come by.[4]

Not everyone agrees with such a diagnosis. Theorists of consociational democracy argue that ethnic differences can be composed by coalitions once all major groups are represented in parliament through proportional representation (and through adoption of a variety of norms of conflict management, in addition to PR). But, as I suggested earlier, the electoral system does not merely represent preexisting tendencies; it also shapes them. Factions that would, under other systems, remain within one political party, for fear of being unable to win seats on their own, may, under PR, be tempted to go it alone. In a severely divided society, with many group and subgroup affiliations and many shades of opinion, list PR is likely to produce a great deal of party fragmentation.

By representing many shades of opinion—and by proliferating those shades of opinion—list PR is indifferent to the goal of choosing the Condorcet winner. And vice versa: Systems that are good at choosing the Condorcet winner leave the interests associated with many losing candidates unrepresented, as PR does not. Note, however, that the Condorcet winner is likely to be a generally moderate candidate. PR winners, on the other hand, may be moderate or not. The whole thrust of PR is to represent all opinions, regardless of their position on the political spectrum. Sartori's descriptive phrase, "polarized pluralism," is apt where the spectrum is broad or there is more than one spectrum, as there is when class cleavages coexist with but do not overlap with ethnic, religious, and regional cleavages.

A system that chooses the Condorcet winner may thus also foster interethnic conciliation, simply by favoring moderates or compromise candidates over extremists. The Lebanese system appears to do this by favoring candidates who can gain some support from voters outside their own group. The same goes for systems that require regionally well-distributed support, in addition to a plurality, for victory: They make it probable that a candidate who manages to achieve both requirements has broad appeal and so is unlikely to be an extremist, popular only with his or her own segment of the population.

The alternative vote also favors moderates. AV is an electoral system that, unlike first-past-the-post, requires 50 percent of the vote plus one for victory. Where no candidate receives 50 percent of voters' first preferences, AV requires that the candidate with the fewest first-preference votes be eliminated and that that candidate's second-preference votes be redistributed as if they were first preferences. The process is repeated until a candidate receives 50 percent. In this way, victory goes to candidates who have some support outside the core of supporters who accord them first preferences. A variation on this is the Coombs rule, under which, if no candidate has 50 percent of first preferences, the candidate with the largest number of last preferences, rather than the smallest number of first preferences, is eliminated first, and the process is carried out until a 50-percent-plus-one winner is found. Coombs is asserted to be better than the alternative vote at choosing the Condorcet winner.[5]

Note, however, that neither the alternative vote nor Coombs will produce proportional results, if by that phrase we mean proportionality of first-preference votes to seats. But, of course, under such preferential systems, it makes no sense to judge proportionality by first-preference votes alone. The whole point of the system is to count second and subsequent preferences of voters, rather than to discard them, as they are discarded by first-past-the-post and list PR alike. Proportionality is generally indifferent to moderation, and moderation is indifferent to proportionality. These are two quite different goals.

If preferential systems such as the alternative vote or Coombs are intended to reflect the full array of voter preferences, they may also shape those preferences, and they may shape the behavior of the parties competing under them. The key to this is the 50 percent threshold for victory in each constituency. As parties recognize that they may not be able by themselves to secure 50 percent of the vote in a given constituency or across a run of constituencies, they are likely to form coalitions before the election in order to exchange second and subsequent preferences. If they do not do this, their opponents will. Something of an analogous sort (but usually with less intensity) occurs under first-past-the-post, for a party wishing to be the plurality winner may try to become a broadly aggregative organization that encompasses a range of views, tendencies, and social groups. Nevertheless, the plurality and majority thresholds may create altogether different incentives for parties in a fragmented party system. In a four-way contest under the plurality rule, a party can win with as little as 26 or 30 or 35 percent of the vote; and, in recurrent three-way and four-way races, it may secure 40 or even 50 percent of the seats on the strength of a much smaller percentage of the total vote. Such a party need not broaden out its support unduly, and it need not compromise with other social groups, in order to win the election. But where the threshold for victory in each constituency is 50 percent and the party system is fragmented, there are powerful incentives for parties to make agreements with each other for the exchange of second and subsequent preferences. The success of such exchanges is likely to determine the winner.

Such preferential systems thus encourage the formation of preelectoral coalitions, and those coalitions in turn depend upon the ability of parties to compromise their differences. Hence the conciliatory thrust of systems of this sort under the conditions specified.

Another preferential system, the single transferable vote, provides fewer such incentives. That is because the threshold for success is governed by a different formula. STV operates in multimember constituencies. To be elected, a candidate must achieve a quota, as follows:

$$\text{Quota} = \frac{1}{\text{Number of Seats} + 1} + 1$$

In other words, a candidate is deemed elected if, in a four-member constituency, he or she receives one vote more than one-fifth of the votes. Such a low threshold provides few incentives to interparty agreements to transfer votes, even though perhaps the last seat in a constituency may be decided on transferred votes, as votes above the quota for victory are transferred in accordance with the second and subsequent preferences of voters providing those surplus votes. Overall, then, STV provides weaker incentives to compromise than preferential systems with majority thresholds do.

If parties do not seek votes (in this case in the form of second and subsequent preferences) from voters whose primary allegiance is to another party, an important consequence follows. In socially polarized settings, parties may not need to moderate their positions, and their supporters need not be cognizant of the claims of other social groups. After the election, of course, interparty arrangements may have to be made in order to govern. Under list PR or STV or first-past-the-post, in conditions of party fragmentation, postelectoral coalitions will probably be necessary, but they will not be based on the sort of understanding that is required of parties that make preelectoral coalitions in order to maximize their share of the vote, rather than merely to put together enough seats to form a government.

That is not to say that STV does not serve any useful functions. In general, it produces relatively proportional results, if proportionality is measured by first preferences, although that proportionality depends heavily on how many seats each constituency has (the more seats, the more proportional the results). And since STV is constituency-based, it provides some of the same constituency responsiveness that first-past-the-post or AV does, although, of course, multimember seats and low thresholds may mitigate the need of candidates to cater to the interests of those who belong to groups with which they themselves are not identified. Constituency-list PR is also a system that provides for accountability to constituents and a kind of local focus that national-list PR does not provide.

Attending to Vital Details

So far I have discussed electoral systems in terms of their goals, as if the major differences in outcome derived entirely from differences among features inherent in those systems. But a major caveat must be introduced here. Electoral outcomes are produced not just by systems, but by the preexisting pattern of social cleavages, whether single or multiple, bipolar or multipolar. Is there only one axis of difference in the society that will be reflected in the party system, or are there more than one? To what extent do the various cleavages overlap? Are there two or three or many positions at which voters locate themselves along each axis? And then there are the specific features of electoral arrangements in a polity. These can truly skew the results in one direction or another. For constituency-based systems, constituency delimitation and apportionment are inordinately important. Are constituency boundaries drawn so as to maximize homogeneity or heterogeneity along the relevant axis? The exigencies of securing election will vary accordingly. Are boundaries drawn so that some groups waste votes to elect favored candidates by large majorities, while other groups are able to use their votes more efficiently? Are constituencies more or less equal or unequal in population? Malapportionment—that is, unequal population of constituencies—is a major source of electoral unfairness.

For list PR, an analogous issue is whether there is a low (1 or 2 percent) or high (5 percent or more) threshold for a party to secure representation. A system in which any party with one percent of the vote can win a seat or seats in parliament provides great inducements for parties to split into their component factions, and it may enable very small parties that can make or break governments to have disproportionate impact in determining policy and receiving patronage, as small parties do in Israel. Ironically, the more perfect the proportionality built into such a system, the more disproportionate the ultimate policy results may be.

Very high thresholds in PR systems can produce even more capricious results. If the electorate is fragmented, a number of parties may fall under the threshold and secure no seats at all, inadvertently providing a large seat bonus to the parties above the threshold. The most striking example of this phenomenon is the 2002 Turkish election, in which the Islamic-rooted Justice and Development Party won a large majority of seats on a minority of votes, and so many parties failed to clear the 10 percent threshold that 46 percent of all votes were wasted.[6]

This should suffice to show that the details matter. Electoral systems need to be tailored closely to what those who design them want them to do. Of course, most of the time those who design such systems want them to produce results that favor the interests they prefer. My point is that there are other ways to evaluate electoral systems and the specific arrangements made pursuant to them. And very likely, no matter what the intentions of the designers, there will be some unanticipated consequences.

In every analysis, the way to proceed is to ask what goals should be fostered, which goals should be preferred over others, and what the likely effects of various alternatives really are. No one can answer these questions without an extended analysis that links electoral reasoning to the party system and the pattern of social cleavages.

There are ways to subvert even the most carefully chosen electoral system. One very common way concerns the boundaries and size of constituencies. Constituencies with vastly different numbers of voters are a prime source of disproportional outcomes. Constituencies whose boundaries have been delimited to advantage one ethnic group over another can undo the effects of electoral systems that have ethnically conciliatory features. Boundaries drawn to favor incumbents can make necessary political change impossible to achieve. It is, therefore, crucially important, not merely to choose an apt electoral system, but to make certain that boundaries are delimited by governmental bodies that are as neutral, professional, and independent as possible.

Constituency delimitation has some special requirements where systems are adopted with interethnic or interreligious conciliation as the primary goal. Whether the alternative vote or the Coombs rule or a Lebanese-style system is chosen, constituencies must be demarcated to assure that they are heterogeneous in composition.

The same attention to detail is required to make the Nigerian-style presidential electoral system work effectively. The 1978 Nigerian system required the winning candidate to gain a plurality plus at least 25 percent of the vote in no fewer than two-thirds of the states. While this system creates incentives for broadly distributed support, it also opens the possibility that no candidate will secure the requisite regional distribution to be elected. It is, therefore, necessary to provide a clear and decisive fallback provision to choose a president if this contingency occurs. The Indonesian constitution makers recently opted for a 50-percent-plus-one threshold plus a provincial distribution requirement, thereby making it especially difficult for any candidate to win on the first round if there are several candidates. It is important not to set thresholds for victory so high as to undo the benefits of the system being adopted. Electoral choice, in short, cannot stop at the level of the electoral system alone but must extend to all the details of implementing it so as to gain the benefits of the system that is preferred.

Although I have just spoken of "the system that is preferred," not all participants will necessarily prefer the same system. Those advantaged by the status quo will tend to prefer it, while those disadvantaged by it may prefer various alternatives, depending on their own interests and predictions about the likely effects of one system or another. When the Japanese changed their system in 1994, many opposition politicians preferred a plurality system that might produce a competitive two-party system, but others wanted a proportional system that would guarantee the survival of minority parties. The result was the Japanese hybrid described above.

The choice of electoral system, therefore, inevitably involves conflicting preferences and uncertain forecasts about effects. And the very process of choosing a new system has its own exigencies. The need to secure a majority for passage may accord disproportionate influence to a few legislators with distinctive interests and so skew the reform one way or another. However great may be the clarity about goals at the outset, the perfectly coherent electoral reform is difficult to achieve.

NOTES

I am indebted to IKMAS and to its director, Professor Ragaya Mat Zin, for hospitality during the time an earlier draft of this paper was written and to the Fulbright Senior Specialist Program for making my stay there possible.

1. The cumulative vote has been described as a system that contains centrifugal incentives—that is, reasons for candidates to differentiate themselves by taking positions away from the political center. Gary W. Cox, "Centripetal and Centrifugal Incentives in Electoral Systems," *American Journal of Political Science* 34 (November 1990): 903–35.

2. For one among many assessments, see Charles Cameron et al., "Do Majority-Minority Districts Maximize Substantive Black Representation in Congress?" *American Political Science Review* 90 (December 1996): 794–812.

3. See Michael F. Thies, "Changing How the Japanese Vote: The Promise and Pitfalls of the 1994 Electoral Reform," in John Fuh-sheng Hsieh and David Newman, eds., *How Asia Votes* (London: Chatham House, 2002), 92–117.

4. Sartori first made these points in "European Political Parties: The Case of Polarized Pluralism," in Joseph LaPalombara and Myron Weiner, eds., *Political Parties and Political Development* (Princeton: Princeton University Press, 1966), 137–76. Sartori pursued this theme in his *Parties and Party Systems: A Framework for Analysis* (New York: Cambridge University Press, 1976), and has more recently discussed it in *Comparative Constitutional Engineering: An Inquiry into Structures, Incentives and Outcomes* 2nd ed. (New York: New York University Press, 1997). See also Gary W. Cox, "Centripetal and Centrifugal Incentives in Electoral Systems," 921–22.

5. Bernard Grofman and Scott Feld, "If You Like the Alternative Vote (a.k.a. the Instant Runoff), Then You'll Really Like the Coombs Rule," unpublished paper, University of California–Irvine, 1 March 2002.

6. Soli Özel, "Turkey at the Polls: After the Tsunami," *Journal of Democracy* 14 (April 2003): 80–94.

2

A GLOBAL SNAPSHOT

Richard W. Soudriette and Andrew Ellis

Richard W. Soudriette *has been president of IFES (established as the International Foundation for Election Systems) since 1988. The author of numerous articles, he is currently coauthoring a book on the importance of election management in advancing democracy.* **Andrew Ellis,** *head of the Electoral Processes Team at International IDEA in Stockholm, is coauthor of* Electoral System Design: The New International IDEA Handbook. *He has previously worked for the National Democratic Institute and the European Commission. This essay originally appeared in the April 2006 issue of the* Journal of Democracy.

Today the voting booth has become the internationally accepted instrument of political change. In 1974, there were only 39 electoral democracies—that is, countries where multiparty national elections took place on a regular basis. By 2006, there were at least 120 countries that could be regarded as electoral democracies in one form or another.

Designing an electoral system is an easily identifiable, fundamental step in building a sustainable democracy. When thinking about electoral-system design, it is imperative to consider a country's historical, cultural, and sociological traditions and characteristics. Systems that work well in one country at one time may not do so in another country or even in the same country at another time. Developing countries that inherited the electoral model of their colonial masters, sometimes without debate, may not have the electoral systems that best serve their needs.

Elections are not an element of the democratic process that can be considered in isolation. The effective functioning of electoral systems is linked to political-party systems, constitutional development, the provisions governing legislative bodies, and other institutional-framework issues. The success of any system also requires its free acceptance as legitimate by the people themselves. There is a diverse array of systems in practice around the world, and sorting through the advantages and disadvantages of each is no easy task. A very useful guide to the world's electoral systems is *Electoral System Design: The New International IDEA Handbook,*[1] upon which we draw freely in the pages that follow.

The World of Electoral Systems

As Table 1 on the following pages indicates, the electoral systems used to choose national legislatures are plentiful and diverse. For more than half a century, such noted scholars as Maurice Duverger, Giovanni Sartori, Arend Lijphart, Donald Horowitz, Andrew Reynolds, and Benjamin Reilly have wrestled with the topic of electoral systems and their impact on democracy. Building on their work and that of others, we can classify electoral systems into four broad categories.

Plurality/majority. Candidates are elected on the basis of a plurality or majority of votes, usually in single-member districts (which are represented in the legislative body by only a single representative). There are five major types within this category: First Past the Post (FPTP), the Two-Round System (TRS), the Alternative Vote (AV), the Block Vote (BV), and the Party-Block Vote (PBV). FPTP is the most widely used of these systems, followed by TRS. Almost all countries that choose presidents by direct popular election use either FPTP or TRS for this purpose. There is much greater variation, however, in the systems used to elect national legislatures.

In the FPTP system, practiced in single-member districts, the winner is the candidate who receives more votes than anyone else, even if it is less than a majority. The Two-Round System, as the name implies, requires a second round of voting if no candidate in the first round wins a certain set percentage, usually an absolute majority (50 percent + 1 vote). Depending on the type of TRS, two or more of the leading candidates in the first round may contest the second round; if more than two candidates are allowed to enter the second round, the winner is the candidate with the most votes, even if less than an absolute majority.

The AV system, usually practiced in single-member districts, is a "preferential" voting system in which voters rank candidates in order according to their preference. A candidate who wins an absolute majority of first preferences wins the seat; if no candidate wins an absolute majority of first preferences, then the candidates who received the fewest number of first preferences are eliminated, and their votes are redistributed among the remaining candidates until one achieves an absolute majority.

The BV system, used in multimember districts (which are represented in a legislative body by more than one representative), gives electors as many votes as there are seats to be filled in their district, and candidates with the highest vote totals win. In the PBV system, also used in

TABLE 1—THE ELECTORAL SYSTEMS OF INDEPENDENT COUNTRIES

COUNTRY	NATIONAL LEGISLATURE	PRESIDENT	COUNTRY	NATIONAL LEGISLATURE	PRESIDENT
Afghanistan	Other (SNTV)	TRS	Equatorial Guinea	PR (List)	FPTP
Albania	Mixed (MMP)	—	Eritrea	T	T
Algeria	PR (List)	TRS	Estonia	PR (List)	—
Andorra	Mixed (PS)	—	Ethiopia	P/M (FPTP)	—
Angola	PR (List)	TRS	Fiji	P/M (AV)	—
Antigua & Barbuda	P/M (FPTP)	—	Finland	PR (List)	TRS
Argentina	PR (List)	TRS	France	P/M (TRS)	TRS
Armenia	Mixed (PS)	TRS	Gabon	P/M (TRS)	TRS
Australia	P/M (AV)	—	The Gambia	P/M (FPTP)	TRS
Austria	PR (List)	TRS	Georgia	Mixed (PS)	TRS
Azerbaijan	Mixed (PS)	TRS	Germany	Mixed (MMP)	—
Bahamas	P/M (FPTP)	—	Ghana	P/M (FPTP)	TRS
Bahrain	P/M (TRS)	—	Greece	PR (List)	—
Bangladesh	P/M (FPTP)	—	Grenada	P/M (FPTP)	—
Barbados	P/M (FPTP)	—	Guatemala	PR (List)	TRS
Belarus	P/M (TRS)	TRS	Guinea	Mixed (PS)	TRS
Belgium	PR (List)	—	Guinea-Bissau	PR (List)	TRS
Belize	P/M (FPTP)	—	Guyana	PR (List)	FPTP
Benin	PR (List)	TRS	Haiti	P/M (TRS)	TRS
Bhutan	N	—	Honduras	PR (List)	FPTP
Bolivia	Mixed (MMP)	TRS	Hungary	Mixed (MMP)	—
Bosnia-Herzegovina	PR (List)	FPTP	Iceland	PR (List)	FPTP
Botswana	P/M (FPTP)	—	India	P/M (FPTP)	—
Brazil	PR (List)	TRS	Indonesia	PR (List)	TRS
Brunei	N	—	Iran	P/M (TRS)	TRS
Bulgaria	PR (List)	TRS	Iraq	PR (List)	—
Burkina Faso	PR (List)	TRS	Ireland	PR (STV)	AV
Burma	P/M (FPTP)	—	Israel	PR (List)	—
Burundi	PR (List)	—	Italy	Mixed (MMP)	—
Cambodia	PR (List)	—	Jamaica	P/M (FPTP)	—
Cameroon	P/M & PR	FPTP	Japan	Mixed (PS)	—
Canada	P/M (FPTP)	—	Jordan	Other (SNTV)	—
Cape Verde	PR (List)	TRS	Kazakhstan	Mixed (PS)	TRS
Central African Rep.	P/M (TRS)	TRS	Kenya	P/M (FPTP)	TRS
Chad	P/M & PR	TRS	Kiribati	P/M (TRS)	FPTP
Chile	PR (List)	TRS	Kuwait	P/M (BV)	—
China	N	—	Kyrgyzstan	P/M (TRS)	TRS
Colombia	PR(List)	TRS	Laos	P/M (BV)	—
Comoros	P/M(TRS)	FPTP	Latvia	PR (List)	—
Congo (Brazzaville)	P/M (TRS)	FPTP	Lebanon	P/M (BV)	—
Congo (Kinshasa)	T	T	Lesotho	Mixed (MMP)	—
Costa Rica	PR (List)	TRS	Liberia	P/M (FPTP)	TRS
Côte d'Ivoire	P/M	TRS	Libya	N	—
Croatia	PR (List)	TRS	Liechtenstein	PR (List)	—
Cuba	P/M(TRS)	—	Lithuania	Mixed (PS)	TRS
Cyprus	PR (List)	TRS	Luxembourg	PR (List)	—
Czech Republic	PR (List)	—	Macedonia	PR (List)	TRS
Denmark	PR (List)	—	Madagascar	P/M & PR	TRS
Djibouti	P/M (PBV)	TRS	Malawi	P/M (FPTP)	FPTP
Dominica	P/M(FPTP)	—	Malaysia	P/M (FPTP)	—
Dominican Republic	PR (List)	TRS	Maldives	P/M (BV)	—
East Timor	Mixed (PS)	TRS	Mali	P/M (TRS)	TRS
Ecuador	PR (List)	TRS	Malta	PR (STV)	—
Egypt	P/M (TRS)	—	Marshall Islands	P/M	—
El Salvador	PR (List)	TRS	Mauritania	P/M (TRS)	TRS

Country	National Legislature	President	Country	National Legislature	President
Mauritius	P/M (BV)	—	Sweden	PR (List)	—
Mexico	Mixed (MMP)	FPTP	Switzerland	PR (List)	—
Micronesia	P/M (FPTP)	—	Syria	P/M (BV)	—
Moldova	PR (List)	—	Taiwan	Mixed (PS)	FPTP
Monaco	Mixed (PS)	—	Tajikistan	Mixed (PS)	TRS
Mongolia	P/M (TRS)	TRS	Tanzania	P/M (FPTP)	TRS
Morocco	PR (List)	—	Thailand	Mixed (PS)	—
Mozambique	PR (List)	TRS	Togo	P/M (TRS)	TRS
Namibia	PR (List)	TRS	Tonga	P/M (BV)	—
Nauru	Other (MBC)	—	Trinidad & Tobago	P/M (FPTP)	—
Nepal	P/M (FPTP)	—	Tunisia	Mixed (PS)	FPTP
Netherlands	PR (List)	—	Turkey	PR (List)	—
New Zealand	Mixed (MMP)	—	Turkmenistan	P/M (TRS)	TRS
Nicaragua	PR (List)	TRS	Tuvalu	P/M (BV)	—
Niger	P/M & PR	TRS	Uganda	P/M (FPTP)	TRS
Nigeria	P/M (FPTP)	TRS	Ukraine	Mixed (PS)	TRS
North Korea	P/M (TRS)	—	United Arab Emirates	N	—
Norway	PR (List)	—	United Kingdom	P/M (FPTP)	—
Oman	P/M (FPTP)	—	United States	P/M (FPTP)	FPTP
Pakistan	Mixed (PS)	—	Uruguay	PR (List)	TRS
Palau	P/M (FPTP)	TRS	Uzbekistan	P/M (TRS)	TRS
Panama	P/M & PR	FPTP	Vanuatu	Other (SNTV)	—
Papua New Guinea	P/M (AV)	—	Venezuela	Mixed (MMP)	FPTP
Paraguay	PR (List)	FPTP	Vietnam	P/M (TRS)	—
Peru	PR (List)	TRS	Yemen	P/M (FPTP)	TRS
Philippines	Mixed (PS)	FPTP	Zambia	P/M (FPTP)	FPTP
Poland	PR (List)	TRS	Zimbabwe	P/M (FPTP)	TRS
Portugal	PR (List)	TRS			
Qatar	N	—			
Romania	PR (List)	TRS	**P/M–Plurality/Majority**		
Russia	Mixed (PS)	TRS	FPTP–First Past the Post		
Rwanda	PR (List)	FPTP	TRS–Two Round System		
St. Kitts & Nevis	P/M (FPTP)	—	AV–Alternative Vote		
St. Lucia	P/M (FPTP)	—	BV–Block Vote		
St. Vincent	P/M (FPTP)	—	PBV–Party Block Vote		
Samoa	P/M	—	SV–Supplementary Vote		
San Marino	PR (List)	—	**PR–Proportional Representation**		
São Tomé & Príncipe	PR (List)	TRS	List–List Proportional Representation		
Saudi Arabia	N	—	STV–Single Transferable Vote		
Senegal	Mixed (PS)	TRS	**Mixed**		
Serbia & Montenegro	T	T	PS–Parallel System		
Seychelles	Mixed (PS)	TRS	MMP–Mixed Member Proportional		
Sierra Leone	PR (List)	TRS	**Other**		
Singapore	P/M	FPTP	SNTV–Single Non-Transferable Vote		
Slovakia	PR (List)	TRS	LV–Limited Vote		
Slovenia	PR (List)	TRS	MBC–Modified Borda Count		
Solomon Islands	P/M (FPTP)	—	**N–No provisions for direct elections**		
Somalia	T	T	**T–Country in transition** (new electoral sys-		
South Africa	PR (List)	—	tem not decided at time of publication)		
South Korea	Mixed (PS)	FPTP			
Spain	PR (List)	—			
Sri Lanka	PR (List)	SV	This table is a modified version of a more		
Sudan	P/M (FPTP)	TRS	extensive one that appears in *Electoral Sys-*		
Suriname	PR (List)	—	*tem Design: The New International IDEA*		
Swaziland	P/M (FPTP)	—	*Handbook* (2005).		

multimember districts, electors vote for party lists rather than individuals, and the party that garners the most votes wins all the seats. These two systems may be regarded as "hypermajoritarian," in that they tend to translate small advantages in votes into larger advantages in seats.

Plurality/majority systems are used in many countries around the world. Along with the United Kingdom and many of its former colonies, including India and Canada, the United States has long embraced the FPTP system. TRS, on the other hand, is used by France and many countries historically influenced by France. AV is used on the national level in Australia, Fiji, and Papua New Guinea. BV is used in 11 countries or territories spread across the globe, mostly in smaller entities where parties are weak. PBV is used in Cameroon, Chad, Djibouti, and Singapore.

Proportional representation (PR). The main goal of PR is to transfer the share of votes received by a party into a corresponding proportion of seats in the legislative body. It is used only in multimember districts. There are two main types of PR systems: List PR and the Single Transferable Vote (STV). List PR is much more common worldwide than STV.

Under List PR, seats are allocated to political parties on the basis of votes cast for party lists, with the percentage of votes at the ballot box roughly translating into the same percentage of legislative seats. List PR is put into practice in different ways. In "closed-list" systems, voters can vote only for party lists, and cannot express any preference for individual candidates. In "open-list" systems, voters may express a preference for candidates within the party lists, while in "free-list" systems they may even express a preference for a candidate outside the party list that they have chosen.

Under the STV system, voters rank candidates. The quota of votes required for victory is determined, and any candidate who receives at least that amount immediately wins a seat. The least successful candidates are then weeded out and their votes are redistributed. Votes from successful candidates that are above the quota are also redistributed. The redistribution continues until the remaining seats are filled.

List PR, widely used in Western Europe, Latin America, and Africa, is employed by more than one-third of the world's countries and territories—more than any other system. It is interesting to note, however, that FPTP is used by almost twice as many *people* in the world as List PR (43.5 percent of people living in countries that have direct elections, versus 23.9 percent), in large part because FPTP is used in such large countries as India and the United States. The STV system, though popular with political scientists, is used on the national level only in the Republic of Ireland and Malta.

Mixed. Under mixed systems, there are two groups of elected members: one group elected under a plurality/majority system, the other under a PR system. The elections for the two groups of members can be linked to produce a relatively proportional result (Mixed-Member Pro-

TABLE 2—CHANGES TO ELECTORAL SYSTEMS (1993–2004)

OLD SYSTEM	NEW SYSTEM				Total (old systems)
	Plurality/ Majority	PR	Mixed	Other	
Plurality/Majority	Bermuda Fiji Mongolia Montserrat Papua NG	Iraq Moldova Rwanda Sierra Leone South Africa	Lesotho Monaco New Zealand Philippines Russia Thailand Ukraine	Afghanistan Jordan	19
PR	Madagascar		Bolivia Italy Venezuela		4
Mixed		Croatia Macedonia	Mexico		3
Other			Japan		1
Total (new systems)	6	7	12	2	27

portional, or MMP) or conducted independently of each other (Parallel System, or PS).

The MMP system first developed in post–World War II Germany is now also used in Albania, Bolivia, Hungary, Italy, Lesotho, Mexico, New Zealand, and Venezuela. The Parallel System is used in 21 countries across the globe, including the Russian Federation and Japan.

Other. Some other systems, such as the Single Non-Transferable Vote (SNTV), the Limited Vote (LV), and the Borda Count (BC), do not fit neatly into any of these categories. In translating votes into seats, these systems tend to have effects somewhere between those of the plurality/ majority and PR systems. SNTV was installed for parliamentary elections in Afghanistan in 2005, though it is a much criticized system. LV is used by Spain to elect its upper house, while only Nauru uses BC.

Trends in Electoral-System Changes

Mapping changes between 1993 and 2004 in a total of 213 countries and territories, International IDEA's *Electoral System Design* handbook found 27 changes of electoral system type (not included in the 27 is Kyrgyzstan, which made a change and then changed back). These are summarized in Table 2 above.

These data show a trend away from plurality/majority systems toward proportional-representation systems. The most common change was from systems of plurality/majority to mixed systems (7 countries).

Table 2 understates the degree of change in electoral-system arrangements around the world. In addition to the 13 percent of countries and territories that have made a change in their system type, many others have made changes within their existing system—for example, by changing the number of members elected from each electoral district, by introducing or changing threshold vote levels that parties or candidates are required to achieve to be allowed representation, or by introducing or restricting voter choice between candidates in party-list–based systems. While such changes may look technical in nature, they can have profound effects on who is elected and thus on the way in which the political system works.

In most cases where the system type itself has changed, a major crisis of representation has been necessary to trigger the change. In Papua New Guinea, more than half the winners in the 2002 parliamentary elections polled less than 20 percent of the vote, which inevitably raised questions about the legitimacy of those elected. The subsequent change from FPTP to AV in Papua New Guinea in 2003 was hardly surprising. Crises can also occur in established democracies. In two successive general elections in New Zealand, the party with the most votes nonetheless found itself in opposition; ultimately, after two referenda were held in the 1990s, the system was changed from FPTP to MMP. In Italy and Japan, the loss of confidence in the whole political system engendered by endemic corruption scandals also led to electoral system changes; Italy changed from List PR to MMP in 1993, and Japan from SNTV to the Parallel System in 1994.

System changes also arise in transitions to democracy—sometimes when the transition is peaceful and domestically driven, and almost always when the transition follows violent conflict and is internationally driven. Iraq is a prime recent example of this. The Two-Round System for parliamentary elections, used during the time of the monarchy and as the framework for the sham elections of the Saddam Hussein era, was replaced by a List PR system in 2004—a change proposed by the United Nations and embraced by the interim Iraqi government.[2]

In Latin America, there has increasingly been a trend toward MMP, with Bolivia, Venezuela, and Mexico all moving in this direction. In the aftermath of the breakup of the Soviet Union, many countries of the former Soviet bloc, such as Estonia, Bulgaria, Poland, Moldova, and Romania, turned to List-PR systems. Other countries, including Hungary, Lithuania, Russia, and Ukraine, have introduced mixed systems, whereby at least half of their parliamentary seats are elected by FPTP and the remainder by PR.

What might explain this general trend toward greater proportionality? PR systems may be particularly valuable in countries where there is a real need to reflect ethnic, economic, or social diversity, or which are seeking to ensure that not only parties with substantial support but also relatively small groups are represented in the elected assembly. Generally, more women and ethnic minorities are elected to legislatures under proportional electoral systems. Strong democracies have grown up in many European countries that have chosen to use List-PR systems, including the Nordic countries and the Netherlands. In 1922, the Republic of Ireland adopted STV, which has helped to produce one of the strongest and most vibrant democracies in Europe.

There have been some notable exceptions to the overall trend toward greater proportionality; Afghanistan in particular has bucked this trend. By definition, proportionality requires identifiable parties or groupings that can be proportionally represented. In Afghanistan, concerns about participation by political groups linked to warlords, combined with the negative connotation of the concept of party (left over from the communist years), led to the presidential election being conducted on a nonpartisan basis. All presidential candidates ran as independent candidates in a Two-Round System. In the run-up to the 2005 parliamentary elections for the 249-member Wolesi Jirga (the directly elected lower house of the Afghan legislature), extensive discussions were held to decide which electoral system to use. Eventually, the SNTV system was chosen. Newly elected president Hamid Karzai was committed to maintaining nonpartisanship in the system. Sixty-eight of the 249 seats were reserved for women. No parties were allowed, and all candidates ran as independents.[3]

The wholesale change of an electoral system is hard to achieve. Most countries' electoral systems are governed by ordinary laws, and thus systems may be altered within the legislative bodies. A number of countries, however, have somehow incorporated details of their electoral systems into their constitutions, and constitutions are usually more difficult to change than ordinary laws. Nonetheless, whether the electoral system is controlled by the constitution or by ordinary laws, political will on the part of elites is needed to change electoral systems, and political elites will often not seriously consider significantly changing a system unless they perceive some benefit to themselves.

Even if the appropriate political actors recognize the need for electoral-system reform, another problem arises in choosing the best electoral system to replace the old. In Mexico, the creation of a Parallel System in 1994 led to the most disproportional result the country ever had with a mixed system (the system was later changed again, to MMP). Additionally, because electoral systems are so complex, long-term benefits from electoral-system change are difficult to assess.

The Effects of Electoral-System Change

Implementing a new electoral system is a complex task. In selecting an electoral system, a vital consideration is the question of its impact on the administration of elections. How will elections actually be carried out under an electoral system in a given country, and what effects will they have, given the facts on the ground?

Many factors must be taken into account when considering which electoral system to implement and how a system can be effectively administered in a country. Five key factors to consider are: 1) electoral boundaries; 2) voter education; 3) the modernization of election equipment; 4) ballot papers and counting; and 5) long-term sustainability.

1) Electoral boundaries. The process of delineating district boundaries is a fundamentally political task: All boundaries create political winners and losers. In plurality/majority systems in particular, the design of districts is a challenging and daunting task. Many countries that use FPTP, like Canada and Britain, are required to develop boundaries for single-member districts on the basis of a regular boundary delimitation process. If this must be done prior to each parliamentary election, it is an expensive and time-consuming process. If it is less regular, significant discrepancies in the size of electoral districts can result. In the United States, for example, boundaries of congressional districts are determined by each of the fifty state legislatures using data generated from the decennial national census. The drawing of these boundaries has always been a volatile and politically charged matter.

Any process that defines boundaries requires substantial time and consultation if it is to be accepted as fair by electoral participants. This means that it is rarely possible to define new electoral districts during democratic transitions, when political momentum and the euphoria of transition create well-nigh irresistible pressures for elections to take place on fast timetables. In addition, almost all political participants in any negotiations over a new institutional framework know that concessions are more valuable the later they are made; it is thus almost inevitable that the time available for processes of boundary definition—and indeed for other aspects of election organization—will be eaten away.

2) Voter education. In newly established democracies, legislators do not always have a good grasp of the concept of "their constituents." At the same time, voters may not fully understand that they are electing legislators to represent them and their communities. In countries with high levels of illiteracy, such as Afghanistan, these concepts can be especially difficult to convey without adequate voter and civic education efforts. Trying to explain the methodology of voting in countries with low literacy levels can be challenging when more complex systems are chosen.

3) Modernization of election equipment. With the growing international trend toward modernization of voting equipment, the selection of electoral systems is one factor that can heavily impact election administration. In India, the introduction of electronic voting machines has helped make elections successful. India's current FPTP system for the election of parliamentarians made it possible for the Indian Election Commission to develop a very effective and low-cost electronic system; under some other electoral systems, the development of a successful electronic voting system would have been much more difficult.

The electoral authorities in the Republic of Ireland spent millions of dollars in 2004 to introduce a new electronic voting system for parliamentary elections. Ireland uses the Single Transferable Vote, however, a system that requires voters to express a series of preferences on the ballot paper. At the last minute, a decision was made to scrap the electronic voting system due to concerns that it was not sufficiently voter-friendly. Instead, Ireland returned to the traditional paper ballot for the 2004 parliamentary elections.

4) Ballot papers and counting. It is essential for election administrators to organize voter-friendly elections, though it is important to remember that administrators can only operate within the confines of the constitution and the electoral law. The ease of voting-equipment use and of voting procedure can help to enhance the integrity of the election process in the eyes of the voter, as well as lay a positive foundation for the future. An example of a system that does not meet these criteria is found in Fiji. The legislative ballot allows voters to vote either in one section of the ballot paper for a party (and see their vote transferred to other candidates according to preferences submitted by that party) or in a second section for individual candidates. If the voter chooses to vote for individual candidates, preferences must be expressed for at least three-quarters of the candidates on the ballot paper. In the first two elections held so far under this system, well over 10 percent of the votes cast have been invalid.

In Iraq's December 2005 National Assembly elections, a total of 996 parties and political entities were on the ballot, presenting a total of 7,655 candidates. Voters were faced with mammoth bedsheet-sized ballots and faced a daunting task in making their final selection and casting their votes. Due to the number of political entities on the ballot, the Independent Election Commission of Iraq (IECI) had to purchase specially designed ballot boxes to accommodate the extremely large ballots. Counting was a slow and tedious process. As a result, it took nearly one month for all of the votes to be counted and for the IECI to release final results. The design of the electoral system enhanced inclusiveness but had heavy costs in the ease of voting and timely counting—a good example of the way in which desirable qualities of electoral systems sometimes tug in opposite directions. Electoral-system design ultimately involves a set of choices: designers must choose which desirable qualities are of highest value and which of secondary importance.

5) Long-term sustainability. Long-term sustainability of the electoral process needs to be considered, especially when relatively complex electoral systems are under consideration. When a first-time democratic election is organized by an international transitional presence, or with substantial international technical assistance and funds, almost anything can be made to work. At a second or third election, when external resources no longer flow so freely, the organization of a sustainable electoral process is dependent on the financial resources available within the national budget and the human resources of the country—both of which may be limited and subject to other urgent demands. While too much simplicity in electoral-system design in transitions can ignore potential constructive approaches to state building, too much complexity may lead to ineffectiveness in the longer term.

The 1948 Universal Declaration of Human Rights recognizes the right to vote as a fundamental human right. Electoral systems provide the framework that guarantees people the right to have a voice in how they are governed. Countries need to consider historical, cultural, and social factors in the choice of an electoral system and to engage stakeholders in the discussion to increase the likelihood that the electorate will accept the legitimacy of elections. Criteria for choice can include building stable and efficient governments; enabling effective legislative opposition and oversight to develop; supporting accountability of governments and of individual elected members for their performance; developing vibrant political parties; and providing incentives for conflict mitigation. Together with other design aims such as strengthening civil society and encouraging press freedom, the choices made are fundamental to laying the foundation for a culture of democracy.

Ill-conceived electoral systems can undermine popular support for democratic governance, while well-designed electoral systems can help to establish systems that encourage popular participation and ensure the long-term success of democracy. As former Philippine president Fidel Ramos once said, "Governments may come and go, but the people remain. It is the majesty of people power that we exalt when we build functioning and free electoral systems."

NOTES

1. Andrew Reynolds, Ben Reilly, and Andrew Ellis, *Electoral System Design: The New International IDEA Handbook* (Stockholm: IDEA, 2005), available online at *www.idea.int.*

2. For more information on Iraq's electoral-system change, see the chapter by Adeed Dawisha and Larry Diamond on pp. 224–38 of this volume.

3. For more information on Afghanistan's SNTV system, see the chapter by Andrew Reynolds on pp. 210–23 of this volume.

3

DEALING WITH DIVIDED SOCIETIES

Benjamin Reilly

Benjamin Reilly *is director of the Centre for Democratic Institutions at the Australian National University.* He is the author of several books, including Democracy in Divided Societies: Electoral Engineering for Conflict Management *(2001), which treats in greater detail some of the issues discussed in this essay. He also consults widely on issues of electoral reform. Funding from the United States Institute of Peace supported the research for this essay. The essay originally appeared in the April 2002 issue of the* Journal of Democracy.

What kinds of electoral systems can help democracy survive in countries split by deep cleavages of race, religion, language, or ethnicity? As is well-known, politicians in such "divided societies" often have strong incentives to "play the ethnic card" at election time, using communal appeals to mobilize voters. "Outbidding"—increasingly extreme rhetoric and demands—can offer rewards greater than those of moderation. In such circumstances, politics can quickly turn centrifugal, as the center is pulled apart by extremist forces and "winner-take-all" rules the day. The failure of democracy is often the result.[1]

Any strategy for building sustainable democracy in divided societies must place a premium on avoiding this depressingly familiar pattern and must instead find ways to promote interethnic accommodation, multiethnic political parties, and moderate, centrist politics. Because elections help shape broader norms of political behavior, scholars and practitioners alike agree that electoral systems can play a powerful role in promoting both democracy and successful conflict management. For example, by changing the incentives and payoffs available to political actors in their search for electoral victory, astutely crafted electoral rules can make some types of behavior more politically rewarding than others. Over the past two decades, such "electoral engineering" has become increasingly attractive for those attempting to build democracy in divided societies.[2]

While political scientists agree broadly that electoral systems do much
to shape the wider political arena, they disagree deeply about which
electoral systems are most appropriate for divided societies.

Two schools of thought predominate. The scholarly orthodoxy has
long argued that some form of proportional representation (PR) is needed
in cases of deep-rooted ethnic divisions. PR is a key element of *consociational* approaches, which emphasize the need to develop mechanisms for elite power-sharing if democracy is to survive ethnic or other
conflicts. Arend Lijphart, the scholar most associated with the consociational model, developed this prescription from a detailed examination of the features of power-sharing democracy in some continental
European countries (the Netherlands, Belgium, and Switzerland), and
there is disagreement over how well these measures can work (if at all)
when applied to ethnic conflict in developing countries.[3] Yet there is
little doubt that among scholars consociationalism represents the dominant model of democracy for divided societies. In terms of electoral
systems, consociationalists argue that party-list PR is the best choice, as
it enables all significant ethnic groups, including minorities, to "define
themselves" into ethnically based parties and thereby gain representation in the parliament in proportion to their numbers in the community
as a whole.[4]

The "Preferential" Option

In contrast to this orthodoxy, some critics argue that the best way to
mitigate the destructive patterns of divided societies is not to encourage the formation of ethnic parties, thereby replicating existing ethnic
divisions in the legislature, but rather to utilize electoral systems that
encourage cooperation and accommodation among rival groups, and
therefore work to reduce the salience of ethnicity. One core strategy,
advocated by Donald Horowitz, is to design electoral rules that promote
reciprocal vote-pooling, bargaining, and accommodation across group
lines.[5] Presidential elections in Nigeria, for example, require the winning candidate to gain support from different regions, thus helping to
diminish claims of narrow parochialism or regionalism. Lebanon's electoral system attempts to defuse the importance of ethnicity by
pre-assigning ethnic proportions in each constituency, thus requiring
parties to present ethnically mixed slates of candidates for election and
making voters base their choices on issues other than ethnicity.

Yet the most powerful electoral systems for encouraging accommodation are those that make politicians reciprocally dependent on votes
from groups other than their own. This essay examines the empirical
record of one such electoral innovation as a tool of conflict management: the use of "preferential" electoral systems that enable voters to
rank-order their choices among different parties or candidates on the

ballot paper. All preferential electoral systems share a common, distinguishing feature: They enable electors to indicate how they would vote if their favored candidate was defeated and they had to choose among those remaining. Such systems include the alternative vote (AV) and the single transferable vote (STV).

AV is a majoritarian system used in single-member electoral districts that requires the winning candidate to gain not just a plurality but an absolute majority of votes. If no candidate has an absolute majority of first preferences, the candidate with the lowest number of first-preference votes is eliminated and his or her ballots are redistributed to the remaining candidates according to the lower preferences marked. This process of sequential elimination and transfer of votes continues until a majority winner emerges.

STV, by contrast, is a proportional system based around multimember districts that, depending on the number of members elected in each district, can allow even small minorities access to representation. Voters rank candidates in order of preference on the ballot in the same manner as AV. The count begins by determining the "quota" of votes required to elect a single candidate.[6] Any candidate who has more first preferences than the quota is immediately elected. If no one has achieved the quota, the candidate with the lowest number of first preferences is eliminated, and his or her second and later preferences are redistributed to the candidates left in the race. At the same time, the "surplus" votes of elected candidates (that is, their votes above the quota) are redistributed at a reduced value according to the lower preferences on the ballots, until all seats for the constituency are filled.

Because they enable electors to rank candidates in their order of preference, such systems can encourage politicians in divided societies to campaign not just for first-preference votes from their own community, but for second-choice votes from other groups as well—thus providing parties and candidates with an incentive to "pool votes" across ethnic lines. To attract second-level support, candidates may need to make crossethnic appeals and demonstrate their capacity to represent groups other than their own. Alternately, where a moderate or nonethnic "middle" part of the electorate exists, candidates may need to move to the center on policy issues to attract these voters.

Either way, negotiations between rival candidates and their supporters for reciprocal vote transfers can greatly increase the chances that votes will shift from ethnic parties to nonethnic ones—thus encouraging, even in deeply divided societies, the formation and strengthening of a core of moderate middle sentiment within the electorate as a whole. Such negotiations can also stimulate the development of alliances between parties and aid the development of multiethnic parties or coalitions of parties. Scholars have increasingly found that aggregative party systems can help new or transitional democracies achieve stability.

This broad approach to conflict management has been dubbed "centripetalism" because "the explicit aim is to engineer a centripetal spin to the political system—to pull the parties toward moderate, compromising policies and to discover and reinforce the center of a deeply divided political spectrum."[7] A centripetal political system or strategy is designed to focus competition at the moderate center rather than the extremes by making politicians do more than just shop for votes in their own community.

Accordingly, I use the term centripetalism as a shorthand for three related but distinct phenomena: 1) the provision of *electoral incentives* for campaigning politicians to reach out to and attract votes from ethnic groups other than their own, thus encouraging candidates to moderate their political rhetoric on potentially divisive issues and forcing them to broaden their policy positions; 2) the presence of an *arena of bargaining,* in which political actors from different groups have an incentive to come together and cut deals on reciprocal electoral support, and hence perhaps on other more substantial issues as well; and 3) the development of *centrist, aggregative, and multiethnic political parties* or coalitions of parties that are capable of making crossethnic appeals and presenting a complex and diverse range of policy options to the electorate.

Five Cases

A recurring criticism of centripetalism is that there are insufficient real-world examples to support the case for using preferential voting as an agent of conflict management in ethnically divided societies.[8] Recent years, however, have seen some remarkable experiments in the use of centripetal electoral rules to encourage interethnic accommodation in divided societies as diverse as Northern Ireland, Estonia, Fiji, and Papua New Guinea. Elsewhere, new democracies like Indonesia and Bosnia are actively considering such systems, and even such established democracies as Australia, the United Kingdom, and the United States are showing increasing interest in the utility of preferential voting as a means of aggregating like-minded interests and combating "vote-splitting" and extremist forces.[9] A common theme is the desire to "engineer" political behavior by changing the incentives to which campaigning politicians must respond. The following pages briefly survey the combined evidence on this issue to date.

Northern Ireland. Northern Ireland is probably the best-known recent example of centripetal institutions encouraging intercommunal accommodation in a divided society, via the use of a preferential electoral system at the crucial 1998 elections held under the Good Friday peace process. After 30 years of sectarian violence between Northern Ireland's Catholic ("nationalist") and Protestant ("unionist") communities, the Good Friday peace agreement of April 1998 provided for a range of new institutions aimed at managing the conflict—among them power-sharing elections, held under STV rules, to a new Northern Ireland Assembly. Although previous elections under similar rules had been held in 1973 and 1982 without achieving the desired effect, the 1998 election resulted, for the first time in Northern Ireland's history, in the formation of a "pro-peace" government in which nationalists and unionists share power.

The use of preference voting assisted the peace process in a number of ways. First, it provided direct incentives for the major parties to moderate their positions in the hope of attracting lower-order preference votes from moderate voters. The possibility of picking up lower-order transfers was instrumental, for example, in moving Sinn Fein away from violence and toward less extreme policy positions. This movement was rewarded by moderation-inclined voters—as the increased flow of lower-order preferences to Sinn Fein from more centrist nationalist parties such as the Social Democratic and Labour Party (SDLP) at the 1998 poll indicated. Similarly, on the unionist side, STV encouraged those voting for anti-agreement unionist parties to transfer their lower-order votes to other unionist parties and candidates, many of them pro-agreement.

These vote transfers benefited the center, allowing pro-agreement communal parties—such as the Catholic SDLP or the Protestant Ulster Unionists (UUP) and Progressive Unionists (PUP)—to gain lower-order votes from other pro-agreement forces. The UUP clearly profited from the system, as it gained 26 percent of the parliamentary seats with only 21 percent of the first-preference votes. This process also benefited some of the nonsectarian "middle" parties like the Alliance and the Women's Coalition, which received lower-order votes from both sides of the political divide and consequently were proportionately overrepresented in the new assembly.

These trends had a beneficial influence both upon the types of political alliances that could be formed and on the eventual composition of the new Assembly, more than 70 percent of which was made up of pro-agreement parties. In fact, vote transfers were essential in converting a bare anti-agreement unionist voter majority into a pro-agreement unionist parliamentary majority. Of course, as Northern Ireland's rocky history underlines, this may not be enough for the peace process to succeed—but it raises its chances of doing so.

Estonia. Another example of the use of STV in a divided society comes from Estonia, which is split between a majority (60 percent) Estonian-speaking community and a minority (35 percent) Russian-speaking one. Estonia used an STV electoral system for its first post-Soviet national election in 1990. In contrast to Northern Ireland, however, analysis of this "one-off" redemocratization election suggests little in the way of crossethnic voting or vote-pooling between the two communities. Studies found that most Russian electors voted predominantly for liberal democratic "Russian" parties, and their second preferences "went overwhelmingly to reactionary imperialist Russian candidates rather than liberal but ethnically Estonian ones. Likewise, voters with Estonian first preferences continued with Estonian names."[10] While there was some evidence of vote transfers crossing ethnic lines, particularly support for Estonian candidates by non-Estonian voters, it is not clear whether this was a reaction to electoral incentives.

Yet there is also evidence from Estonia that using STV early in the transition did help encourage the development of an aggregative, multiethnic party system—itself a crucial agent of conflict management in divided societies. Some analyses found that STV's combination of proportional outcomes with individual (rather than group-based) candidacy promoted a broad-based party system in Estonia and restricted incentives for parties to form purely along ethnic lines.[11] Other comparative studies of electoral-system choice in Eastern Europe have concluded that optimum strategies of electoral-system design in divided societies should attempt to represent groups fairly while promoting candidate-based (rather than group- or party-based) voting—and hence that STV may be "just the institutional trick" for preventing politicized ethnic conflicts in new democracies.[12]

Had STV been maintained on an ongoing basis in Estonia, it is likely that electoral strategies would have become more sophisticated as political actors learned about the system and its effects. But this was not to be: In 1992, the new parliament abandoned STV and adopted a variant of list PR after several leading parties calculated that such a change would help them. The political effect of STV upon Estonian politics is thus difficult to evaluate, given the quickly changing conditions and the way it was adopted as a political compromise and then discarded for similar reasons. Rein Taagepera points to two general lessons: First, even a country with as limited a recent experience with free elections as Estonia had no problems with the relatively complex STV ballot, and second, "whichever electoral rules one adopts, keep them for at least two elections before getting into the revamping game."[13]

Australia. One of the most interesting recent examples of the use of preferential voting to foil political extremism comes from the unlikely setting of Australia, one of the world's most stable democracies. Although not a divided society, Australia has an extremely diverse population, with almost 40 percent being immigrants or the offspring of immigrants, many of whom come from non–English-speaking countries in Southern Europe, the Middle East, and Asia. Preferential-voting systems are used for all Australian jurisdictions, in the form of single-member AV systems in the lower house and proportional STV systems in the Senate. Over the years, preferential voting has tended to push the Australian political system away from extremes and toward the moderate middle, while also ensuring the election of governments that, in most cases, enjoy majority support. It has also enabled parties to develop partnership arrangements—with the long-running coalition agreement between the conservative Liberal and National parties being the most prominent, but not the only, example. In recent years the other major party, the Australian Labor Party, has also benefited from preference flows from left-leaning minor parties such as the Greens and the Australian Democrats.[14]

In most cases, the effect of such vote transfers has been to aggregate common interests on either the labor or conservative side of politics, rather than align those interests against a common enemy. One graphic exception to this rule, however, occurred in the 1998 federal election, due to the rising power of Pauline Hanson and her One Nation party. One Nation represented a distinctively Australian version of the populist right-wing racist parties that had appeared in many European countries during the 1990s. First elected to the House of Representatives in 1996, Hanson campaigned on a platform of ending immigration, removing benefits and subsidies to Aborigines and other disadvantaged groups, drastically cutting taxes, raising tariffs, ending all foreign aid, and removing Australia from international bodies such as the United Nations.

Following a protracted period of national and international media attention, the major Australian parties decided to join forces to eliminate what they saw as a dangerous aberration in the political system. One potent way of doing this was by suggesting to their supporters a specific distribution of lower-order preferences. At the 1998 election in Hanson's Queensland district, both major parties instructed their supporters to place her *last* when marking their ballot (in contrast to the more familiar tactic of suggesting that their major-party opponent be placed last).

The result was an instructive lesson in the application of AV rules to defeat an extremist candidate who commands significant core support but ultimately repels more voters than he or she attracts. In a field of nine candidates, Hanson achieved the highest number of first preferences—36 percent—but received very few preference transfers. As the count progressed, almost three-quarters of the Labor candidate's preferences went to a Liberal, who won the seat with 53.4 percent of the overall (preference-distributed) vote, even though he only polled *third* on first preferences. This result, which was repeated in a less dramatic fashion in other districts around the country, saw One Nation largely eliminated from federal politics (although it did win one seat in the Senate). By contrast, under a plurality system Hanson would almost certainly have beaten a divided field of more moderate candidates and taken a seat in the federal parliament. The Australian example thus demonstrates a preventive form of conflict management: the capacity of AV to privilege centrist interests and centripetal political strategies in a potentially divisive situation.

Fiji. One of the most comprehensive recent attempts at electoral engineering using centripetal approaches has taken place in Fiji, a South Pacific island country of approximately 750,000 people divided almost equally between indigenous and Indian Fijians. Fiji's indigenous population is a mixture of the Melanesian and Polynesian groups found throughout the Pacific islands, while Fiji's Indian citizens are mostly the descendants of indentured laborers who came from southern India to work on Fiji's sugar plantations in the nineteenth century under British colonialism. Fijian society and politics have long been characterized by the uneasy coexistence of these two communities, with Indo-Fijians predominating in certain key areas of the economy (particularly the sugarcane industry) and indigenous Fijians owning 90 percent of the land but holding limited economic power.

In 1997, ten years after two military coups brought down an elected government seen as overly close to the Indian community—and in the face of economic stagnation, increasing Indian immigration, and mounting international pressure—a new power-sharing constitution was promulgated that attempted to push Fiji "gradually but decisively" toward multiethnic politics. It featured an innovative package of electoral and power-sharing arrangements designed to promote the development of open and multiethnic political competition, including an AV voting system. By making politicians from one group reliant on votes from the other group for their electoral success, AV could, it was argued, encourage a degree of vote-pooling between rival ethnic parties that would promote accommodation between (and within) Fiji's deeply divided Indian and indigenous Fijian communities.[15]

Fiji's 1999 parliamentary election, the first held under the new constitution, provided a practical test for the new system. Early signs were encouraging: Political parties from both sides of the ethnic divide reacted to the changed incentives by making preelection alliances. This meant that the election was effectively fought between two large multiethnic coalitions rather than between monoethnic parties as in the past. Parties representing the interests of Fiji's three designated ethnic groups—indigenous Fijians, Indo-Fijians, and "general" electors (European, Chinese, and other minorities)—formed the core of both of these coalitions. Since crossethnic preference exchanges underpinned both coalitions, the new rules also prompted the development of new bargaining arenas that brought together former adversaries from across the ethnic divide, encouraging a degree of crosscultural communication that had been conspicuously absent at previous elections.[16]

At the election itself, an unexpectedly strong vote for the Fiji Labour Party, combined with a fragmented indigenous Fijian vote, resulted in a surprise landslide victory for one of these groupings, the so-called People's Coalition. Mahendra Chaudhry, the Labour leader, thus became Fiji's first Indo-Fijian prime minister. Labour ran largely on a multiethnic, class-based platform and was the only party to gain a good spread of votes in both rural and urban areas, although it was a poor performer in contests for the Fijian communal seats.

A number of other parties appeared to suffer at the hands of the system, however, leading to an imbalanced parliament dominated by Labour and its allies. Popular discontent on the part of many indigenous Fijians at the presence of an Indo-Fijian prime minister continued to simmer, and Chaudhry's sometimes outspoken advocacy of Indo-Fijian rights served to deepen mistrust over such key issues as land ownership. In May 2000, exactly one year after the 1999 election, a group of gunmen headed by failed part-Fijian businessman George Speight burst into the parliament building and took the new government hostage, claiming a need to restore indigenous Fijian paramountcy to the political system. By the time the hostages were released and Speight and his supporters arrested, Fiji had returned to military rule.

In August 2001, however, Fiji went back to the polls under the 1997 Constitution. Again, the election campaign was fought out by two broad coalitions—this time, the moderates and the conservatives. This election, held under the same AV electoral system, resulted in a quite different outcome, with the incumbent government of military-appointed indigenous Fijian prime minister Laisenia Qarase emerging victorious.

As this uncertain history shows, preferential voting has had mixed success in stimulating the core objective of peaceful multiethnic politics in Fiji. On the positive side, the new opportunities for interelite bargaining and crossethnic vote pooling were exploited by party elites from both communities. In combination with the expectations of places at the power-sharing cabinet table, this served to cool significantly the rhetoric of the 1999 campaign. But the outcome of the 1999 election was highly disproportional, with the Fiji Labour Party dominating. At the 2001 election, however, these imbalances were less in evidence, but so was crossethnic political behavior. Overall, the introduction of preferential voting appears to have played a modest but ambiguous role in breaking the old habits of monoethnic politics in Fiji. Whether it will serve to promote multiethnic politics in the future remains to be seen.

Papua New Guinea. Another Pacific country, Papua New Guinea, offers perhaps the most compelling case for the use of preferential voting as a means of conflict management in ethnically diverse societies. Papua New Guinea is a country of exceptional ethnic fragmentation, with some 840 languages spoken by several thousand competitive ethnic "micropolities," reflecting enormous ethnic, cultural, and regional divisions. Indeed, more languages are spoken by Papua New Guinea's 5.1 million people than in all of Africa. Despite its amazingly fragmented society, Papua New Guinea also has one of the longest records of continuous democracy in the developing world, having maintained a highly competitive and participatory form of democratic governance since 1964.[17]

In terms of electoral systems, Papua New Guinea's first three elections—in 1964, 1968, and 1972—were conducted under AV rules inherited from Australia, its colonial administrator until independence in 1975. These rules were replaced at independence by a plurality system—a move that had devastating consequences for the nascent political system.

Politics in Papua New Guinea is strongly influenced by the fractionalized nature of traditional society, which is composed of several thousand competing "clans"—extended family units—that form the primary (and sometimes the only) unit of political loyalty. Electoral contests are focused on the mobilization of clan and tribal groups, rather than around issues of public policy or ideology, and thus often have the effect of underlining the significance of basic clan and ethnic attachments. Since independence, elections have also encouraged a "retribalization" of ethnic groups, in which the economic importance of gaining political office has led to increasingly rigid group boundaries and burgeoning interethnic armed conflict.[18] Elections are thus one of the primary ways in which traditional enmities are mobilized in contemporary Papua New Guinea.

This was the case under both AV and plurality elections, and it remains the case today. The difference in pre-independence elections held under AV rules was that the electoral system appeared to encourage a degree of vote-pooling, cooperation, and accommodation among the country's many small tribal groups, rather than the violent competition that has become the norm over the past decade. Vote-pooling in pre-independence elections took place in three primary ways, all of which were predicated on the assumption that most voters would invariably give their first preference to their own clan or "home" candidate. The most common and successful method was for candidates who had limited home support to campaign widely for second-preference support among rival groups. For this strategy to succeed, candidates needed to be able to sell themselves as the second-best choice—which meant, in general, someone who would look after all groups fairly—and to campaign as much for second preferences as for first ones. A second strategy was for candidates with significant existing support bases to reach out to selected allies for secondary support. Traditional tribal contacts and allegiances could thus be utilized to create majority victors. A third strategy, increasingly common by independence, was for groups and candidates to form mutual alliances, sometimes campaigning together and urging voters to cast reciprocal preferences. Not only were these alliances a response to the incentives presented by AV for campaigning on a common platform, they also appear to have encouraged political organizing and can thus be seen as the forerunners to the establishment of political parties.

All of these patterns disappeared in 1975 when preferential voting, seen as a colonial imposition from Australia, was replaced with a plurality system. With no incentives for cooperation, elections almost immediately became zero-sum contests between rival tribal groups. Most seats were contested by scores of clan-backed candidates, resulting in winners being elected on the basis of increasingly minuscule vote shares. At the most recent national election in 1997, over half of all seats were won with less than 20 percent of the vote, and 15 with less than 10 percent. Related factors of electoral violence and "vote splitting"— friendly candidates with little hope of winning the seat standing in order to "split" an opposition vote—have also became a problem under the plurality system. Under AV, the winning candidates in many electorates were those who cultivated the preferences of voters outside their own local area. Today, such spreading of the net is almost inconceivable in many parts of Papua New Guinea, as the very real physical risks of campaigning in a hostile area tend to overshadow the (marginal) possibilities of picking up significant numbers of votes there.[19]

Not surprisingly, this state of affairs has encouraged a strong push for a return to the pre-independence AV electoral system. In January 2002, following several failed attempts, Papua New Guinea's parliament voted decisively to return to a form of "limited" preferential voting for elections after 2002, with voters required to list at least three preferences. Along with moves to strengthen executive government, weed out corruption in politics, and promote the development of political parties, this move was seen as part of a last-ditch effort to turn around Papua New Guinea's vibrant but chronically unstable democracy. The main benefits of the electoral system reforms, however, are likely to be changes in electoral behavior and a reduction in conflicts and tribal violence at the local level.

Evaluating the Evidence

All of these cases provide important empirical evidence for evaluating claims that preferential electoral systems can, under certain circumstances, promote cooperation among competing groups in divided societies. This in itself is an important conclusion, as a recurring criticism of centripetal theories in general, and of the case for preferential voting in particular, has been a perceived lack of real-world examples. Apparently similar institutional designs, however, also appear to have had markedly different impacts in different countries. In Northern Ireland, for example, it is clear that vote transfers assisted the process of moderation in the breakthrough 1998 election. But the evidence from elections held under similar rules in 1973 or 1982—or, for that matter, from Estonia's 1990 election—is much more ambiguous. Similarly, Papua New Guinea's experience with AV in the 1960s and 1970s was markedly more successful than that of its Pacific neighbor, Fiji, more recently. Why?

A key facilitating condition appears to be the presence of a core group of *moderates,* both among the political leadership and in the electorate at large. Centripetal strategies for conflict management assume that there is sufficient moderate sentiment within a community for crossethnic voting to be possible. In some circumstances, the presence of vote-pooling institutions may even encourage the development of this type of moderate core, via repeated interelite interaction within bargaining arenas. But it cannot invent moderation where none exists. It is likely that a major factor in the success or failure of centripetalism in Northern Ireland was the lack of a moderate core in earlier elections and its clear presence in 1998. This is reflected in part by the fact that, in the 1998 election, far more votes were transferred from sectarian to nonsectarian "middle" parties than across the ethnic divide per se.[20]

The argument that preferential election rules induce moderation rests on the assumption that politicians are rational actors who will do what needs to be done to gain election. Under different types of preferential-voting rules, however, "what needs to be done" varies considerably, depending on the electoral formula in place and the social makeup of the electorate. For example, if candidates are confident of achieving an absolute majority or winning the required quota of first preferences, they need only focus on maximizing votes from their own supporters in order to win the seat. In cases where no candidate has outright majority support, however, the role of second and later preferences becomes crucial to gaining an overall majority. Thus some scholars such as Horowitz favor majoritarian forms of preferential voting like AV over the proportional variant of STV, since the former's threshold for immediate victory is higher. In addition, Horowitz's case for "vote pooling" is based on the purported possibility of crossethnic voting—that is, the assumption that even in deeply divided societies some electors will be prepared to give some votes, even if only lower-order ones, to members of another ethnic group. In Northern Ireland, however, while vote transfers played an important role in promoting accommodation, these ran predominantly from anti-agreement to pro-agreement parties on the same side of the sectarian divide, or from sectarian to nonsectarian "middle" parties, rather than across the communal cleavage between unionists and nationalists.

Second, *continuity of experience* appears to be a critical variable. The evidence suggests that successive elections held under the same rules encourage a gradual process of political learning. Structural incentives need to be kept constant over several elections before the effects of any electoral package can be judged—particularly with preferential systems, where the routines of deal-making and preference-swapping by politicians, and the understanding of these devices by voters, take time to emerge. In the world's two longest-running cases of preferential voting—Australia and Ireland—it took many years for the full strategic potential of vote-transfers to became clear to politicians and voters alike (in fact, rates of preference-swapping in Australian elections have increased steadily over recent decades), while Estonia's preferential system may have been so short-lived that voters and politicians never became adjusted to it.

Third, the *social context* in which elections are held appears all-important. Countries like Northern Ireland and Estonia feature "bipolar" splits between two large and relatively cohesive ethnic groups, both of which were effectively guaranteed representation under STV's proportional election rules. But in 1998, Northern Ireland also had a third group: the middle, nonsectarian parties that were not clearly bound to either community. By advantaging the representation of this group, STV promoted outcomes that would not have been likely under AV or other majority systems, or under party-list PR. In other cases, however, where there is greater ethnic heterogeneity or a much smaller nonethnic center, STV may not work so well—indeed, it did not work well in Northern Ireland's previous elections. All this suggests that a key element of any electoral-engineering prescription must be a careful understanding of the prevailing social and demographic conditions—particularly the size, number, and dispersion of ethnic groups.

The importance of ethnic demography is highlighted by the cases of Fiji and Papua New Guinea. In Fiji, most open electoral districts—which are supposed to encapsulate a "good proportion" of members of both major communities—are drawn in such a way as to become the exclusive preserve of one ethnic group or the other. Thus genuine opportunities for interethnic cooperation at the constituency level are rare, and most contests provide no opportunity at all for crossethnic campaigns, appeals, or outcomes. Indeed, only six seats were genuinely competitive between ethnic groups in the 1999 election, while in the rest clear Indian or Fijian majorities prevailed.[21]

Contrast this with the situation in Papua New Guinea, where the extreme fragmentation of traditional society means that most districts feature dozens of small tribal ethnopolities. To be elected under a preferential majority system like AV, candidates had no option but to amass votes from a range of groups beyond their own. Under such conditions, candidates had a strong incentive to behave accommodatingly toward rival groups. Not surprisingly, electoral violence was much rarer under the AV system than under the more recent plurality rules, which lacks such incentives.

Such cases remind us that divided societies, like Tolstoy's unhappy families, tend to be divided in different ways. Yet it is surprising how many "one-size-fits-all" conflict-management packages have been recommended for divided societies without sufficient understanding of the structure of the society itself. Differences in ethnic demography need to be matched by differences in constitutional designs across different regions. African minorities, for example, have been found to be

more highly concentrated in contiguous geographical areas than minorities in other regions, making it difficult to create ethnically
heterogenous electorates.[22] Contrast this with the highly intermixed
patterns of ethnic settlement found in many parts of Europe (the Baltics),
Asia (India, Singapore, Malaysia), and the Caribbean (Guyana, Suriname,
Trinidad and Tobago), in which members of various ethnic groups tend
to have more day-to-day contact with one another. In such contexts,
electoral districts are likely to be ethnically heterogeneous, and ethnic
identities will often be mitigated by other crosscutting cleavages, so
that centripetal designs which encourage parties to seek the support of
various ethnic groups may very well break down interethnic antago-
nisms and promote the development of broad, multiethnic parties. Such
prosaic details can determine the success of centripetal approaches to
the management of ethnic conflict.

NOTES

1. For good discussions of the interaction between ethnicity and electoral politics, see Donald L. Horowitz, *Ethnic Groups in Conflict* (Berkeley: University of
California Press, 1985); Larry Diamond and Marc F. Plattner, eds., *Nationalism,
Ethnic Conflict, and Democracy* (Baltimore: Johns Hopkins University Press, 1994);
and Timothy D. Sisk, *Power Sharing and International Mediation in Ethnic Conflicts* (Washington, D.C.: U.S. Institute of Peace Press, 1996).

2. See, for example, Arend Lijphart, *Democracy in Plural Societies: A Com-
parative Exploration* (New Haven: Yale University Press, 1977); Donald L.
Horowitz, *A Democratic South Africa? Constitutional Engineering in a Divided
Society* (Berkeley: University of California Press, 1991); Giovanni Sartori, *Com-
parative Constitutional Engineering: An Inquiry into Structures, Incentives and
Outcomes* (London: Macmillan, 1994); and Benjamin Reilly and Andrew Reynolds,
Electoral Systems and Conflict in Divided Societies (Washington, D.C.: National
Research Council, 1999).

3. See Arend Lijphart, *Democracy in Plural Societies*; and Timothy D. Sisk,
Power Sharing and International Mediation in Ethnic Conflicts, 27–45. See also
Donald L. Horowitz, "Making Moderation Pay: The Comparative Politics of Ethnic
Conflict Management," in Joseph V. Montville, ed., *Conflict and Peacemaking in
Multiethnic Societies* (New York: Lexington Books, 1991), 451–76.

4. Arend Lijphart, "Electoral Systems, Party Systems and Conflict Management
in Segmented Societies," in R.A. Schrire, ed., *Critical Choices for South Africa: An
Agenda for the 1990s* (Cape Town: Oxford University Press, 1990), 10–13.

5. See Donald L. Horowitz, *Ethnic Groups in Conflict*; and Donald L. Horowitz,
"Making Moderation Pay."

6. The formula used divides the total number of votes in the count by one more
than the number of seats to be elected, and then adds one to the result. For example,
if there are 6,000 votes and five members to be elected, the quota for election is
6,000/(5+1) + 1, or 1,001 votes.

7. Timothy D. Sisk, *Democratization in South Africa: The Elusive Social Contract* (Princeton: Princeton University Press, 1995), 19.

8. See Timothy D. Sisk, *Power Sharing and International Mediation in Ethnic Conflicts*, 44, 62; and Arend Lijphart, "The Alternative Vote: A Realistic Alternative for South Africa?" *Politikon* 18 (June 1991): 91–101.

9. In 1998, the British government's Jenkins Commission unveiled a proposal for "AV plus": a mixed system with 80 percent of seats elected by AV, and the remaining 20 percent elected from a PR list to balance proportionality. In May 2000, a form of preferential voting was used for London's first-ever mayoral elections. In the United States, preferential voting is becoming an increasingly prominent electoral-reform option in a number of states, including New Mexico and California. On 5 March 2002, voters in San Francisco passed an initiative adopting the alternative vote for all future city elections.

10. Rein Taagepera, "STV in Transitional Estonia," *Representation* 34 (Winter 1996–97): 31.

11. See John T. Ishiyama, "Electoral Rules and Party Nomination Strategies in Ethnically Cleaved Societies: The Estonian Transitional Election of 1990," *Communist and Post-Communist Studies* 27 (June 1994): 177–92.

12. John T. Ishiyama, "Institutions and Ethnopolitical Conflict in Post-Communist Politics," *Nationalism and Ethnic Politics* 6 (Autumn 2000): 65.

13. Rein Taagepera, "STV in Transitional Estonia," 36.

14. See Benjamin Reilly, "Preferential Voting and Its Political Consequences," in Marian Sawer, ed., *Elections: Full, Free and Fair* (Sydney: Federation Press, 2001).

15. See Constitution Review Commission 1996, *The Fiji Islands: Towards a United Future* (Suva: Parliament of Fiji, 1996).

16. See Brij V. Lal, *A Time to Change: The Fiji General Elections of 1999*, Department of Political and Social Change Discussion Paper 23, Australian National University, 1999, 6.

17. See Benjamin Reilly, "Democracy, Ethnic Fragmentation, and Internal Conflict: Confused Theories, Faulty Data, and the 'Crucial Case' of Papua New Guinea," *International Security* 25 (Winter 2000–2001): 162–85.

18. Andrew Strathern, "Violence and Political Change in Papua New Guinea," *Pacific Studies* 16 (December 1993): 41–60.

19. Bill Standish, "Elections in Simbu: Towards Gunpoint Democracy?" in Yaw Saffu, ed., *The 1992 PNG Election: Change and Continuity in Electoral Politics* (Canberra: Australian National University, 1996).

20. See Richard Simmott, "Centrist politics makes modest but significant progress: cross-community transfers were low," *Irish Times* (Dublin), 29 June 1998.

21. See Nigel Roberts, "Living up to Expectations? The New Fijian Electoral System and the 1999 General Election," paper presented to Citizens Constitutional Forum, Suva, Fiji, 18 July 1999.

22. James R. Scarritt, "Communal Conflict and Contention for Power in Africa South of the Sahara," in Ted Robert Gurr, ed., *Minorities at Risk: A Global View of Ethnopolitical Conflicts* (Washington, D.C.: U.S. Institute of Peace Press, 1993).

4

THE CASE FOR POWER SHARING

Arend Lijphart

Arend Lijphart is research professor emeritus of political science at the University of California, San Diego. He is the author of Patterns of Democracy: Government Forms and Performance in Thirty-Six Countries *(1999) and many other studies of democratic institutions, the governance of deeply divided societies, and electoral systems. This essay originally appeared in the April 2004 issue of the* Journal of Democracy.

Over the past half-century, democratic constitutional design has undergone a sea change. After the Second World War, newly independent countries tended simply to copy the basic constitutional rules of their former colonial masters, without seriously considering alternatives. Today, constitution writers choose more deliberately among a wide array of constitutional models, with various advantages and disadvantages. While at first glance this appears to be a beneficial development, it has actually been a mixed blessing: Since they now have to deal with more alternatives than they can readily handle, constitution writers risk making ill-advised decisions. In my opinion, scholarly experts can be more helpful to constitution writers by formulating specific recommendations and guidelines than by overwhelming those who must make the decision with a barrage of possibilities and options.

This essay presents a set of such recommendations, focusing in particular on the constitutional needs of countries with deep ethnic and other cleavages. In such deeply divided societies the interests and demands of communal groups can be accommodated only by the establishment of power sharing, and my recommendations will indicate as precisely as possible which particular power-sharing rules and institutions are optimal and why. (Such rules and institutions may be useful in less intense forms in many other societies as well.)

Most experts on divided societies and constitutional engineering broadly agree that deep societal divisions pose a grave problem for democracy, and that it is therefore generally more difficult to establish and maintain democratic government in divided than in homogeneous countries. The experts also agree that the problem of ethnic and other deep divisions is greater in countries that are not yet democratic or fully democratic than in well-established democracies, and that such divisions present a major obstacle to democratization in the twenty-first century. On these two points, scholarly agreement appears to be universal.

A third point of broad, if not absolute, agreement is that the successful establishment of democratic government in divided societies requires two key elements: power sharing and group autonomy. Power sharing denotes the participation of representatives of all significant communal groups in political decision making, especially at the executive level; group autonomy means that these groups have authority to run their own internal affairs, especially in the areas of education and culture. These two characteristics are the primary attributes of the kind of democratic system that is often referred to as power-sharing democracy or, to use a technical political-science term, "consociational" democracy.[1] A host of scholars have analyzed the central role of these two features and are sympathetic to their adoption by divided societies.[2] But agreement extends far beyond the consociational school. A good example is Ted Robert Gurr, who in *Minorities at Risk: A Global View of Ethnopolitical Conflicts* clearly does not take his inspiration from consociational theory (in fact, he barely mentions it), but based on massive empirical analysis reaches the conclusion that the interests and demands of communal groups can usually be accommodated "by some combination of the policies and institutions of *autonomy* and *power sharing.*"[3]

The consensus on the importance of power sharing has recently been exemplified by commentators' reactions to the creation of the Governing Council in Iraq: The Council has been criticized on a variety of grounds, but no one has questioned its broadly representative composition. The strength of the power-sharing model has also been confirmed by its frequent practical applications. Long before scholars began analyzing the phenomenon of power-sharing democracy in the 1960s, politicians and constitution writers had designed power-sharing solutions for the problems of their divided societies (for example, in Austria, Canada, Colombia, Cyprus, India, Lebanon, Malaysia, the Netherlands, and Switzerland). Political scientists merely discovered what political practitioners had repeatedly—and independently of both academic experts and one another—invented years earlier.

Critics of Power Sharing

The power-sharing model has received a great deal of criticism since it became a topic of scholarly discourse three decades ago. Some critics have argued that power-sharing democracy is not ideally democratic or effective; others have focused on methodological and measurement issues.[4] But it is important to note that very few critics have presented serious alternatives to the power-sharing model. One exception can be found in the early critique by Brian Barry, who in the case of Northern Ireland recommended "cooperation without cooptation"—straightforward majority rule in which both majority and minority would simply promise to behave moderately.[5] Barry's proposal would have meant that Northern Ireland's Protestant majority, however moderate, would be in power permanently, and that the Catholic minority would always play the role of the "loyal" opposition. Applied to the case of the Iraqi Governing Council, Barry's alternative to power sharing would call for a Council composed mainly or exclusively of moderate members of the Shi'ite majority, with the excluded Sunnis and Kurds in opposition. This is a primitive solution to ethnic tensions and extremism, and it is naïve to expect minorities condemned to permanent opposition to remain loyal, moderate, and constructive. Barry's suggestion therefore cannot be—and, in practice, has not been—a serious alternative to power sharing.

The only other approach that has attracted considerable attention is Donald L. Horowitz's proposal to design various electoral mechanisms (especially the use of the "alternative vote" or "instant runoff") that would encourage the election of moderate representatives.[6] It resembles Barry's proposal in that it aims for moderation rather than broad representation in the legislature and the executive, except that Horowitz tries to devise a method to induce the moderation that Barry simply hopes for. If applied to the Iraqi Governing Council, Horowitz's model would generate a body consisting mainly of members of the Shi'ite majority, with the proviso that most of these representatives would be chosen in such a way that they would be sympathetic to the interests of the Sunni and Kurdish minorities. It is hard to imagine that, in the long run, the two minorities would be satisfied with this kind of moderate Shi'ite representation, instead of representation by members of their own communities. And it is equally hard to imagine that Kurdish and Sunni members of a broadly representative constituent assembly would ever agree to a constitution that would set up such a system.

Horowitz's alternative-vote proposal suffers from several other weaknesses, but it is not necessary to analyze them in this article.[7] The main point that is relevant here is that it has found almost no support from either academic experts or constitution writers. Its sole, and only partial, practical application to legislative elections in an ethnically divided society was the short-lived and ill-fated Fijian constitutional system, which tried to combine the alternative vote with power-sharing; it was adopted in 1999 and collapsed in 2000.[8] With all due respect to the originality of his ideas and the enthusiasm with which he has defended them, Horowitz's arguments do not seem to have sparked a great deal of assent or emulation.[9]

"One Size Fits All"?

In sum, power sharing has proven to be the only democratic model that appears to have much chance of being adopted in divided societies, which in turn makes it unhelpful to ask constitution writers to contemplate alternatives to it. More than enough potential confusion and distraction are already inherent in the consideration of the many alternatives *within* power sharing. Contrary to Horowitz's claim that power-sharing democracy is a crude "one size fits all" model,[10] the power-sharing systems adopted prior to 1960 (cited earlier), as well as more recent cases (such as Belgium, Bosnia, Czechoslovakia, Northern Ireland, and South Africa), show enormous variation. For example, broad representation in the executive has been achieved by a constitutional requirement that it be composed of equal numbers of the two major ethnolinguistic groups (Belgium); by granting all parties with a minimum of 5 percent of the legislative seats the right to be represented in the cabinet (South Africa, 1994–99); by the equal representation of the two main parties in the cabinet and an alternation between the two parties in the presidency (Colombia, 1958–64); and by permanently earmarking the presidency for one group and the prime ministership for another (Lebanon).

All of these options are not equally advantageous, however, and do not work equally well in practice, because the relative success of a power-sharing system is contingent upon the specific mechanisms devised to yield the broad representation that constitutes its core. In fact, the biggest failures of power-sharing systems, as in Cyprus in 1963 and Lebanon in 1975, must be attributed not to the lack of sufficient power sharing but to constitution writers' choice of unsatisfactory rules and institutions.

These failures highlight the way in which scholarly experts can help constitution writers by developing recommendations regarding power-sharing rules and institutions. In this sense, Horowitz's "one size fits all" charge should serve as an inspiration to try to specify the optimal form of power sharing. While the power-sharing model should be adapted according to the particular features of the country at hand, it is not true that *everything* depends on these individual characteristics. In the following sections I outline nine areas of constitutional choice and provide my recommendations in each area. These constitute a "one size" power-sharing model that offers the best fit for most divided societies regardless of their individual circumstances and characteristics.

1) The legislative electoral system. The most important choice facing constitution writers is that of a legislative electoral system, for which the three broad categories are proportional representation (PR), majoritarian systems, and intermediate systems. For divided societies, ensuring the election of a broadly representative legislature should be the crucial consideration, and PR is undoubtedly the optimal way of doing so.

Within the category of majoritarian systems, a good case could be made for Horowitz's alternative-vote proposal, which I agree is superior to both the plurality method and the two-ballot majority runoff.[11] Nevertheless, there is a scholarly consensus against majoritarian systems in divided societies. As Larry Diamond explains:

> If any generalization about institutional design is sustainable . . . it is that majoritarian systems are ill-advised for countries with deep ethnic, regional, religious, or other emotional and polarizing divisions. Where cleavage groups are sharply defined and group identities (and intergroup insecurities and suspicions) deeply felt, the overriding imperative is to avoid broad and indefinite exclusion from power of any significant group.[12]

The intermediate category can be subdivided further into semiproportional systems, "mixed" systems, and finally, majoritarian systems that offer guaranteed representation to particular minorities. Semiproportional systems—like the cumulative and limited vote (which have been primarily used at the state and local levels in the United States) and the single nontransferable vote (used in Japan until 1993)[13]—may be able to yield minority representation, but never as accurately and consistently as PR. Unlike these rare semiproportional systems, mixed systems have become quite popular since the early 1990s.[14] In some of the mixed systems (such as Germany's and New Zealand's) the PR component overrides the plurality component, and these should therefore be regarded not as mixed but as PR systems. To the extent that the PR component is not, or is only partly, compensatory (as in Japan, Hungary, and Italy), the results will necessarily be less than fully proportional—and minority representation less accurate and secure. Plurality combined with guaranteed representation for specified minorities (as in India and Lebanon) necessarily entails the potentially invidious determination of which groups are entitled to guaranteed representation and which are not. In contrast, the beauty of PR is that in addition to producing proportionality and minority representation, it treats all groups— ethnic, racial, religious, or even noncommunal groups—in a completely equal and evenhanded fashion. Why deviate from full PR at all?

2) Guidelines within PR. Once the choice is narrowed down to PR, constitution writers need to settle on a particular type within that system. PR is still a very broad category, which spans a vast spectrum of complex possibilities and alternatives. How can the options be narrowed further? I recommend that highest priority be given to the selection of a PR system that is simple to understand and operate—a criterion that is especially important for new democracies. From that simplicity criterion, several desiderata can be derived: a high, but not necessarily perfect, degree of proportionality; multimember districts that are not too large, in order to avoid creating too much distance between voters and their representatives; list PR, in which parties present lists of candidates to the voters, instead of the rarely used single transferable vote, in which voters have to rank order individual candidates; and closed or almost closed lists, in which voters mainly choose parties instead of individual candidates within the list. List PR with closed lists can encourage the formation and maintenance of strong and cohesive political parties.

One attractive model along these lines is the list-PR system used in Denmark, which has 17 districts that elect an average of eight representatives each from partly open lists. The districts are small enough for minority parties with more than 8 percent of the vote to stand a good chance of being elected.[15] In addition to the 135 representatives elected in these districts, there are 40 national compensatory seats that are apportioned to parties (with a minimum of 2 percent of the national vote) in a way that aims to maximize overall national proportionality.[16] The Danish model is advantageous for divided societies, because the compensatory seats plus the low 2 percent threshold give small minorities that are not geographically concentrated a reasonable chance to be represented in the national legislature. While I favor the idea of maximizing proportionality, however, this system does to some extent detract from the goal of keeping the electoral system as simple and transparent as possible. Moreover, national compensatory seats obviously make little sense in those divided societies where nationwide parties have not yet developed.

3) Parliamentary or presidential government. The next important decision facing constitution writers is whether to set up a parliamentary, presidential, or semipresidential form of government. In countries with deep ethnic and other cleavages, the choice should be based on the different systems' relative potential for power sharing in the executive. As the cabinet in a parliamentary system is a collegial decision-making body—as opposed to the presidential one-person executive with a purely advisory cabinet—it offers the optimal setting for forming a broad power-sharing executive. A second advantage of parliamentary systems is that there is no need for presidential elections, which are necessarily majoritarian in nature. As Juan Linz states in his well-known critique of presidential government, "Perhaps the most important implication of presidentialism is that it introduces a strong element of zero-sum game into democratic politics with rules that tend toward a 'winner-take-all' outcome."[17] Presidential election campaigns also encourage the politics of personality and overshadow the politics of competing parties and party programs. In representative democracy, parties provide the vital link between voters and the government, and in divided societies they are crucial in voicing the interests of communal groups. Seymour Martin Lipset has recently emphasized this point again by calling political parties "indispensable" in democracies and by recalling E.E. Schattschneider's famous pronouncement that "modern democracy is unthinkable save in terms of parties."[18]

Two further problems of presidentialism emphasized by Linz are frequent executive-legislative stalemates and the rigidity of presidential terms of office. Stalemates are likely to occur because president and legislature can both claim the democratic legitimacy of being popularly elected, but the president and the majority of the legislature may belong to different parties or may have divergent preferences even if they belong to the same party. The rigidity inherent in presidentialism is that presidents are elected for fixed periods that often cannot be extended because of term limits, and that cannot easily be shortened even if the president proves to be incompetent, becomes seriously ill, or is beset by scandals of various kinds. Parliamentary systems, with their provisions for votes of confidence, snap elections, and so on, do not suffer from this problem.

Semipresidential systems represent only a slight improvement over pure presidentialism. Although there can be considerable power sharing among president, prime minister, and cabinet, the zero-sum nature of presidential elections remains. Semipresidential systems actually make it possible for the president to be even more powerful than in most pure presidential systems. In France, the best-known example of semipresidentialism, the president usually exercises predominant power; the 1962–74 and 1981–86 periods have even been called "hyperpresidential" phases.[19] The stalemate problem is partly solved in semipresidential systems by making it possible for the system to shift from a mainly presidential to a mainly parliamentary mode if the president loses the support of his party or governing coalition in the legislature. In the Latin American presidential democracies, constitutional reformers have often advocated semipresidential instead of parliamentary government, but only for reasons of convenience: A change to parliamentarism seems too big a step in countries with strong presidentialist traditions. While such traditional and sentimental constraints may have to be taken into account in constitutional negotiations, parliamentary government should be the general guideline for constitution writers in divided societies.

There is a strong scholarly consensus in favor of parliamentary government. In the extensive literature on this subject, the relatively few critics have questioned only parts of the pro-parliamentary consensus. Pointing to the case of U.S. presidentialism, for instance, they have noted that the stalemate problem has not been as serious as Linz and others have alleged—without, however, challenging the validity of the other charges against presidential government.[20]

4) Power sharing in the executive. The collegial cabinets in parliamentary systems facilitate the formation of power-sharing executives, but they do not by themselves guarantee that power sharing will be instituted. Belgium and South Africa exemplify the two principal methods of doing so. In Belgium, the constitution stipulates that the cabinet must comprise equal numbers of Dutch-speakers and French-speakers. The disadvantage of this approach is that it requires specifying the groups entitled to a share in power, and hence the same discriminatory choices inherent in electoral systems with guaranteed representation for particular minorities. In South Africa there was so much disagreement and controversy about racial and ethnic classifications that these could not be used as a basis for arranging executive power sharing in the 1994 interim constitution. Instead, power sharing was mandated in terms of political parties: Any party, ethnic or not, with a minimum of 5 percent of the seats in parliament was granted the right to participate in the cabinet on a proportional basis.[21] For similar situations in other countries, the South African solution provides an attractive model. But when there are no fundamental disagreements about specifying the ethnic groups entitled to a share of cabinet power, the Belgian model has two important advantages. First, it allows for power sharing without mandating a grand coalition of all significant parties and therefore without eliminating significant partisan opposition in parliament. Second, it allows for slight deviation from strictly proportional power sharing by giving some overrepresentation to the smaller groups, which may be desirable in countries where an ethnic majority faces one or more ethnic minority groups.

5) Cabinet stability. Constitution writers may worry about one potential problem of parliamentary systems: The fact that cabinets depend on majority support in parliament and can be dismissed by parliamentary votes of no-confidence may lead to cabinet instability—and, as a result, regime instability. The weight of this problem should not be overestimated; the vast majority of stable democracies have parliamentary rather than presidential or semipresidential forms of government.[22] Moreover, the position of cabinets vis-à-vis legislatures can be strengthened by constitutional provisions designed to this effect. One such provision is the constructive vote of no confidence, adopted in the 1949 constitution of West Germany, which stipulates that the prime minister (chancellor) can be dismissed by parliament only if a new prime minister is elected simultaneously. This eliminates the risk of a cabinet being voted out of office by a "negative" legislative majority that is unable to form an alternative cabinet. Spain and Papua New Guinea have adopted similar requirements for a constructive vote of no confidence. The disadvantage of this provision is that it may create an executive that cannot be dismissed by parliament but does not have a parliamentary majority to pass its legislative program—the same kind of stalemate that plagues presidential systems. A suggested solution to this potential problem was included in the 1958 constitution of the French Fifth Republic in the form of a provision that the cabinet has the right to make its legislative proposals matters of confidence, and these proposals are adopted automatically unless an absolute majority of the legislature votes to dismiss the cabinet. No constitution has yet tried to combine the German and French rules, but such a combination could undoubtedly give strong protection to cabinets and their legislative effectiveness—without depriving the parliamentary majority of its fundamental right to dismiss the cabinet and replace it with a new one in which parliament has greater confidence.

6) *Selecting the head of state.* In parliamentary systems, the prime minister usually serves only as head of government, while a constitutional monarch or a mainly ceremonial president occupies the position of head of state. Assuming that no monarch is available, constitution writers need to decide how the president should be chosen. My advice is twofold: to make sure that the presidency will be a primarily ceremonial office with very limited political power, and not to elect the president by popular vote. Popular election provides democratic legitimacy and, especially in combination with more than minimal powers specified in the constitution, can tempt presidents to become active political participants—potentially transforming the parliamentary system into a semipresidential one. The preferable alternative is election by parliament.

A particularly attractive model was the constitutional amendment proposed as part of changing the Australian parliamentary system from a monarchy to a republic, which specified that the new president would be appointed on the joint nomination of the prime minister and the leader of the opposition, and confirmed by a two-thirds majority of a joint session of the two houses of parliament. The idea behind the two-thirds rule was to encourage the selection of a president who would be nonpartisan and nonpolitical. (Australian voters defeated the entire proposal in a 1999 referendum mainly because a majority of the pro-republicans strongly—and unwisely—preferred the popular election of the president.) In my opinion, the best solution is the South African system of not having a separate head of state at all: There the president is in fact mainly a prime minister, subject to parliamentary confidence, who simultaneously serves as head of state.

7) *Federalism and decentralization.* For divided societies with geographically concentrated communal groups, a federal system is undoubtedly an excellent way to provide autonomy for these groups. My specific recommendation regards the second (federal) legislative chamber that is usually provided for in federal systems. This is often a politically powerful chamber in which less populous units of the federation are overrepresented (consider, for example, the United States Senate, which gives two seats to tiny Wyoming as well as gigantic California). For parliamentary systems, two legislative chambers with equal, or substantially equal, powers and different compositions is not a workable arrangement: It makes too difficult the forming of cabinets that have the

confidence of both chambers, as the 1975 Australian constitutional crisis showed: The opposition-controlled Senate refused to pass the budget in an attempt to force the cabinet's resignation, although the cabinet continued to have the solid backing of the House of Representatives. Moreover, a high degree of smaller-unit overrepresentation in the federal chamber violates the democratic principle of "one person, one vote." In this respect, the German and Indian federal models are more attractive than the American, Swiss, and Australian ones.

Generally, it is advisable that the federation be relatively decentralized and that its component units (states or provinces) be relatively small—both to increase the prospects that each unit will be relatively homogeneous and to avoid dominance by large states on the federal level. Beyond this, a great many decisions need to be made regarding details that will vary from country to country (such as exactly where the state boundaries should be drawn). Experts have no clear advice to offer on how much decentralization is desirable within the federation, and there is no consensus among them as to whether the American, Canadian, Indian, Australian, German, Swiss, or Austrian model is most worthy of being emulated.

8) Nonterritorial autonomy. In divided societies where the communal groups are not geographically concentrated, autonomy can also be arranged on a nonterritorial basis. Where there are significant religious divisions, for example, the different religious groups are often intent on maintaining control of their own schools. A solution that has worked well in India, Belgium, and the Netherlands is to provide educational autonomy by giving equal state financial support to all schools, public and private, as long as basic educational standards are met. While this goes against the principle of separating church and state, it allows for the state to be completely neutral in matters of education.

9) Power sharing beyond the cabinet and parliament. In divided societies, broad representation of all communal groups is essential not only in cabinets and parliaments, but also in the civil service, judiciary, police, and military. This aim can be achieved by instituting ethnic or religious quotas, but these do not necessarily have to be rigid. For example, instead of mandating that a particular group be given exactly 20 percent representation, a more flexible rule could specify a target of 15 to 25 percent. I have found, however, that such quotas are often unnecessary; it is sufficient to have an explicit constitutional provision in favor of the general objective of broad representation and to rely on the power-sharing cabinet and the proportionally constituted parliament for the practical implementation of this goal.

Other Issues

As far as several other potentially contentious issues are concerned, my advice would be to start out with the modal patterns found in the world's established democracies, such as a two-thirds majority requirement for amending the constitution (with possibly a higher threshold for amending minority rights and autonomy), a size of the lower house of the legislature that is approximately the cube root of the country's population size[23] (which means that a country with about 25 million inhabitants, such as Iraq, "should" have a lower house of about 140 representatives), and legislative terms of four years.

While approval by referendum can provide the necessary democratic legitimacy for a newly drafted constitution, I recommend a constitutional provision to limit the number of referenda. One main form of referendum entails the right to draft legislation and constitutional amendments by popular initiative and to force a direct popular vote on such propositions. This is a blunt majoritarian instrument that may well be used against minorities. On the other hand, the Swiss example has shown that a referendum called by a small minority of voters to challenge a law passed by the majority of the elected representatives may have the desirable effect of boosting power sharing. Even if the effort fails, it forces the majority to pay the cost of a referendum campaign; hence the potential calling of a referendum by a minority is a strong stimulus for the majority to be heedful of minority views. Nevertheless, my recommendation is for extreme caution with regard to referenda, and the fact that frequent referenda occur in only three democracies—the United States, Switzerland, and, especially since about 1980, Italy—underscores this guideline.

Constitution writers will have to resolve many other issues that I have not mentioned, and on which I do not have specific recommendations: for example, the protection of civil rights, whether to set up a special constitutional court, and how to make a constitutional or supreme court a forceful protector of the constitution and of civil rights without making it too interventionist and intrusive. And as constitution writers face the difficult and time-consuming task of resolving these issues, it is all the more important that experts not burden or distract them with lengthy discussions on the relative advantages and disadvantages of flawed alternatives like presidentialism and non-PR systems.

I am not arguing that constitution writers should adopt all my recommendations without *any* examination of various alternatives. I recognize that the interests and agendas of particular parties and politicians may make them consider other alternatives, that a country's history and traditions will influence those who must draft its basic law, and that professional advice is almost always—and very wisely—sought from more than one constitutional expert. Even so, I would contend that my recommendations are not merely based on my own preferences, but on a strong scholarly consensus and solid empirical evidence, and that at the very least they should form a starting point in constitutional negotiations.

NOTES

I am grateful to the Bellagio Study and Conference Center of the Rockefeller Foundation for offering me the opportunity to work on this project while I was a resident of the Center in May–June 2003, and to Roberto Belloni, Torbjörn Bergman, Joseph H. Brooks, Florian Bieber, Jorgen Elklit, Svante Ersson, John McGarry, Brendan O'Leary, Mogens N. Pedersen, Hugh B. Price, and Timothy D. Sisk for their valuable advice. Some of the ideas presented in this article were first published in my chapter "The Wave of Power-Sharing Democracy," in Andrew Reynolds, ed., *The Architecture of Democracy: Constitutional Design, Conflict Management, and Democracy* (Oxford: Oxford University Press, 2002), 37–54; and in *Democracy in the Twenty-First Century: Can We Be Optimistic?* Uhlenbeck Lecture No. 18 (Wassenaar: Netherlands Institute for Advanced Study, 2000).

1. The secondary characteristics are proportionality, especially in legislative elections (in order to ensure a broadly representative legislature—similar to the aim of effecting a broadly constituted executive) and a minority veto on the most vital issues that affect the rights and autonomy of minorities.

2. Some of these scholars are Dirk Berg-Schlosser, William T. Bluhm, Laurence J. Boulle, Hans Daalder, Edward Dew, Robert H. Dix, Alan Dowty, Jonathan Fraenkel, Hermann Giliomee, Theodor Hanf, Jonathan Hartlyn, Martin O. Heisler, Luc Huyse, Thomas A. Koelble, Gerhard Lehmbruch, Franz Lehner, W. Arthur Lewis, Val R. Lorwin, Diane K. Mauzy, John McGarry, Kenneth D. McRae, Antoine N. Messarra, R.S. Milne, S.J.R. Noel, Eric A. Nordlinger, Brendan O'Leary, G. Bingham Powell, Jr., Andrew Reynolds, F. van Zyl Slabbert, Jürg Steiner, Albert J. Venter, Karl von Vorys, David Welsh, and Steven B. Wolinetz. Their most important writings on the subject (if published before the mid-1980s) can be found in the bibliography of Arend Lijphart, *Power-Sharing in South Africa* (Berkeley: Institute of International Studies, University of California, 1985), 137–71.

3. Ted Robert Gurr, *Minorities at Risk: A Global View of Ethnopolitical Conflicts* (Washington, D.C.: U.S. Institute of Peace Press, 1993), 292, italics added.

4. I have responded to these criticisms at length elsewhere. See especially Arend Lijphart, "The Wave of Power-Sharing Democracy," in Andrew Reynolds, ed., *The Architecture of Democracy: Constitutional Design, Conflict Management, and Democracy* (Oxford: Oxford University Press, 2002), 40–47; and Arend Lijphart, *Power-Sharing in South Africa,* 83–117.

5. Brian Barry, "The Consociational Model and Its Dangers," *European Journal of Political Research* 3 (December 1975): 406.

6. Donald L. Horowitz, *A Democratic South Africa? Constitutional Engineering in a Divided Society* (Berkeley: University of California Press, 1991), 188–203; and "Electoral Systems: A Primer for Decision Makers," *Journal of Democracy* 14 (October 2003): 122–23. In alternative-vote systems, voters are asked to rank order the candidates. If a candidate receives an absolute majority of first preferences, he or she is elected; if not, the weakest candidate is eliminated, and the ballots are redistributed according to second preferences. This process continues until one of the candidates receives a majority of the votes.

7. For a detailed critique, see Arend Lijphart, "The Alternative Vote: A Realistic Alternative for South Africa?" *Politikon* 18 (June 1991): 91–101; and Arend Lijphart, "Multiethnic Democracy," in Seymour Martin Lipset, ed., *The Encyclopedia of Democracy* (Washington, D.C.: Congressional Quarterly, 1995), 863–64.

8. The alternative vote was also used for the 1982 and 1988 presidential elections in Sri Lanka and for the 2000 presidential elections in the Republika Srpska

in Bosnia. Nigeria has used a similar system favored by Horowitz (requiring a plurality plus at least 25 percent of the votes in at least two-thirds of the states for victory) for its presidential elections. The third and sixth guidelines that I describe in the present essay recommend a parliamentary system without a popularly elected president—and therefore no direct presidential elections at all.

9. Benjamin Reilly has come to Horowitz's defense, but only with significant qualifications; for instance, Reilly dissents from Horowitz's advocacy of the alternative vote for the key case of South Africa. See Reilly, *Democracy in Divided Societies: Electoral Engineering for Conflict Management* (Cambridge: Cambridge University Press, 2001). Andreas Wimmer advocates the alternative vote for Iraq in "Democracy and Ethno-Religious Conflict in Iraq," *Survival* 45 (Winter 2003–2004): 111–34.

10. Donald L. Horowitz, "Constitutional Design: Proposals versus Processes," in Andrew Reynolds, ed., *The Architecture of Democracy*, 25.

11. In contrast with plurality, the alternative vote (instant runoff) ensures that the winning candidate has been elected by a majority of the voters, and it does so more accurately than the majority-runoff method and without the need for two rounds of voting.

12. Larry Diamond, *Developing Democracy: Toward Consolidation* (Baltimore: Johns Hopkins University Press, 1999), 104.

13. All three of these systems use multimember election districts. The cumulative vote resembles multimember district plurality in which each voter has as many votes as there are seats in a district, but, unlike plurality, the voter is allowed to cumulate his or her vote on one or a few of the candidates. In limited-vote systems, voters have fewer votes than the number of district seats. The single nontransferable vote is a special case of the limited vote in which the number of votes cast by each voter is reduced to one.

14. See Matthew Soberg Shugart and Martin P. Wattenberg, eds., *Mixed-Member Electoral Systems: The Best of Both Worlds?* (Oxford: Oxford University Press, 2001).

15. This estimate is based on the $T=0.75(M+1)$ equation—in which T is the effective threshold and M the number of representatives elected in a district—suggested by Rein Taagepera; see Arend Lijphart, "Electoral Systems," in Seymour Martin Lipset, ed., *Encyclopedia of Democracy*, 417. There is considerable variation around the average of 8 representatives per district, but 9 of the 17 districts are very close to this average, with between 6 and 9 seats. The open-list rules are very complex and, in my opinion, make the lists too open. In addition to the 175 seats described here, Greenland and the Faeroe Islands elect two representatives each. I should also point out that my recommendation of the Danish model entails a bit of a paradox: It is a system that is very suitable for ethnically and religiously divided countries, although Denmark itself happens to be one of the most homogeneous countries in the world.

16. Parties below the 2 percent threshold may still benefit from the compensatory seats if certain other requirements are met, such as winning at least one district seat.

17. Juan J. Linz, "Presidential or Parliamentary Democracy: Does It Make a Difference?" in Juan J. Linz and Arturo Valenzuela, eds., *The Failure of Presidential Democracy* (Baltimore: Johns Hopkins University Press, 1994), 18.

18. Seymour Martin Lipset, "The Indispensability of Political Parties," *Journal of Democracy* 11 (January 2000): 48–55; E.E. Schattschneider, *Party Government* (New York: Rinehart, 1942), 1.

19. John T.S. Keeler and Martin A. Schain, "Institutions, Political Poker, and Regime Evolution in France," in Kurt von Mettenheim, ed., *Presidential Institutions and Democratic Politics: Comparing Regional and National Contexts* (Baltimore: Johns Hopkins University Press, 1997), 95–97. Horowitz favors a president elected by the alternative vote or a similar vote-pooling method, but in other respects his president does not differ from presidents in pure presidential systems; see his *A Democratic South Africa?*, 205–14.

20. Scholars have also indicated methods to minimize the problem of presidential-legislative deadlock—for instance, by holding presidential and legislative elections concurrently and electing the president by plurality instead of the more usual majority-runoff method. Such measures may indeed be able to ameliorate the problem to some extent, but cannot solve it entirely. See Matthew Soberg Shugart and John M. Carey, *Presidents and Assemblies: Constitutional Design and Electoral Dynamics* (Cambridge: Cambridge University Press, 1992); and Mark P. Jones, *Electoral Laws and the Survival of Presidential Democracies* (Notre Dame: University of Notre Dame Press, 1995).

21. The 1998 Good Friday Agreement provides for a similar power-sharing executive for Northern Ireland.

22. In my comparative study of the world's stable democracies, defined as countries that were continuously democratic from 1977 to 1996 (and had populations greater than 250,000), 30 of the 36 stable democracies had parliamentary systems. See Lijphart, *Patterns of Democracy: Government Forms and Performance in Thirty-Six Countries* (New Haven: Yale University Press, 1999).

23. This pattern was discovered by Rein Taagepera; see his "The Size of National Assemblies," *Social Science Research* 1 (December 1972): 385–401.

5

THE IMPACT OF FEDERALISM

R. Kent Weaver

R. Kent Weaver *is professor of public policy and government at George-*
town University and a senior fellow in the Governance Studies Pro-
gram at the Brookings Institution. He has written widely on institutional
and electoral reform issues in industrial democracies, and is the editor
of The Collapse of Canada? *(1992) and the coeditor of* Do Institutions
Matter? Government Capabilities in the United States and Abroad
(1993). This essay originally appeared in the April 2002 issue of the
Journal of Democracy.

Federalism and electoral rules are usually seen as two distinct mechanisms for managing societal conflict in general and territorial conflicts
in particular. Electoral rules that provide some element of proportionality in legislative elections, for example, are frequently viewed as a
"consociational" mechanism that allows many different groups to express their interests rather than polarizing them around a single
dominant cleavage. Such electoral rules can be particularly effective at
protecting minority interests when they are combined with other consociational features, including oversized coalitions with informal norms
of cabinet selection (in parliamentary systems) that reach across major
cleavages.

Federalism, on the other hand, is viewed as a quite different mechanism for limiting the rule of national majorities: Instead of building
consensus across cleavage lines at the national level, conflict is managed by *devolving* decisions to geographic subunits, where decision
making in turn may be managed through either majoritarian or major-
ity-limiting mechanisms. Devolution may in fact leave regional minority groups—such as Spanish speakers in Catalonia, francophones in
Ontario and the Canadian prairie provinces, or Catholics in Northern
Ireland—less protected than they would be if the central government
were to take a more active role.

As this simple example suggests, the interaction between federalism and electoral rules needs to be carefully examined. Electoral systems can vary in an almost infinite number of ways. In reviewing the institutional effects of different sets of electoral rules, it is helpful to begin with the polar opposite cases—single-member-plurality (SMP) systems, also known as first-past-the-post, and closed-list proportional representation (PR)—and then discuss intermediate cases. The focus here will be on legislative elections rather than selection rules for the chief executive in systems where the latter is separately elected.

Single-member plurality. SMP electoral rules, as the name implies, involve one-person legislative districts in which the candidate who receives the most votes is declared elected, regardless of whether that vote share is a majority or not. The very large academic literature on electoral systems has identified a number of consequences associated with SMP electoral rules:

• SMP tends to restrict the number of political parties that are potential contenders for office, and creates a tendency toward a two-party system—for example, in the United Kingdom, the United States, and New Zealand (prior to 1996).

• SMP facilitates the creation of single-party majority governments by turning pluralities of votes into a majority of legislative seats, although this outcome is by no means guaranteed. Furthermore, it is less likely to occur when territorially based cleavages allow minor parties to gain a significant share of legislative seats because their supporters are concentrated in specific regions.

• SMP leads to some votes being "worth more" than others in vote-to-seat conversions. In particular, relatively small parties whose support is diffused across the whole political system without a territorial stronghold are likely to be severely punished, while parties of a similar size with geographically concentrated support may get a bonus.

• SMP tends to lead to centrist, nonideological, pragmatic, "brokerage" politics as parties compete for the "median voter." Yet significant policy swings may occur when there is a change in government if parties move away from median-voter positions on some issues.

• SMP increases incentives for strategic voting, since a vote for a minor-party candidate may be wasted, leading to a voter's least preferred candidate getting elected.

Critics of SMP have noted that it may have a number of additional (mostly harmful) consequences. When used at the national level, it may exacerbate regional cleavages, since it tends to exaggerate the advantage enjoyed by the largest political party in a region in vote-seat conversions and to punish smaller parties. In combination with the tendency of SMP to promote single-party majority governments (in parliamentary systems), there is a danger that in a country with strong territorially based cleavages one region may end up dramatically overrepresented in the governing party, while another region may end up with virtually no representatives in the governing-party caucus or the cabinet. Perceptions of regional exclusion are therefore reinforced.

When used in territorial subunits, SMP electoral rules may allow the majority social group in that territory to govern alone, thereby excluding ethnic, linguistic, or religious minorities from political power (as in Northern Ireland prior to the imposition of direct rule from London). SMP may also allow a political party that is ambivalent or even hostile to national unity to gain a strong power base through control of a single-party majority government in a state or province, which can then be used to promote autonomist or even separatist policies and popular sentiment.

It should be noted that SMP is something of a dinosaur: Most parliamentary systems in the advanced industrial world—even those without severe territorially based cleavages—have moved away from strict single-member first-past-the-post systems, generally to some sort of proportional representation. New Zealand, for example, recently moved to a German-style system of mixed-member proportional representation (discussed below). Even the United Kingdom has adopted elements of proportionality for elections to the Scottish Parliament, the Welsh Assembly, and the European Parliament, and a debate has been opened about introducing it for House of Commons elections.

Proportional representation. At the other end of the spectrum of electoral systems are those using proportional representation. Ballots are cast in multimember districts for a party list rather than an individual candidate, and the party receives seats based on its share of the vote in that district. There are of course many variations among proportional representation systems, most notably in three areas: the number of seats filled in each electoral district (district magnitude); whether or not there is a legal minimum threshold that a party must pass in order to win any seats; and whether voters have any choice over individual candidates or must simply endorse a pre-ordered party list. Overall, proportional representation generally has the following effects:

• PR increases the number of parties that are likely to compete in elections, although the magnitude of the increase depends on the specific electoral rules, notably the threshold and the size of electoral districts.

• Due to the proliferation of parties, PR increases the number of "non-throwaway" choices available to voters, although the number again varies depending on district magnitude and legal thresholds.

• PR makes it extremely unlikely that a single party will gain a majority of seats in the legislature, thus making either minority or coalition governments the norm in parliamentary systems.

• PR therefore increases the probability that the composition of a government and its policies will be decided not by the election but after it, during negotiations among party leaders. This outcome may be mitigated, however, by pre-electoral alliances and common electoral programs.

• In most cases, PR weakens the ability of legislators in parties that operate nationwide to act (and to be seen by constituents to act) as regional representatives, since they are likely to be bound by party discipline. PR also weakens individual legislators' incentive to act as providers of constituency services, since the ability of voters to reward individual MPs is lessened (although this effect is weaker in open-list systems).

• PR tends to lead to programmatic parties that seek to make distinctive appeals to relatively narrow shares of the electorate.

Proportional representation may also interact with federalism in important ways. For example, we might expect that federalism would reinforce PR's tendency to produce a profusion of parties. The combination might especially spur movement toward territorially focused parties, since the entry barriers for small parties are relatively low and the chance that a modest-sized party may share power at one or both levels of government is higher than under SMP.

Intermediate and mixed systems. A number of intermediate alternatives exist between SMP and PR. The alternative vote (AV), used in elections for the Australian House of Representatives, uses single-member districts but compels voters to list not just a single choice but a ranked set of choices; votes for the least-favored candidates are redistributed in stages until one candidate wins a majority. The two-round majority system used in elections for the French Chamber of Deputies also employs single-member districts and in most cases produces majority support for a single candidate. Both systems are likely to stimulate the existence of more than two parties both within and across districts, but fewer than under PR rules. The single transferable vote (STV) operates in multimember districts as in PR, but voters rank individual candidates without regard to party, thus weakening party leaders' control over the selection of legislators. Because of the practical difficulties of vote counting and allocation under STV, however, both the district magnitude and the number of parties are only modestly greater than under SMP.

Complexities in vote counting under AV and STV, and the added expense of two-round elections, have limited the appeal of these intermediate options. Instead, electoral reform in recent years has focused on the development of mixed electoral systems, with a combination of single-member districts and seats awarded by proportional representation. Two attributes of such systems are critical in determining the incentives for party fragmentation and the prospects for single-party majority government: 1) the ratio between the number of single-member seats and PR seats; and 2) whether PR seats are awarded as a completely separate tier from the SMP tier or in order to compensate parties that did poorly in vote-seat conversions in the SMP seats. Where the two types of seats are relatively equal in number and awarded on a compensatory basis, as in Germany and New Zealand, something close to full proportionality in translation of seats into votes is achieved. Indeed, such systems are generally known as a mixed-member proportional (MMP) systems.[1]

While MMP tends to yield fewer parties than most pure proportional systems (especially when combined with high electoral thresholds as in Germany), the prospects for single-party majority government under MMP are nonetheless minimal. Where the percentage of PR seats is small and they are awarded parallel to SMP seats rather than on a compensatory basis, the number of political parties is likely to be smaller and the prospects for single-party majority government higher. This option is generally referred to as mixed-member majoritarian (MMM).

Patterns of Federalism

Before examining how electoral rules affect party systems and governance in federations, it is important to get a general lay of the land. The Table on the following pages provides a preliminary list of electoral rules for national lower and upper chambers, national executives, and provincial legislatures in a number of federal systems. Several patterns and nonpatterns are evident in the Table. Most generally, there is no clear cross-national relationship linking a federal system to a particular set of electoral rules at either the national or subnational levels. Federalism coexists with a variety of electoral systems—with separation of powers or parliamentarism, with varying degrees of proportionality, and with concurrent or non-concurrent elections—at both the national and territorial levels.

Not only is federalism consistent with many electoral systems, but the Table shows that it is also consistent with a wide variation in the "effective number of parties" in the lower chambers of national legislatures.[2] Previous research suggests that institutional variables (notably district magnitudes, electoral thresholds, and the presence or absence of concurrent presidential elections decided by plurality), as well as the degree of ethnolinguistic fractionalization in a country, have a very strong impact on the effective number of parties: Both electoral rules that do not discriminate against relatively small parties and more complex patterns of social fragmentation expand the number of legislative parties.

We might also expect federalism to have an impact on the effective number of parties. In particular, federalism may stimulate the growth of province- or region-specific parties that compete and win seats federally, thereby fragmenting party representation in the national legislature. This effect is likely to vary, however, depending on whether or not federal and provincial elections take place simultaneously. In general, we would expect concurrent elections to stimulate votes for parties that operate and have some chance of winning at both levels of government.

Concurrent elections may also allow more efficiency in campaign organization and advertising.

Yet there is little evidence that federalism has an *independent* effect on the degree of fragmentation in a legislature. Indeed, two federations with concurrent federal and state elections—the United States and Brazil—currently have among the lowest and highest effective number of legislative parties, respectively. Federations with nonconcurrent federal and subfederal elections also vary dramatically in their effective number of parties.

There is a very strong association, evident in the Table, between federalism and having a two-chamber national legislature, with the territorial subunits generally playing a distinctive role in the upper chamber. While unicameralism is common at both the national and subnational levels worldwide, all of the countries shown in the Table are bicameral at the national level, as are virtually all federations worldwide—the tiny Federated States of Micronesia is a rare exception. Canada is also a partial exception, since its upper chamber is a vestigial body appointed by the federal prime minister, and it is no accident that the Canadian Senate has persistently been seen as a problematic political institution. The United Kingdom, with its hereditary and appointive House of Lords—also a vestigial body—is another partial exception.

Upper chambers in national legislatures vary widely both in their selection rules and in the degree to which their powers approach or equal those of lower chambers. Despite this diversity, electoral rules in upper chambers almost always reinforce the role of those legislators as representatives of provincial interests by having them selected on a province-wide basis, even where the lower-chamber elections occur in much smaller electoral districts. The most common situation is that territorial subunits serve as the electoral districts for upper-chamber elections, either in single-member districts as in the United States or in multimember districts as in Australia and Switzerland.

In several countries, provinces play a direct role in selecting members of the national upper chamber. This can take several forms. In the case of the German Bundesrat, the *Länder* delegations are direct appointees of the *Land* governments. Provincial legislatures (rather than executives) choose most members of the Indian Rajya Sabha; autonomous community legislatures choose a minority of members of the Spanish Senate; and the Belgian Senate is a hybrid of directly elected members, those delegated by regional councils, and additional members appointed by the first two groups. This suggests a further conclusion about upper chambers in federations: They are more likely than lower chambers to have their members selected in several quite distinct ways.

Moreover, the representation of territorial subunits in upper chambers is frequently disproportionate to population, either with complete equality across units, as in the United States and Australia, or with rules that divide

TABLE—LEGISLATIVE CHARACTERISTICS IN SELECTED FEDERATIONS

COUNTRY	NATIONAL LOWER CHAMBER		NATIONAL UPPER CHAMBER		NATIONAL EXECUTIVE	SUBNATIONAL LEGISLATURE	SYNCHRONIZATION OF NATIONAL AND SUBNATIONAL ELECTIONS
	ELECTORAL RULES	EFFECTIVE NO. OF LEGISLATIVE PARTIES	ELECTORAL RULES	DISPROPORTIONALITY IN REPRESENTATION OF TERRITORIAL SUBUNITS			
Australia	AV	2.38	STV by states; equal representation of states	Moderate	Leader of party(ies) with plurality or majority of seats	Bicameral legislatures in 5 of 6 states: mostly AV in lower chamber; upper chambers are AV in some states, STV in others	No
Belgium	PR	7.01	Combination of directly elected, indirectly elected by linguistic community councils, and co-opted	Low	Leader of a party in a coalition having majority of seats	PR	No, except in 1999
Brazil	PR; very highly disproportional representation of states	8.69	PR by states; equal representation of states	Extremely High	President separately elected by two-round majority	Statewide PR	Yes
Canada	SMP in highly disproportional districts	1.69	Vestigial body is appointed by federal Prime Minister	Moderate	Leader of party with plurality or majority of seats; always single-party cabinets	SMP with moderately disproportional seat allocation	No
Germany	MMP	3.16	Appointed by *Land* governments; weighted representation of *Länder*	Moderate	Leader of party(ies) with plurality or majority of seats	MMP	No

ABBREVIATIONS FOR ELECTORAL RULES:
AV: Alternative vote
MMM: Mixed-member majoritarian
MMP: Mixed-member proportional
SMP: Single-member plurality
STV: Single transferable vote

TABLE—LEGISLATIVE CHARACTERISTICS IN SELECTED FEDERATIONS (CONT'D)

COUNTRY	NATIONAL LOWER CHAMBER		NATIONAL UPPER CHAMBER		NATIONAL EXECUTIVE	SUBNATIONAL LEGISLATURE	SYNCHRONIZATION OF NATIONAL AND SUBNATIONAL ELECTIONS
	ELECTORAL RULES	EFFECTIVE NO. OF LEGISLATIVE PARTIES	ELECTORAL RULES	DISPROPORTIONALITY IN REPRESENTATION OF TERRITORIAL SUBUNITS			
India	SMP	1.69	Mostly elected by state legislatures by STV for fixed terms; minority nominated by President; weighted representation of states	Low	Leader of party(ies) with plurality or majority of seats	SMP; some states have two chambers	No
Spain	PR with many small districts	2.81	208 directly elected; 44 appointed by parliaments of autonomous communities; weighted representation; fixed terms	Moderate	Leader of party(ies) with plurality or majority of seats	PR	Varies
Switzerland	PR by cantons, but effectively SMP in single-seat cantons	5.26	Equal representation of cantons, half representation of demi-cantons; cantons set their own selection rules	High	Collegial executive chosen for fixed term by bicameral legislature	Varies; mostly PR	No
United Kingdom	SMP	2.09	Vestigial hereditary and appointive body	N/A	Leader of party(ies) with plurality or majority of seats	MMP	No
United States	SMP in highly proportional districts	1.95	Two seat SMP with staggered elections	Very High	President chosen by plurality election in highly disproportional, state-focused system	Bicameral legislatures in 49 of 50 states: all SMP in highly proportional districts	Partial

Sources: Data on effective number of legislative parties are from Octavio Amorim Neto and Gary W. Cox, "Electoral Institutions, Cleavage Structures, and the Number of Parties," *American Journal of Political Science* 41 (January 1997): 149–74. Data on disproportionality in upper chambers are from the Gini indexes in Alfred Stepan, "Federalism and Democracy: Beyond the U.S. Model," *Journal of Democracy* 10 (October 1999): 19–34. Indexes of less than 0.15 are coded as low disproportionality, 0.16 to 0.40 as moderate, 0.41 to 0.50 as high, and 0.51 or greater as very high.

states into a small number of categories that tend to overrepresent the smallest and underrepresent the largest units, as in Germany. The degree of disproportionality in representing territorial units in upper chambers varies broadly, ranging from close to perfect proportionality in Belgium, Austria, and India to extreme disproportionality in Brazil and Argentina.

There are probably two distinct reasons for the strong affinity between federalism and disproportional upper chambers in the national legislature. The first is that federal systems frequently coexist with major ethnic, religious, or linguistic divisions, and minority groups seek protection not just through consociational mechanisms (if they exist) but also through the "limited government" checks and balances of an upper chamber in which minority regions (if not minority groups) are overrepresented. The second reason is that many federations (notably Australia, Canada, and the United States) were formed from the union of preexisting political units. Politicians from those units did not want to see their influence extinguished in the new national institutions, and those from smaller units were particularly concerned that their jurisdictions not be dominated by the larger units in the new federation.

Electoral rules for each chamber are almost always uniform across territorial subunits. In other words, representatives from all subunits are elected following the same sets of rules, even though they may not represent equal numbers of voters. There are exceptions, perhaps the best known of which is the use of the single transferable vote in Northern Ireland for elections to the House of Commons, while single-member plurality is used in other areas. In the United States, many states moved to direct election of senators before the passage of the Seventeenth Amendment to the Constitution: Thus two different systems existed simultaneously during this transition. In Switzerland, most members of the lower chamber are elected according to PR, but plurality elections are used in five small cantons. In addition, the cantons set their own election rules for the Council of States, although all currently use proportional representation. Nonetheless, asymmetrical electoral rules for specific territorial subunits in upper chambers are definitely the exception rather than the rule.

The extent to which legislators in upper chambers actually function as representatives of regional interests varies substantially, however, even if they are elected from province-wide districts. Party discipline is fairly high in most of these bodies, meaning that representation of regional interests takes place primarily in the formulation of legislation rather than in votes on its adoption, as well as through the development of regionally focused parties. In Australia, for example, the fact that a different electoral system is used for the Senate (single transferable vote rather than the alternative vote, as in the House of Representatives) has had a clear impact on policy—the governing party or coalition has never had a Senate majority in recent years, and has therefore been forced to negotiate with smaller parties to win approval for its legislative program. But the combination of party discipline, the prevalence of class and ideological cleavages over regional ones, and the absence of regionalist parties means that Australian senators do not act as representatives of the interests of their states.

Finally, it should be noted that because representation ratios for territorial subunits tend to be embedded in constitutions, over time small rural subunits (and interests) may become increasingly overrepresented relative to urban interests.

Subnational Legislatures

Several patterns (and nonpatterns) are also evident when one examines legislatures in territorial subunits. First, as noted earlier, there is, at a minimum, a strong "family resemblance" between legislative-chamber electoral rules at the national level and those at the subnational level. The most obvious cross-level similarity is in the choice of a parliamentary system versus the separation of executive and legislative powers: Countries almost always make the same choice at both levels. Furthermore, within this broad category, there is a tendency to make very similar choices in terms of degree of proportionality, openness or closedness of lists in PR systems, and so on. In some cases, most notably Brazil, there is a common electoral law that operates at both the national and state levels. More frequently, however, these similarities appear to result simply from common institutional inheritances, and perhaps from a reluctance on the part of political elites to make electoral rules too difficult for ordinary voters to understand.

Yet family resemblances have been strained in recent years by several factors that have led to increasingly diverse electoral systems within individual countries. One particularly important factor behind this trend is the rise of a supranational parliamentary institution, the European Parliament. As a result of an EU directive to use proportional representation for elections to the European Parliament, countries like the United Kingdom that had formerly used SMP found themselves hosting on a regular basis elections using a different set of rules. Second, moves toward devolution, especially in Western Europe, have created a need for new electoral arrangements—sometimes with different cleavage-management tasks at the subnational level that appear to call for different electoral rules than those which operate at the national level. Third, the growth of mixed systems, along with widespread perceptions among electoral experts that these rules might be an effective "middle road" between SMP and PR, has also fueled increased diversity of rules within countries. Fourth, perceptions in countries like Japan and Italy that existing electoral rules have had negative consequences have spurred a search for new arrangements that are not always pursued at all levels of government. Thus the United Kingdom, for example, currently uses SMP in elections for the House of Commons, PR for the European Parliament (except in Northern Ireland, where the single transferable vote is used for both), STV for the Northern Ireland Assembly, and MMP for the Scottish Parliament and the Welsh Assembly.

A second pattern evident across subnational legislatures is the strong degree of uniformity in the electoral rules of individual subunits within countries. Again, there are exceptions: Louisiana with its two-round majority elections, some experiments with the alternative vote and the single transferable vote in western Canadian provinces prior to the 1960s, differences across Australian states in whether all choices must be filled out in their alternative-vote ballots, the use of straight proportional representation rather than a mixed-member system in elections for three *Land* legislatures in Germany, and so on. But uniformity is the norm, even in multinational federations that are asymmetrical in the constitutional powers that they assign to specific territorial subunits.

A third very clear pattern is the low degree of synchronization between national elections and state and local elections. In general, we would expect simultaneous national and subnational elections to foster closer cooperation between candidates and political apparatuses at the two levels, as well as less of a disjunction between party systems and the messages conveyed by parties operating at the two levels. The low degree of inter-level electoral synchronization observed here appears to be largely a by-product of the fact that most federations in the advanced industrial countries are parliamentary systems at both levels, with electoral cycles at each level varying (within fixed outer limits) based on calculations of electoral advantage by those holding the reins of government and their capacity to maintain a legislative majority. Parliamentarism and federalism need not lead to unsynchronized elections, however. This is shown by the case of Sweden, where electoral rules require elections by a specific date even if an intermediate, unplanned election has been held since the last scheduled balloting. This system has preserved a high degree of certainty in electoral timing and the complete synchronization of national and subnational elections.

Implications for Governability

Electoral rules may have several implications for the governability of federations. As noted earlier, single-member-plurality electoral rules may severely punish parties with broad national appeal but not enough support to win pluralities in any region, while disproportionately rewarding regionally concentrated parties if they are able to win plurality victories throughout their regions. An even more serious problem is associated with plurality electoral rules in countries with severe regional cleavages: Because the system requires winning pluralities in individual districts, even political parties that win a majority of seats in the legislature overall may be shut out entirely from regions where their popular support is relatively weak.

This effect is particularly troubling when it involves the governing party, for weak representation of a region in the caucus of the governing party may feed a vicious cycle in which a region's perceived underrepresentation in government further exacerbates regional alienation. Perhaps the clearest and most persistent case of such regional underrepresentation in government is found in Canada. The Canadian electoral system has produced severe underrepresentation of one or more regions in the governing party much of the time, most notably of Quebec within the Conservative Party prior to 1984 and of the Western provinces within the Liberal Party. Overall, countries with proportional or semiproportional electoral systems, such as Germany and Spain, are far less likely to experience severe regional underrepresentation in the governing-party caucus than countries with single-member-plurality (the United Kingdom, Canada) or alternative-vote (Australia) systems.

Several factors in addition to electoral rules also seem to affect the prospects for severe underrepresentation in government. One is the size of the subnational jurisdiction: Extremely small jurisdictions, with only one or a few members of the legislature (for example, the city-state of Bremen in Germany), are far less likely than larger jurisdictions to achieve proportionality in electoral outcomes. A second factor, not surprisingly, is the degree to which cleavages have a strong regional component. In Australia, despite the alternative-vote electoral system, severe regional underrepresentation is a phenomenon confined largely to very low-population jurisdictions, because cleavages are stronger along class and ideological lines than by region.

Federalism may also lead to the development of territorially based subnational parties, usually founded on linguistic differences or strong regional cultural identities. In Spain, for example, the growth of regionally oriented parties followed the creation of Spain's various autonomous communities, although such parties dominate only in the two regions with exceptionally strong identities (Catalonia and the Basque region). Regionalist parties like the South Tyrolean People's Party in the South Tyrol province of Italy and the Convergencia i Unio electoral coalition in Catalonia frequently participate in, and sometimes dominate, subnational assemblies in parts of Europe where minority languages are dominant.

Of more importance for the question of governability, however, are situations in which such parties not only represent the interests of a particular territorially based interest group but seek to alter national borders, either through secession to form a new state or irredentism to join another state. I will refer to such parties as "antisystem" parties. The boundary line between regionalist and separatist or irredentist parties is not always clear in practice, of course: The Social Democratic and Labour Party in Northern Ireland, for example, supports eventual union with the

Irish Republic but eschews violence and favors consensual approaches, while Sinn Fein, the political wing of the Irish Republican Army, has only recently moved toward a more gradualist position. Italy's Northern League, which has vacillated between support for Northern separation and support for federalism, is another ambiguous case.

In general, we might expect antisystem parties to be more likely to emerge under PR (especially where electoral thresholds are low), because the barriers to entry faced by new parties are relatively weak. Yet evidence from the industrialized Western countries does not permit any firm conclusions on this issue. Belgium's extreme form of proportional representation has facilitated the emergence of the Flemish nationalist Vlaams Blok as a significant presence in both the federal and Flanders legislatures, but it is not a part of the government in either. In Scotland, the SMP-based elections to the British Parliament have consistently discriminated against the Scottish Nationalist Party. The Nationalists did indeed fare much better in the 1999 elections to the Scottish Parliament, which were held under MMP rules. Thus SMP electoral rules do appear to have dampened both votes and vote-to-seat conversions for the Scottish Nationalists.

Evidence regarding the impact of Canada's SMP electoral rules on the growth of antisystem parties suggests that such rules can cut both ways. In the 1960s and early 1970s, Canada's system clearly discriminated against political parties promoting sovereignty for Quebec. In 1976, however, those same rules gave the Parti Québécois control of Quebec's National Assembly thanks to a plurality of the overall vote and an electoral platform that emphasized "good government" over attaining sovereignty. Since that time, the Parti Québécois has won three more National Assembly majorities, but never a majority of the popular vote. Indeed, SMP electoral rules particularly benefit the Parti Québécois, since under this system, the votes of immense majorities for the Liberals in Montreal-area constituencies, with many anglophones and persons whose first language is neither French nor English, are "wasted." In the November 1998 provincial election, the Parti Québécois won 76 of 125 seats in the Quebec National Assembly, even though the Quebec Liberal Party won 1 percent more of the popular vote. In federal politics, the pro-sovereignty Bloc Québécois won the second largest number of seats in the House of Commons in the 1993 federal election, using its concentration of plurality victories (it ran candidates only in Quebec) to win 18 percent of all Commons seats—54 of Quebec's 75—with only 13.5 percent of the national vote. In short, SMP electoral rules may discourage secessionist parties in their early stages, but they may provide such parties a major boost once they attain sufficient size to start winning a substantial number of victories in individual constituencies.

The Italian situation of electoral coalitions within a mixed-member-majoritarian system may in fact be the most likely to promote antisystem parties. Relatively small parties that do not fit clearly on one side of the left-right divide but have a concentrated regional base are able to win single-member districts in the plurality part of the election contest. Because there are strong incentives to build a broad coalition that can win a majority of seats in both chambers of the Italian Parliament, these small regional parties may be in a strong position either to provide the crucial majority-forming partner for one of the two fairly evenly divided coalitions, or to win good deals in preelection pacts and thus share power if their coalition wins. This is in fact what happened with the Northern League in both 1994 and 2001.

It is extremely difficult to define and develop measures of political violence that are reliable cross-nationally. Moreover, expectations about the effects of electoral rules on political violence are far from obvious. One plausible hypothesis holds that political minorities and groups outside the political mainstream are driven to political violence because under SMP electoral rules they see no prospect for achieving their objectives through normal political channels.

Evidence for this proposition is quite limited, however. Arend Lijphart, for example, finds in a study of 36 democracies that, once levels of economic development, social pluralism, and population size are controlled for, relationships between "consensus democracy" institutions and the level of political violence are quite weak, with much of the variance accounted for by two outliers: the United Kingdom (because of Northern Ireland) and Jamaica (because of violence surrounding the 1980 election).[3] Majoritarian electoral rules for the Northern Ireland Parliament in Stormont, along with widespread gerrymandering practices designed to marginalize Catholic influence, have received at least part of the blame for the violence in Northern Ireland. Yet many other factors, such as widespread employment discrimination, seem at least as important as electoral rules. And the argument is even less persuasive in other countries. The movement to gain additional autonomy for Quebec has been almost entirely devoid of violence, except for a brief outburst in 1968–70. Political violence has been far more evident in Belgium (with PR elections) than in Canada (with SMP elections). Italy, too, underwent a bout of political violence in the 1960s in the German-speaking South Tyrol region. In short, factors other than majoritarian electoral rules are probably far more important in explaining why a minority group turns to political violence. And changes in areas other than electoral reforms (for example, increased autonomy for provincial governments in jurisdictions where minority groups predominate) are probably more important in containing it.

Lessons for New Democracies

This review of electoral systems and their effects on governability in European and North American federations suggests that federalism is compatible with a variety of electoral rules at both the national and territorial levels. Countries that choose more proportional systems for their national legislatures generally make similar choices for territorial legislatures as well. That said, however, many countries in Europe are developing increasingly diverse sets of electoral rules across different levels of governments.

Single-member-plurality electoral rules do have some distinctive risks in terms of governing federations. In particular, when compared to PR systems, SMP electoral rules appear significantly more likely to create a high risk of territorial exclusion from the governing-party caucus at the national level in parliamentary systems. The effect of SMP electoral rules in fostering antisystem secessionist or irredentist parties is more ambiguous, however. Such rules appear to raise the barriers to anti-system parties that enjoy modest levels of support, but to favor them once their voter support has reached around 35 to 40 percent. Yet both of these effects are highly contingent on other factors—notably on the existence of strong and persistent regionally based cleavages. Finally, the effects of electoral arrangements on stimulating political violence appear to be weak at best.

Overall, the experience of the industrialized democracies suggests no single "best design" of electoral rules for governing federations that should be adopted by new democracies. Past institutional choices influence the range of options that elites are likely to see as viable, as does the need to make election administration simple and less susceptible to fraud, and to make the system intelligible to voters. Perhaps most important, the precise conflict-management tasks faced by new democracies vary widely across countries. Elites in new democracies thus will—and should—make very different choices in designing electoral systems. What is essential is that their choices be well-adapted to national circumstances and able to be perceived as fair over time, rather than based upon short-term calculations of electoral self-interest.

NOTES

1. See Matthew Soberg Shugart and Martin Wattenberg, eds., *Mixed-Member Electoral Systems: The Best of Both Worlds?* (New York: Oxford University Press, 2001).

2. On the definition and calculation of the effective number of parties, see Rein Taagepera and Matthew Soberg Shugart, *Seats and Votes: The Effects and Determinants of Electoral Systems* (New Haven: Yale University Press, 1989), 78–80.

3. Arend Lijphart, *Patterns of Democracy: Government Forms and Performance in Thirty-Six Countries* (New Haven: Yale University Press, 1999), 271.

II

Is Proportional Representation Best?

6

CONSTITUTIONAL CHOICES FOR NEW DEMOCRACIES

Arend Lijphart

Arend Lijphart is research professor emeritus of political science at the University of California, San Diego. He is the author of Patterns of Democracy: Government Forms and Performance in Thirty-Six Countries *(1999) and many other studies of democratic institutions, the governance of deeply divided societies, and electoral systems. This essay originally appeared in the Winter 1991 issue of the* Journal of Democracy.

Two fundamental choices that confront architects of new democratic constitutions are those between plurality elections and proportional representation (PR) and between parliamentary and presidential forms of government. The merits of presidentialism and parliamentarism were extensively debated by Juan J. Linz, Seymour Martin Lipset, and Donald L. Horowitz in the Fall 1990 issue of the *Journal of Democracy.*[1] I strongly concur with Horowitz's contention that the electoral system is an equally vital element in democratic constitutional design, and therefore that it is of crucial importance to evaluate these two sets of choices in relation with each other. Such an analysis, as I will try to show, indicates that the combination of parliamentarism with proportional representation should be an especially attractive one to newly democratic and democratizing countries.

The comparative study of democracies has shown that the type of electoral system is significantly related to the development of a country's party system, its type of executive (one-party vs. coalition cabinets), and the relationship between its executive and legislature. Countries that use the plurality method of election (almost always applied, at the national level, in single-member districts) are likely to have two-party systems, one-party governments, and executives that are dominant in relation to their legislatures. These are the main characteristics of the Westminster or *majoritarian* model of democracy, in which power is concentrated in the hands of the majority party. Con-

Figure—Four Basic Types of Democracy

	PRESIDENTIAL	PARLIAMENTARY
PLURALITY ELECTIONS	United States Philippines	United Kingdom Old Commonwealth India Malaysia Jamaica
PROPORTIONAL REPRESENTATION	Latin America	Western Europe

versely, PR is likely to be associated with multiparty systems, coalition governments (including, in many cases, broad and inclusive coalitions), and more equal executive-legislative power relations. These latter characteristics typify the *consensus* model of democracy, which, instead of relying on pure and concentrated majority rule, tries to limit, divide, separate, and share power in a variety of ways.[2]

Three further points should be made about these two sets of related traits. First, the relationships are mutual. For instance, plurality elections favor the maintenance of a two-party system; but an existing two-party system also favors the maintenance of plurality, which gives the two principal parties great advantages that they are unlikely to abandon. Second, if democratic political engineers desire to promote either the majoritarian cluster of characteristics (plurality, a two-party system, and a dominant, one-party cabinet) or the consensus cluster (PR, multipartism, coalition government, and a stronger legislature), the most practical way to do so is by choosing the appropriate electoral system. Giovanni Sartori has aptly called electoral systems "the most specific manipulative instrument of politics."[3] Third, important variations exist among PR systems. Without going into all the technical details, a useful distinction can be made between *extreme* PR, which poses few barriers to small parties, and *moderate* PR. The latter limits the influence of minor parties through such means as applying PR in small districts instead of large districts or nationwide balloting, and requiring parties to receive a minimum percentage of the vote in order to gain representation, such as the 5 percent threshold in Germany. The Dutch, Israeli, and Italian systems exemplify extreme PR and the German and Swedish systems, moderate PR.

The second basic constitutional choice, between parliamentary and presidential forms of government, also affects the majoritarian or consensus character of the political system. Presidentialism yields majoritarian effects on the party system and on the type of executive, but a consensus effect on executive-legislative relations. By formally separating the executive and legislative powers, presidential systems generally promote a rough executive-legislative balance of power. On the other hand, presidentialism tends to foster a two-party system, as the presidency is the biggest political prize to be won, and only the largest parties have a chance to win it. This advantage for the big parties often carries over into legislative elections as well (especially if presidential and legislative elections are held simultaneously), even if the legislative elections are conducted under PR rules. Presidentialism usually produces cabinets composed solely of members of the governing party. In fact, presidential systems concentrate executive power to an even greater degree than does a one-party parliamentary cabinet—not just in a single *party* but in a single *person.*

Explaining Past Choices

My aim is not simply to describe alternative democratic systems and their majoritarian or consensus characteristics, but also to make some practical recommendations for democratic constitutional engineers. What are the main advantages and disadvantages of plurality and PR and of presidentialism and parliamentarism? One way to approach this question is to investigate why contemporary democracies made the constitutional choices they did.

The Figure illustrates the four combinations of basic characteristics and the countries and regions where they prevail. The purest examples of the combination of presidentialism and plurality are the United States and democracies heavily influenced by the United States, such as the Philippines and Puerto Rico. Latin American countries have overwhelmingly opted for presidential–PR systems. Parliamentary–plurality systems exist in the United Kingdom and many former British colonies, including India, Malaysia, Jamaica, and the countries of the so-called Old Commonwealth (Canada, Australia, and New Zealand). Finally, parliamentary–PR systems are concentrated in Western Europe. Clearly, the overall pattern is to a large extent determined by geographic, cultural, and colonial factors—a point to which I shall return shortly.

Very few contemporary democracies cannot be accommodated by this classification. The major exceptions are democracies that fall in between the pure presidential and pure parliamentary types (France and Switzerland), and those that use electoral methods other than pure PR or plurality (Ireland, Japan, and, again, France).[4]

Two important factors influenced the adoption of PR in continental Europe. One was the problem of ethnic and religious minorities; PR was designed to provide minority representation and thereby to counteract potential threats to national unity and political stability. "It was no accident," Stein Rokkan writes, "that the earliest moves toward proportional representation (PR) came in the ethnically most heterogeneous countries." The second factor was the dynamic of the democratization process. PR was adopted "through a convergence of pressures from below and from above. The rising working class wanted to lower the thresholds of representation in order to gain access to the legislatures, and the most threatened of the old-established parties demanded PR to protect their position against the new waves of mobilized voters created by universal suffrage."[5] Both factors are relevant for contemporary constitution making, especially for the many countries where there are deep ethnic cleavages or where new democratic forces need to be reconciled with the old antidemocratic groups.

The process of democratization also originally determined whether parliamentary or presidential institutions were adopted. As Douglas V. Verney has pointed out, there were two basic ways in which monarchical power could be democratized: by taking away most of the monarch's personal political prerogatives and making his cabinet responsible to the popularly elected legislature, thus creating a parliamentary system; or by removing the hereditary monarch and substituting a new, democratically elected "monarch," thus creating a presidential system.[6]

Other historical causes have been voluntary imitations of successful democracies and the dominant influence of colonial powers. As the Figure shows very clearly, Britain's influence as an imperial power has been enormously important. The U.S. presidential model was widely imitated in Latin America in the nineteenth century. And early in the twentieth century, PR spread quickly in continental Europe and Latin America, not only for reasons of partisan accommodation and minority protection, but also because it was widely perceived to be the most democratic method of election and hence the "wave of the democratic future."

This sentiment in favor of PR raises the controversial question of the *quality* of democracy achieved in the four alternative systems. The term "quality" refers to the degree to which a system meets such democratic norms as representativeness, accountability, equality, and participation. The claims and counterclaims are too well-known to require lengthy treatment here, but it is worth emphasizing that the differences between the opposing camps are not as great as is often supposed. First of all, PR and plurality advocates disagree not so much about the respective effects of the two electoral methods as about the weight to be attached to these effects. Both sides agree that PR yields greater proportionality and minority representation and that plurality promotes two-party systems and one-party executives. Partisans disagree on which of these results is preferable, with the plurality side claiming that only in two-party systems can clear accountability for government policy be achieved.

In addition, both sides argue about the *effectiveness* of the two systems. Proportionalists value minority representation not just for its democratic quality but also for its ability to maintain unity and peace in divided societies. Similarly, proponents of plurality favor one-party cabinets not just because of their democratic accountability but also because of the firm leadership and effective policy making that they allegedly provide. There also appears to be a slight difference in the relative emphasis that the two sides place on quality and effectiveness. Proportionalists tend to attach greater importance to the *representativeness* of government, while plurality advocates view the *capacity to govern* as the more vital consideration.

Finally, while the debate between presidentialists and parliamentarists has not been as fierce, it clearly parallels the debate over electoral systems. Once again, the claims and counterclaims revolve around both quality and effectiveness. Presidentialists regard the direct popular election of the chief executive as a democratic asset, while parliamentarists think of the concentration of executive power in the hands of a single official as less than optimally democratic. But here the question of effectiveness has been the more seriously debated issue, with the president's strong and effective leadership role being emphasized by one side and the danger of executive-legislative conflict and stalemate by the other.

Evaluating Democratic Performance

How can the actual performance of the different types of democracies be evaluated? It is extremely difficult to find quantifiable measures of democratic performance, and therefore political scientists have rarely attempted a systematic assessment. The major exception is G. Bingham Powell's pioneering study evaluating the capacity of various democracies to maintain public order (as measured by the incidence of riots and deaths from political violence) and their levels of citizen participation (as measured by electoral turnout).[7] Following Powell's example, I will examine these and other aspects of democratic performance, including democratic representation and responsiveness, economic equality, and macroeconomic management.

Due to the difficulty of finding reliable data outside the OECD countries to measure such aspects of performance, I have limited the analysis to the advanced industrial democracies. In any event, the Latin American democracies, given their lower levels of economic development, cannot be considered comparable cases. This means that one of the four basic alternatives—the presidential–PR form of democracy prevalent only in Latin America—must be omitted from our analysis.

Although this limitation is unfortunate, few observers would seriously argue that a strong case can be made for this particular type of democracy. With the clear exception of Costa Rica and the partial exceptions of Venezuela and Colombia, the political stability and economic performance of Latin American democracies have been far from satisfactory. As Juan Linz has argued, Latin American presidential systems have been particularly prone to executive-legislative deadlock and ineffective leadership.[8] Moreover, Scott Mainwaring has shown persuasively that this problem becomes especially serious when presidents do not have majority support in their legislatures.[9] Thus the Latin

American model of presidentialism combined with PR legislative elections remains a particularly unattractive option.

The other three alternatives—presidential–plurality, parliamentary–plurality, and parliamentary–PR systems—are all represented among the firmly established Western democracies. I focus on the 14 cases that unambiguously fit these three categories. The United States is the one example of presidentialism combined with plurality. There are four cases of parliamentarism–plurality (Australia, Canada, New Zealand, and the United Kingdom), and nine democracies of the parliamentary–PR type (Austria, Belgium, Denmark, Finland, Germany, Italy, the Netherlands, Norway, and Sweden). Seven long-term, stable democracies are excluded from the analysis either because they do not fit comfortably into any one of the three categories (France, Ireland, Japan, and Switzerland), or because they are too vulnerable to external factors (Israel, Iceland, and Luxembourg).

Since a major purpose of PR is to facilitate minority representation, one would expect the PR systems to outperform plurality systems in this respect. There is little doubt that this is indeed the case. For instance, where ethnic minorities have formed ethnic political parties, as in Belgium and Finland, PR has enabled them to gain virtually perfect proportional representation. Because there are so many different kinds of ethnic and religious minorities in the democracies under analysis, it is difficult to measure systematically the *degree* to which PR succeeds in providing more representatives for minorities than does plurality. It is possible, however, to compare the representation of women—a minority in political rather than strictly numerical terms—systematically across countries. The first column of Table 1 shows the percentages of female members in the lower (or only) houses of the national legislatures in these 14 democracies during the early 1980s. The 16.4 percent average for the parliamentary–PR systems is about four times higher than the 4.1 percent for the United States or the 4.0 percent average for the parliamentary–plurality countries. To be sure, the higher social standing of women in the four Nordic countries accounts for part of the difference, but the average of 9.4 percent in the five other parliamentary–PR countries remains more than twice as high as in the plurality countries.

Does higher representation of women result in the advancement of their interests? Harold L. Wilensky's careful rating of democracies with regard to the innovativeness and expansiveness of their family policies—a matter of special concern to women—indicates that it does.[10] On a 13-point scale (from a maximum of 12 to a minimum of 0), the scores of these countries range from 11 to 1. The differences among the three groups (as shown in the second column of Table 1) are striking: The PR countries have an average score of 7.89, whereas the parliamentary–plurality countries have an average of just 2.50, and the U.S. only a slightly higher score of 3.00. Here again, the Nordic countries have the

TABLE 1—WOMEN'S LEGISLATIVE REPRESENTATION, INNOVATIVE
FAMILY POLICY, VOTING TURNOUT, INCOME INEQUALITY, AND THE
DAHL RATING OF DEMOCRATIC QUALITY

TYPE OF DEMOCRACY	Women's Rep. 1980–82	Family Policy 1976–80	Voting Turnout 1971–80	Income Top 20% 1985	Dahl Rating 1969
Presidential–Plurality[1]	4.1	3.00	54.2%	39.9%	3.0
Parliamentary–Plurality[2]	4.0	2.50	75.3%	42.9%	4.8
Parliamentary–PR[3]	16.4	7.89	84.5%	39.0%	2.2

[1] The one presidential–plurality democracy is the United States.
[2] The four parliamentary–plurality democracies are Australia, Canada, New Zealand, and the United Kingdom.
[3] The nine parliamentary–PR democracies are Austria, Belgium, Denmark, Finland, Germany, Italy, the Netherlands, Norway, and Sweden.
Sources: Based on Wilma Rule, "Electoral Systems, Contextual Factors and Women's Opportunity for Election to Parliament in Twenty-Three Democracies," *Western Political Quarterly* 40 (September 1987): 483; Harold L. Wilensky, "Common Problems, Divergent Policies: An 18-Nation Study of Family Policy," *Public Affairs Report* 31 (May 1990): 2; personal communication by Harold L. Wilensky to the author, dated 18 October 1990; Robert W. Jackman, "Political Institutions and Voter Turnout in the Industrial Democracies," *American Political Science Review* 81 (June 1987): 420; World Bank, *World Development Report 1989* (New York: Oxford University Press, 1989), 223; Robert A. Dahl, *Polyarchy: Participation and Opposition* (New Haven: Yale University Press, 1971), 232.

highest scores, but the 6.80 average of the non-Nordic PR countries is still well above that of the plurality countries.

The last three columns of Table 1 show indicators of democratic quality. The third column lists the most reliable figures on electoral participation (in the 1970s); countries with compulsory voting (Australia, Belgium, and Italy) are not included in the averages. Compared with the extremely low voter turnout of 54.2 percent in the United States, the parliamentary–plurality systems perform a great deal better (about 75 percent). But the average in the parliamentary–PR systems is still higher, at slightly above 84 percent. Since the maximum turnout that is realistically attainable is around 90 percent (as indicated by the turnouts in countries with compulsory voting), the difference between 75 and 84 percent is particularly striking.

Another democratic goal is political equality, which is more likely to prevail in the absence of great economic inequalities. The fourth column of Table 1 presents the World Bank's percentages of total income earned by the top 20 percent of households in the mid-1980s.[11] They show a slightly less unequal distribution of income in the parliamentary–PR than in the parliamentary–plurality systems, with the United States in an intermediate position.

Finally, the fifth column reports Robert A. Dahl's ranking of democracies according to ten indicators of democratic quality, such as freedom of the press, freedom of association, competitive party systems, strong parties and interest groups, and effective legislatures.[12] The stable democracies range from a highest rating of 1 to a low of 6. There is a slight pro-PR bias in Dahl's ranking (he includes a number-of-parties

TABLE 2—ECONOMIC GROWTH, INFLATION, AND UNEMPLOYMENT (1961–1988)

TYPE OF DEMOCRACY	Economic Growth (percent)	Inflation (percent)	Unemployment (percent)
Presidential–Plurality	3.3	5.1	6.1
Parliamentary–Plurality	3.4	7.5	6.1
Parliamentary–PR	3.5	6.3	4.4

Sources: OECD Economic Outlook, No. 26 (December 1979), 131; No. 30 (December 1981), 131, 140, 142; No. 46 (December 1989), 166, 176, 182.

variable that rates multiparty systems somewhat higher than two-party systems), but even when we discount this bias we find striking differences between the parliamentary–PR and parliamentary–plurality countries: six of the former are given the highest score, whereas most of the latter receive the next to lowest score of 5.

No such clear differences are apparent when we examine the effect of the type of democracy on the maintenance of public order and peace. Parliamentary–plurality systems had the lowest incidence of riots during the period 1948–77, but the highest incidence of political deaths; the latter figure, however, derives almost entirely from the high number of political deaths in the United Kingdom, principally as a result of the Northern Ireland problem. A more elaborate statistical analysis shows that societal division is a much more important factor than type of democracy in explaining variation in the incidence of political riots and deaths in the 13 parliamentary countries.[13]

A major argument in favor of plurality systems has been that they favor "strong" one-party governments that can pursue "effective" public policies. One key area of government activity in which this pattern should manifest itself is the management of the economy. Thus advocates of plurality systems received a rude shock in 1987 when the average per capita GDP in Italy (a PR and multiparty democracy with notoriously uncohesive and unstable governments) surpassed that of the United Kingdom, typically regarded as the very model of strong and effective government. If Italy had discovered large amounts of oil in the Mediterranean, we would undoubtedly explain its superior economic performance in terms of this fortuitous factor. But it was not Italy but Britain that discovered the oil!

Economic success is obviously not solely determined by government policy. When we examine economic performance over a long period of time, however, the effects of external influences are minimized, especially if we focus on countries with similar levels of economic development. Table 2 presents OECD figures from the 1960s through the 1980s for the three most important aspects of macroeconomic performance—average annual economic growth, inflation, and unemployment rates.

Although Italy's economic growth has indeed been better than that of Britain, the parliamentary–plurality and parliamentary–PR countries as groups do not differ much from each other or from the United States. The slightly higher growth rates in the parliamentary–PR systems cannot be considered significant. With regard to inflation, the United States has the best record, followed by the parliamentary–PR systems. The most sizable differences appear in unemployment levels; here the parliamentary–PR countries perform significantly better than the plurality countries.[14] Comparing the parliamentary–plurality and parliamentary–PR countries on all three indicators, we find that the performance of the latter is uniformly better.

Lessons for Developing Countries

Political scientists tend to think that plurality systems such as the United Kingdom and the United States are superior with regard to democratic quality and governmental effectiveness—a tendency best explained by the fact that political science has always been an Anglo-American–oriented discipline. This prevailing opinion is largely contradicted, however, by the empirical evidence presented above. Wherever significant differences appear, the parliamentary–PR systems almost invariably post the best records, particularly with respect to representation, protection of minority interests, voter participation, and control of unemployment.

This finding contains an important lesson for democratic constitutional engineers: the parliamentary–PR option is one that should be given serious consideration. Yet a word of caution is also in order, since parliamentary–PR democracies differ greatly among themselves. Moderate PR and moderate multipartism, as in Germany and Sweden, offer more attractive models than the extreme PR and multiparty systems of Italy and the Netherlands. As previously noted, though, even Italy has a respectable record of democratic performance.

But are these conclusions relevant to newly democratic and democratizing countries in Asia, Africa, Latin America, and Eastern Europe, which are trying to make democracy work in the face of economic underdevelopment and ethnic divisions? Do not these difficult conditions require strong executive leadership in the form of a powerful president or a Westminster-style, dominant one-party cabinet?

With regard to the problem of deep ethnic cleavages, these doubts can be easily laid to rest. Divided societies, both in the West and elsewhere, need peaceful coexistence among the contending ethnic groups. This requires conciliation and compromise, goals that in turn require the greatest possible inclusion of representatives of these groups in the decision-making process. Such power sharing can be arranged much more easily in parliamentary and PR systems than in presidential and plurality systems. A president almost inevitably belongs to one ethnic group, and hence presidential systems are particularly inimical to ethnic power sharing. And while Westminster-style parliamentary systems feature collegial cabinets, these tend not to be ethnically inclusive, particularly when there is a majority ethnic group. It is significant that the British government, in spite of its strong majoritarian traditions, recognized the need for consensus and power sharing in religiously and ethnically divided Northern Ireland. Since 1973, British policy has been to try to solve the Northern Ireland problem by means of PR elections and an inclusive coalition government.

As Horowitz has pointed out, it may be possible to alleviate the problems of presidentialism by requiring that a president be elected with a stated minimum of support from different groups, as in Nigeria.[15] But this is a palliative that cannot compare with the advantages of a truly collective and inclusive executive. Similarly, the example of Malaysia shows that a parliamentary system can have a broad multiparty and multiethnic coalition cabinet in spite of plurality elections, but this requires elaborate preelection pacts among the parties. These exceptions prove the rule: the ethnic power sharing that has been attainable in Nigeria and Malaysia only on a limited basis and through very special arrangements is a natural and straightforward result of parliamentary–PR forms of democracy.

PR and Economic Policy Making

The question of which form of democracy is most conducive to economic development is more difficult to answer. We simply do not have enough cases of durable Third World democracies representing the different systems (not to mention the lack of reliable economic data) to make an unequivocal evaluation. However, the conventional wisdom that economic development requires the unified and decisive leadership of a strong president or a Westminster-style dominant cabinet is highly suspect. First of all, if an inclusive executive that must do more bargaining and conciliation were less effective at economic policy making than a dominant and exclusive executive, then presumably an authoritarian government free of legislative interference or internal dissent would be optimal. This reasoning—a frequent excuse for the overthrow of democratic governments in the Third World in the 1960s and 1970s—has now been thoroughly discredited. To be sure, we do have a few examples of economic miracles wrought by authoritarian regimes, such as those in South Korea or Taiwan, but these are more than counterbalanced by the sorry economic records of just about all the nondemocratic governments in Africa, Latin America, and Eastern Europe.

Second, many British scholars, notably the eminent political scientist S.E. Finer, have come to the conclusion that economic development requires not so much a *strong* hand as a *steady* one. Reflecting on the poor economic performance of post–World War II Britain, they have argued that each of the governing parties indeed provided reasonably strong leadership in economic policy making but that alternations in governments were too "absolute and abrupt," occurring "between two sharply polarized parties each eager to repeal a large amount of its predecessor's legislation." What is needed, they argue, is "greater stability and continuity" and "greater moderation in policy," which could be provided by a shift to PR and to coalition governments much more likely to be centrist in orientation.[16] This argument would appear to be equally applicable both to developed and developing countries.

Third, the case for strong presidential or Westminster-style governments is most compelling where rapid decision making is essential. This means that in foreign and defense policy parliamentary–PR systems may be at a disadvantage. But in economic policy making speed is not particularly important—quick decisions are not necessarily wise ones.

Why then do we persist in distrusting the economic effectiveness of democratic systems that engage in broad consultation and bargaining aimed at a high degree of consensus? One reason is that multiparty and coalition governments *seem* to be messy, quarrelsome, and inefficient in contrast to the clear authority of strong presidents and strong one-party cabinets. But we should not let ourselves be deceived by these superficial appearances. A closer look at presidential systems reveals that the most successful cases—such as the United States, Costa Rica, and pre-1970 Chile—are at least equally quarrelsome and, in fact, are prone to paralysis and deadlock rather than steady and effective economic policy making. In any case, the argument should not be about governmental aesthetics but about actual performance. The undeniable elegance of the Westminster model is not a valid reason for adopting it.

The widespread skepticism about the economic capability of parliamentary–PR systems stems from confusing governmental strength with effectiveness. In the short run, one-party cabinets or presidents may well be able to formulate economic policy with greater ease and speed. In the long run, however, policies supported by a broad consensus are more likely to be successfully carried out and to remain on course than policies imposed by a "strong" government against the wishes of important interest groups.

To sum up, the parliamentary–PR form of democracy is clearly better than the major alternatives in accommodating ethnic differences, and it has a slight edge in economic policy making as well. The argument that considerations of governmental effectiveness mandate the rejection of parliamentary–PR democracy for developing countries is simply not tenable. Constitution makers in new democracies would do themselves and their countries a great disservice by ignoring this attractive democratic model.

NOTES

I gratefully acknowledge the assistance and advice of Robert W. Jackman, G. Bingham Powell, Jr., Harold L. Wilensky, and Kaare Strom, the research assistance of Markus Crepaz, and the financial support of the Committee on Research of the Academic Senate of the University of California at San Diego.

1. Donald L. Horowitz, "Comparing Democratic Systems," Seymour Martin Lipset, "The Centrality of Political Culture," and Juan J. Linz, "The Virtues of Parliamentarism," *Journal of Democracy* 1 (Fall 1990): 73–91. A third set of important decisions concerns institutional arrangements that are related to the difference between federal and unitary forms of government: the degree of government centralization, unicameralism or bicameralism, rules for constitutional amendment, and judicial review. Empirical analysis shows that these factors tend to be related; federal countries are more likely to be decentralized, to have significant bicameralism, and to have "rigid" constitutions that are difficult to amend and protected by judicial review.

2. For a fuller discussion of the differences between majoritarian and consensus government, see Arend Lijphart, *Democracies: Patterns of Majoritarian and Consensus Government in Twenty-One Countries* (New Haven: Yale University Press, 1984).

3. Giovanni Sartori, "Political Development and Political Engineering," in John D. Montgomery and Alfred O. Hirschman, eds., *Public Policy,* (Cambridge: Harvard University Press, 1968), 273.

4. The first scholar to emphasize the close connection between culture and these constitutional arrangements was G. Bingham Powell, Jr. in his *Contemporary Democracies: Participation, Stability, and Violence* (Cambridge: Harvard University Press, 1982), 67. In my previous writings, I have sometimes classified Finland as a presidential or semipresidential system, but I now agree with Powell (pp. 56–57) that, although the directly elected Finnish president has special authority in foreign policy, Finland operates like a parliamentary system in most other respects. Among the exceptions, Ireland is a doubtful case; I regard its system of the single transferable vote as mainly a PR method, but other authors have classified it as a plurality system. And I include Australia in the parliamentary-plurality group, because its alternative-vote system, while not identical with plurality, operates in a similar fashion.

5. Stein Rokkan, *Citizens, Elections, Parties: Approaches to the Comparative Study of the Processes of Development* (Oslo: Universitetsforlaget, 1970), 157.

6. Douglas V. Verney, *The Analysis of Political Systems* (London: Routledge and Kegan Paul, 1959), 18–23, 42–43.

7. G. Bingham Powell, Jr., *Contemporary Democracies,* 12–29 and 111–74.

8. Juan J. Linz, "The Perils of Presidentialism," *Journal of Democracy* 1 (Winter 1990): 51–69.

9. Scott Mainwaring, "Presidentialism in Latin America," *Latin American Research Review* 25 (1990): 167–70.

10. Wilensky's ratings are based on a five-point scale (from 4 to 0) "for each of three policy clusters: existence and length of maternity and parental leave, paid and unpaid; availability and accessibility of public daycare programs and government effort to expand daycare; and flexibility of retirement systems. They measure government action to assure care of children and maximize choices in balancing

work and family demands for everyone." See Harold L. Wilensky, "Common Problems, Divergent Policies: An 18-Nation Study of Family Policy," *Public Affairs Report* 31 (May 1990): 2.

11. Because of missing data, Austria is not included in the parliamentary–PR average.

12. Robert A. Dahl, *Polyarchy: Participation and Opposition* (New Haven: Yale University Press, 1971), 231–45.

13. This multiple-correlation analysis shows that societal division, as measured by the degree of organizational exclusiveness of ethnic and religious groups, explains 33 percent of the variance in riots and 25 percent of the variance in political deaths. The additional explanation by type of democracy is only 2 percent for riots (with plurality countries slightly more orderly) and 13 percent for deaths (with the PR countries slightly more peaceful).

14. Comparable unemployment data for Austria, Denmark, and New Zealand are not available, and these countries are therefore not included in the unemployment figures in Table 2.

15. Donald L. Horowitz, "Comparing Democratic Systems," 76–77.

16. S.E. Finer, "Adversary Politics and Electoral Reform," in S.E. Finer, ed., *Adversary Politics and Electoral Reform* (London: Anthony Wigram, 1975), 30–31.

7

THE PROBLEM WITH PR

Guy Lardeyret

Guy Lardeyret is president of the Paris-based Institut pour la Démocratie, a nongovernmental organization that is currently providing advice and support to heads of state, government officials, or party leaders in about 20 countries in Asia, Africa, the Middle East, Eastern Europe, and South America. The essay originally appeared in the Summer 1991 issue of the Journal of Democracy.

Arend Lijphart's article on "Constitutional Choices for New Democracies" (pp. 73–85 above) attempts to provide scientific evidence for the superiority of proportional representation (PR) to the system of plurality elections. The author presents a comparative analysis designed to show that regimes based on plurality elections do not measure up to parliamentary–PR regimes in terms of "democratic performance."

Lijphart considers the effects of electoral systems on eight variables, which we will consider successively. The first correlation suggests that PR favors the representation of "minorities" and pressure groups. As clearly shown by the statistics, women legislators are more numerous in Nordic countries, which also tend to spend more money on family policies. Although tradition plays a role, the phenomenon is made possible by PR: candidate slates are chosen by party leaders, who are more easily influenced by strong women's movements.

The relationship between PR and voter participation is not as clear. If it were calculated on the European basis (as a proportion of registered voters), U.S. voter turnout would be similar to that of Western Europe. Moreover, Lijphart's figures would look quite different if he had not made some questionable decisions in categorizing countries. France, for instance, might be counted as a presidential–plurality democracy alongside the United States. Germany (whose mixed electoral system has majoritarian effects) belongs among the parliamentary–plurality regimes, while Spain and Portugal (which Lijphart ignores) should be included among the third group, the parliamentary–PR democracies.

Lijphart's next set of figures indicates that northern European countries have a more equal distribution of income, which is not surprising. If there is a link between the electoral system and the greater degree of economic equality in these countries, it may not have much to do with democracy. When conservatives win elections in such countries as Sweden, Denmark, Norway, and Finland, they must form coalitions with other parties, which makes it hard for them to pursue their democratically mandated program of reducing the welfare state.

Lijphart's use of Robert Dahl's system for rating "democratic quality" raises the question of what criteria best measure democratic performance. If the index includes variables such as turnout (as measured in the U.S.), the number of parties, and the strength of interest groups, it introduces a strong bias in favor of PR with this sample of countries.

Finally, the correlations with inflation, economic growth, and unemployment (underestimated in Nordic countries because of highly protected jobs) are difficult to exploit. These indicators are much more powerfully influenced by many other important factors.

Consequences of Electoral Systems

Lijphart accepts from the beginning a fundamental hypothesis—namely, that the electoral system largely determines the party system and through it the structure of the government. Thus, countries where PR is the rule end up with multipartism and coalition governments, while plurality elections favor the two-party system and single-party governments. But as Lijphart notes, opinions diverge on how the party system affects the exercise of democratic governance. It is precisely on this point that it would have been fruitful for Lijphart to test the hypothesis against empirical data.

Such an analysis would have clearly shown that bipartism favors governmental stability and decision-making capacity as well as periodic alternations in power. Multipartism, on the other hand, is positively correlated with ephemeral governments, periods when the chief executive office goes unfilled, repeated elections, and long tenures in office for fixed groups of key politicians. The more parties a country has, moreover, the greater is the incidence of these phenomena.

When the government rests on a homogeneous majority, it remains in power for the duration of its mandated term (stability); can apply its program (efficiency); and is likely, should it falter, to lose power to a strong and united opposition (alternation). By contrast, the coalition governments so common in PR systems often cannot survive serious disagreement over particular measures (instability); need inordinate amounts of time to build new coalitions (executive vacancy); and when they fall apart, call new elections that generally return the same people (nonalternation).

The contention that PR favors the representation of "minorities" is true, in a sense: PR gives any well-organized pressure group—be it a union, a religion, an ethnic group, a profession, or an ideological faction—a chance to win seats. A party that polarizes one important issue of common interest like environmental protection will attract votes.

Dividing the electorate in this way tends to exacerbate the conflicts in a society. For example, the introduction of PR in local and European elections in France during the 1980s made possible the growing prominence of Jean-Marie Le Pen's National Front (FN), a far-right party that condemns immigration. The Front's rise has in turn sparked the formation of a number of left-wing "antiracist" groups that are no less intolerant than the FN itself. This unhealthy situation can be attributed largely to PR.

It can also be shown that PR is dangerous for countries faced with ethnic or cultural divisions. In Belgium, for instance, linguistic parties sprang up after PR was introduced early in this century. Belgian politics became little more than a feud between the Flemings and the French-speaking Walloons. Without the monarchy to cement its national unity, Belgium could have fallen apart.

The risks of coalition governments should also be recalled. Such governments are often reluctant to make unpopular decisions because of the resistance of some coalition partner. The Palestinian problem in Israel will probably never be solved unless Israel's electoral law is changed or extraordinary foreign pressure is exerted.

Proportional representation tends to give small parties disproportionate power because such parties control the "swing" seats needed to make up a majority coalition. Germany's Free Democratic Party, for instance, has been able to participate in all governments since World War II. Sometimes coalitions can be political absurdities: In Greece recently, the right forged an alliance with the communists in order to keep the socialists out of the government. The political annals of the Scandinavian countries offer numerous examples of cases where the only party to have made significant gains in a given election was unable to find partners and had to remain in opposition.

Even more problematic is PR's tendency to give extremist parties a chance to participate in government. Such a party may eliminate its coalition partners by an internal coup, as Mussolini's Fascists did in Italy in the 1920s. Without PR, the Communists and the Nazis would probably not have been able to storm onto the German political scene as they did in the 1930s.

An election is not a poll aimed at giving the most accurate representation of all the various opinions or interests at play in a given society. Were that the case—there being no fixed limit to the possible divisions in a society—the most democratic assembly would be one where each member represented a sharply defined interest or particular ideological nuance. Such an assembly would present an absurd caricature of democratic government.

An electoral system is intended to give citizens the power to decide who shall rule and according to what policy. It should produce an efficient government, supported by the bulk of the citizens. Plurality elections force the parties to coalesce before the balloting occurs. They must synthesize the divergent interests and opinions of as many voters as possible, offer the electors a coherent program for governing, and prove their ability to gather a majority. Parties in plurality systems tend to be moderate because most votes are to be gained among the undecided voters of the center.

Proportional representation places the responsibility of choosing both the personnel and the policy of the new government on party leaders, deliberating out of public view and after all the votes have been cast. What distinguishes one system from the other thus has less to do with "consensus" than with differences in their methods of forging political compromises. The method of plurality elections is more democratic as well as more efficient, because the decisions are taken by the citizens themselves. The choice is clear, and the contract is limited in time.

Rediscovering the Westminster Model

Once a homogeneous majority exists in parliament, there is no need, strictly speaking, for the direct election of a separate chief executive. The head of the majority party in parliament can do the job, and this avoids the risk of conflict between the two sources of democratic legitimacy. The parliamentary majority provides competent ministers who remain in touch with the legislature. The executive has the initiative in proposing legislation; the legislators' main role is to improve bills through amendments, and not to obstruct policies that have received the support of the electorate.

We thus rediscover the Westminster model, which has been working smoothly for the past 300 years in England, while France has changed regimes 20 times in two centuries and is still experimenting with various possible combinations of electoral systems with parliamentary and presidential regimes. France's greatest single institutional advance came in 1958, when the faltering parliamentary–PR Fourth Republic gave way to the presidential-de-facto-plurality Fifth Republic under Charles de Gaulle. Yet serious conflicts of competence emerged between the president and the prime minister during the "cohabitation" period of 1986–88, when for the first time in the history of the Fifth Republic, a president from one party (Socialist François Mitterrand) was teamed with a premier from another (Gaullist Jacques Chirac). This situation, which could soon recur, creates pressure for a move toward the parliamentary–plurality model.

There is now massive evidence that, among the four possible combinations of institutions (presidential or parliamentary) and electoral systems (PR or plurality), the order of rank according to standards of both efficiency and democracy is the following: the Westminster model, presidential–plurality, parliamentary–PR, and presidential–PR. Among the PR systems, the worst is pure PR (Italy, Israel), and the least bad is PR with majoritarian devices (Germany, Greece).

It is almost impossible to get rid of PR, because doing so requires asking independent parties to cooperate in their own liquidation. The coalition of threatened parties will almost always be strong enough to thwart electoral reform, which must then await a major national crisis. The shift from presidentialism to parliamentarism is fairly easy in semi-presidential regimes. Portugal has recently made this move, and Finland has done practically the same thing, which may soon be confirmed by a constitutional change (not that one is indispensable: parties can agree not to nominate their leaders as presidential candidates).

This helps to explain the institutional problems which, as Lijphart acknowledges, can be observed in Latin America. Electoral divisions in parliament tend to reinforce the power of the president. Political competition then focuses on the presidency to a degree that can encourage military coups. One way to avoid that risk is the establishment of a presidential party that entrenches itself in both the state apparatus and many sectors of society. The classic case is Paraguay, where President Alfredo Stroessner stayed in office for 35 years at the head of his Colorado Party machine. To prohibit the reelection of the president simply shifts the power to the ruling party, as Mexicans have learned under the longstanding rule of the PRI.

Building a Democracy

Although the electoral system is a major determinant of a political regime—albeit one curiously omitted in most constitutions—it would be a mistake for new democracies to assume that good democratic performance can be ensured by choosing the right electoral system, or that democracy can be simply defined as a political system where the rulers are freely elected (although that is certainly a necessary condition). Although Boris Yeltsin was freely elected president of the Russian Republic, the RSFSR is still not a democracy.

To become a democracy, a regime must meet two fundamental conditions. Because sovereignty resides with the citizens, who delegate power only to solve problems of common concern, a democracy must above all respect the distinction between the private and public spheres.[1] The transition to democracy in most of the countries of Eastern Europe will depend primarily on their capacity to disengage the state from economic and social life. It is much more difficult to restore the springs of individual initiative, which have been destroyed by years of stifling bureaucracy and irresponsibility, than to ratify a formal constitution. On the other hand, countries such as Korea, Taiwan, or Singapore, where an authoritarian regime has allowed the growth of an effervescent private and economic life, can easily become democratic as soon as free and fair elections are organized.

The second great principle to follow in building a democracy is to diffuse power by dividing control over the public sphere among various levels and centers of authority. The rule here is that decisions should be taken at the level closest to the citizen. Switzerland presents a splendid example of this principle in action. Decentralization can also be spread by competence, with decisions delegated to people concerned with the subject. To set the executive and legislative branches directly against one another, whether at the local or the national level, is more likely to cause inefficiency than political equilibrium. When a country contains populations from widely differing cultures, each intent upon its autonomy, federalism (usually involving a second legislative chamber) is the best institutional solution. A good constitution will find ways to establish these prerequisites of democracy, along with an independent judiciary to guarantee the rule of law.

Ethnic divisions present especially thorny difficulties in Africa. Despite the existence of interesting local democratic traditions in many parts of the continent, national elections there tend to degenerate into ethnic contests over legislative seats and public offices. The best way to counteract these propensities is to oblige members of each group to run against one another on (transethnic) political and ideological grounds in single-member districts. The worst way is to adopt PR, which tends to reproduce ethnic cleavages in the legislature.

In this regard, the unique case of South Africa becomes especially intriguing. The "white tribe" has installed a political regime that basically respects the first two conditions of democracy. As the country moves toward fuller democracy, it remains to be seen whether South Africa's new citizens will array themselves along cleavages of ideology or ethnicity. South Africa's prospects will be grim if it cannot build big and moderate multiethnic parties. There can be no question that a system of plurality elections offers the best conditions for the growth of such parties.

Lijphart's article proves at least that political scientists still have a long way to go even to reach a consensus, much less to discover the definitive truth—if it exists—on this fundamental issue.

NOTES

1. For a thorough analysis of the concept of democracy, see Jean Baechler, *Democracy: An Analytical Survey* (New York: UNESCO, 1995).

8

PR AND DEMOCRATIC STATECRAFT

Quentin L. Quade

Quentin L. Quade *(d. 1999) was professor of political science at Marquette University in Milwaukee, Wisconsin, where he also served as dean of the graduate school (1968–72) and executive vice-president (1974–90).* His writings include more than 60 essays in journals such as the Review of Politics, Freedom at Issue, First Things, Thought, *and* Parliamentary Affairs. *This essay originally appeared in the Summer 1991 issue of the* Journal of Democracy.

In "Constitutional Choices for New Democracies," Arend Lijphart sets out to describe and evaluate some of the primary institutional alternatives available to new democracies. Lijphart knows that the choice of electoral system is especially important, since it will likely determine whether many or few parties will compete, and whether coalition or single-party governments will result. He also knows that once chosen, the electoral system will be hard to change. Lijphart favors proportional representation (PR), welcomes proliferated parties, and esteems coalitions. I have publicly defended the opposite view. I urge plurality voting in single-member districts, hope and expect that this will encourage a two-party system, and applaud the single-party government that would result.[1]

How is it that two democrats with similar starting points like Lijphart and myself could come up with such starkly contrasting practical advice for newly emerging democracies? As in real estate, the key is to inspect the premises. Even a brief and selective inspection, as this one must be, will show why our recommendations differ so sharply, and why I think Lijphart's position rests on questionable, even utopian, foundations.

Advocates of proportional representation typically describe it as more "fair" and more "just." Lijphart's article says PR produces "consensus" politics, promotes "conciliation and compromise," and is more "representative" than plurality voting. In fact, each of these good words applied to PR begs a question and calls for a rarely given philosophical argument to establish a meaning for "fair," "just," "representative," and so on. No such arguments are presented or even summarized by Lijphart. The only thing certain about PR is that it will tend to re-create society's divisions and locate them in the legislature. That is its purpose, logic, and result.[2]

Whether a system that encourages party proliferation is any of the good things its proponents call it—fairer, more just, more representative—depends on a theory of statecraft and democratic form. What is the purpose of the state? Does the adoption of democracy eliminate or even lessen the traditional requirements of state action? In particular, does democratic statecraft have a diminished responsibility to synthesize society's parts, unify and defend its people, or identify and pursue the common good—meaning those values that no particular part of society will ever seek as its own but on which all particular parts depend? Or does democratic politics exist to do all the things states exist for, but to do them in a new way, a responsible and accountable way? If it does, then the first test of fairness, justice, and representation that democratic politics must pass will be the test of excellence in state action. The second and no less important test will be that of accountability. But for Lijphart and his fellow PR advocates, the first question appears to be: how well are society's natural divisions re-created and relocated in the legislature? Where he equates the number of women in legislatures with representation of women's interests, for example, Lijphart uses the term "representation" as identical to re-creation. In his uncritical implicit reliance on the "picture theory" of legislative representation, Lijphart writes as if Edmund Burke had never lived.

To prove that PR's tendency to re-create divisions and proliferate parties is indeed a good thing, an extended argument is required. It must explain how a political system will be "fair" if it succumbs to the centrifugal pull of interests, how it can advance the general welfare if it "represents" only minute and particular aspects of society, and how a government cobbled together out of postelection splinters by a secretive process of interparty bartering can be considered responsible and accountable. Only by doing this can PR advocates escape the charge of question-begging.

Easy Cases and Unfounded Speculations

I have suggested that PR advocates generally, and Lijphart in particular, tend to make their work easy by eliding from PR's tendency to re-create societal divisions to an unexamined designation of such re-creation as good. Another labor-saving approach, greatly evident in Lijphart's article, is to build the argument for PR on easy cases developed in unusually auspicious circumstances.

It is axiomatic that the difficulty of the tests a political system faces will be commensurate with the severity of the prepolitical conditions it must confront. I refer to such obvious variables as economic health or sickness, ethnic tension or harmony, religious cleavages or unity, geopolitical peril or security. It is also obvious that a relatively weak political structure may work under "fair-weather" prepolitical conditions, while a stronger system may founder if it must endure unusually foul prepolitical weather. Thus, if one could know for sure that nation X would never confront any but the most peaceful circumstances, the strength of its political structure would be of little concern. Such an idyllic environment would leave ample room for error; even if the government were prone to stumble, the natural buoyancy of society would save the state from falling.

Much of my difference with Lijphart derives from his inclination to test PR in too-easy cases. Most of his "successful" examples of PR are drawn from very small societies. Some, like the Scandinavian countries, are nearly homogeneous, with low levels of racial, ethnic, or religious turbulence. Nor have they experienced any severe economic stress during the period of Lijphart's observations. Moreover, all the positive examples from the era he studies have lived under the umbrella of American military protection, an artificial and temporary condition that has spared them most of the stresses of balance-of-power machinations. Many also were beneficiaries of the Marshall Plan, which spurred an era of unprecedented economic recovery and growth in Western Europe.

Lijphart's list of examples contains mostly fair-weather cases; the favorable conditions they enjoyed bear scant resemblance to the arduous circumstances that now confront struggling new democracies. Nor does his list include any of the obvious and dramatic cases in which PR clearly contributed to governmental weakness and systemic collapse. Pre-Mussolini Italy, with its splintered parties and political gridlock, would be a worthy example. France's Fourth Republic (1945-1958), chronically crippled and finally made suicidal by its inability to deal with colonial and domestic problems, would be another. Finally, the Weimar Republic, where coalition was endemic and weakness perpetual, might be the best of all test cases for PR. F.A. Hermens definitively established PR's direct contribution to the regime's inability to develop moderate strength and to rid itself of its extremist elements.[3] As Herman Finer once observed, PR's version of "justice"—lodging social splinters in the legislature—kept both Nazism and Communism alive so that together they could murder the Weimar Republic.[4] "Conciliation and compromise" were conspicuous by their absence.

It seems strange to me that a list of PR examples contains only the beneficiaries of sunny prepolitical conditions. It seems stranger still that it makes no reference to illustrations of PR's most calamitous effects.

In addition to its unwarranted ascription of "good" words to PR and its reliance on easy cases, Lijphart's effort suffers from a third difficulty.

To put the case broadly, Lijphart presumes to know things that the evidence simply does not indicate. He imagines, for instance, that Italy's relative economic success over the last few decades, Germany's evident success during the same period, and Britain's relative weakness can all be appreciably attributed to the shape of the central political institutions in each country. If that were true, then one could infer that splintered parties and weak, unstable coalitions (as in Italy) are as good as or better than majority-forming parties that produce strong single-party governments (as in Britain).

Though Lijphart says that the "empirical evidence" suggests all this, it actually suggests nothing of the sort. Instead, the empirical evidence should remind us of the numerous and sometimes mysterious variables that one must take into account when considering such complex social and economic realities. As previously noted, all we know *for certain* about electoral systems is that PR tends to proliferate parties, while plurality voting encourages two-party arrangements. All we know *for certain* about coalitions is that they are subject to stress and dissolution more than a single-party majority would be (witness Italy in the spring of 1991 as it deposed its forty-ninth postwar government); and that to govern they must form postelection groupings outside of public view (no member of Italy's electorate voted for its fiftieth government). Abstract logic—plus experience with cases like Weimar Germany and the Fourth French Republic—suggests that coalitions will be a less secure basis for governance than would be a single-party majority. Such majorities are clearly able to act, even while constantly debating and maneuvering against an opposition striving to become the next government.

But what of Italy's economic good fortune, Germany's robustness, Britain's pale comparison? One could attribute these conditions to their respective political institutions only by arguing *post hoc, ergo propter hoc*. Such an argument simply ignores the array of other variables that any objective analysis should bring to mind. I have mentioned already the artificiality of the foreign-affairs responsibilities that have confronted Italy and Germany in the age of the Marshall Plan and the NATO alliance, as well as the jump-start that the former gave to their economies. I would also note that policies which encourage economic growth can be adopted by weak governments, while strong governments are not assured of making all the right decisions. It is not unreasonable to suggest, for example, that Germany's economic strength since the Marshall Plan derives in great part from the horrible economic lessons learned during the PR-induced paralysis of the Weimar period. Certainly the deep-seated German fear of inflation is derived from those experiences. It would be a mistake to attribute Germany's cautious monetary policy to the country's contemporary system of modified PR when in fact this penchant for caution is a negative lesson from Germany's ruinous pre-Hitler PR experience.

By the same token, attempts to attribute Britain's relatively pallid economic record to its majority-forming system are entirely unconvincing. Britain has performed poorly by comparison to some other countries—a weak showing that is traceable in part to poor decisions and not just difficult circumstances. But wise decisions are not guaranteed by *any* political system, and the impact of unpromising circumstances should not be underestimated. Britain, after all, went into World War II in substantial decline, and emerged from it greatly weakened. It did not receive the same massive help from the Marshall Plan that others did. It had to endure the rapid dissolution of a massive overseas empire that was tightly interwoven with the fabric of its economy. Decolonization has required not merely economic adaptation, but a seismic social-psychological adjustment as well. On top of all this is the extraordinarily thorny prepolitical problem posed by the Irish question.

The point of this litany is this: While Britain's economic performance in the postwar era can hardly be called a triumph of the Westminster model, neither can it be explained simply as one of that model's failures. The array of influences on those countries that have done better, the degree to which an economy operates independently of day-to-day political influence, and the large number of debilitating conditions Britain has confronted all make it simply unrealistic to cite the British political system as the main debilitator of the British economy. It is wise, as a rule, never to speculate when you can ascertain. Among this rule's many corollaries is this one: Never fail to speculate when you cannot ascertain, but never imagine you have ascertained when in fact you are only speculating. The causal relationships that Lijphart claims his "empirical evidence" has established turn out, upon closer inspection, to be purely speculative.

The Virtues of Plurality Systems

Lijphart's dedication to PR rests on his assumption that we can get all of PR's alleged virtues (re-creationist representation, all voices heard, consensus, compromise, and so on) without any of its alleged vices (invitation to extremism, governmental weakness and instability, political unrealism, unaccountability to the electorate, and so on). But both analysis and history strongly suggest that you cannot buy it that way. Even if fair-weather conditions make PR tolerable over some period of time, it is unlikely that modern mass nation-states will forever or even for long have such happy circumstances before them. The natural centrifugal stresses and strains in human existence that call the state into being argue for majority-based systems to ensure its capacity for action. And if popular control is to be genuine, the people need to be able to see who is doing what and what each side has to offer, and to make serious judgments between them.

Plurality voting encourages the competing parties to adopt a major-ity-forming attitude. The parties incline to be moderate, to seek conciliation, to round off their rough edges—in short, to do *before* the election, in the public view, the very tasks that Lijphart applauds PR systems for doing *after* the election. Majorities formed in plurality sys-tems are more likely to be strong enough to sustain effective government without becoming unresponsive and rigid, for majorities thus formed are innately fickle, always falling apart, always needing rebuilding.

Moreover, well-chosen policies, including respect for subsidiarity, can foster vibrant local governments and civil societies, thus encourag-ing the very multiplicity for which PR strives without incurring the deleterious effects of governmental weakness and unaccountability. In contrast to Lijphart, I maintain that PR's true virtues (accommodation of differences, a hundred flowers blooming, and so on) can be had with-out any of its debilitating vices under a majority-forming plurality sys-tem. That being the case, why run the well-known risks of PR? Emerging democracies, facing very difficult prepolitical circumstances, need the best political structures they can get. The best combine great capacity for action with clear accountability and thus provide power-made-re-sponsible. This happy combination is most likely to occur in majority-forming electoral systems operating within parliamentary structures. Of course, even the best arrangements cannot guarantee success in this imperfect world, any more than inferior systems make wise policy im-possible. But the best systems will ensure both that the paralysis of government itself does not become the chief problem before the nation, and that it will be the voters who truly elect and depose governments.

NOTES

1. Compare my essay "Democracies-to-Be: Getting It Right the First Time," in *Freedom at Issue* 113 (March–April 1990): 4–8.

2. Since societal divisions are potentially innumerable, one sometimes finds PR advocates like Lijphart introducing distinctions between "extreme" and "moder-ate" forms of PR. In the latter, PR's natural tendencies are frustrated by devices that give government a better chance to form and function—a repudiation, however unacknowledged, of the logic of PR.

3. F.A. Hermens, *Democracy or Anarchy? A Study of Proportional Representa-tion* (Notre Dame, Indiana: University of Notre Dame Press, 1941).

4. Herman Finer, *Governments of Greater European Powers* (New York: Henry Holt, 1956), 623.

9

DOUBLE-CHECKING
THE EVIDENCE

Arend Lijphart

Arend Lijphart *is research professor emeritus of political science at the University of California, San Diego. He is the author of* Patterns of Democracy: Government Forms and Performance in Thirty-Six Countries *(1999) and many other studies of democratic institutions, the governance of deeply divided societies, and electoral systems. This essay originally appeared in the Summer 1991 issue of the* Journal of Democracy.

In my article "Constitutional Choices for New Democracies," I presented systematic empirical evidence concerning the relative performance of various types of democratic systems in an effort to transcend the usual vague and untestable claims and counterclaims that surround this topic. I compared four parliamentary-plurality democracies (the United Kingdom, Canada, Australia, and New Zealand) with nine parliamentary-proportional representation (PR) democracies (Germany, Italy, Austria, the Netherlands, Belgium, and four Nordic countries—Sweden, Denmark, Norway, Finland) with regard to their performance records on minority representation and protection, democratic quality, the maintenance of public order and peace, and the management of the economy.

I found that, where differences between the two groups of democracies appeared, the parliamentary-PR systems showed the better performance. There were sizeable differences with regard to minority representation (as measured by the representation of women in national parliaments), the protection of minority interests (measured by innovative family policy), democratic quality (measured by voter turnout), and control of unemployment; smaller differences on income inequality and control of inflation; and little or no difference with regard to the maintenance of public order (as measured by riots and deaths from political violence) and economic growth. Since, according to the conventional—but also rather old-fashioned—wisdom, PR may be superior to plurality as far as minority representation is concerned but leads to less effective decision making, even my finding of minor or no differences on some of the performance indicators must be counted in favor of the parliamentary-PR type.

Guy Lardeyret and Quentin L. Quade, both eloquent exponents of this conventional wisdom, raise a series of objections to my analysis and conclusions—very welcome challenges because they present an opportunity to double-check the validity of my evidence. Lardeyret and Quade argue that 1) the differences in governmental performance may be explained by other factors than the type of democracy, and hence that they do not prove any parliamentary-PR superiority; 2) that, when other important effects of the different types of democracy are considered, plurality systems are superior; 3) that some of my findings are the result of incorrect measurement; and 4) that my findings are biased by my choice and classification of the countries included in the analysis. I shall demonstrate, however, that whenever their objections can be tested against the facts, they turn out to be invalid.

Alternative Explanations

I agree with Lardeyret's and Quade's argument that economic success is not solely determined by government policy; I said as much in my original article. There are obviously many external and fortuitous factors that influence a country's economic performance. Neither do I disagree with Quade's argument that several special circumstances have had a negative effect on Britain. On the other hand, some of the PR countries suffered similar setbacks: The Netherlands and Belgium also lost sizeable colonial empires, the "seismic social-psychological" shock of decolonization suffered by Britain was no greater than the shock of defeat and division suffered by Germany, and ethnic strife has plagued Belgium as well as the Celtic periphery of the United Kingdom. But my comparison was not just between Britain and one or more PR countries; I compared the four parliamentary-plurality democracies as a group with the group of nine parliamentary-PR countries. I assumed that when the economic performance of groups of democracies is examined over a long period of time, and when all of the countries studied have similar levels of economic development, external and fortuitous influences tend to even out. In the absence of any plausible suggestion that, as a group, the parliamentary-PR countries enjoyed unusual economic advantages from the 1960s through the 1980s—and neither Lardeyret nor Quade offers any such suggestion—my assumption and hence my findings concerning differences in economic performance remain valid.

Lardeyret and Quade do mention a few things that might provide a basis for alternative explanations: the special characteristics of the Nordic countries, the advantage of having a constitutional monarchy, the difference between moderate and extreme PR, and the advantage of U.S. military protection. All of these can be tested empirically. Lardeyret claims that unemployment in the Nordic countries is underestimated because of "highly protected jobs" and that income inequality is relatively modest because of unusual handicaps that conservative parties must contend with in these countries. Whether these factors change my findings can be checked easily by excluding the Nordic countries and comparing the non-Nordic parliamentary-PR countries with the parliamentary-plurality countries. Average unemployment in the Nordic countries was indeed lower than in the non-Nordic countries—2.7 percent compared with 5.7 percent—but the latter percentage is still slightly better than the 6.1 percent for the parliamentary-plurality countries. As far as income inequality is concerned, there is virtually no difference between the Nordic and non-Nordic parliamentary-PR countries—39.0 and 38.9 percent, respectively—both of which score lower than the 42.9 percent in the parliamentary-plurality democracies.

When we compare monarchies with republics, the first point to be made is that, if a constitutional monarchy is an advantage, all of the parliamentary-plurality countries enjoy this advantage, whereas only about half of the parliamentary-PR democracies do. Second, when we compare the monarchical countries (Belgium, the Netherlands, Sweden, Norway, and Denmark) with the republican PR countries (Germany, Italy, Austria, and Finland), their growth rates are virtually identical and their inflation rates exactly the same. Only their unemployment rates differ somewhat: the monarchies have a 4.0 percent average unemployment rate compared with 4.9 percent in the nonmonarchical countries; again, the latter percentage is still better than the 6.1 percent average of the parliamentary-plurality countries. On all of the indicators of minority representation and protection and of democratic quality, there are slight differences between the monarchical and non-monarchical groups, but both still clearly outperform the parliamentary-plurality countries.

Is PR's Achilles' heel revealed when we focus on the countries that have extreme PR (Italy, the Netherlands, Denmark, and Finland) and contrast these with the more moderate PR systems (Germany, Sweden, Norway, Belgium, and Austria)? The empirical evidence disproves this. The inflation and unemployment rates in the extreme PR group are indeed higher (7.4 and 5.5 versus 5.4 and 3.6 percent) but still at least a bit lower than the 7.5 and 6.1 percent in the parliamentary-plurality systems; their growth rates are virtually identical. On the four indicators of representation and democratic quality, the differences are slight, and both groups of PR countries remain way ahead of the parliamentary-plurality countries. My own firm preference remains for moderate PR, but the dangers of extreme PR must not be exaggerated.

As Quade correctly states, the parliamentary-PR countries have had the advantage of living under "the umbrella of American military protection"—but so have all four of the parliamentary-plurality countries. In fact, the only slight exceptions are in the PR group: Sweden's neutral but strongly armed posture entailed heavy military expenditures, and Finland lived in precarious dependence on Soviet restraint. On the whole, however, American military protection benefited all 13 parliamentary democracies more or less equally, and therefore cannot explain any differences in their performance records.

Alternative Standards and Classifications

Partly in addition to and partly instead of the measures that I used to evaluate the performance of different types of democracy, Lardeyret and Quade state that democracies should be judged in terms of factors like accountability, government stability, decision-making capacity, and the ability to avoid "repeated elections." There are several problems with these suggestions. First of all, while accountability is certainly an important aspect of democratic government, it cannot be measured objectively. Second, it is not at all clear that coalition governments are less responsible and accountable than one-party governments. Quade's description of coalition cabinets as governments "cobbled together out of postelection splinters by a secretive process of interparty bartering" may apply to a few exceptional cases like Israel (which combines extreme PR with an evenly split and polarized electorate), but for most PR countries it is a grossly overdrawn caricature. In fact, once they are formed, coalition cabinets tend to be a good deal *less* secretive and more open than one-party cabinets.

Third, government stability can be measured in terms of average cabinet duration. On the basis of previously collected figures, my calculation shows that the average cabinet life in the parliamentary-plurality countries is about twice that in the parliamentary-PR systems.[1] Longer cabinet duration, Lardeyret assumes, means greater decision-making strength because of greater continuity in government personnel. But when coalition cabinets change they usually do not change as much as the radically alternating cabinets in the parliamentary-plurality countries. Lardeyret admits this when he complains about the "long tenures in office for fixed groups of key politicians" in the PR countries. Fourth, if Lardeyret is right about the superior decision-making capacity of parliamentary-plurality governments, the only convincing proof is that their decisions result in more effective policies. This brings us back to the evaluation of government performance in terms of successful macroeconomic policy making and the successful maintenance of public order. As we have already seen, this hard evidence does not show any parliamentary-plurality superiority.

Lardeyret's complaint about unnecessarily frequent elections in the parliamentary-PR systems suggests an additional useful measure of democratic performance—and one that, happily, can be measured and tested easily. In the 29-year period from 1960 to 1988—the same period for which two of the three OECD economic indicators were collected—the parliamentary-plurality countries conducted an average of 10.0 national legislative elections, compared with an average of 8.8 in the parliamentary-PR countries.[2] The frequency of elections is actually *smaller* in the PR systems, contrary to Lardeyret's assertion, although the difference is slight. However, Lardeyret's hypothesis is clearly disproved by this simple test.

Lardeyret and Quade have only a few disagreements with my measurements. One question that Lardeyret does raise is the measurement of voter turnout: The U.S. voter-turnout figure would be considerably higher if counted as a proportion of registered voters. He is quite right on this point, but all of my turnout figures are percentages of eligible voters—which means that all countries are treated equally. Moreover, if turnout figures are used as a measure of democratic quality, the low figure for the United States accurately reflects not only an unusually high degree of political apathy but also the fact that voting is deliberately discouraged by the government by means of onerous registration procedures.

Quade questions my equation of "the number of women in legislatures with representation of women's interests." But I did not equate the two at all: I used a separate measure (the innovativeness and expansiveness of family policy, which is of special concern to women) to test whether women's interests were actually better taken care of in the PR countries—and I found that this was indeed the case.

Finally, Lardeyret questions my use of Robert Dahl's ratings of democratic quality because of their alleged pro-PR bias. I already admitted a slight bias of this kind in my original article, but I decided to use the Dahl ratings anyway since they are the most careful overall ratings that are available. However, since they are obviously less objective than my other indicators, I shall not insist on their being used as evidence.

Quade criticizes my favorable judgment of the parliamentary-PR combination by pointing out some examples in which PR did not work well, especially the two cases that are often regarded as spectacular failures of democracy: the Weimar Republic and the French Fourth Republic. Nobody can disagree with the assessment that the Weimar Republic was a failure, but it is less clear that PR was the decisive factor or that plurality would have been able to save Weimar democracy. Moreover, Weimar was a semi-presidential rather than a parliamentary system. In France, the Fourth Republic indeed did not work well, but a reasonable argument can be made that relatively small reforms within the parliamentary-PR framework might have cured the problems and that the radical shift to semi-presidentialism and away from PR was not absolutely necessary. And examples of PR failures can be matched by examples of the failure of plurality systems, such as the failed democracies of West Africa. Sir Arthur Lewis, who served as an economic advisor to these governments, became convinced that "the surest way to kill the idea of democracy" in these divided societies "is to adopt the Anglo-American electoral system of first-past-the-post [plurality]."[3]

Lardeyret does not question my focus on stable contemporary democracies, but argues instead that some of these countries should have been classified differently. Although France is neither fully presidential nor fully plurality, I accept his suggestion that it is close enough on both counts to be classified alongside the United States. I agree that Spain and Portugal belong in the parliamentary-PR category, but comparable data are lacking since the two countries were not yet democratic during the full period covered by the empirical evidence. I disagree that Germany lacks PR and should be classified as a plurality system; it is almost entirely PR in terms of how Bundestag seats are allocated to the parties, though its 5 percent threshold makes it a moderate PR system.

But let us concede Germany to the plurality category; my analysis still stands. Lardeyret's counter-hypothesis is that in "the order of rank according to standards of both efficiency and democracy," the two plurality systems (parliamentary and presidential) are ahead of the parliamentary-PR systems. This can be tested by comparing the seven plurality systems (the parliamentary-plurality countries plus the United States, France, and, arguably, Germany) with eight PR systems (all of the parliamentary-PR systems except Germany). Thus reclassified, the PR countries still have the better record with regard to control of unemployment (4.6 percent versus 5.5 percent average unemployment) and do not differ much with regard to growth (3.5 versus 3.4 percent) and inflation (6.6 versus 6.5 percent). On the indicators of minority representation and protection and of democratic quality, the PR countries are still far ahead of the plurality systems: 17.5 versus 4.5 percent women in parliament; a score of 8.0 versus 4.4 on family policy; 84.5 versus 73.5 percent on voter turnout; and 38.9 versus 41.9 percent of total income earned by the top 20 percent of households. The evidence clearly disproves Lardeyret's counter-hypothesis.

Choices and Changes

The demonstrable advantages of parliamentarism and PR appear to be appreciated by the citizens and politicians of democratic countries. In many, if not most, presidential countries, there is widespread dissatisfaction with the operation of presidentialism and sizeable support for a shift to a parliamentary form of government; the contrary sentiment can be found in hardly any parliamentary democracy. Similarly, there is great unhappiness about how plurality elections work and strong sentiment for a shift to PR in most democracies that use plurality, but few calls for plurality in PR countries. One important reason for this pattern is that the divisive, winner-take-all nature of plurality and presidentialism is widely understood. From the turn of the century on, democracies with ethnic or other deep cleavages have repeatedly turned to PR in order to accommodate such differences. Lardeyret's recommendation of plurality elections for South Africa and other deeply divided countries is therefore particularly dangerous.

Another important reason for PR's popularity is the feeling that disproportional election results are inherently unfair and undemocratic. None of postwar Britain's governing parties was put in power by a majority of the voters; all of these parties gained power in spite of the fact that most of the voters voted against them. Lardeyret's and Quade's opinion that electoral disproportionality is unimportant is simply not shared by most democrats. As a recent editorial in the *Economist* puts it, "since the perception of fairness is the acid test for a democracy—the very basis of its legitimacy—the unfairness argument overrules all others."[4]

Fundamental constitutional changes are difficult to effect and therefore rare, but the prevailing pattern of democratic sentiment makes shifts from plurality to PR more likely than the other way around. The reason for this is not, as Lardeyret suggests, that "it is almost impossible to get rid of PR, because doing so requires asking independent parties to cooperate in their own liquidation." On the contrary, this is the main reason why the big parties that benefit from the plurality rule will try to keep it. In PR systems, the large parties usually have enough votes to shift to a system that would greatly benefit them, especially because, as Lardeyret correctly observes, the electoral system is "curiously omitted in most [written] constitutions." That they rarely try to do so cannot be explained in terms of narrow partisan self-interest; the feeling that scrapping PR is undemocratic and dangerous plays a major role. Both the empirical evidence and the weight of opinion in existing democracies make a strong case for the proposition that PR and parliamentarism are also the wisest options for new democracies.

NOTES

1. Arend Lijphart, *Democracies: Patterns of Majoritarian and Consensus Government in Twenty-One Countries* (New Haven: Yale University Press, 1984), 83. A cabinet is defined as the same cabinet if its party composition does not change; on the basis of this definition and for the 1945–80 period, average cabinet life in the four parliamentary-plurality countries was 88 months and in the parliamentary–PR countries, 44 months.

2. The dates of parliamentary elections for the 13 countries can be found in the respective country chapters of Thomas T. Mackie and Richard Rose, *The International Almanac of Electoral History*, 3rd ed. (London: Macmillan, 1991).

3. W. Arthur Lewis, *Politics in West Africa* (London: Allen and Unwin, 1965), 71.

4. *Economist,* 11 May 1991, 13.

10

THE PRIMACY OF THE PARTICULAR

Ken Gladdish

Ken Gladdish *(d. 2003) taught comparative European politics at the University of Reading in England, where he was head of the department of politics for four years until his retirement in 1994. He wrote extensively on the Netherlands, also on Portugal, and more generally on representation, ethnicity, and the etiology of political science. This essay originally appeared in the January 1993 issue of the* Journal of Democracy.

A little more than three generations ago, the eminent British political scientist Sir Henry Maine discussed what he referred to as "that extreme form of popular government which is called democracy." He wrote not as an opponent of the form but as an inquirer into its success, which seemed to him "to have arisen rather from skillfully applying the curb to popular impulses than from giving them the rein."[1] This view, which today may appear unfashionably paternalistic, can be redeemed by stressing the word "impulses." Few contemporary governments would regard it as either sensible or necessary to respond to each and every fluctuation of public opinion in between the settled contests that now determine and legitimate periods of rule by competing sets of politicians. But the question of how these contests should be staged, in terms of the method for translating votes into legislative seats, still leaves much room for argument.

That it is a topical argument is as evident in long-established democratic polities like France and Britain as in the emerging democracies of Eastern and Central Europe, or indeed in the moves toward multiparty politics that have recently occurred in many states which date their independence to the post-1945 collapse of European colonialism.

In the recent debate in the *Journal of Democracy* among Arend Lijphart, Guy Lardeyret, and Quentin L. Quade that followed Lijphart's original article, two opposing positions were presented.[2] Lijphart advocated strict proportionality in the allocation of popular representation. His two critics catalogued the perils of such close attention to the unmediated arithmetic of party support and endorsed plurality elections. The arguments of the protagonists, however, implied an uncomfortable absolutism, for all rested on the presupposition that a particular electoral system can be advanced as universally superior to all alternatives. This notion had already been challenged in an earlier essay in the *Journal of Democracy* by Larry Diamond. Writing on "Three Paradoxes of Democracy," Diamond had drawn attention to the problem of "representativeness versus governability" and contended that "each country must find its own way of resolving this universal tension."[3]

My purpose is to expand upon that sage contention, which I shall seek to do in three ways: First, by questioning the starkness with which the alternatives were earlier presented; second, by resisting the amputation of electoral systems from the whole body politic; and third, by considering some examples that may suggest greater subtlety in value judgments than attachment to general prescriptions easily allows.

A Range of Formulas

In the first place, the choice does not lie *tout court* between plurality and proportional representation (PR). There is a range of formulas that is so elaborate as to make each set of national arrangements virtually *sui generis*.[4] When, for example, we consider systems that are not based upon mere plurality (and note that plurality systems differ in important ways), we confront provisions as distinct as the additional-member system in Germany, the alternative vote in Australia, and the single transferable vote in Ireland.[5] Furthermore, even where proportionality is embraced as a goal, actual practices extend from Portugal's regional system, with its large variations in the size of constituencies, to the nationwide PR system found in the Netherlands. There is therefore a real danger of setting up a debate that is grossly reductionist in its essential terms. But that is only part of the problem. Lijphart can certainly be commended for his broad-brush search for objective measurements of the various outcomes of different systems. This is a vastly different undertaking, however, from endeavoring to decide which of the two highly generalized alternatives is the ultimate answer.

This is very clearly brought out by the efforts of each of the three debaters to press his case. Two difficulties here seem insuperable. The first—and this is something that the interlocutors themselves largely concede—is the impossibility of separating out the influence of electoral systems from all the other forces that can affect a polity over time. The second is that electoral systems cannot simply be pulled out of a drawer in the way that one might choose a cooking recipe. Each national case is highly circumstantial and reflects both history in all its manifestations and, more specifically, the consequences of particular patterns of political mobilization.

In the Netherlands, on which Lijphart is a widely recognized expert, nationwide PR came about for a number of reasons. Prominent among these was the perceived failure of a plurality system to deliver coherent results, given the fragmented nature of Dutch political competition by the second decade of the present century. This is not of course to argue that the eventual choice was wholly determined by this circumstance, for debate continues in the Netherlands today about the efficacy and desirability of nationwide PR. But it does suggest that the notion of a circumstance-free choice is at odds with reality.

Furthermore, even if it could be convincingly demonstrated (which on the evidence of the debate so far seems unlikely) that PR systems consistently outperform plurality systems, or vice versa, it would still be naive to insist that the apparently more enlightened method should be universally adopted.

Of course, one can explore, as an exercise in comparative politics, the extent to which electoral systems seem to play a significant role in the performance of different polities. If the general findings were persuasive, they would then become an instructive reference for politicians and others who must decide the exact "rules" of the electoral "game" in their various countries. But this merely reemphasizes the point that each polity is distinct, and must therefore work out its own formula.

In Britain today, there is renewed debate about the wisdom of retaining a plurality system based upon single-member constituencies. Many ingredients are discernible in the cases for and against, but the dominant concern is whether "simple" plurality still provides for a reasonably frequent alternation of parties in government. If this particular anxiety, the result of four successive Conservative victories, had not arisen, the debate would almost certainly not be so high on the agenda. The current concern therefore reflects a highly circumstantial feature peculiar to a particular run of recent electoral outcomes. What is most significant is that there is no consensus on what might replace the traditional plurality system, given that each of the alternative prospects would have important consequences for the complexion of both representation and government.[6] It may be that, in the eyes of God, there is a "perfect" electoral system for Britain. But we do not know what it is, and even if we did, there may be costs that significant groups would be unprepared to pay to secure it.

The latter point, concerning costs, must be taken into account when considering why polities do or do not adopt particular arrangements. For there is a fundamental dichotomy that runs through all discussions about how popular votes should be related to the distribution of seats in a legislature: in systems based on popular sovereignty, the people need to be both represented and governed. In each and every democracy, some appropriate relationship between these two needs must be established; it seems obvious that the solutions chosen will vary considerably from country to country.

Nevertheless, one general statement can be confidently made about the prime difference between plurality systems and PR systems: The former tend to limit significant representation in the assembly to two parties, thus facilitating single-party majority government, while the latter, subject to whatever thresholds might be imposed, provide for the legislative representation of all measurable contenders. To put it most simply, plurality systems reduce the prospect of legislative fragmentation; proportional systems increase it.

The Netherlands, France, and Germany

Having questioned the grounds on which the debate has so far proceeded, I shall now attempt to demonstrate the importance of particular cases rather than the persuasive force of general propositions. Let us begin with the previously mentioned example of the Netherlands. Even as it was adopting universal suffrage, the Netherlands replaced its constituency system by a formula of nationwide PR. The main circumstance prompting this change was the sheer geometry of political mobilization, which meant that contests in single-member seats had become unmanageable.[7] By 1914, five significant political groupings were competing on an increasingly national basis, and ad hoc alliances formed to produce majorities in individual constituencies were unable to solve the problem of coherent representation. It seemed inevitable therefore that some other method of staging the national electoral competition would have to be adopted.

The solution of nationwide PR was a resort to the arithmetic of overall party strengths at the cost of a direct linkage between voters and representatives. That this has been no light cost is evidenced by the continuing Dutch debate, which surfaced dramatically in the latter half of the 1960s, about the need to address the problem of linkage. Under nationwide PR, Dutch MPs have no constituents and Dutch voters have no local representatives in the legislature. As several commentators have explained, this has serious consequences for the conduct of national politics.[8]

A further cost is that the meticulous registration of party strengths, with no minimum threshold, results in a multiparty legislature from which governments have to be forged, often with considerable delay and with no reference back to voters. It so happens that, for a number of reasons, this seems not to cause undue damage to governmental continuity.[9] But the reasons are highly specific to Dutch political practice and—dare one use the term?—culture. In other polities it is likely that such prolonged cabinet formations, and the sometimes painful delivery of unexpected governments via the midwifery of party leaders acting in the wake of elections, could cause considerable dislocation and disaffection.

If we turn to the much discussed case of contemporary France, other matters come into view. Although the precise classification of successive French electoral systems has become an academic cottage industry, it is clear enough that under the Fifth Republic single-bloc legislative majorities were sought by the device of second ballots in single-member constituencies.[10] What is more open to conjecture is exactly what ensued from the adoption of PR with department-wide districts for the 1986 elections to the National Assembly. John Frears contends that this move "generated a storm from political elites, indifference from the public, and a commitment from the new government to get rid of it again."[11] In the same vein, Roy Pierce and Thomas Rochon hold that it "was widely interpreted as a move to avert electoral disaster by the Socialist party, by preventing the two main rightist parties from together winning a large majority of the seats in the Assembly."[12]

The Right did, in the event, secure a legislative majority. The Socialists were not destroyed, though they lost a quarter of their seats. What has attracted most comment, however, is that Jean-Marie Le Pen's National Front was able to secure as many seats as the Communists. Whereas, according to Frears, "If the two-round system had been maintained, the National Front would have won virtually no parliamentary seats though winning the same number of votes."[13]

Here we confront a frequent objection to PR that applies even to mild specimens like Mitterand's provision for departmental lists. Lardeyret regards the success of the National Front, and the emergence of extreme opponents to it, as "an unhealthy situation [that] can be attributed largely to PR." But surely the real question is another one: Socialist motivations apart, what would have been the best electoral formula for dealing with not only the threat of extremism, but all the other circumstances of French politics in the mid-1980s?

As already noted, all electoral systems have costs—a fact that was not exactly highlighted by the earlier contributors. The French situation may appear somewhat peculiar to an outsider in that powerholders seem able to shuffle electoral systems at will (Greece would be a similar instance). While such maneuverings might conceivably be regarded as commendable attempts to respond to the fluctuations of political mobilization, there is ample evidence that less pure instincts are at work in both countries.

Clearly, profound issues arise when the consequences of any given electoral system are confronted. A provision that has attracted much enthusiasm on the part of electoral reformers in plurality systems is the German additional-member formula, which the Federal Republic adopted at the time of its formation in 1949. This recipe provides both for constituency representatives chosen in plurality elections and for representation in terms of national party strengths. It includes a threshold applying to both constituency and national party support, so that a party has to achieve at least 5 percent of the total number of votes cast in order to secure seats in the Bundestag. This level of support, but often little more, has been recurrently achieved by the Free Democratic Party (FDP), which accordingly occupies a pivotal position between the much larger forces of the Christian Democratic Union (CDU) and of the Social Democratic Party (SPD). As Gordon Smith explains, "The strategic position in the party system occupied by the Free Democratic Party . . . gives the party a weight quite out of proportion to its parliamentary representation."[14] From this pivotal position, the FDP has been able to exert a powerful influence on the formation and operation of governments. Indeed, it has been able to change the whole complexion of government without benefit of elections, as when the FDP abandoned its coalition with the SPD in 1982 and ushered the CDU into office.

Disproportionate leverage wielded by small but strategically positioned "fulcrum" parties like the FDP is not an inherent feature of PR systems. It is generally lacking in the Scandinavian countries, for instance. Where such parties do exist, moreover, their power derives more from the particular geometry of mobilization patterns (which produce political situations where majorities cannot be formed without the inclusion of smaller parties) than from PR as such. But plurality systems, given their tendency to marginalize third parties, do make the rise of fulcrum parties less likely, which is one reason for the resistance to PR in Britain.

The New Systems of Central Europe

If we turn from established West European systems to the admittedly still larval systems of Central Europe, we find an interesting variety of cases. In the Czech and Slovak Federative Republic, postcommunist elections were held in June 1990 for both the bicameral Federal Assembly and the respective Czech and Slovak National Councils. A party-list system was adopted in all three cases, but there was concern about two issues.[15] One was a fear of the sort of fragmentation that beset interwar legislatures; the other was an anxiety about overweening party machines, another feature of earlier practice. Several devices were therefore adopted to impede these possibilities. They included, though the detail is complex, what amounted to a 5-percent threshold for the federal parliament and the Czech assembly and a provision for preferential voting within party lists.

Hyperfragmentation was indeed avoided, though this could be largely ascribed to Civic Forum's success in gaining widespread support as a transitional political movement closely identified with the Velvet Revolution. The Forum gained some two-thirds of the seats in each house of the Federal Assembly as well as in the Czech National Council.

Despite the prognostications of pollsters and commentators, the results of the second Federal Assembly elections, held in June 1992, also reflected a consolidation of the leading Czech and Slovak formations (Civic Democracy and the Movement for a Democratic Slovakia, respectively).[16] Yet this very same consolidation has served to promote the impending split of the 74-year-old federation into a Czech republic and a separate Slovakia. Hindsight thus reveals that the bogeyman was less party fragmentation than national fission, though it would hardly be plausible to argue that a system designed to produce less consolidation in each of the two parts of the federation would have offered a more constructive approach.

The case of Poland, though alarming, is a more straightforward example of the problems of electoral mechanics. There the October 1991 elections for the Sejm resulted in the emergence of 29 parliamentary parties, the largest of which obtained less that 13 percent of the total vote and less than 14 percent of the available seats.[17] Turnout was a mere 42 percent. The elections were held on the basis of proportional representation, without a threshold, in 37 districts with between 7 and 17 seats each. A further 15 percent of the total seats (69 out of 460) were allocated nationally with a 5-percent threshold and a requirement of support in at least five districts.[18] It took almost two months of intensive interparty negotiation before a government could be assembled, and there has subsequently been a succession of governmental changes.

The Czech and Polish experiences exemplify the uncertainties of the early phases of transition from an effectively one-party to a competitive system. But each transition has its own problems and peculiarities, and electoral mechanisms remain merely one facet of the prism of political competition. In Hungary, the pace of the political transition away from the one-party system fell somewhere between the long march led by Solidarity in Poland and the abrupt Velvet Revolution in Prague. More than three years elapsed between the beginning of intense debate, negotiation, and organizing work in mid-1987 and the first multiparty parliamentary elections in April 1990, as Hungarians dismantled communism and put together a new constitution.

Roundtable talks in the fall of 1989 hammered out the electoral system for the first free elections in postcommunist Hungary. A Hungarian political analyst has characterized the outcome as follows:

The historical parties (Smallholders, Social Democrats, Christian Democrats) favored proportional representation with county-based party lists, which was used in 1945 and 1947. However, the general mood in the country, especially among the MPs in the parliament, made it impossible to abolish the existing local constituency representation. Since there were no huge popular movements behind the new political parties, their legitimacy was limited. The local notables and the citizens did not want to let the whole nomination process be controlled by party bureaucracies. The long debate and the general mood made it impossible to introduce any election system based on a single principle. Therefore the electoral system became a combination of different principles and techniques. The 386 seats of the unicameral Hungarian parliament were divided into three categories: 176 were to be elected in single-member constituencies, 152 from regional party lists, and 58 from national party lists.[19]

In single-member constituencies, a second ballot was required where no candidate received an absolute majority in the first round. On the second ballot, a plurality would suffice for election. The regional party-list seats and the national seats were subject to a 4-percent threshold. The whole formula was intended to help prevent party proliferation. That it had its costs is indisputable: Turnout was unimpressive, and hardly any constituency seats were filled on the first ballot. Given the complexity of the electoral provisions, it would be hard to determine how proportional the results actually were in terms of the ratio of seats to initial party votes. Nevertheless, they did deliver a parliament with only six parties, which enabled a majority coalition to be formed by an alliance of the largest single party and two ancillaries.

Merits and Defects

My examples so far have tended to suggest that various forms of PR produce outcomes that are less than optimal from the standpoint of stable, coherent, and effective government. None of this, however, should be taken as pointing to the absurdly simple-minded conclusion that PR is always the wrong choice. For not only can PR work well in certain national contexts (such as Norway, Sweden, and the Netherlands), but plurality systems (as in Britain) can display grave defects of their own.

Britain, like the United States, is a land of single-member legislative districts and first-past-the-post elections. To win, a candidate need not secure an overall majority of votes in the constituency. That will, of course, be the case if only two candidates compete; in practice, however, three or more contenders seek election in most British constituencies. Candidates may therefore be elected with just over a third of the votes cast where there are three contenders, or just over a quarter where there are four, and so on.

Two serious problems arise under the British system. The first, and the one most commonly cited by critics, is the lack of provision for proportionality between total national party votes and party parliamentary seats. It is invariably the smallest of the three significant national parties, the Liberal Democrats (formerly the Liberals), which is the most heavily penalized. In the April 1992 parliamentary elections, which were fairly typical, the Liberal Democrats gained 17.8 percent of the total national vote, but having obtained a plurality in only 20 constituencies, they secured a mere 3 percent of the seats in the House of Commons. Since the system is not designed to deliver proportionality, exact equivalents of national votes and seats are rare for the two larger parties as well.[20] On the other hand, the system does usually manage to produce single-party majority governments. Of all the elections held in Britain since 1945, only one (the February 1974 balloting that returned Harold Wilson to Number 10 Downing Street at the head of a Labour-Liberal coalition) has failed to return one party with an overall legislative majority.

The less frequently voiced criticism of the British system stresses the apathy it seems to breed among the vast majority of voters, who may reasonably feel that it matters little whether or not they vote. In April 1992, only 52 of 651 parliamentary seats changed hands across parties. In perhaps a further 50 seats there may have been a possibility of an upset. In more than five hundred seats, therefore, no change was remotely likely; this is the case in every election. In a fully proportional system, all votes would go toward the distribution of legislative seats. Even though there might not be dramatic overall changes from election to election, such a set-up would do much more than the current one does to justify the act of voting.

From a standpoint that is concerned purely with translating votes into representation, a proportional system may appear, at least in principle, to deliver the democratic goods. If parties are the sole vehicle of popular representation, and if government is based, as it is in all genuinely parliamentary systems, upon relative party strengths in the legislature, there may seem little to justify any system that narrows the range of electoral choices. In practice, however, there are formidable arguments, both general and specific, against proportionality.

The most general argument emphasizes the threat that proportionality can pose to governmental coherence. The process of forming a majority government after proportionality has delivered a highly fragmented legislature is subject to several types of difficulties. The first occurs when long periods of interparty haggling follow parliamentary elections. In the Netherlands, as we saw, prolonged delays in the formation of cabinets have become a normal and not very troublesome feature of national politics. A more worrisome example of delay in cabinet formation would be the recent experience in Belgium, where five months elapsed between the parliamentary election of November 1991 and the creation of a new government. Such severe paralysis cannot be attributed simply to PR, of course, nor does it mean that a plurality system would necessarily be better for Belgium. But it is a troubling instance of a political hiatus arising from fragmentation.

A second kind of difficulty arises when odd coalitions form out of sheer expediency, as with the combination between the Portuguese Socialist Party and its most right-wing opponent, the Social Democratic Center Party, in 1977–78. What is interesting in the Portuguese case is that the very same electoral system (party lists in varied-size districts) that produced this egregious example also delivered single-party majority governments after elections in both 1987 and 1991.[21]

A third type of problem emerges when it proves impossible to form a majority government at all, and a minority administration results. The Scandinavian countries—notably Denmark, which has had only three

majority governments since 1945—offer many instances of this dubious phenomenon. Poland today is another case in point.

A further problem of coalition formation in fragmented legislatures
is that of accountability to voters when coalitions form only after the
elections are over. There is much comment about this on record in the
Dutch case.[22] The argument here has two barrels. The first is that voters
in such circumstances cannot know the full consequences of their choice
of party. This can to some extent be countered by the contention that in
all systems voters cannot calculate the precise outcome of casting their
vote. The second charge—that such "unsignaled" coalitions lack a democratic mandate—is more difficult to refute because it strikes near the
heart of the notion of popular sovereignty. To combine two or more
parties, each of which represents an *exclusive* choice by individual voters, where there has been no prior pact known to the electorate, does
seem to raise serious questions about governmental legitimacy.

It so happens that the Dutch case also exemplifies the problem, already cited in respect to Germany, of the enormous leverage available
to parties that command the center. The major confessional parties in
the Netherlands, amalgamated since 1975 under the banner of the Christian Democratic Appeal, have for most of this century largely determined
the complexion of each and every coalition cabinet. Until the 1960s,
this reflected their regularly demonstrated ability to amass about half of
both the votes cast and the seats contested, making them the country's
principal political grouping. Yet even their relative decline to around
one-third of the national vote has not robbed them of this decisive
leverage, and so they continue to preside from the center.

The Test of Practicality

Another question for debate is that of the linkage—or the lack thereof—
between voter and representative. The basic structure of parliamentary
representation in Britain was established long before the development of
either national mass-based parties or universal suffrage. Although it has
been modified in recent times, the system's essential characteristic remains that of locality representation. This ostensibly means that each
citizen, however he or she may have voted (or not voted), has a representative in the legislature to whom grievances can be directly addressed.
This follows from the assumption that each MP serves on behalf of all the
interests and concerns within his or her constituency. Given the current
primacy of national party strategies, that assumption may now be dubious, but it endures within the minds of citizens and legislators alike.
Indeed, in a recent survey of the attitudes of British MPs toward electoral
reform, the majority of respondents placed this aspect of the representational system at the top of their list of that system's virtues.[23]

The concrete benefits of locality representation may be variously evaluated, but it is undeniable that where proportionality leaves local-ity representation out of account, then relations between the citizen and the legislature are affected. This is one reason why so-called mixed systems, like the German additional-member system, have attracted the interest of reformers in a pluralist system like Britain's.

The final item in the critic's arsenal of charges against proportional-ity is its potential for giving scope to fringe parties (as already noted above with regard to France). The literature on this topic is vast indeed, ranging through the emergence of fascism in the interwar period to the threats posed by the extreme left and right (and now by fundamental-ism) in the post-1945 era. The literature can only grow, for the debate is perennially open-ended. If an electoral system operates so as to exclude expressions of antidemocratic sentiment, does that not also mean shut-ting out the lesser voices of democratic sentiment? Can the problem not be tackled by other means, such as the German Basic Law's proscription of antidemocratic parties? Whatever judgment an impartial referee might reach on this vexed question, it remains a comfort to those who live under long-established plurality systems that the likelihood of an anti-democratic movement gaining significant legislative influence in their countries is small indeed.

Any sensible tribunal weighing the relative merits and demerits of proportionality (in its many possible forms) and plurality (also capable of variations) would refuse to rule on purely or even largely theoretical grounds. The best test is one of practicality and aptness relative to national circumstance. The most relevant of these—the one that must be given the most weight in the evaluation of alternative electoral mecha-nisms—is the existing pattern of political mobilization. No reformer, however convinced of the elegance of a particular scheme or provision, could sanely try to graft it onto a polity whose dynamics would make the reform unworkable, damaging, absurd, disruptive, or catastrophic. It is surely one of the tasks of political scientists to analyze the effects of different electoral provisions, but it cannot be in their province to rec-ommend recipes *in vacuo.*

The problems of orchestrating free, fair, and open competition for political power can be especially great in relatively new, resource-strapped states. In such circumstances, one would have to be bold beyond measure to offer general prescriptions for representation. Yet one may still nurse a hope that the debate which this journal has so usefully promoted will be of heuristic value to decision makers in societies where representative government is a new item on the agenda.

NOTES

1. Sir Henry Maine, *Popular Government* (London: John Murray, 1885), vii, xi.

2. See Arend Lijphart, "Constitutional Choices for New Democracies," *Journal*

of Democracy 2 (Winter 1991): 72–84; and Guy Lardeyret, "The Problem with PR," Quentin L. Quade, "PR and Democratic Statecraft," and Arend Lijphart, "Double-Checking the Evidence," *Journal of Democracy* 2 (Summer 1991): 30–48.

3. Larry Diamond, "Three Paradoxes of Democracy," *Journal of Democracy* 1 (Summer 1990): 54.

4. An official of the British Electoral Reform Society claimed recently that he knew of three hundred different formulas.

5. All three systems are constituency-based. The additional-member system distributes additional seats in proportion to the national configuration of party support. The alternative vote is a preference system that enables voters to rank candidates in their order of preference and then redistributes the second (or subsequent) preferences of those who voted for the weakest contenders so that a majority is achieved. The single transferable vote operates similarly to the alternative vote, but in multimember constituencies.

6. Current serious proposals include all three systems cited above. There is little discernible support for party-list approaches on either a regional or national basis.

7. See H. Daalder, "Extreme Proportional Representation: The Dutch Experience" in S.E. Finer, ed., *Adversary Politics and Electoral Reform* (London: Anthony Wigram, 1975), and K.R. Gladdish, "The Netherlands" in Vernon Bogdanor, ed., *Representatives of the People? Parliamentarians and Constituents in Western Democracies* (Aldershot, England: Gower, 1985).

8. See K.R. Gladdish, *Governing from the Centre: Politics and Policy-Making in the Netherlands* (London: C. Hurst, 1991), ch. 6.

9. See K.R. Gladdish, "Governing the Dutch," *Acta Politica* 25 (October 1990): 389–402.

10. See Alistair Cole and Peter Campbell, *French Electoral Systems and Elections Since 1789* (Aldershot, England: Gower, 1989).

11. Howard Penniman, ed., *France at the Polls, 1981 and 1986* (Durham, N.C.: Duke University Press, 1988), 211.

12. Howard Penniman, ed., *France at the Polls,* 181.

13. Howard Penniman, ed., *France at the Polls,* 214.

14. Gordon Smith, William Paterson, and Peter Merkl, eds., *Developments in West German Politics* (London: Macmillan, 1989), 71.

15. See Judy Batt, "After Czechoslovakia's Velvet Poll," *World Today* 46 (August–September 1990): 141–43.

16. *Economist,* 13 June 1992.

17. David Warszawski, "The Elections: Don't Let's Be Shocked," *East European Reporter,* January–February 1992, 19–21.

18. Krzysztof Jasiewicz, "From Solidarity to Fragmentation," *Journal of Democracy* 3 (April 1992): 55–69. Jasiewicz has grave doubts whether juggling with the electoral system would have avoided hyperfragmentation, though from his consideration of alternatives it does seem that it might have been significantly reduced.

19. A. Körösényi, "The Hungarian Parliamentary Elections 1990" in A. Bozóki, A. Körösényi, and G. Schopflin, eds., *Post-Communist Transition: Emerging Pluralism in Hungary* (London: Pinter, 1992).

20. In the case of the April 1992 election, John Curtice has called attention to a surprising quirk in the mathematics: "For the first time ever the system wholly failed to deliver a bonus in seats to the winner. Instead, so far as the Conservatives and Labour are concerned, it acted in a purely proportional way." *Guardian,* 13 April 1992. Clearly what happened—ostensibly for the first time—could have happened on any previous occasion. This prompts the reflection that proportionality is not excluded in a plurality system. It is merely made highly uncertain.

21. A former member of the Portuguese parliament recently delivered the following verdict on the electoral system: "The four main political parties . . . dispute elections according to rules that reduce the individual deputies more to the role of party officials than of representatives of the electorate." She then warned: "Indeed, the functioning of the proportional system in Portugal should be a true object lesson for those naif Britons who believe its introduction might improve British institutions." Patricia Lança, "The Land of Mild Customs," *Salisbury Review,* June 1992, 29.

22. See K.R. Gladdish, "Two-Party versus Multi-Party: The Netherlands and Britain," *Acta Politica* 7 (July 1972): 342–61, and K.R. Gladdish, "Two-Party versus Multi-Party: The Netherlands and Britain," *Parliamentary Affairs* 26 (June–August 1973): 454–70.

23. K.R. Gladdish, A.T.W. Liddell, and P.J. Giddings, "MPs' Perceptions of the British Electoral System" (University of Reading Politics Group Research Paper No. 1, 1984).

III

Country and Regional Experiences

11

CONSTITUTIONAL ENGINEERING IN SOUTHERN AFRICA

Andrew Reynolds

Andrew Reynolds *is associate professor of political science at the University of North Carolina at Chapel Hill. He has consulted on issues of electoral and constitutional design for a wide array of countries. His latest book is* The Architecture of Democracy: Constitutional Design, Conflict Management, and Democracy *(2002). This essay originally appeared in the April 1995 issue of the* Journal of Democracy.

The flurry of democratization that the world has seen since the late 1980s has engendered a running debate—some of it conducted in the pages of this journal—about how fledgling democracies can best design constitutions that give rise to political harmony and stability.[1] In the context of this debate about "constitutional engineering," electoral-system design is increasingly being recognized as a key lever that can be used to promote political accommodation and stability in ethnically divided societies.

Most scholars agree that the choice of an electoral system has powerful political consequences; where they differ is in their basic prescriptions for newly democratizing states. The evidence from the emerging democracies of southern Africa strongly suggests that divided societies need proportional representation (PR) rather than plurality elections, and a parliamentary rather than a presidential form of government. A simple parliamentary–PR system, however, is not enough: these fragile democracies are better served by a type of PR that maximizes the geographic representativeness of MPs, as well as their accountability to the voters. Although appropriate electoral laws are insufficient to ensure stability and good governance in divided societies, poorly designed laws can entrench societal divisions and exacerbate preexisting conflict.

The prevailing academic wind is clearly blowing in favor of PR— and against plurality elections—for ethnically divided states. As W. Arthur Lewis asserted in his seminal Whidden Lecture of 1965, "The surest way to kill the idea of democracy in a plural society is to adopt the Anglo-American system of first-past-the-post." According to Lewis, the vagaries of plurality elections would produce racially exclusive and geographically parochial governments that would exploit a "mandate" from a plurality of the electorate in order to discriminate systematically against minorities: "If you belong to a minority in a new state, and are being asked to accept parliamentary democracy, you can hardly build much faith in the system if you win 30 percent of those votes and get only 20 percent of the seats, or no seats at all. If minorities are to accept Parliament, they must be adequately represented in Parliament."[2]

Supporting this view is Arend Lijphart, who argues not only that divided societies need PR in order to protect minority interests, but that PR systems (in conjunction with parliamentarism) "almost invariably post the best records, particularly with respect to representation . . . voter participation, and control of unemployment."[3] Timothy Sisk also identifies a "consensus on PR" in the debate over electoral-system design for South Africa, a consensus born of that country's overwhelming need for governmental structures that facilitate political accommodation: "Threatened as they are by the centrifugal politics of extremist outbidding, divided societies like South Africa need institutions that pave the way for moderation and compromise."[4]

A number of prominent scholars, however, come down on the other side of the debate. Guy Lardeyret argues that the best way to counteract the tendency for electoral competition to follow ethnic lines is to "oblige members of each group to run against one another on (transethnic) political and ideological grounds in single-member districts," while "the worst way is to adopt PR, which tends to reproduce ethnic cleavages in the legislature." Lardeyret believes that South Africa's prospects will be grim without the development of "big and moderate multiethnic parties" and posits that plurality elections would be most likely to give rise to such parties.[5] His reasoning is echoed by Donald Horowitz, who argues that "vote-pooling," in which parties are encouraged to appeal across societal divides, "lies at the heart of intergroup compromise in severely divided societies."[6] Vote-pooling, argues Horowitz, is best achieved through the "alternative-vote" electoral system, a modification of single-member-district plurality that involves reallocation of voters' second and subsequent preferences until a candidate attains a majority.

Recent Developments

In the last five years, southern Africa has been the scene of constitutional changes unmatched since the end of European colonialism in the 1960s. Namibia became a multiparty democracy in 1989, with independence from South Africa formally declared in 1990; Zambia moved to a democratic system in 1991. South Africa and Malawi completed their remarkable democratic transitions in 1994, and Mozambique held what were generally considered to be free and fair elections at the end of that same year. Of the remaining southern African states, Zimbabwe, Botswana, and Lesotho have experienced varying degrees of political competition, while Angola has taken tentative steps toward a new constitutional arrangement and an end to civil strife. Only President Mobutu Sese Seko of Zaire continues to buck the trend of failing authoritarian rulers, maintaining power despite his legalization of opposition parties in 1990.

At present, the most "electorally democratic" states in southern Africa include Malawi, Namibia, South Africa, and Zambia. Zimbabwe has also had relatively free, fair, and regular elections since 1980, but electoral competition has been truncated since 1987. Of these five, Malawi, Zimbabwe, and Zambia can be categorized as presidential–plurality systems under Lijphart's "basic types of democracy," while South Africa is a parliamentary–PR system.[7] President Nelson Mandela's title is actually a misnomer: even though the 1994 elections for the South African National Assembly were strongly reminiscent of a presidential campaign, Mandela was not directly elected, and has classic prime-ministerial powers derived from his leadership of the largest party in parliament. Namibia began its democratic life in a similar situation, with "President" Sam Nujoma leading the nation, but moved to a genuine presidential–PR system in December 1994.

The argument that plurality elections exacerbate regional and ethnic polarization draws considerable strength from the experiences of the fledgling democracies of southern Africa.

Malawi. The results of Malawi's May 1994 multiparty elections showed each of the three main political parties to be overwhelmingly dominant in its core region, and exceedingly weak in the remaining two regions. The number of seats that each party won in a given region, however, did not closely reflect the percentage of votes that it polled there. The Alliance for Democracy (AFORD), led by Chakufwa Chihana, won *every* seat in the northern region even though *non*-AFORD candidates managed to capture nearly 15 percent of the vote there. The Malawi Congress Party (MCP) of then-President Hastings Kamuzu Banda won fully 75 percent of the seats in the central region while receiving slightly more than 60 percent of the vote. In the southern region, the United Democratic Front (UDF) of successful presidential candidate Bakili Muluzi won 95 percent of the seats with just three-quarters of the popular vote. The overall proportion of seats that each party gained in the National Assembly was surprisingly close to the percentage of the popular vote that it captured nationwide, but the distribution of seats created a false picture of homogeneous regional bastions that could derail efforts to build political unity across ethnic groups.

Zimbabwe and Zambia. The virtual disappearance of a vigorous political opposition in Zimbabwe and Zambia in recent years provides ample evidence of the threat that plurality elections can pose to the emergence of new parties in fledgling democracies. Jonathan Moyo maintains that the danger to democracy in Zimbabwe was revealed most clearly in 1990, when the opposition parties were rewarded with only two parliamentary seats despite polling 20 percent of the popular vote. According to Moyo's calculations, had the elections been conducted under a list form of PR, the opposition could have expected to win 23 parliamentary seats—a far more solid foundation from which to critique government policy.[8] In Zambia's 1991 plurality elections, Frederick Chiluba's Movement for Multiparty Democracy (MMD) won 125 of the 150 parliamentary seats—enough to rule unhindered as well as to amend the constitution unilaterally. In the words of journalist Jowie Mwiinga, "there has been little organized pressure on the President to clean up his government, thanks to the absence of either a meaningful opposition or an independent press."[9]

   South Africa. Use of a plurality system in the 1994 elections for the South African National Assembly would have had a number of negative consequences.[10] The immediate result would have been a denial of parliamentary representation to minority interests. Despite their geographic pockets of electoral support, the Freedom Front (which won 9 seats in the actual election), Democratic Party (7 seats), Pan-Africanist Congress (5 seats), and African Christian Democratic Party (2 seats) would have failed to win a single parliamentary seat. Although all these parties together constitute only 6 percent of the new South African National Assembly, they have an importance within the structures of government that is disproportionate to their numerical strength. General Constand Viljoen's Freedom Front represents a highly volatile Afrikaner-heartland constituency that could easily have fallen into the hands of white-supremacist demagogues such as Eugene Terre'blanche had its representatives been shut out of the political process. Similarly, the predominantly Xhosa Pan-Africanist Congress of Azania (PAC) is a party torn between the ballot box and the AK-47. Had the PAC been denied parliamentary representation, its armed terrorist wing might have gained the upper hand, posing a severe threat to stability in South Africa in the immediate postelection period. The significance of the place obtained in parliament by the small, liberal Democratic Party (DP) is also not to be underestimated. Its leaders were crucial to the crafting of the liberal elements of the interim constitution, and its presence in the new National Assembly is necessary to ensure that such tolerance remains the official creed of the land.

   The list-PR system actually used in the South African elections was probably neither an advantage nor a disadvantage to the midsized National Party (NP) and Inkatha Freedom Party (IFP), for the "national referendum" nature of the campaign led to a two-party battle between the old and the new: the African National Congress (ANC) versus the IFP in the KwaZulu-Natal province, and the ANC versus the NP in the rest of the country. Given the ethnically homogeneous nature of constituencies and the strong geographic concentrations of popular support in South Africa, the NP would have won only slightly fewer, and the IFP slightly more, seats under a single-member-constituency system than under PR. Yet the anomalies of the Anglo-American electoral system—summed up by Vernon Bogdanor's statement that "the number of seats which a party wins in a general election depends not only upon how many votes the party receives but also upon *where* these votes are cast"—would have led the ANC to win all of the parliamentary seats in the Northern and Eastern Transvaal, North-West, and Eastern Cape and all but one of the seats in the Orange Free State.[11] In the Western Cape, the NP would have captured over 80 percent of the seats with just over half of the popular vote. Clearly, these results would have exacerbated ethnic and regional polarization, jeopardizing the development of a stable political system in South Africa. Plurality might have done its greatest harm in precluding the emergence of nonracial or smaller minority parties without roots in the old constitutional arrangement.

Proportional Representation in Action

Proportional representation has undoubtedly been an integral part of efforts at power-sharing and ethnic accommodation in both South Africa and Namibia. Yet PR alone would not have ensured multiparty government in South Africa, as a dominant single party could have formed an administration unilaterally had the interim constitution not exhibited *consociational* features.[12] What PR did was realize Article 88 of that constitution, which guaranteed all parties with more than 5 percent of the seats in the National Assembly a proportionate share of the cabinet portfolios. List PR thus helped F.W. de Klerk's NP win 6 of the 27 cabinet portfolios, and the Zulu-based IFP, 3 portfolios. Real sharing of power was ensured when an NP member was named to head the finance ministry and Chief Mangosuthu Buthelezi, head of the IFP, was appointed minister of home affairs. Thus in South Africa PR helped fulfill one of Lijphart's basic principles of consociational democracy—a "government by 'grand coalition,' that is, by a broadly representative coalition of all significant groups."[13]

In the Namibian elections of 1989 as in the 1994 South African voting, PR ensured that there were few "wasted votes." In Namibia, 99 percent of the votes cast went toward electing a representative; the figure was even higher in South Africa. This high level of efficiency was due primarily to the low threshold of representation needed to win a parliamentary seat under the national list-PR system (0.7 percent in Namibia, 0.2 percent in South Africa). Lijphart has argued that, for new democracies, "moderate PR [with its high threshold] and moderate multipartism, as in Germany and Sweden, offer more attractive models than the extreme PR [with its low threshold] and multiparty systems of Italy and the Netherlands," reasoning that a highly fragmented party system would be detrimental to the formation of coalitions and subsequent governmental stability.[14] The evidence from southern Africa, however, suggests that the costs of excluding small but significant parties through a high (say, 5 percent) threshold far outweigh the benefits. Even a 3 percent threshold would have excluded some of the most important political factions from the first South African National Assembly, and would have denied representation to all but the three largest parties in Namibia. In the earliest stages of a new democracy, the need for all significant groups to feel included in the system outweighs concern about the obstacles that may face coalition-builders in subsequently elected parliaments.

Proportional representation has also allowed the South African parliament to be fairly reflective of South African society as a whole. The national lists, which were "closed" in the sense that the electorate was unable to alter or reorder them, allowed parties to present ethnically heterogeneous groups of candidates with anticipated cross-cutting appeal. The resulting National Assembly was 52 percent Black, 32 percent White, 8 percent Indian, and 7 percent Coloured, as compared to an electorate that was estimated to be 73 percent Black, 15 percent White, 3 percent Indian, and 9 percent Coloured. South Africans of Indian extraction fared particularly well, gaining more than 30 MPs and 4 cabinet ministers. Moreover, an influx of female MPs representing the ANC—they now constitute almost a third of their parliamentary party[15]—brought the percentage of women in the new National Assembly to 24 percent of the total, one of the highest percentages in the world.[16] On the basis of evidence from the United Kingdom and other countries with winner-take-all electoral systems, it seems fair to surmise that use of plurality elections in South Africa would have resulted in a much less heterogeneous and more polarized National Assembly, with whites of various parties representing majority white constituencies, Xhosas representing Xhosas, and Zulus representing Zulus.

A Few Criticisms—and Rebuttals

The strongest recent criticism of the PR prescription for emerging democracies has come from Lardeyret, who lists five ways in which PR supposedly impedes conflict resolution in a divided society.[17] First, he argues, PR tends to allow the representation of extremist groups (he cites as an example the French National Front), which in turn breed opposing extremist parties that may also gain representation. In fact, however, PR merely helps to fulfill minority parties' desire for representation, rather than promoting new parties, and reflects the actual size of, rather than exaggerates, such parties' support base. Moreover, as noted above, in the most severely divided societies, allowing fringe parties to gain parliamentary representation may actually help the democratic polity to coopt extremists, giving them an incentive to press their case with ballots rather than bullets.

Lardeyret's second criticism is that the experience of Belgium indicates that PR is dangerous for countries faced with ethnic or cultural divisions. He claims that in Belgium, "linguistic parties sprang up after PR was introduced early in this century," making Belgian politics "little more than a feud between the Flemings and the French-speaking Walloons."[18] Here again, Lardeyret is mistaking reflection for causation: Belgian politics would have evolved along linguistic and, to a lesser extent, religious lines regardless of the particular electoral system chosen. The early evidence from southern Africa indicates that PR has exerted pressure for parties to be *less* rather than more ethnically exclusive. In the new South African National Assembly, almost a third of the 130 white members of parliament represent the ANC, and F.W. de Klerk's NP gained more votes from nonwhites than from whites.

Lardeyret's third criticism of PR for new democracies is that the multiparty coalition governments it usually produces run the risks of instability and inability to implement coherent policies. This argument is perhaps the most convincing. South Africa's new government carries the burden of huge expectations, and the factionalized nature of Mandela's "cabinet of national unity" may indeed hobble decision making. Yet here as elsewhere in southern Africa, the alternative of control by a single party, with its majoritarian excesses, would be worse. No government, not even a single-party government, would be able to "deliver the goods" if civil society were perpetually on the verge of permanent breakdown. Furthermore, Lijphart has shown that governments elected through PR are no less effective than those elected by other systems. Indeed, parliamentary–PR systems do better in terms of governmental longevity, voter participation, and economic performance.[19]

Another criticism offered by Lardeyret is that PR not only allows small extremist parties into parliament, but also gives them too much leverage, as they often control the "swing" seats that can make or break a would-be majority coalition. This may be true, but as the cases of South Africa and Namibia clearly show, including minorities—no matter how extremist—in the democratic political order is a better alternative than banishing them to the fringes of the system.

Lardeyret claims that plurality elections are more likely than PR to give rise to moderate parties, for under such a system parties are forced to compete constantly for undecided centrist voters. Not only do Britain's Thatcher-led Tory governments (1979–90) and South Africa's NP governments (1948–94) fly in the face of such reasoning, but one would not expect to see much moderation in a plurality system where a dominant party can count on easily winning an absolute majority, as is currently the situation in South Africa, Zimbabwe, Zambia, and Namibia. In southern Africa, only Malawi lacks a single dominant party; and, as mentioned above, the Malawian electorate is divided along regional and ethnic lines, leaving few undecided voters floating in the center.

The high level of geographic representativeness and accountability to the voters that single-member constituencies can provide has long been invoked as an advantage of plurality elections over PR. It is true that the large size of multimember list-PR constituencies can virtually destroy the link between a representative and a specific geographic area (in the South African case, each 20 members represent an average of 2.5 million electors). Roelf Meyer, the minister for constitutional development, claimed that this was a "serious weakness," and that "any new constitution must make provision for clearly designated representatives."[20] The use of closed party lists in South Africa and Namibia is indeed problematic, for the MPs that emerge are far more beholden to party bosses in national party headquarters than to local communities or society as a whole. In order to remedy this without violating the basic proportionality of parliament, the constitutional engineer can use smaller multimember constituencies (with perhaps between 5 and 12 members) designed to dovetail with traditional geographic and societal boundaries, as well as open lists, in which voters choose among candidates as well as parties. In South Africa, the principal objection to such a system was made by members of the ANC, who argued that voting for individuals rather than parties would be too complicated for many of the country's illiterate voters. Yet such a system would still only entail placing one mark by one name and symbol, and the low level of spoiled ballots (less than 1 percent) in the 1994 elections suggests that educational illiteracy is not necessarily synonymous with political illiteracy.

While increasing geographical representativeness and accountability, such an adaptation of simple list PR would also maintain the overall benefits that PR offers to diverse societies. Multimember constituencies would still be able to provide a choice of representative for citizens to approach concerning constituency casework problems. In practice, this would mean that constituents might be able to approach either an Ndebele or a Shona MP in Matabeleland, Zimbabwe; a Chewa, Lomwe, or Yao MP in Lilongwe, Malawi; or a Zulu, Xhosa, White, or Indian MP in southern KwaZulu, South Africa. Finally, such a constituency-based list-PR system would serve as a further incentive for parties to be ethnically accommodating—that is, to present a diverse slate of candidates as a means of maximizing both their total vote and their number of parliamentary seats.

Presidentialism versus Parliamentarism

After the choice of electoral system, the second fundamental choice facing new democracies is that between a presidential and a parliamentary form of government. As this debate is conducted in the context of southern Africa, opinions may be too easily colored by the performance of former African presidents, whether they were democratically elected or not. Prior to the most recent wave of democratization, the political reputation of African presidents ranged from poor to atrocious. All of the countries discussed here have endured painful presidential histories, which one might think would make them eager to avoid vesting one individual with much power. Yet in 1985 Zimbabwe went to a directly elected presidency, as did Malawi nine years later. Namibia moved from an indirectly elected president to a directly elected one in 1994, and South Africa, by naming what is really its prime minister the "executive state president," has created the appearance of presidential control if not the reality.

Good constitutional design for divided societies dictates against directly elected presidents for the emerging democracies of southern Africa. Lijphart has warned that while "the combination of parliamentarism with proportional representation should be an especially attractive one to newly democratic and democratizing countries," the Latin American experience shows that a presidentialist-PR system should be avoided.[21] Matthew Shugart and John Carey have identified three key traits of presidentialism that often have negative consequences: temporal rigidity, majoritarianism, and dual democratic legitimacy.[22] Of these three, majoritarianism is by far the most damaging to stability in ethnically divided societies. The winner-take-all nature of a directly elected executive office in itself militates against presidentialism in southern Africa. In a divided society without a history of stable democracy, there is no assurance that the loser or losers of a presidential race will accept defeat in what amounts to a zero-sum game. As the recent experiences of Angola and Nigeria show, there is little hope for elaborate constitutional mechanisms designed to promote power-sharing if a fragile new democracy is shattered at the first hurdle. Ann Reid of the U.S. State Department laid the blame for the collapse of peace plans in Angola and the bloody conflict that ensued largely on the country's presidential system: Given that "both [José Eduardo] Dos Santos and [Jonas] Savimbi were vying for the only prize worth having," it was inevitable that Savimbi would resume his violent struggle after losing the election.[23] In Nigeria, the all-or-nothing structure of the 1993 presidential race made it easier than it otherwise would have been for the military to succeed in annulling the election before the final results had been officially announced: unsuccessful candidates and political factions had no immediate stake in the political outcome, and many readily acquiesced in the annulment in the hope of being able to contest again. Ian Campbell claims, moreover, that Nigerian presidentialism caused a marked increase in electoral corruption in the run-up to the vote. "It was suggested that the problem was the 'size of the jackpot,' with the selection process [for presidential candidates] being seen as an 'investment opportunity' and the presidency as the source of instant wealth."[24]

Another danger of a presidential system is that a directly elected president tends to be pressured into ethnic or regional exclusivity. Such presidents have a great incentive to offer special privileges to their own ethnic or regional group as a means of ensuring reelection through a simple majority or plurality of votes. The risk to democratic stability is particularly great in Malawi, Namibia, and Zimbabwe. In Malawi, Bakili Muluzi won the 1994 presidential election with 47.2 percent of the vote, much of it coming in the form of a huge vote share in his native southern region. In the South, which accounts for half of the voting population, Muluzi won 78 percent of the votes cast, while in the central and northern regions he polled only 27.8 percent and 4.5 percent, respectively. As mentioned above, Malawian politics is sharply divided along regional lines, and any constitutional structure that allows one region to be permanently excluded from power will destabilize the state as a whole. President Muluzi may well turn out to embrace a strategy of nation-building, distributing resources fairly across the country, but such a positive outcome will have been due to the virtue of the man rather than the institutional structure of the office. The dynamics of Malawi's presidential system invite Muluzi to pamper the South, do only enough to maintain a third of the votes from the central region, and largely ignore the voters in the North.

In Namibia, Dirk Mudge, former leader of the opposition Democratic Turnhalle Alliance (DTA), articulated similar fears about presidentialism:

> Politically, the proposal for a directly elected president is unsound and dangerous, because it denies the existence of a multiparty system. A parliamentary head of state who is mandated by parliament becomes a symbol of unity and conciliation, since in the exercise of his executive powers he needs to follow the wishes of the representatives of the people.[25]

In fact, in Namibia's first democratic elections in 1989, a full 70 percent of Sam Nujoma's national vote of 57.3 percent came from his ethnic base of Ovamboland. In the 22 electoral districts outside of Ovamboland, the DTA outpolled Nujoma's party, the South West Africa People's Organization (SWAPO), by 181,000 to 159,000 votes. In the presidential election of December 1994, Nujoma again rode to victory on the back of an overwhelming share of the Ovambo vote, with his 72 percent of the popular vote being strongly concentrated in the heavily Ovambo-populated northern regions of the country.

The actions of Robert Mugabe in Zimbabwe have clearly shown how a powerful directly elected president can politically marginalize a given ethnic group. For seven years after its first accession to power in 1980, Mugabe's Shona-based Zimbabwe African National Union-Patriotic Front (ZANU-PF) effectively excluded Joshua Nkomo's Ndebele-based

Patriotic Front-Zimbabwe African People's Union (PF-ZAPU) from political power. In 1987, they signed a unity agreement giving three PF-ZAPU leaders cabinet posts in return for acquiescence to one-party rule. In fact, Zimbabwe's presidential system, combined with the numerical dominance of the Shona, would have allowed Mugabe to maintain his ethnically exclusionary government even without the accord with Nkomo.

If we accept Lijphart's hypothesis that consensual rather than majoritarian democracy is what is needed in divided (or plural) societies, then vesting a single individual with all executive power is clearly detrimental to constructive power-sharing arrangements. The interim South African constitution has partly overcome this problem by creating a "triumvirate" of leaders from parties representing over 80 percent of the electorate. President Mandela is assisted in carrying out his executive functions by two deputy presidents—Thabo Mbeki of the ANC and F.W. de Klerk of the opposition NP. Such creative power-sharing mechanisms—available in a parliamentary system—can make the difference between stable democracy and spiraling ethnic conflict.

Shugart and Carey offer "premier-presidentialism" as a persuasive alternative to presidentialism. In such systems, the presence of a prime minister tempers the president's "exaggerated sense of mandate." Moreover, the president can dissolve parliament and call new elections when crises arise, which mitigates the problem of rigid terms. Because of its majoritarianism, however, premier-presidentialism is as inappropriate to the southern African democracies as straightforward presidentialism. As Shugart and Carey note, "Because the cabinet is subject to parliamentary confidence, it will not be as narrowly representative of the president's interests as will a presidential cabinet, *unless, of course, there is majority support in parliament for the president's narrow interests.*"[26]

When the results of elections in Malawi, Namibia, Zimbabwe, and South Africa are reinterpreted under a hypothetical premier-presidentialist system, it is clear that such a system would still allow one party to dominate both the executive and legislative branches of government and govern in an ethnically exclusive way. The presence of a statutory multiparty cabinet, as now exists in South Africa, might ease the problem, but as Scott Mainwaring has observed, this too is unattractive in practice: "Multiparty presidentialism is more likely to produce immobilizing executive/legislative deadlock than either parliamentary systems or two-party presidentialism."[27] Such deadlock carries with it the danger of popular discontent with the new power-sharing government, which might well overwhelm any executive achievements in the realm of ethnic accommodation.

Perhaps the South African practice of electing a parliamentary government, headed by a prime minister, and then bestowing upon that leader the title of state president is the most constructive route to follow.

Along with inclusive proportional representation and minority-majority power-sharing arrangements within the cabinet, the country thereby also gains a national figurehead who can serve as a rallying point. President Mandela's legitimacy is based on his leadership of a majority parliamentary party and an executive branch that represents over 90 percent of the country's voters—a far stronger foundation than the simple plurality of the electorate that legitimates a directly elected president.

Finding the Least Imperfect System

No electoral system or any other constitutional mechanism is a panacea. The task of the constitutional engineer is to find the least imperfect system and then adapt it to the needs of an emerging democracy, achieving a balance between a representative parliament and a coherent government; an understandable ballot and a broad range of voter choice; and a proportional parliament and solid links between representatives and specific geographic areas. Although electoral-system design is only one cog in the intricate constitutional machine, a misshapen cog may cause the whole structure to grind to a halt.

Divided societies and those without solid democratic histories may be particularly susceptible to instability if the electoral-system design fails to meet any of the following criteria:

• *Representativeness.* If an electoral system is to maximize legitimacy and ensure a degree of electoral consent to any government formation, it must carry out the will of the entire electorate, not just the majority.

• *Accessibility.* The legislature will be representative only to the extent that people feel included in the political process. When people feel that their vote makes a difference, they are more likely to work for change within the system instead of supporting antisystem parties and organizations that feed on societal instability.

• *Provision of incentives for conciliatory behavior.* The electoral system must promote an environment of compromise and reconciliation, rather than exacerbate existing conflict. This does not mean enforced consensus, but rather the mutual recognition of opposing viewpoints.

• *Accountability.* The electoral system must promote a high degree of accountability of government and MPs to their constituents. The amount of influence that voters have over their representatives depends on both the size of geographic constituencies and the extent to which voters can choose among candidates, as opposed to parties.

• *Encouragement of cross-cutting parties.* Prospects for stability are maximized by an electoral system that engenders parties rooted in shared perspectives on issues and political values rather than ethnic, linguistic, or geographic factors.

The early evidence from southern Africa indicates that PR systems uniformly outperform their plurality counterparts with respect to the first three criteria listed above. Clearly, accountability is a problem in the large-district, closed-list form of PR used in South Africa and Namibia; the use of smaller multimember PR constituencies in conjunction with open lists could alleviate this problem. To date there is little evidence of the encouragement of cross-cutting parties under either plurality or PR in southern Africa, but presumably the evolution of such parties is best facilitated by the broad-based party lists necessary under PR. Finally, the experiences of Malawi, Zimbabwe, and Nigeria show that investing substantial executive control in a directly elected president is detrimental to stability in a multiparty government. For these reasons, parliamentary–PR systems of government are best for the fragile new democracies of southern Africa as well as for other African states such as Angola, Mozambique, and Zaire—that have yet to make the transition to democracy.

NOTES

This essay is based on research supported by a grant from the National Science Foundation of the United States (SBR-9321864).

1. See Arend Lijphart, "Constitutional Choices for New Democracies," *Journal of Democracy* 2 (Winter 1991): 72–84; Guy Lardeyret, "The Problem with PR," *Journal of Democracy* 2 (Summer 1991): 30–35; Quentin L. Quade, "PR and Democratic Statecraft," *Journal of Democracy* 2 (Summer 1991): 36–41; Ken Gladdish, "The Primacy of the Particular," *Journal of Democracy* 4 (January 1993): 53–65; Vernon Bogdanor, "Israel Debates Reform," *Journal of Democracy* 4 (January 1993): 66–78; and Timothy Sisk, "South Africa Seeks New Ground Rules," *Journal of Democracy* 4 (January 1993): 79–91.

2. W. Arthur Lewis, *Politics in West Africa* (London: Allen and Unwin, 1965), 71, 72.

3. Arend Lijphart, "Constitutional Choices for New Democracies," 81.

4. Timothy Sisk, "South Africa Seeks New Ground Rules," 88.

5. Guy Lardeyret, "The Problem with PR," 35.

6. Donald Horowitz, *A Democratic South Africa? Constitutional Engineering in a Divided Society* (Berkeley: University of California Press, 1991), 167.

7. Arend Lijphart, "Constitutional Choices for New Democracies," 74.

8. Jonathan N. Moyo, *Voting for Democracy: Electoral Politics in Zimbabwe* (Harare: University of Zimbabwe Publications, 1992), 158.

9. Jowie Mwiinga, "Chill for Chiluba," *Africa Report* 39 (March–April 1994): 60.

10. The analysis that follows is presented in more detail in Andrew Reynolds, "Re-running the South African and Malawian Parliamentary Elections Under Alternative Electoral System Formulae" (paper to be presented at a conference on "Elections in Africa" sponsored by the United States Institute of Peace, Washing-

ton, D.C., May 1995). The results presented here were calculated on the basis of equal-sized single-member districts within the nine provinces, and voting data from the 343 counting districts used in the actual election. It was assumed that voting preferences would not have been significantly affected by the varying incentives provided by different electoral systems.

11. Vernon Bogdanor, *What Is Proportional Representation?* (Oxford: Martin Robertson, 1984), 44.

12. The extent to which the interim South African constitution is consociational could be the focus of an important debate. Although the method of constituting the "government of national unity" is classically consociational, minority parties do not have a formal blocking veto, and the absence of executive power-sharing in any new constitution would make the government considerably more majoritarian in nature.

13. Arend Lijphart, "Prospects for Power-Sharing in the New South Africa," in Andrew Reynolds, ed., *Election '94 South Africa: The Campaigns, Results and Future Prospects* (New York: St. Martin's, 1994), 222.

14. Arend Lijphart, "Constitutional Choices for New Democracies," 81.

15. In drawing up its national and provincial lists, the ANC used a quota system that entitled women to a third of the places.

16. Among established democracies, only the four Scandinavian nations and the Netherlands have a higher percentage of female MPs than South Africa. See Wilma Rule, "Women's Underrepresentation and Electoral Systems," *PS: Political Science and Politics* 27 (December 1994): 689–92.

17. Guy Lardeyret, "The Problem with PR," 32–33.

18. Guy Lardeyret, "The Problem with PR," 32.

19. Arend Lijphart, "Constitutional Choices for New Democracies," 81.

20. Editorial, *Natal Witness* (Pietermaritzburg), 18 August 1994.

21. Arend Lijphart, "Constitutional Choices for New Democracies," 72.

22. Matthew Shugart and John Carey, *Presidents and Assemblies: Constitutional Design and Electoral Dynamics* (New York: Cambridge University Press, 1992), 28–43.

23. Ann Reid, "Conflict Resolution in Africa: Lessons from Angola," *INR Foreign Affairs Brief* (Bureau of Intelligence and Research, U.S. Department of State, Washington, D.C., 6 April 1993), 2.

24. Ian Campbell, "Nigeria's Failed Transition: The 1993 Presidential Election," *Journal of Contemporary African Studies* 12 (1994): 182.

25. Quoted in Lionel Cliffe et al., *The Transition to Independence in Namibia* (Boulder, Colo.: Lynne Rienner, 1994), 208.

26. Matthew Shugart and John Carey, *Presidents and Assemblies,* 49–51 (emphasis added).

27. Scott Mainwaring, "Presidentialism, Multipartism, and Democracy: The Difficult Combination," *Comparative Political Studies* 6 (July 1993): 200.

12

COMMENT: ELECTIONS IN AGRARIAN SOCIETIES

Joel D. Barkan

Joel D. Barkan *is professor emeritus of political science at the University of Iowa and senior associate at the Center for Strategic and International Studies in Washington, D.C. He has written extensively on democratization and economic reform in East Africa, and on African elections. His current work in this area focuses on the application of GIS technology to problems of electoral design and is reported in the November 2006 issue of the* American Journal of Political Science. *This essay originally appeared in the October 1995 issue of the* Journal of Democracy.

The recent transitions to democracy in Namibia and South Africa have prompted renewed claims by advocates of proportional representation (PR) that it is the most appropriate electoral formula for plural societies in Africa and elsewhere. Their argument, as presented by Andrew Reynolds (pp. 121–34 above) and earlier by Arend Lijphart, contains four essential elements.[1] First, PR is the "fairest" method of electing members of national legislatures—particularly in comparison with formulas that elect legislators from single-member districts (SMDs)—because it ensures that the percentage of seats won by a political party is virtually the same as its percentage of the popular vote. Parties receiving a plurality or a majority of the vote are therefore not overrepresented in the legislature, while parties receiving a minority of the vote gain representation equal to their voting strength. As a result, PR also protects minority interests.

Second, PR is inclusive, because it ensures that all significant players in the political system, including potential spoilers, are represented in the legislature. PR thus enhances the prospects that all players will support the constitutional order by participating in its elections and principal institutions. Such support is particularly important during the early stages of new or recently restored democratic rule, when the institutionalization of the new constitutional order is incomplete. Third, PR facilitates arrangements of power-sharing or consociational democracy, enabling most political forces to participate in governance. Fourth—and this last benefit results from the first three—PR greatly enhances the prospects for democratization in plural societies, in which political cleavages run deep and mirror ethnic, racial, linguistic, or religious divisions.

Although the recent experience of southern Africa appears to support the argument for PR, the advantages of this system—particularly for the rest of the continent and other similar societies—are not as clear-cut as they seem. In agrarian societies, in which the overwhelming majority of the people derive their livelihood from the land, PR does *not* produce electoral results that are significantly "fairer" or more inclusive than plurality elections based on SMDs. PR is not, therefore, an essential feature of consociational government, but rather one method of facilitating power-sharing within the executive branch.

PR also has serious disadvantages, one of which should be of particular concern to any would-be constitutional engineer for an agrarian society. Because under the purest forms of PR legislative seats are allocated from party lists according to each party's proportion of the total national vote, individual MPs do not identify with, nor can they be held accountable to, the residents of a specific geographic constituency. Yet in agrarian societies, this lack of linkage between representatives and constituents greatly reduces the prospects for the consolidation of democratic rule.

Voting Behavior Among Rural Populations

In agrarian societies, with their low levels of occupational specialization and class identity, most people define their interests and differentiate themselves from one another on the basis of where they live, rather than what they do. They have a strong attachment to the place where they reside and affection for their neighbors. When it comes to elections, they focus on the basic needs of their local community and surrounding region—whether they have adequate water, schools, and health-care facilities, whether there is a farm-to-market road, whether the producer price for the agricultural commodity grown in the area yields a fair return to local farmers, and so on. Inhabitants of a particular rural area usually have a common set of political interests, and they vote accordingly. This explains the high geographic concentration of the vote for competing parties in the recent round of multiparty elections in Africa. Except in urban areas, whose inhabitants come from many different regions and tend to have a relatively strong sense of occupational and class identity, people who live in the same place vote for the same political party.[2] In agrarian societies, people evaluate parties and candidates in terms of their potential for, or past record of, constituency service.[3]

Yet PR systematically frustrates such voter expectations. Not only are MPs not responsible for addressing the needs of specific localities, but their political careers depend primarily on satisfying their party's leadership, which determines their rankings on the party list for the next election. In agrarian societies, and particularly in Africa, the use of PR risks the development of what Goran Hyden has termed "the suspended state"—a state that is disconnected from the population and eventually loses its authority and its ability to govern.[4]

Electoral Formulas and Democratization

Democratization hinges on the simultaneous development of two different relationships: 1) *representation* of citizens by their chosen leaders, a relationship characterized by dialogue and accountability; and 2) *tolerance, bargaining,* and *compromise* among rival political groups. The former links elites and nonelites who have a common political interest, and constitutes the "vertical" dimension of democracy. The latter obtains mainly between leaders of opposing interests, and constitutes the "horizontal" dimension of democracy.

The relative importance of these two dimensions is different during transitions to democracy and during democratic consolidation. Because transitions involve the establishment of a new constitutional order that must be embraced by all significant factions, they are marked by intense bargaining among rival elites. At this stage, relatively little emphasis is placed on the quality of representation. It is more or less taken for granted that key elites are bargaining on behalf of their respective constituencies. For example, in the negotiations over South Africa's transition to democracy, few questioned the extent to which Nelson Mandela and Cyril Ramaphosa, on the one hand, or F.W. de Klerk and Roelf Meyer, on the other, spoke for the rank and file of the African National Congress (ANC) and the National Party (NP), respectively.

Consolidation, on the other hand, is a long-term process during which democratic practice is gradually institutionalized. Indeed, it can be said that the process of consolidation never ceases, because for democracy to survive, successive generations of citizens and elites must reaffirm the nation's commitment to it.[5] Hence consolidation requires the *continuous* fulfillment of both the vertical and horizontal dimensions of democracy, and any electoral formula that does not sustain both undermines the prospects for democracy over the long term. It is clear, then, that PR has both advantages and disadvantages. While it can facilitate transitions to democracy in plural societies, when these societies are also agrarian it impedes consolidation by failing to sustain democracy's vertical component.

The experience of southern Africa offers substantial evidence of PR's primary shortcoming, and has given rise to calls for the system's abolition or modification. PR was used in Namibia for that country's first all-race elections in November 1989. The elections were held to establish a Constituent Assembly, which became the National Assembly (or lower house of parliament) upon Namibia's independence from South Africa in March 1990. Seventy-two seats were allocated on the basis of the total nationwide vote of the contesting parties—that is, the party vote in a single national constituency. The same variation of PR was used for Namibia's second parliamentary elections in December 1994. In between, Namibians elected 13 regional councils (in November 1992) from 95 SMDs. Each council, in turn, elected two of its members to an upper house of parliament, the National Council. The outcomes are instructive.

The South West African People's Organisation (SWAPO) obtained majorities of 57.3 percent and 73.9 percent in the first two parliamentary elections, and has governed since independence. The principal opposition party, the Democratic Turnhalle Alliance (DTA), obtained 28.6 percent of the vote in 1989 and 20.8 percent in 1994, while the United Democratic Front (UDF) obtained 5.6 percent and 2.7 percent. The use of PR resulted in an allocation of seats to each party that closely approximated that party's percentage of the vote.

With more than two-thirds of the seats in the National Assembly, SWAPO has the power to amend Namibia's constitution. Thus PR by itself has failed to provide sufficient minority representation to block constitutional changes that could be injurious to minority interests. Nor has PR guaranteed the inclusion of minority representatives in the executive branch—the essence of consociational democracy. Rather, it is the self-restraint of the majority government of President Sam Nujoma, along with international pressure, that has been responsible for the protection of minority interests—particularly the property rights of Namibia's white population.[6] Self-restraint and commitment to a policy of national reconciliation have also resulted in the appointment of opposition party members to minor posts in the government and to the position of attorney general.

Most significantly, Namibia's ethnic and racial minorities, which supported the DTA and the UDF, would be no worse off and possibly better off under an electoral system based on SMDs. Because the vote in the 1994 parliamentary elections was tabulated and reported by each of the 95 constituencies that elected the regional councils, it is possible to estimate the distribution of seats that would have occurred had the elections been run under an SMD formula. The results show SWAPO obtaining a plurality or majority of the vote in 67.4 percent of the 95 districts, the DTA obtaining a plurality or majority in 29.5 percent, and the UDF in 3.2 percent.[7] *The distribution of seats is thus substantially the same under the two systems.* Advocates of PR claim that SMD plurality overrepresents parties that obtain a plurality or majority of the vote; yet the Namibian case shows that it can also underrepresent the majority party, and thus may provide better protection of minority interests than PR.

For example, the DTA—the party of Namibia's white community and ethnic minorities—obtained only 20.8 percent of the vote in the 1994 election, but would have "won" 29.5 percent of the seats had each councilmanic district elected a representative to the legislature. Moreover, SMD systems can be fine-tuned so as to reduce (or maintain) the associated disparity between vote shares and seats won, as explained below.

The Namibian case also demonstrates the failure of PR to provide appropriate representation for the residents of agrarian societies. Interviews conducted by myself and two colleagues with more than three dozen regional councillors in July 1994 consistently revealed that members of the National Assembly rarely make an appearance in the rural areas, because they have no constituency to which they are accountable. It is the regional councillors—precisely because they are elected from geographically defined constituencies and are physically accessible within their districts—to whom citizens bring their problems and those of their communities.[8] This is hardly surprising. In agrarian societies, in which most residents are peasant farmers who move about on foot, by bicycle, or by public transportation, the most effective representation is based on face-to-face contact in the countryside or small towns.

It is also not surprising that this difference in quality of representation between PR and district-based systems is becoming a political issue in Namibia and within SWAPO. Owing to the failure of PR to facilitate a continuous dialogue between MPs and the rural population, regional councillors want an end to PR for elections to the National Assembly, as well as a devolution of power to the regional councils. Some also believe that a change to an SMD system would enable them to challenge incumbent MPs successfully at the next parliamentary election. For the same reasons, incumbent MPs and the SWAPO leadership oppose a change of electoral system. The disagreement over electoral approach also reflects a "generation gap": councillors tend to be five to ten years younger than MPs. The divisions are likely to have deepened by the time of the next elections in 1999.

These shortcomings of PR resulted in similar calls for district-based voting in South Africa less than one year after that country's first all-race elections, which were conducted under a "two-tier" version of PR. Under the South African system, 200 seats in the National Assembly are allocated on the basis of the party vote nationwide, and 200 are allocated on the basis of the party vote in each of nine regions.[9] This version of PR has resulted in each party's gaining a proportion of seats that is virtually identical to its percentage of the total vote, with the largest parties guaranteed participation in the government proportionate to their vote.[10] Yet the absence of a representational link between individual MPs and specific geographic constituencies has been apparent from the start. Recognizing the disadvantages of this situation, the ANC announced in October 1994 that it was establishing an informal system of constituency-based representation by assigning MPs and cabinet ministers to designated areas and providing them with the financial support needed to maintain a presence there.[11] Historically, the ANC has favored an SMD system, but it modified its position to support the present system when it calculated that it would do no worse under "two-tier" PR. The NP has also announced that it wants a partial return to constituency-based elections in 1999.[12]

Leaders of South Africa's two largest parties feel comfortable in calling for an end to or a modification of PR largely because they have concluded that a constituency-based formula would provide substantially similar electoral results, without PR's disadvantages. Small parties, such as the Pan-Africanist Congress (PAC), the Democratic Party (DP), and the Freedom Front (FF), may be wiped out under an SMD system, while the fortunes of the regionally based Inkatha Freedom Party (IFP) are unlikely to change. It would also appear that the NP, which favors a continuation of power-sharing after 1999, realizes that such arrangements do not require PR. Indeed, the current power-sharing arrangement in South Africa is based not on PR per se, but on the number of seats each party obtains in the National Assembly. If an SMD formula yields roughly the same distribution of seats as PR, consociational democracy can be maintained.

The Same Distribution of Seats

Ironically, some of the best evidence for the similarity of the distribution of legislative seats under SMD plurality and PR has been assembled by Andrew Reynolds, a staunch proponent of PR. In a valuable essay in which he "re-runs" the recent elections in South Africa and Malawi, Reynolds shows that the choice of electoral formula is not nearly as significant in agrarian societies as it is in advanced industrial societies.[13] Reynolds's data, along with my own figures for the most recent parliamentary elections in Kenya and Namibia, are presented in the table.[14]

The table presents the results of four elections in four African countries: South Africa (April 1994), Namibia (December 1994), Malawi (May 1994), and Kenya (December 1992). South Africa's and Namibia's elections were run under PR, and Malawi's and Kenya's were run under SMD plurality. The table allows for comparison of the percentage of seats that each party *actually obtained* under the electoral formula used for the election in question with its percentage of the vote, as well as with the percentage of seats that the party *would have obtained* under alternative electoral formulas. Thus the distributions of seats obtained via PR in South Africa and Namibia can be compared with the distributions that would have resulted under SMD plurality, while the distributions of seats obtained via SMD plurality in Malawi and Kenya can be compared with the vote shares obtained by the parties—percentages that would

TABLE—DISTRIBUTIONS OF VOTES & SEATS UNDER PR & SMD FORMULAS

ELECTION	PARTY[1]	PERCENTAGE OF VOTE	PERCENTAGE OF SEATS		
			NATIONAL-LIST PR	EXISTING SMDs	EQUAL SMDs[2]
South Africa (April 1994)	ANC	62.7	63.0	NA	70.8
	NP	20.4	20.5	NA	17.0
	IFP	10.5	10.8	NA	12.3
	FF	2.2	2.2	NA	–
	DP	1.7	1.8	NA	–
	PAC	1.3	1.3	NA	–
	ID	–	**0.3**	NA	**6.7**
Namibia (December 1994)	SWAPO	73.9	73.6	67.4	73.9
	DTA	20.8	20.8	29.5	23.9
	UDF	2.7	4.2	3.2	2.2
	Other	3.1	1.4	–	–
	ID	–	**1.1**	**7.7**	**2.2**
Malawi (May 1994)	UDF	46.4	NA	48.0	NA
	MCP	33.7	NA	31.6	NA
	AFORD	18.9	NA	20.3	NA
	ID	–	NA	**2.1**	NA
Kenya (December 1992)	KANU	29.7	NA	53.2	44.6
	FORD-A	24.2	NA	16.5	22.3
	FORD-K	20.8	NA	16.5	17.0
	DP	22.2	NA	12.2	15.4
	Other	3.1	NA	1.6	0.5
	ID	–	NA	**19.1**	**12.0**
IDs (average) for selected established democracies with SMD plurality systems	Canada				11.3
	N.Zealand				10.7
	UK				10.5
	USA				5.4

[1] *South Africa:* ANC, African National Congress; DP, Democratic Party; FF, Freedom Front; IFP, Inkatha Freedom Party; NP, National Party; PAC, Pan-Africanist Congress. *Namibia:* DTA, Democratic Turnhalle Alliance; SWAPO, South West African People's Organisation; UDF, United Democratic Front. *Malawi:* AFORD, Alliance for Democracy; MCP, Malawi Congress Party; UDF, United Democratic Front. *Kenya:* DP, Democratic Party; FORD-A, Forum for Restoration of Democracy–Asili; FORD-K, Forum for Restoration of Democracy–Kenya; KANU, Kenya African National Union.
[2] Data for South Africa based on election results as reported in 341 counting districts as presented by Andrew Reynolds in "Re-running the 1994 South African and Malawian Parliamentary Elections Under Alternative Electoral System Formulae," in Timothy Sisk and Andrew Reynolds, eds., *Elections and Conflict Resolution in Africa* (Washington, D.C.: U.S. Institute of Peace Press, forthcoming). Data for Namibia based on election results as reported in 95 councilmanic districts adjusted for population variations among districts. Data for Kenya based on election results in 188 parliamentary constituencies adjusted for population variations among districts. Data for the established democracies from Arend Lijphart, *Electoral Systems and Party Systems* (New York: Oxford University Press, 1994), 160–62.
Note: Percentages do not always total 100 due to rounding.

have been approximated by PR. Data for the SMD system are presented in one or both of two versions—actual results (as they occurred in Malawi and Kenya) and estimated results (for South Africa, Namibia, and Kenya) had all districts contained the same number of voters. Finally, the Table presents an Index of Disproportionality (ID) for each formula for which a distribution of seats was calculated, as well as for recent elections in four advanced democracies that employ SMD plurality. The closer the ID is to zero, the closer the electoral formula comes to translating each party's percentage of the vote into exactly the same percentage of seats. Thus the higher the ID, the greater the disproportionality of the outcome. The ID typically ranges from near zero to 20.[15]

The Table underscores three basic points. First, except in the case of Kenya, PR and SMD plurality yield substantially the same distribution of seats. Both formulas do a good job of translating percentage of the vote into percentage of seats. Second, PR is the superior method if achieving a proportional outcome is the main purpose of an election. As argued above, however, the mere mathematical translation of votes into seats does not guarantee the establishment of a continuous process of representation after the election. When it comes to the quality of representation, SMD plurality is the superior formula. The question, then, is whether the superiority of representation offered by SMD plurality is worth the cost of a modest distortion in the translation of votes into seats.

Third, the deficiencies of SMD plurality are mitigated when all districts contain the same number of voters. In Namibia, the average number of voters per district is 5,236, but the number of voters in the existing councilmanic districts varies from 1,051 to 13,592. Here, an SMD system based on districts of equal size would result in an ID nearly as low as the current PR system. Such a system would also reduce the level of disproportionality in Kenya, where the average number of registered voters per district is 25,544, but the actual number varies from 2,872 to 65,887. While the resulting ID is not as low as that for Namibia, it is near that of several advanced democracies. Most important, the creation of equal-sized districts in Kenya would reverse the most serious shortcoming of the present SMD system (but one that also "protects" the minority interests of Kenya's smallest and least developed ethnic groups): a legislative majority for a party that obtained only 30 percent of the vote. Creating more and thus smaller and more compact districts would further reduce the level of disproportionality associated with SMD plurality.

Explaining Disproportionality

The level of disproportionality depends not so much on the choice of electoral formula as on three other variables: 1) the extent to which voters of different parties are geographically concentrated or dispersed; 2) the extent of variation in the number of voters per district; and 3) the number and compactness of electoral districts. This is why, in the context of agrarian societies, SMD systems yield (or can be designed to yield) distributions of seats that are close to those obtained via PR.

As explained above, voters in agrarian societies tend to vote in geographic blocs that are highly homogeneous. As a result, it is not unusual for parties to obtain more than 90 percent of the vote in some areas and less than 10 or 15 percent in others. What appears from a distance to be a multiparty system is in actuality a collection of regional one-party systems. Malawi and Namibia are near-perfect examples of this tendency. By contrast, multiparty systems in advanced industrial societies are characterized by a geographic dispersion of the vote. Although different regions are viewed as bastions of different parties, the degree of hegemony is much less than in developing nations, because most areas harbor voters from across the political spectrum. Newly industrialized countries (NICs) fall somewhere in between these two extremes, manifesting a pattern of bloc voting in many rural areas combined with more heterogeneous patterns elsewhere.

The more agrarian the society, then, the higher the geographic concentration of the vote and the more closely the distribution of seats under an SMD system will mirror the distribution of the total vote, as well as the distribution of seats that would be obtained under PR. Conversely, the more industrialized the society, the more geographically dispersed will be the vote, and the greater the discrepancy between the distribution of seats obtained under SMD plurality and that obtained via PR. In sum, SMD systems are likely to have a low ID in agrarian societies, but a moderate to high ID in industrialized societies.[16] Moreover, the extent of disproportionality associated with SMD systems can be reduced by creating more districts, thus making all districts smaller and more compact. This raises the level of social homogeneity within all districts, and thus increases the extent to which residents support one party or another.

Because advocates of PR and consociational democracy such as Arend Lijphart have tended to focus their examinations of electoral systems on advanced democracies and thus on industrial and postindustrial societies, it is not surprising that they have failed to appreciate the extent to which SMD plurality and PR yield similar results in developing countries. Nor, for the same reason, have they been sensitive to the extent to which SMD systems in agrarian societies can be refined to reduce the extent of disproportionality. Finally, advocates of PR have not fully considered the way in which rural voters approach the electoral process. Proponents of PR place a low emphasis on the need for geographically based representation, because in societies dominated by interest-group or corporate politics, such representation is no longer required to maintain a democratic constitutional order.

Conceding the need for geographic representation, Andrew Reynolds has argued that a modified system of PR based on multimember districts would overcome PR's principal defect in agrarian societies. If such a system is to facilitate face-to-face contact between citizens and representatives, however, it would require districts so small in size and population as to reduce the number of representatives per district to the point that allocating seats on the principle of proportionality would be either unnecessary or unfeasible. For example, if PR is modified to allocate from three to six seats in each of a series of small multimember districts, why bother? The allocation of such a small number of seats may yield results that are less proportional than those of SMD plurality. They would certainly be less proportional than those of ordinary PR.[17]

Advocates of PR and defenders of SMD plurality run the risk of talking past each other. In fact, each formula is particularly appropriate for one subset of political systems, but not necessarily for all systems. For agrarian societies—especially those of Africa, the world's least developed continent, where the return to democracy is at a critical stage—SMD systems may yet provide an essential ingredient of democracy, without which its consolidation is unlikely to occur: effective representation. In this context, any call for the replacement of constituency-based voting with PR is likely to be premature.

NOTES

1. See Andrew Reynolds, "Constitutional Engineering in Southern Africa," *Journal of Democracy* 6 (April 1995): 86–99; and Arend Lijphart, *Power-Sharing in South Africa* (Berkeley, Calif.: Institute of International Studies, 1985) and *Electoral Systems and Party Systems* (New York: Oxford University Press, 1994).

2. See Joel D. Barkan, "Kenya: Lessons from a Flawed Election," *Journal of Democracy* 4 (July 1993): 85–99; and Andrew Reynolds, "Re-running the 1994 South African and Malawian Parliamentary Elections Under Alternative Electoral System Formulae," in Timothy Sisk and Andrew Reynolds, eds., *Elections and Conflict Resolution in Africa* (Washington, D.C.: U.S. Institute of Peace Press, forthcoming). While ethnicity is undoubtedly an important factor in the high geographic concentration of the vote in many African countries, there is substantial evidence—from Kenya and elsewhere—that it is not the only one.

3. Joel D. Barkan, "Legislators, Elections and Political Linkage," in Barkan, ed., *Politics and Public Policy in Kenya and Tanzania* (New York: Praeger, 1984), 71–101.

4. Goran Hyden, *No Shortcuts to Progress: African Development Management in Perspective* (Berkeley: University of California Press, 1981), 7.

5. As Samuel P. Huntington wrote nearly three decades ago, the institutionalization of any political practice—democratic or otherwise—requires that each element of that practice (e.g., the regular holding of elections, the legislative or judicial process, and so on) be valued by those who engage in that particular practice as well as those outside of it. See Samuel P. Huntington, *Political Order in Changing Societies* (New Haven: Yale University Press, 1968).

6. International donors and investors have made clear to the Namibian government that any reversal of constitutional guarantees of property rights or of multipartism would drive away both investment and aid.

7. It should be remembered that these 95 councilmanic constituencies play no

role in the present application of PR, other than to serve as counting areas for the tabulation of the national vote. Thus the number of seats in the National Assembly is not 95 but 72. To facilitate comparison of the outcomes of PR and SMD plurality, all actual or hypothetical distributions of seats have been expressed as percentages.

8. Joel D. Barkan, Gretchen Bauer, and Carol Lynn Martin, *The Consolidation of Democracy in Namibia: Assessment and Recommendations* (report prepared for the United States Agency for International Development by Associates in Rural Development, Inc., Burlington, Vermont, July 1994).

9. Seats within the nine regional legislatures are also allocated on the basis of the party vote within the regions.

10. One cabinet position is allocated for every 20 seats held by a political party.

11. *Sunday Times* (Johannesburg), 9 October 1994, as cited in *South Africa News Update*, 11–17 October 1994.

12. *Citizen* (Johannesburg), 20 January 1995, as cited in *South Africa News Update*, 17–23 January 1995.

13. Andrew Reynolds, "Re-running the 1994 South African and Malawian Parliamentary Elections."

14. I wish to thank Andrew Reynolds for sharing his insights and data with me. I am also grateful to Judith Geist for sharing her data on the 1992 Kenya election.

15. Several methods exist for measuring the extent to which an electoral formula yields a distribution of seats that diverges from the distribution of the vote. Following both Andrew Reynolds and Arend Lijphart, I use the least squares index developed by Michael Gallagher. For a full discussion of the various methods of calculating disproportionality, including Gallagher's, see Arend Lijphart, *Electoral Systems and Party Systems,* ch. 3.

16. The only exceptions to this rule are those cases where support for contesting parties is dispersed as a result of some factor, such as religion or language, that divides residents of the same rural communities. The impact of caste in India or of religion in Uganda would be examples of this phenomenon. Conversely, the high geographic concentration of the vote in South Africa, the most industrialized country on the continent, is in large part a legacy of apartheid laws (e.g., the Group Areas Act), which dictated where members of different races and ethnic groups could live.

17. See, for example, Andrew Reynolds's own calculations for the application of this option to Malawi in "Re-running the 1994 South African and Malawian Parliamentary Elections."

13

REJOINDER: THE CASE FOR PROPORTIONALITY

Andrew Reynolds

Andrew Reynolds *is associate professor of political science at the University of North Carolina at Chapel Hill. He has consulted on issues of electoral and constitutional design for a wide array of countries. His latest book is* The Architecture of Democracy: Constitutional Design, Conflict Management, and Democracy *(2002). This essay originally appeared in the October 1995 issue of the* Journal of Democracy.

In "Elections in Agrarian Societies" (pp. 135–45 above), Joel Barkan offers a strong challenge to the newly emerging conventional wisdom that proportional representation (PR) is the best electoral formula for the fledgling—and often highly divided—democracies of Africa. First, he criticizes PR for weakening (or even severing) the link between individual MPs and constituents. This hinders the development of the "vertical" dimension of democracy (that is, the representative relationship between elites and nonelites with a common political interest), "greatly reduc[ing] the prospects for the consolidation of democratic rule" (p. 136). For Barkan, the relationship between representative and voter that obtains within a single-member district (SMD) best reflects the nature of agrarian societies in Africa, in which the strongest ties are those of kinship, neighborhood, and land, and people "define their [political] interests . . . on the basis of where they live" (p. 136). While accepting that some degree of proportionality (indicating the protection of minority interests) is a normative good, he argues that the patterns of geographically polarized voting seen in agrarian societies enable SMD plurality systems to produce parliaments that are reasonably reflective of the distribution of the nationwide popular vote. Thus one can retain one of the underpinnings of consociational government (a proportionally constituted parliament) while avoiding the main drawback of PR: the detachment and lack of accountability of representatives elected from party lists.

It is true that when voting patterns closely follow cleavages among groups defined by ascriptive traits (such as race, ethnicity, language, or religion), and when different groups cluster in different areas, elections held under SMD plurality can produce highly proportional results. As Barkan notes, the 1994 general election in Malawi gave rise to a parliament that closely mirrored the distribution of the national vote among the three main parties. An election's Index of Disproportionality (ID) measures the degree to which the distribution of parliamentary seats among parties diverges from the distribution of votes, with zero representing a perfectly proportional outcome. The score on that index for the Malawian election (2.1) was lower than the figures for plurality elections in all but three of the established democracies for which data are presented in Arend Lijphart's comprehensive *Electoral Systems and Party Systems,* which covers the period from 1945 to 1990.[1] Similarly, the regionally polarized parliamentary election of 1985 in Zimbabwe produced an ID of 2.5, and my own "re-running" of the 1994 parliamentary elections in South Africa and Namibia (which were held under PR systems) indicated that SMD plurality would have produced relatively proportional results, with IDs of 6.7 and 4.0, respectively.[2]

The ID for a given election tells us much about parliamentary composition. High IDs indicate a high likelihood that: 1) minority parties are receiving little or no representation; 2) larger parties are gaining "seat bonuses" over and above their share of the popular vote; 3) governments with 100 percent of the executive power are being catapulted into office with less than 50 percent of the popular vote; and 4) governments based on a simple majority of the popular vote are being awarded supermajority powers (as in South Africa, where the use of a plurality system would have provided the African National Congress [ANC], which received 62 percent of the vote, with two-thirds of the seats in the National Assembly—enough to write the new constitution unfettered).

Atypical Cases

The evidence from Malawi in 1994 and Zimbabwe in 1985 (and the hypothetical evidence from South Africa and Namibia) seems to indicate that, in southern Africa, SMD plurality can provide "the best of both worlds"—a proportionally constituted parliament, along with the representational advantages of a district-based system. Barkan claims that "in agrarian societies . . . PR does *not* produce electoral results that are significantly 'fairer' or more inclusive than plurality elections based on SMDs" (p. 136). Yet the results from Malawi and Zimbabwe have not been mirrored in established democracies, in Africa as a whole, or within southern Africa itself. At the end of the day, these are atypical cases, and we must take care not to be blinded by them.

The five countries using SMD plurality for democratic elections in southern Africa since 1965 have, on average, experienced IDs in line

TABLE 1—AVERAGE IDS OF SMD PLURALITY & PR ELECTIONS

	SOUTHERN AFRICA	AFRICA	ESTABLISHED DEMOCRACIES
SMD Plurality	11.0[a]	12.9[c]	9.8[e]
PR	3.7[b]	4.8[d]	2.9[f]

[a] Thirteen elections: Botswana, 1965–94; Lesotho, 1993; Malawi, 1994; Zambia, 1991; Zimbabwe, 1985 (common roll), 1990, 1995.
[b] Six elections: Angola, 1992; Mozambique, 1994; Namibia, 1989, 1994; South Africa, 1994, Zimbabwe 1980.
[c] Twenty elections: Botswana, 1965–94; Gambia, 1966–92; Kenya, 1992; Lesotho, 1993, Malawi, 1994, Zambia, 1991; Zimbabwe, 1985–95.
[d] Thirteen elections: Angola, 1992; Benin, 1991; Burkina Faso, 1992; Burundi, 1993; Cape Verde, 1991; Madagascar, 1993; Mozambique, 1994; Namibia, 1989, 1994; Niger, 1993, 1995; South Africa, 1994; Zimbabwe, 1980.
[e] Calculated from data for 78 elections held under plurality in five countries: Canada, 1945–88; India, 1952–84; New Zealand, 1946–90; United Kingdom, 1945–92; United States, 1946–94.
[f] Calculated from data for 212 elections held under various PR formulas in 17 countries: Austria, 1945–90; Belgium, 1946–87; Costa Rica, 1953–90; Denmark, 1945–88; Finland, 1945–87; Germany, 1945–87; Iceland, 1946–87; Ireland, 1948–89; Israel, 1949–88; Italy, 1946–87; Luxembourg, 1945–89; Malta, 1947–87; Netherlands, 1946–89; Norway, 1945–89; Portugal, 1975–89; Sweden, 1948–88; Switzerland, 1947–87.
Note: Method of calculation: least squares index developed by Michael Gallagher. See his "Proportionality, Disproportionality and Electoral Systems," *Electoral Studies* 10 (1991): 33–51.
Sources: For Africa as a whole, author's calculations based on data presented in Shaheen Mozaffar, "The Political Originas and Consequences of Electoral Systems in Africa: A Preliminary Analysis" (paper presented at a conference on "Comparative Democratic Elections," Kennedy School of Government, Harvard University, May 1995); for established democracies, calculations based on data presented in Arend Lijphart, *Electoral Systems and Party Systems* (New York: Oxford University Press, 1994), and updated by Reynolds.

with plurality elections in the rest of the world (Table 1). The results have been slightly more proportional than those for Africa as a whole but slightly less proportional than those for the established democracies—Britain and the inheritors of her "first-past-the-post" electoral system. Furthermore, the figures for PR elections show that, despite the low IDs for plurality in Malawi and Zimbabwe, when it comes to translating votes into seats, PR is not just marginally superior to SMD plurality but substantially so. The evidence from throughout Africa suggests that the use of an electoral system based on SMDs does not ensure the proportionality of electoral results. This is true even in agrarian societies, where voting patterns are geographically concentrated. It follows that if proportionality is a necessary feature of consociational democracy, plurality cannot be relied on to secure it.

Even if plurality elections in fledgling democracies produced reasonably proportional results across the board, there would still be worrying threats to democratic consolidation. First, the experience of South Africa illustrates that the inclusion within parliament of small minority parties can play a crucial stabilizing role in the early years of democratization of a divided society. Clearly, the presence of the Afrikaner Freedom Front (FF), Pan-Africanist Congress (PAC), and Democratic Party (DP) in the first nonracial South African parliament has been conducive to an atmosphere of reconciliation. As I noted in "Constitutional Engineering in Southern Africa," this measure of political inclusiveness would not have been achieved had the April 1994 elections been run on a plurality system rather than a PR system.

Second, if over the longer term economic and class mobility increases and ethnic and regional divisions fade, as most people hope, the resulting integration of neighborhoods and reduction in the political importance of primordial ties will likely bring about a decline in the geographic polarization of voting. This weakening of regional bloc voting will give rise to all the vagaries of plurality that more homogeneous societies such as Britain and the United States have been forced to endure. Such vagaries include the exclusion of substantially supported third parties from representation and the winning of parliamentary majorities by parties with fewer votes than their opponents. It is often claimed that while the more stable and established Western democracies can tolerate these representational anomalies, they could prove fatal in Africa, where democracy is—and will be for many years to come—fragile at best. If the Malawian Congress Party (MCP) of former president Hastings Kamuzu Banda had won a parliamentary majority in 1994 with only 34 percent of the vote, against the 46 percent won by the United Democratic Front (UDF), one can only imagine the civil strife that would have erupted. Nor is this wild speculation without historical foundation. In the whites-only general election in South Africa in 1948, D.F. Malan's Nationalist–Afrikaner coalition came to power with 79 of the 150 seats in parliament despite polling only 42 percent of the vote. Jan Smuts's United–Labour coalition gained 52 percent of the popular vote but only 71 parliamentary seats.

Perhaps most important, the use of plurality in southern Africa freezes the party system to such a degree that the alternation of parties in government and opposition is not perceived as a likely or natural occurrence. This is true even when levels of disproportionality are not high. As Table 2 illustrates, elections held under SMD plurality in southern Africa have provided a paucity of truly competitive seats—the lifeblood of the Westminster system of government.

All five southern African plurality elections described in Table 2 reveal the classic elements of a de facto one-party state, in which governing parties are insulated from electoral challenges. In Malawi, Zambia, and Zimbabwe, the largest parties won their seats with huge segments of the vote, making them largely invulnerable. Marginal seats are those won with a margin of victory (whether a plurality or a majority) of less than 10 percent of the valid vote. These are considered "battleground seats"—which way they go determines which party forms a government. In the elections of the five established democracies, between one-fifth and one-third of the seats were considered marginal. In southern Africa, however, competitive seats have never amounted to more than a tiny fraction of the legislative body. In Zimbabwe, no seat

TABLE 2—MARGINAL SEATS IN RECENT SMD PLURALITY
ELECTIONS

	ELECTION	NUMBER OF MARGINALS	% OF TOTAL SEATS	LARGEST PARTY	AVERAGE VOTE IN SEATS WON
Southern Africa	Zimbabwe, 1995	1	0.8	ZANU-PF	82%
	Zimbabwe, 1990	4	3.3	ZANU-PF	81%
	Zimbabwe, 1985	3	3.7	ZANU-PF	91%
	Malawi, 1994	7	3.9	UDF	72%
	Zambia, 1991	6	4.0	MMD	81%
Established Democracies	USA, 1994	88	20.2	Republican	65%
	Canada, 1993	63	21.4	Liberal	56%
	UK, 1992	171	26.3	Conservative	52%
	India, 1980	157	29.7	Congress	52%
	New Zealand, 1993	30	30.3	National	44%

Note: Marginal seats are defined as those seats won with a margin of victory of less than 10 percent of the total valid vote. Figures are for lower houses of parliament only.

defended by a candidate of the incumbent party has ever changed hands. In effect, the use of plurality systems in heterogeneous societies freezes the number of seats won, creating an environment in which only a political earthquake can jar the patterns of party-vote concentration.

This finding is a serious blow to the case for plurality in Africa, for such majoritarian prescriptions rely on at least the perception that power can change hands from election to election. If plurality leads to a de facto one-party state, there are no incentives for losing parties to remain loyal opposition parties. In the deeply divided societies of Africa, this poses the greatest possible threat to democracy in its initial stages. In contrast, PR systems may display sensitivity to evolving vote patterns by facilitating shifting government coalitions or forcing a single-party cabinet to include other parties when the ruling party's support falls below an absolute majority of the population.

Remedying the Problems of PR

As Barkan points out, accountability and dialogue between representatives and constituents are crucial to any properly functioning democracy. And it is true that the type of national, large-district PR used in South Africa and Namibia has weakened the link between elites and nonelites, giving rise to fears of a "'suspended state' . . . disconnected from the population" (p. 137). Yet instituting an electoral system based on SMDs may not always be the best way to overcome such obstacles to the fulfillment of the vertical dimension of democracy. First, the overwhelming regional concentration of voting patterns throughout Africa gives rise to SMDs that are little more than pocket boroughs of this or that party. One intuitive hypothesis is that the less competitive the seat, the lower the quality of the candidates, and therefore the less responsive the elected MP will be to his or her constituents' needs. This "yellow dog" syndrome (so called because voters would sooner elect a yellow dog than someone from an opposing party) has been noted throughout the democracies that traditionally have used SMD plurality, especially the United States (where the term was coined) and the United Kingdom.

Second, adequate constituency representation is not simply a matter of advocating the interests of 50, 60, or even 80 percent of a given community; it is about allowing supporters of both majority and minority parties within a certain area to have their views articulated in parliament. In Africa, SMD plurality has accentuated regional fiefdoms of party dominance to the extent that 25 percent of the voters of Zambia's Eastern Province (who happened not to support the United National Independence Party [UNIP]), 15 percent of Malawi's Northern Region (who voted against the Alliance for Democracy [AFORD]), and virtually the entire opposition vote of Zimbabwe (which hovered around 19 percent in both 1990 and 1995) are prevented from having a direct say in legislative affairs. The constitutional engineer who seeks to craft a dynamic and inclusive representative democracy must look somewhere in between the extremes of the remote and unaccountable representation that characterizes national-list PR and the exclusionary and all too often complacent representation provided by MPs elected from "safe" SMDs.

The debate currently taking place within South Africa's Constitutional Assembly highlights both the dissatisfaction with large-district list PR and the ways in which PR systems can be adapted to provide more accountable and responsive representation. In South Africa, two options are now on the table. The first is to introduce SMDs for electing a proportion of the National Assembly (perhaps half), with the rest of the MPs being elected from regionally based lists. This would resemble the German system in that, overall, the National Assembly would reflect near proportionality between votes cast and seats won, but a single person would represent each district.

Although this "mixed-member" system might seem attractive, it has two key flaws. First, because of plurality's tendency to exaggerate regional fiefdoms, it is quite probable that certain parties would dominate all of the SMD seats, leaving minority-party MPs to be elected only from the "top-up" pool of members from regional lists. For example, throughout South Africa's Orange Free State, urban and rural constituencies would be represented solely by ANC members, while minority representatives would be elected from the more detached party lists. This leads to the second problem of the mixed-member system: the creation of two classes of MPs, the first group elected from districts tied to local parties and local voters and responsive to constituents' concerns, and the second group elected from the lists and therefore accountable chiefly to party bosses in national headquarters.

The second option is to reduce the size of the multimember districts (MMDs) of list PR and provide voters with more sophisticated choices on the ballot. In *Voting for a New South Africa,* I advocated a formula, akin to the Finnish system, by which 300 members of the South African National Assembly would be elected from MMDs ranging from 5 to 12 members in size, and voters could choose among candidates as well as parties.[3] Parties would win seats in proportion to the number of votes they received, but those seats would be filled by the parties' most popular individual candidates. To ensure overall proportionality, 100 seats would be reserved to "top up" each party's share of the parliamentary seats; in order to remedy the problem of detachment, however, these additional members would be drawn from each party's most successful *losing* candidates.

This system is by no means perfect. Yet it retains overall proportionality in parliament and simplicity for the voter, while at the same time enhancing geographic accountability and diversity of representation within regions. An added benefit is that minority votes are not "wasted," as they are in SMD plurality; this might encourage minority parties in regions where one ethnic or linguistic group predominates. Minority representation and party organization within regions are particularly important when provincial powers are strengthened through federalism, as regional minorities are then less able to rely on the intervention of the national state to protect their interests.

Joel Barkan and I agree on a number of important issues. We agree that choosing an electoral system involves a number of trade-offs among consequences that we attempt to predict by assessing evidence from previous elections. We concur that we should not seek a "perfect" electoral system, nor should we propagate one method as the single best system for any context. Rather, electoral rules must be tailored to the specific needs and desires of each individual society. Furthermore, we agree that the inclusion of both minority and majority interests, and therefore some degree of electoral proportionality, is a normative good in fledgling democracies that are divided along ethnic or regional lines.

I would argue, however, that the results of SMD-plurality elections throughout Africa and the rest of the world indicate that this system cannot be relied on to produce a distribution of parliamentary seats that closely mirrors the distribution of the popular vote, and thus will not necessarily facilitate a diverse and inclusive legislative body. Furthermore, plurality's potential to produce extremely disproportional results and legislative anomalies makes it especially unsuitable for the fragile new democracies of Africa. Barkan argues that electoral rules could be written so as to mandate culturally homogeneous districts (*à la* the U.S. Justice Department's guidelines for racially representative districts), but my guess is that these legal gerrymanders would spark the same tension and controversy that have arisen in the United States. Certainly, the list-PR systems currently in effect in Africa exhibit deficits of legitimacy and accountability. But there is no need to throw the baby out with the bathwater. With a little imagination and innovation, PR systems in Africa can be made to provide a solid link between representatives and constituents, thus strengthening the prospects for democratic consolidation. If South Africa, in devising its new constitution, finds a way to elect not only a proportional National Assembly but an accountable and responsive parliament representing all the people, it may again serve as a beacon for the rest of Africa.

NOTES

This essay is based on research supported by the National Science Foundation of the United States (grant SBR-9321864) and the Institute on Global Conflict and Cooperation.

1. Arend Lijphart, *Electoral Systems and Party Systems* (New York: Oxford University Press, 1994).

2. See Andrew Reynolds, "Re-running the 1994 South African and Malawian Parliamentary Elections Under Alternative Electoral System Formulae," in Timothy Sisk and Andrew Reynolds, eds., *Elections and Conflict Resolution in Africa* (Washington, D.C.: U.S. Institute of Peace Press, 1998). The 4.0 figure for Namibia is slightly lower than Barkan's calculation for plurality on the basis of the 95 counting districts. My assessment is based on a combination of the 95 counting districts to provide 72 SMDs of roughly equal size. That calculation leaves the South West People's Organisation (SWAPO) with 55 seats and the Democratic Turnhalle Alliance (DTA) with 17. (I am very grateful to Joel Barkan for sharing his counting-district data with me.)

3. Andrew Reynolds, *Voting for a New South Africa* (Cape Town: Maskew Miller Longman, 1993), 66–103.

14

ELECTORAL REFORM AND STABILITY IN URUGUAY

Jeffrey Cason

Jeffrey Cason is associate professor of political science and dean of international programs at Middlebury College in Vermont. He is coauthor *(with Christopher Barrett) of* Overseas Research: A Practical Guide *(1997), coeditor (with Michael Carter and Frederic Zimmerman) of* Development at a Crossroads: Paths to Sustainability After the Neoliberal Revolution *(1998), and coeditor (with Sunder Ramaswamy) of* Democracy and Development: New Perspectives on an Old Debate *(2003). This essay originally appeared in the April 2000 issue of the* Journal of Democracy.

In November 1999, Uruguay held its fourth consecutive national elections since the demise of its military regime in 1985. In so doing, Uruguayans reaffirmed their strong commitment to democratic political rules, while at the same time adjusting to a set of constitutional reforms that profoundly altered the electoral system. One of the more important reforms instituted a runoff election if no presidential candidate receives an absolute majority in the first round. As expected, a runoff was necessary, and the election was won by Jorge Batlle of the Colorado Party, who had finished second in the first round. Because of the new constitutional rules, Batlle ran in alliance in the runoff with his traditional political rivals to defeat a surprisingly strong challenge from Tabaré Vázquez, the candidate of a leftist coalition. These new electoral rules were seen as a herald of further change to come, but as Uruguayans remind outsiders, change occurs only gradually in this nation of 3.2 million.

The 1999 elections also showed that Uruguay is much less "risk-prone" than it was even a few years ago. Juan Linz and Alfred Stepan argued in 1996 that Uruguay, though a consolidated democracy, remained risk-prone for a variety of reasons, including economic stagnation and an electoral system that combined with party fragmentation and presidentialism to create "legislative impasse and short-lived policy coalitions."[1] Fortunately, however, the constitutional reforms that were approved in late 1996 and inaugurated with the 1999 elections have removed a substantial amount of this risk, both by making the electoral process more straightforward and by providing incentives for the Left to move to the center. Indeed, even if the Left had won this election, it is highly unlikely that democracy would have been threatened. Thus Uruguay remains quite exceptional, in political terms, in Latin America: It is a consolidated and robust democracy in a region prone to instability.

The "Switzerland of Latin America"

Before its authoritarian interlude from 1973 to 1985, Uruguay was perhaps the most stable democracy in Latin America. After a turbulent nineteenth century, a military truce was concluded at the beginning of the twentieth century between the two main political parties, the Partido Colorado and the Partido Nacional (also known as the Blanco party).[2] Soon thereafter, Uruguay developed a welfare state—the first in Latin America—under the leadership of Colorado politician José Batlle y Ordóñez (a great-uncle of the winner of the 1999 election) that led to the country being dubbed the "Switzerland of Latin America." As Charles Guy Gillespie notes, however, this label was not really fitting: "With respect to the rights accorded women, labor, and other groups, as well as the provision of welfare benefits and state intervention in the process of economic growth, Uruguay was far ahead of [Switzerland]."[3] Uruguay's income distribution was remarkably equal in the Latin American context, and political democracy was entrenched early in the century. Apart from a brief period of authoritarian rule in the 1930s, Uruguay seemed to have a democratic vocation; it is still the Latin American country that has lived longest under democratic regimes.[4]

Uruguayan democracy was buttressed by strong parties. Both the Colorado and Blanco parties were formed in the mid-nineteenth century, and each has distinct characteristics. The Colorados are generally more urban, anticlerical, and progressive, whereas the Blancos are more rural and traditional. The Colorados have dominated politics since independence, ruling uninterruptedly for the first half of the twentieth century, losing control (for two terms) to the Blancos only in the 1958 elections.

By the time the Blancos assumed power, however, there was a growing crisis in the Uruguayan economy. The Colorado Party's welfare state rested on an import-substitution industrialization strategy that was quickly exhausted, given Uruguay's small domestic market. Growth began to stagnate in the 1950s; by the 1960s, there was increasing political conflict, reflecting both ailing economy and the general political ferment in Latin America after the Cuban revolution.

This growing political and economic crisis in Uruguay was accompanied by the rise of the political Left. Although various leftist parties were formed early in the twentieth century, it was only in the 1960s that the Left became a more important player in politics. The Left was represented both by legal political parties and (from the mid-1960s on) by an urban guerrilla movement, the Tupamaros. By the late 1960s, the Tupamaros were staging increasingly bold and popular strikes on targets of the traditional political establishment, in turn provoking increased military repression. The ensuing spiral of political violence ended only after the task of defeating the guerrillas was put in the hands of the military (it had been in the hands of the police until 1971). By the end of 1972, the Tupamaros were defeated militarily.

Amidst this increasing political violence from both left and right, Uruguay continued to hold elections, though it was no longer just the two traditional political parties who had strong popular support. At the beginning of the 1970s, the Left became a significant electoral force with the founding of the Frente Amplio (Broad Front, or FA) under the leadership of retired general Liber Seregni. The FA garnered just over 18 percent of the national vote in the 1971 elections, and for the first time the traditional parties saw their combined portion of the vote drop below 90 percent.

This was also the last election that Uruguay would hold for 13 years. In one of Uruguay's political ironies, it was only *after* the Tupamaros had been defeated that the military decided to carry out a coup in June 1973.[5] There was some initial confusion as to the direction the coup would take,[6] but it quickly became obvious that the military were there to stay, even though they did not overthrow the president in office at the time, Juan María Bordaberry. Although Bordaberry remained the nominal head of the executive branch until he was forced out by the military in 1976, for all intents and purposes the military had been calling the shots ever since they dissolved Congress in June 1973.

Nonetheless, the military did feel some need to legitimate their rule, and they held a plebiscite on a new constitution in 1980, confident that they would win. Unlike Pinochet in Chile that same year, however, the Uruguayan generals lost. Thus began a transition to democracy that was consummated in 1984 with the so-called Naval Club Pact, which led to new elections (with some politicians, including Seregni, Blanco Party leader Wilson Ferreira, and Colorado politician Jorge Batlle, prohibited from participating) and the return to civilian rule.

Electoral Systems, Old and New

When democracy was reestablished, Uruguay returned to the electoral system that had been in force before the coup, which was, to say the least, unique. The most remarkable aspect of this system, referred to as the Double Simultaneous Vote (DSV) system, was that individual political parties were permitted to run multiple presidential candidates in the general election. The individual candidate who received the largest number of votes *in the party that received more votes than any other party* was declared the winner of the presidential election. Thus in 1971, for example, Colorado candidate Bordaberry, with only 22.8 percent of the vote, defeated Blanco candidate Wilson Ferreira, who received 26.4 percent, because the Colorados as a whole outpolled the Blancos by 41 to 40.2 percent.

In effect, this system combined the primary and the general elections. It also meant, however, that voters could inadvertently contribute, through their vote for a rival candidate in the same party, to the election of a candidate that they would never have voted for directly. An obvious consequence of this system was that there was a great deal of ideological heterogeneity within the traditional political parties, since there was no incentive for them to define a particular profile.

This system worked relatively efficiently while Uruguay was still basically a two-party system, but it began to break down as the Left gathered strength, particularly after the return to civilian rule in 1984. The emergence of a three-party system meant that the winner of any particular presidential election would have a relatively small percentage of the total vote. For example, the winning candidate won only 28.3 percent of the vote in 1984 (Julio María Sanguinetti of the Colorado Party), 22.5 percent in 1989 (Luis Alberto Lacalle of the Blanco Party), and 24.5 percent in 1994 (once again, Julio María Sanguinetti).[7] These relatively thin mandates called into question the legitimacy of the eventual presidential winner.

Parliamentary elections—always held on the same day as the presidential contest—were also extraordinarily complicated under the old electoral rules. Voters had to cast a ballot for the same party in both the presidential and legislative contests, and legislative seats were allocated on the basis of strict proportional representation (PR). The legislative elections employed a DSV system as well, with each party presenting multiple (closed) lists, both for the Senate and the Chamber of Deputies. Voters simultaneously selected a party and the list of one of the party factions when voting, and each faction received seats in accordance with its share of the vote in the party. Thus, for example, if the Blanco Party, based on its share of the vote, was entitled to 30 seats in the Chamber of Deputies, and its Herrerista faction had received 40 percent of the Blanco vote, then the Herreristas would be entitled to 12 seats in the Chamber. The other 18 seats would go to other factions in the Blanco Party.

Compared to the number of lists for the Chamber of Deputies, the number of Senate lists was small, since the Senate was (and still is) elected on the basis of a single national constituency. For the Chamber of Deputies, the constituencies are the 19 individual departments, so each party had (and still has) multiple lists in each department. In addition, different lists could enter into electoral alliances with one another, accumulating votes among them. For example, if it took 20,000 votes to reach the threshold for representation in the Chamber of Deputies, three different lists that managed to get 7,000 votes each could combine to obtain a seat in the Chamber. The leaders of these lists would come to an agreement before the election regarding who would fill the seat, offering deals ranging from the resignation of the initial officeholder midway through the term in favor of one of the other lists to specific agreements on distribution of state-sector jobs.

Needless to say, this system produced immense fragmentation. In 1994, for example, in an electorate of just over two million voters, the three main parties had 641 lists nationwide for the Chamber of Deputies and 79 different lists in Montevideo alone.[8] Most analysts saw the system as enormously complex and confusing for voters, and the proliferation of lists reinforced clientelistic practices, particularly outside Montevideo.

Despite these problems, however, until 1994 most politicians in the traditional parties were satisfied with the status quo. As Juan J. Linz and Alfred Stepan pointed out, "The only groups that can change this system are the Parliament and the party leaders, yet it is precisely these groups that have been the 'winners' with the system."[9] The system, they argued, could be changed only if there was a perception of crisis, and indeed, such a perception of crisis followed the 1994 elections. These elections had almost been won by the Left, alarming traditional party leaders, who feared not so much that the system was not working but rather that it might in fact work to the detriment of the traditional parties. This led Colorado and Blanco party leaders to propose a constitutional reform to head off a victory by the Left in 1999.

The reform, approved by a narrow margin in a December 1996 referendum, made five basic changes to the electoral system: 1) In April of each presidential election year, parties would have primaries on the same day to select a single presidential candidate for each party. 2) These presidential candidates would then face one another in a first round of voting in October of that year. (Parliamentary elections would be held on the same day as the first round of presidential elections.) 3) If no candidate won an absolute majority in that election, the top two finishers would face each other in a runoff the following month. 4) Municipal elections, which had traditionally been held on the same date as the national elections, would be held in May of the year following the presidential election. 5) In parliamentary elections, the DSV was preserved, but parties could no longer accumulate votes among different lists.[10] Parties could still run multiple lists for legislative posts, but the different lists could no longer give their votes to other lists. This last change had the effect of reducing the total number of lists for the Chamber of Deputies in the 1999 election to 425 nationally, and 33 in Montevideo.[11]

These constitutional changes proved quite contentious for a number of reasons. First, the traditional parties had become accustomed to manipulating the complex electoral system to downplay their internal divisions; under the new system, these divisions would have sharper electoral consequences. Second, the Left viewed the changes as a way to keep it from winning the presidency, since it was clear that it was gaining on the traditional parties. There was a widespread assumption that the Left would probably gain a plurality of the vote in a single-round election in 1999 and that introducing a second round would allow the traditional parties to unite against it in the runoff. Nevertheless, some on the Left supported the reform, since many of the changes—like requiring each party to choose a single presidential candidate—might work to the Left's advantage. In addition, requiring that the eventual president win a runoff election would provide the winner with greater popular legitimacy, which is especially important when the president's party is unlikely to have an absolute majority in parliament. Finally, separating municipal from national elections meant that parties would have to compete with one another at the local level shortly after the national elections, which could make electoral alliances more difficult to forge.

The 1999 Campaign

Because of the changes outlined above, political parties faced a new and untested environment in 1999, and they did not necessarily know how to confront it. In addition, the new electoral rules came into play at a moment when the electorate seemed neatly divided into thirds among the three main parties. The 1994 election had been extremely tight; the Table on page 161 shows the evolution of the vote for the main parties since the 1971 election and indicates the general parity among the three main political forces. Because of Uruguay's strict PR system—and the fact that voters had to cast a party-line vote for Congress and the president—parliamentary representation closely tracked the presidential vote. This parity increased uncertainty, since no party could count on making it to the second round in November.

The new electoral system challenged the traditional parties and the Left in different ways. For the traditional parties, the main difficulty was that for the first time they would now have to present a single candidate in the presidential election. Presenting multiple presidential candidates had allowed them to play down internal party divisions, and the general election had sorted out which particular force within each party was strongest.

This new set of rules hurt the Blanco party most of all. It went through a particularly bloody primary campaign that culminated in the selection of former president Luis Alberto Lacalle (1990–95) as its standard bearer. During the primary campaign, Lacalle's chief opponent, Juan Andrés Ramírez, accused him of corruption during his period in office. After Ramírez lost the primary, he disappeared from politics until just before the first round of the presidential election, sending a signal to other Blanco voters that he did not regard the presidential candidate they had nominated as worthy of their support. Under the previous rules, this problem would not have arisen: There would have been no primary, and both Lacalle and Ramírez would have focused on getting out their own voters for the general election. In the end, this defection proved disastrous for the Blancos.

The Colorados dealt with the new circumstances much more effectively, as the two main challengers in the primary decided to unite behind the winner, Jorge Batlle, who was now running in his fifth presidential campaign. Batlle's vice-presidential running mate was Luis Hierro, who represented the wing of the Colorado party led by outgoing president Julio María Sanguinetti (who was constitutionally prohibited from running for reelection).

The problem for the Left was different. The FA had presented a single presidential ticket ever since its founding in 1971, so this was not a novelty. Yet the fact that the constitution now called for a primary election meant that internal fissures within the party could come to the surface. Senator Danilo Astori decided to challenge the front-runner, former Montevideo mayor Tabaré Vázquez, who had been the presidential candidate of the renamed Encuentro Progresista–Frente Amplio (EP-FA) in the 1994 elections. Though Astori was soundly defeated in the primary, receiving less than 20 percent of the vote, the mere fact of his challenge (and the lingering dispute between "radicals" and "moderates") gave the traditional parties ammunition to use in the general election campaign.

After the candidates were chosen, the parties settled on their general election strategies. The incumbent Colorados mostly kept silent about what they would do; they represented *continuismo*, that is, a continuation of the relatively conservative economic policies of the past decade, which were attacked as "neoliberal" by Colorado opponents. The Blancos, who had been junior partners in the Colorado-led governing coalition for the last five years and had held several cabinet posts, attempted to distance themselves from the government, largely because of the economic recession that Uruguay was suffering during 1999. In the first nine months of the year, GDP declined by 2.5 percent. Industry was hit particularly hard, and unemployment (in the August–October period) increased from 10 percent in 1998 to 11.6 percent in 1999. This recession was largely due to the economic turmoil and the devaluation

TABLE—URUGUAYAN ELECTION RESULTS, 1979–99*

PARTY	1971	1984	1989	1994	1999†
Colorado Party	40.9	41.2	30.3	32.5	32.8
Blanco Party	40.2	35.0	38.9	31.4	22.3
Frente Amplio	18.3	21.3	21.2	30.8	40.1

* Totals given in percentages.
† First-round results, which determined parliamentary representation.

in Brazil, Uruguay's largest market. Finally, the EP-FA adopted an "it's the economy, stupid" strategy. Its advertisements and rhetoric emphasized the economic crisis, and essentially asked: "Do you want five more years of the same old policies? If you don't, vote for the EP-FA."

The first round of elections took place on October 31. As all the opinion polls had indicated, the EP-FA came in first, with 40.1 percent of the valid votes cast.[12] The Colorados followed with 32.8 percent, and the Blancos turned in a disastrous performance, their worst in the twentieth century, finishing with only 22.3 percent. Nuevo Espacio (New Space), a small social-democratic party, received 4.6 percent, and the Unión Cívica got the remaining 0.2 percent.

The EP-FA's vote totals exceeded expectations, but the Colorados beat polling estimates as well. The biggest losers in the election were the Blancos, who saw their party torn apart by the nasty primary battle and are arguably the most difficult party to pin down ideologically. While the EP-FA clearly occupies the left and center-left, and the Colorado Party, the right and center-right, the Blancos are much more dispersed along the ideological spectrum. When it held the presidency in 1990–95, the party generally carried out a conservative economic policy, but it is not united behind such an ideology. It has not only rural but also nationalist roots, and it is not easily pigeon-holed. Important figures in its past could appropriately be described as "progressive nationalists," notably the late Wilson Ferreira, who was one of the most forceful opponents of military rule and was consequently barred from the 1984 presidential election by the military. The new constitutional rules imposing a single presidential candidate made the Blanco party's life more difficult, and some of its votes drained off to the Colorado party (particularly in Montevideo) and to the EP-FA (particularly in the provinces, though to some extent in the capital as well).

One of the major effects of the constitutional reform was to move the EP-FA towards the center, since to win, it could no longer rely on its core supporters. Even before the first round, the EP-FA was moving toward the center, attempting to demonstrate moderation by promising to pay the foreign debt and not to devalue the currency and by making unmistakable noises about the need to govern in a coalition. Moving toward the center was not an easy task, given the splits within the party and some of its previously stated positions.

Indeed, in both the first and second rounds of the election the traditional parties kept pointing to these previous positions, which proved to be the Left's Achilles' heel. The traditional parties emphasized contradictory statements on the part of the Left, and accused it of harboring "intolerant," "Marxist," and "undemocratic" tendencies. Batlle, for example, charged that the EP-FA was trying "to disguise the philosophy behind its economic program," asking rhetorically: "Have they changed? Have they changed because they understood that their ideas were wrong? . . . As far as I'm concerned, they haven't changed."[13] While it was true that the Left suffered from some internal inconsistencies with respect to its economic plan, there was little reason to question its commitment to democracy. Although during the 1960s the leftist Tupamaro guerrillas had denounced "formal" democracy and had taken up arms against it, the Left had also suffered the most from the military dictatorship from 1973 to 1985, and it had joined with the Colorado party in 1984 to ensure a stable transition to democracy.[14] Nevertheless, these charges were an effective campaign tactic, and a certain Cold War rhetoric permeated the campaign.

The Second Round

As the second electoral round unfolded, the traditional parties, as expected, joined forces to prevent an EP-FA victory. Shortly after the first round was over, the Blancos announced that they were "convoking" their voters to vote for the Colorado candidate, Batlle. The Nuevo Espacio left its voters "free" to choose whichever candidate they preferred, but leading party figures (including presidential candidate Rafael Michelini) said that they would vote for Vázquez. After the first round, some observers claimed that Uruguay was on the verge of a new two-party system, though it is too early to arrive at such a conclusion. Clearly, however, the electoral map had changed.

One of the oddities of the second-round campaign was that, unlike in the first round, political campaigning was largely carried out via television and radio; there were few large political rallies, although these had long been a staple of Uruguayan politics. On the part of the Left, this appears to have been the result of a strategy of avoiding "incidents" that could be used to paint them as "intolerant" or "violent." Batlle's campaign, on the other hand, feared that it would be quite difficult to hold political rallies that would join the forces of the Colorados and Blancos, given their historical rivalry. The Batlle campaign played down the candidate's party affiliation, calling for a "unity" campaign that would bring the country together. Both candidates campaigned heavily in the provinces, where the majority of undecided voters lived (only 18 percent of voters in Montevideo had voted for a candidate other than the two finalists, while in the interior 32 percent had done so), and spent their time giving local press conferences and meeting with local political leaders.

The EP-FA's goal was to gain the support of local Blanco leaders who were unhappy with the general trend of their party. EP-FA strategists hoped to exploit three weaknesses. First, they thought that many Blanco voters would find it difficult to support Batlle, a traditional rival. Second, they knew that some Blanco leaders were unhappy with the conservative economic policy advocated by the national party leadership. (The Lacalle government had carried out orthodox economic policies during its time in power in the first half of the 1990s, undercutting those Blancos who preferred a more redistributionist economic policy.) Finally, the EP-FA hoped to exploit the fact that Blancos might find it difficult to vote for the Colorados, whom they would be opposing six months later, and the EP-FA held out the possibility of electoral alliances with "progressive" Blanco leaders in these elections.

In the end, however, these efforts reaped few dividends; the second round, instead of focusing on Uruguay's current economic performance (which would have benefited the opposition), focused on tax policy. The Colorados took the offensive, accusing the EP-FA of intending to raise taxes, largely because of the EP-FA's platform plank calling for a broad-based income tax. Although the EP-FA claimed that this new tax would replace or reduce other taxes (a more narrow "salary tax" and a high—14 to 23 percent—value-added tax), the Colorado attack was effective, and the EP-FA was forced onto the defensive.

In response, the EP-FA accused the Colorados of having no policy to deal with the economic crisis and suggested, in the last few days of the campaign, that the Colorado economic program concealed a "fiscal shock" that would result in increased taxes. EP-FA spokesmen argued that the policies that the Colorados had agreed to adopt as part of their agreement with the Blancos would lead to substantially higher state spending and thus created a need for higher taxes as well. The Colorados denied this, of course, and the EP-FA attack had little effect on undecided voters.

Indeed, it appears that the Left erred in being too specific about its proposed policies, and the Colorados were able to take advantage of this. The subtleties of tax policy do not come across well in a sound-bite election campaign, and it did not help that the Left sent contradictory signals on the exact content of its proposed tax reform. Its general message—a tax reform that would not increase taxes but would make the wealthier pay more—was lost in discussions of technical details that only confused the electorate, particularly the undecided voters who would determine the outcome. The Colorados were quite aware that many of these undecided voters were less educated, identified themselves as being on the center or right politically, and were likely to be susceptible to appeals meant to convince them that their taxes would increase if the EP-FA came to power.[15]

Batlle's platform, unlike that of his opponents, was usefully vague. The general message was "No new taxes." Batlle also devoted a large portion of his speeches and television appearances to discussing the need to keep up with technological changes in the world economy, to increase Uruguay's exports, and to decrease foreign trade barriers in the upcoming World Trade Organization negotiations. These positions were not at all controversial, and Battle's strategy was to stay on this message. By and large, he was quite successful.

The dynamics of the second round were profoundly different from those of the first. In the first round, with competition not only among multiple parties but (given Uruguay's electoral system) among factions within parties, there was a great deal of electoral "noise," as the various factions within each party focused on increasing their share of the vote. As a consequence, there was little need to focus on policy proposals. The second round, on the other hand, made this necessary, and the Colorados were much better prepared for a one-on-one confrontation. Interestingly, however, there was never a debate between the two candidates, despite attempts to schedule one. The Colorados saw their media strategy working quite well without one, and decided not to risk it.

The Colorados won the second round handily, 54 percent to 46 percent. This was a somewhat surprising result, since most of the pre-election polls had shown the candidates as more evenly matched, with the most lopsided poll showing Batlle leading Vázquez 47 to 44 percent. Most of the polls placed the candidates in a statistical dead heat, though there was a discernible trend in favor of Batlle in the waning moments of the campaign. After the election, however, it became clear that most of the voters who had declared themselves undecided or unwilling to answer were in fact planning to vote in favor of Batlle, as the pollsters pointed out after the results were in.[16] This was not surprising, given that most of these voters were Blanco supporters intending to vote for their historical rivals the Colorados—something they might not be willing to admit to pollsters.

It is also evident that one reason why the EP-FA did not substantially boost its vote in the second round (it increased its total by just a bit over 100,000 votes, or less than 5 percent of the total) was that it had already "cannibalized" a great deal of support from the Blancos in the first round. In other words, many of the Blanco voters likely to consider voting for the Left had already done so in October. Conservative Blanco voters were almost certain to vote for Batlle, especially after the their national leadership decided to support his candidacy officially.

It thus became clear that party discipline and loyalty still matter in Uruguay, much more than they do in most other Latin American countries. The Blanco leadership told their voters to vote for Batlle, and it appears that at least 80 percent of them did.[17] There had been talk of a possible "rebellion" on the part of Blanco voters leading them to refuse to vote for Colorados,[18] but by and large, these voters toed the line. If the party leadership had not recommended that they vote for the Colorado candidate, some Blancos might have cast blank ballots, thus helping the Vázquez candidacy. In the end, however, fewer than 2 percent of voters cast blank ballots.

A Strong Commitment to Democracy

Despite the Right's warnings that a triumph by the Left would lead Uruguay down the Cuban road, democracy is quite safe in Uruguay. The country continues to demonstrate the highest level of commitment to democratic institutions in Latin America: Eighty-six percent of its citizens favor democracy over any other system (in other Latin American countries, this ranges from 75 percent in Argentina to 41 percent in Ecuador), and 64 percent of its citizens are satisfied with democracy (elsewhere in the region, this figure ranges from 45 percent in Mexico to 16 percent in Paraguay).[19] There is no sign that this support is declining.

The commitment of Uruguayans to democracy is demonstrated by the solid identification of most voters of all political persuasions with political parties. Voters show an almost fetishistic addiction to polls and electoral speculations. Indeed, it is hard to find a Uruguayan who is not interested in talking about politics at election time. Most will give a rather sophisticated rendering of the possible outcomes and the strength of different factions within each political party, and they will be able to recite the number of votes that are needed to capture a seat in the Chamber of Deputies.

Furthermore, the 1999 elections show that Uruguay's institutional reforms have made it less "risk-prone" in three ways. First, the introduction of a second round in the presidential vote has forced the Left to move toward the center. It is true, of course, that, in order to govern, the Left would have had to move toward the center anyway, even under the old system. International factors and practical considerations would have imposed moderation in any case. The new system, however, has forced the Left to emphasize its moderation as a necessary part of its electoral strategy. This has made the Left appear less threatening, which, in turn, has increased its popular support.

Second, by reducing the number of parliamentary lists, the new electoral rules have created an incentive for parties—particularly the two major parties—to unify. It is no longer possible for factions to survive politically with support from a tiny slice of the electorate, as it was when different lists could combine their votes to achieve parliamentary representation. Factionalism has not been eliminated, of course, but it has been reduced.

Finally, the institutional reforms will make governance easier, since the new electoral rules require coalitions for *electoral* success. In the past, the Colorado and Blanco parties have collaborated to a greater or lesser degree in government, but often this has been an unsteady alliance. With the new electoral rules, the two traditional parties will work together more closely. An important psychological barrier to their cooperation has fallen, with Blanco voters for the first time having crossed party lines to vote for a Colorado candidate in the second round. As all three major parties learn from their experience with the new electoral rules, Uruguay is likely to see its three-party system take on many characteristics of a two-party system as it divides into two major blocs. This promises to provide greater stability and more coherent governance under the leadership of *either* the Left or the Right.

NOTES

I would like to thank Eric Davis, Marcelo Pereira, and Marcelo Rossal for their helpful comments on an earlier draft of this article.

1. Juan J. Linz and Alfred Stepan, *Problems of Democratic Transition and Consolidation: Southern Europe, South America, and Post-Communist Europe* (Baltimore: Johns Hopkins University Press, 1996), 164.

2. See Gerardo Caetano and José Rilla, *Historia Contemporánea del Uruguay: De la Colonia al Mercosur* (Montevideo: Editorial Fin de Siglo, 1994), ch. 4.

3. Charles Guy Gillespie, *Negotiating Democracy: Politicians and Generals in Uruguay* (Cambridge: Cambridge University Press, 1991), 19.

4. Luis Eduardo González, *Political Structures and Democracy in Uruguay* (Notre Dame: University of Notre Dame Press, 1991), 4.

5. See Luis Costa Bonino, *La Crisis del Sistema Político Uruguayo: Partidos Políticos y Democracia Hasta 1973* (Montevideo: Fundación de Cultura Universitaria, 1995), 241–60.

6. See Charles Guy Gillespie, *Negotiating Democracy,* 42–45.

7. Gerardo Caetano and José Rilla, *Historia Contemporánea del Uruguay,* 335–36 and "Así Fueron las Elecciones en 1994," *La República* (Montevideo), 1 November 1999, 11.

8. Felipe Monestier, "Partidos Por Dentro: La Fraccionalización de los Partidos Políticos en el Uruguay (1954–1994)," in Luis Eduardo González, Felipe Monestier, Rosaria Quierolo, and Mariana Sotelo Rico, eds., *Los Partidos Políticos Uruguayos en Tiempos de Cambio* (Montevideo: Fundación de Cultura Universitaria, 1999), 58.

9. Juan J. Linz and Alfred Stepan, *Problems of Democratic Transition and Consolidation,* 164.

10. See Marcelo Pereira, "El Proyecto, sus Pros y sus Contras," *Brecha* (Montevideo), 5 December 1996: 2–3; Ruben Correa Freitas and Cristina Vázquez, *La Reforma Constitucional de 1997: Analisis Constitucional y Administrativo* (Montevideo: Fundación de Cultura Universitaria, 1997); and Miguel Semino, "Panorama del Nuevo Sistema Electoral," in Carlos Mata Prates, ed., *Reflexiones Sobre la Reforma Constitucional de 1996* (Montevideo: Fundación de Cultura Universitaria, 1998).

11. "En todo el país habrá 425 listas," *El Observador* (Montevideo), 5 October 1999, 5.

12. The percentages reported do not include blank and voided ballots, which made up around 2 percent of all votes cast.

13. "Batlle opinó que si Vázquez gana no sólo habrá 'devaluación de la moneda sino también una devaluación de la democracia,'" *Búsqueda* (Montevideo), 7 October 1999, 7.

14. The Tupamaros also became part of the Frente Amplio coalition in 1989. See Charles Guy Gillespie, *Negotiating Democracy*, for an extended discussion of the role of the Left in the transition.

15. Only 35 percent of undecided voters had completed secondary school, compared with 45 percent nationwide. Ideologically, 86 percent of these undecided voters identified themselves as part of the Center or Right, compared with 62 percent nationally. These poll results were reported in "Batlle y Vázquez llegan iguales, aunque el Colorado es favorito," *El Observador* (Montevideo), 25 November 1999, 8–9.

16. "Encuestadores con actitud conservadora," *El Observador* (Montevideo), 30 November 1999, 8.

17. If we assume (conservatively) that half of the Nuevo Espacio voters voted for Batlle in the second round (almost certainly, fewer than half did), then Batlle would have needed more than 80 percent of the Blanco votes to reach his vote total.

18. See Nelson Cesin, "Arriba, arriba, presidente la . . . Batlle," *Brecha* (Montevideo): 12 November 1999, 2–3.

19. These Latinobarómetro poll results from 1996 are reported in Agustín Canzani, "La Década del desencanto," *El Observador* (Montevideo), 20 November 1999.

15

DEVALUING THE VOTE IN LATIN AMERICA

Richard Snyder and David Samuels

Richard Snyder is associate professor of political science at Brown University. He is the author of Politics after Neoliberalism *(2001) and coauthor with Gerardo L. Munck of* Passion, Craft and Method in Comparative Politics *(2006).* David Samuels, *Benjamin E. Lippincott Associate Professor of political science at the University of Minnesota, specializes in Latin American politics and the comparative study of political institutions, with particular emphasis on Brazilian politics, electoral systems, political parties, legislatures, and federalism. This essay originally appeared in the January 2001 issue of the* Journal of Democracy.

Although the exact definition of democracy is vigorously disputed, wide agreement exists that *free and fair elections* are the cornerstone of any democratic system of government. An indispensable characteristic of free and fair elections is that each citizen's vote counts equally. This notion of fairness is embodied in the well-known principle of "one person, one vote" that theorists such as Robert Dahl consider to be an essential ingredient of democracy.[1]

Democratic rule now prevails across Latin America, and most Latin American countries embrace the principle of "one person, one vote" through constitutional provisions that explicitly guarantee the equality of each citizen's vote. Nevertheless, in practice, these same countries often fall far short of achieving such equality. In the lower chambers of their national legislatures, many Latin American countries have extraordinarily high levels of malapportionment—a wide discrepancy between the share of legislative seats and the share of population held by electoral districts. A malapportioned chamber means that the votes of some citizens weigh far more heavily than those of others. Although a longstanding federalist tradition acknowledges the value of having a bicameral legislature with an *upper* chamber that represents territorial units equally, a situation that usually requires a significant degree of malapportionment, there is a broad consensus that at least one chamber should weigh the votes of citizens equally. Thus there is no normative justification for malapportionment in the lower chamber.

Apart from these important normative issues, lower-chamber malapportionment has troubling practical consequences for democracy in Latin America. High levels of lower-chamber malapportionment have contributed to a syndrome characterized by four interrelated elements: 1) a distinct rural and conservative bias in legislatures; 2) a tendency toward estrangement between the executive and legislative branches; 3) a growing capacity for subnational political actors to hold national governments hostage on important policy issues; and 4) the proliferation of subnational authoritarian enclaves. Moreover, in countries with high levels of lower-chamber malapportionment, a malapportioned upper chamber can greatly exacerbate these same problems. Malapportionment thus poses a serious, yet hitherto neglected, challenge to the quality and fairness of democracy in many Latin American countries.

Free and Unfair Elections

The Table on the following page shows the degree of malapportionment in 19 Latin American countries in 1999.[2] The entries indicate the percentage of seats in the legislature that are not apportioned according to the principle of "one person, one vote." Thus a score of 0.00 would indicate a perfectly apportioned chamber in which no citizen's vote weighs more than another's. By contrast, a score of 1.00 would indicate a fully malapportioned chamber in which all of the legislative seats are allocated to a single electoral district with just one voter. And a score of 0.50 would mean that 50 percent of the seats are allocated to districts that would not receive those seats if there were no malapportionment.

The Table shows that the overall level of malapportionment for lower and upper chambers in Latin America is significantly higher than in the rest of the world. Indeed, Latin America has some of the world's most malapportioned legislative chambers. For example, Argentina's Senate has a score of 0.49, making it the world's most malapportioned legislative chamber. Ecuador's lower chamber has a score of 0.20, making it the third most malapportioned lower chamber in the world. Although the Table shows that malapportionment is not a problem everywhere in Latin America, a number of prominent countries—Argentina, Bolivia, Brazil, Chile, Colombia, and Ecuador—do have extremely high levels of lower-chamber malapportionment. These countries together account for almost two-thirds of the population of Latin America, underlining how important a focus on malapportionment is for understanding the problems of democracy in the region.

Most legislatures have some malapportionment, especially in the upper chamber (where one exists).[3] Moreover, countries typically expe-

TABLE—MALAPPORTIONMENT IN LATIN AMERICA, 1999

COUNTRY	LOWER CHAMBER	UPPER CHAMBER
Argentina*	0.14	0.49
Belize	0.08	–
Bolivia	0.17	0.38
Brazil*	0.09	0.40
Chile	0.15	0.31
Colombia	0.13	0.00
Costa Rica	0.02	–
Dominican Republic	0.08	0.38
Ecuador	0.20	–
El Salvador	0.07	–
Guatemala	0.06	–
Honduras	0.04	–
Mexico*	0.06	0.23
Nicaragua	0.06	–
Panama	0.06	–
Paraguay	0.04	0.00
Peru	0.00	–
Uruguay	0.03	0.00
Venezuela*	0.07	0.33
Latin America Average	**0.08**	**0.25**
Average for Advanced Industrial Democracies	**0.04**	**0.18**
World Average Without Latin America	**0.06**	**0.18**
United States*	**0.01**	**0.36**

* Countries with federal systems
Note: A score of 0.00 would indicate perfect apportionment; a score of 1.00 would indicate perfect malapportionment.
Source: David Samuels and Richard Snyder, "The Value of a Vote: Malapportionment in Comparative Perspective," *British Journal of Political Science* 31 (October 2001): 627–49.

rience rising levels of "natural" malapportionment over time because of demographic changes across electoral districts. Nevertheless, many countries—especially the advanced industrial democracies of Western Europe and North America—have achieved low levels of malapportionment in one or both legislative chambers. Low levels of malapportionment in these cases reflect the implementation of procedures for periodic reapportionment. By contrast, the far higher levels of malapportionment characterizing both upper *and* lower chambers in many Latin American countries indicate that they have not implemented such corrective procedures as part of their transitions to democracy.

A Formal Flaw

Given the return to formal democracy in Latin America over the last two decades, much of the debate about the shortcomings of democracy in the region has focused on informal rules and practices. For example, Guillermo O'Donnell calls attention to "brown areas," where the rule of law is extremely attenuated because of a loose fit between formal rules and actual practices. Similarly, Jonathan Fox argues that "semi-clientelist" politics (especially at the local level) are an important obstacle to full-fledged democracy in Latin America.[4]

These informal defects are clearly important. Yet the problems of contemporary Latin American democracies are by no means limited to the informal realm. Formal institutions can also diminish the quality of democracy. A focus on malapportionment highlights how formalized, detailed, and explicit electoral rules in many countries have resulted in large inequalities in the weighting of citizens' votes. Consequently, the limitations of many contemporary Latin American democracies go well beyond the problem that "the games played 'inside' the democratic institutions are different from the ones dictated by their formal rules."[5] Where formal electoral rules lead to unfair electoral results, even games that do abide by the rules may be undemocratic.

Malapportionment should be regarded as a formal institutional flaw that significantly weakens the quality of democracy in many countries in the region,[6] yet it has attracted surprisingly little attention among scholars, politicians, or engaged citizens. In Chile, for example, the current method for electing members to the Chamber of Deputies has been the focus of much analysis and debate because it was designed by General Augusto Pinochet to favor the second-place finisher (typically, the conservative parties' list), but the extreme malapportionment in the system, which is biased against the country's metropolitan region, has attracted little notice. And in Brazil, where the issue of malapportionment has drawn some scholarly attention, a major recent report about proposed political reforms prepared with encouragement from the Cardoso administration contained "not one word about decreasing the malapportionment of the Senate."[7]

This lack of attention highlights an important characteristic of malapportionment: It is often hidden from public view. In contrast to traditional "low-tech" methods for rigging elections, such as vote-buying, ballot-stuffing, and techniques for tampering with the actual counting of votes, which are easier for election monitors and opposition parties to detect, malapportionment has not been perceived as a proximate cause of unfair elections. Because the mechanisms for apportioning legislative seats are often arcane mathematical functions, they do not provide the kind of vivid material that easily lends itself to front-page news or to use as a lightning rod for mobilizing mass indignation. By contrast, lurid charges of ballot-stuffing and vote-buying are far more attractive issues for opposition parties, election losers, and international election monitors. The virtual absence of political debate about malapportionment even in countries where it is most egregious, such as

Argentina, Chile, Ecuador, Bolivia, and Brazil, underscores the hidden nature of this problem.

Although malapportionment has attracted little public attention, it can give some groups important strategic advantages in political competition. Politicians across the world have long recognized this, and they have honed well-known techniques for manipulating how electoral systems are apportioned, including gerrymandering and the preservation of "rotten boroughs." As is the case elsewhere, the use of such blatant methods of manipulating apportionment seems increasingly unlikely in contemporary Latin America. Yet this does not mean that apportionment decisions have been depoliticized, nor does it mean that apportionment procedures are fully democratic.

In contemporary Latin America, unlike in the advanced industrial democracies, high levels of malapportionment readily coexist with the core package of democratic rules and institutions—freedom of association, assembly, and speech; universal suffrage; absence of massive fraud; and contested elections.[8] In a malapportioned system, all citizens can enjoy a free and equal opportunity to formulate and signify their preferences, but they are denied the opportunity to have their preferences weighed equally.[9] Consequently, even genuinely competitive elections held in systems with universal suffrage and where basic civil and political freedoms are effectively guaranteed *may nevertheless be unfair*. This apparent compatibility between malapportionment and the core elements of democratic politics can help sustain an illusion of robust democracy in contexts where the votes of some citizens actually weigh far more than the votes of others.

The Malapportionment Syndrome

The high levels of lower-chamber malapportionment in many Latin American countries have a negative effect on the quality of democracy. Let us now consider in greater detail the four practical consequences of malapportionment noted at the outset of this essay:

1) Rural-conservative bias. Malapportionment has resulted in an overrepresentation of rural interests in both lower and upper chambers of national legislatures in a number of Latin American countries. This rural bias is partially an institutional legacy of efforts by conservative landed elites to undercut the electoral strength of emerging urban classes in the early twentieth century. The military regimes of the 1960s and 1970s, especially in Argentina, Brazil, and Chile, significantly reinforced this rural bias, thereby guaranteeing that it would persist into the contemporary democratic period.[10]

Examples from several countries illustrate how malapportionment fosters a rural bias in legislatures. In Chile, the Santiago and Valparaíso metropolitan areas together encompass 50 percent of the voting population, but they elect only 37 percent of the national Chamber of Deputies. Moreover, the population of Chile's most populous electoral district (Maipu) is five times greater than that of its least populous district (Coihaique), yet both districts get two seats, making one vote in Coihaique worth the same as five votes in Maipu. In Brazil, the six densely populated southern states hold 55 percent of the population but elect only 48 percent of the deputies, and one vote in the country's least populous state (Roraima) has 16 times the weight in electing a deputy of a vote cast in the most populous state (São Paulo). This inequality reaches even greater heights in Ecuador, where the two largest districts (Guayas and Pichincha) hold 45 percent of the population yet command only 23 percent of the seats. One vote in Ecuador's least populous district (Galápagos) has 50 times the weight of a vote cast in the most populous district (Guayas).

This rural bias associated with malapportionment leads to distortions in the ideological balance of national legislatures. In Brazil in 1998, for example, leftist parties captured 26 percent of all votes for federal deputies, but because a large share of those votes was won in underrepresented states, these parties earned only 22 percent of the seats. And in Argentina, overrepresentation of rural provinces has long served to protect the Peronist party and its conservative allies in the lower chamber at the expense of urban interests, including the Peronist party's own urban supporters.[11]

2) Estrangement between the legislative and executive branches. Some scholars praise presidential systems for their ability to combine distinct kinds of representation—the legislature can be "representative of the diversity of the society and polity," while the executive represents the nation as a whole.[12] In the context of highly malapportioned legislatures, however, such combinations can actually lead to paralyzing impasses between the two branches. Because the president's electoral district is essentially the entire nation, presidential candidates have strong incentives to build their electoral coalitions and focus their campaigns in regions with the largest absolute number of voters. Consequently, presidents today seek and gain most of their support from urban constituencies, whereas legislators in malapportioned legislatures are more likely to represent rural interests. This difference in their bases of support can contribute to an estrangement between the executive and legislative branches.

In Brazil, for example, no presidential candidate can hope to win without doing very well in the heavily urban states of São Paulo, Rio de Janeiro, and Minas Gerais, which together have 43 percent of the electorate. Yet because of malapportionment, those three states control only 33 percent of the seats in the Chamber of Deputies. Thus a successful presidential candidate who concentrates his campaign in those states must inevitably cultivate new allies from less populous states in order to construct a viable governing coalition. This is precisely what current president Fernando Henrique Cardoso, who makes his home in São Paulo, has done.

Yet presidents with urban bases of support who face a malapportioned legislature favoring rural regions are not always as successful as Cardoso has been in forging a governing coalition. The distinct geographic support bases for the Brazilian legislative and executive branches led to conflicts that contributed to the collapse of democracy in 1964.[13] A similar process led to the overthrow of President Velasco Ibarra in Ecuador in 1961.[14] These examples suggest that a failure to manage the coalition-building challenges posed by malapportioned legislatures can undermine the stability of democratic regimes.

3) Holding the center hostage. When rural areas are overrepresented in the legislature, a president who wins election with an urban base of support may not be able to govern unless he can build alliances with rural groups. Thus he may face compelling pressures to channel patronage payoffs to rural areas in order to purchase legislative support for his policy proposals.[15] As a result, the president is potentially vulnerable to being held hostage by rural interests.

Moreover, in highly malapportioned systems, an increase in the share of the total population residing in urban areas can ironically *strengthen* the hand of overrepresented rural interests. This is because the amount of pork-barrel funds required to secure electoral support in rural areas should decrease as they acquire relatively smaller populations, thereby making them an attractive source of "cheap" support for coalition-builders at the national level. The pro-rural effects of existing malapportionment, combined with increasing migration from rural to urban areas, have greatly strengthened the influence of rural interests in many Latin American legislatures, even as those societies have become increasingly urbanized.

Edward Gibson and his colleagues have found statistical evidence showing that lower-chamber malapportionment in federal systems tends to distort government spending significantly in ways that favor sparsely populated regions.[16] In countries such as Argentina and Brazil, they argue, the central government strategically directs pork-barrel spending toward overrepresented rural states in order to shore up its majority in the congress. Thus malapportionment has strengthened the capacity of rural interests in these countries to extract fiscal favors from the central government.

4) Proliferation of subnational authoritarian enclaves. Malapportionment also has an important impact on subnational politics in Latin America. In new democracies, overrepresentation of rural districts can contribute to the maintenance—and even the proliferation—of nondemocratic enclaves at the subnational level. Malapportionment can compel democratic elites at the national level to tolerate subnational authoritarian enclaves because these elites rely on overrepresented regions to secure the national legislative majorities they need to achieve their policy goals. Ironically, the ability of leaders at the national level to implement and consolidate democratic reforms in a highly malapportioned system may therefore depend on winning the overvalued support of subnational authoritarian elites. At the same time, overrepresentation of subnational authoritarian enclaves in national legislatures may strengthen the ability of these subnational elites to fend off efforts by external groups seeking to reform local politics. Such a dynamic has been especially apparent in the case of Brazil, where, as Alfred Stepan notes, "Many of the states that are overrepresented in the federal legislature are precisely those states with particularly unequal income distribution and strong traditions of local oligarchic control."[17]

Strategies for Reducing Malapportionment

Is there a cure for the malapportionment syndrome? Can Latin American countries solve the problem of high malapportionment? We address these questions by considering the strengths and limitations of two strategies for reducing malapportionment that have been employed successfully by many countries around the world: 1) judicial oversight of reapportionment and 2) electoral-law reform.

1) Judicial oversight of reapportionment. Courts play a central role in the reapportionment of electoral systems in several countries, most notably the United States. Until the 1960s, the U.S. House of Representatives had significant levels of malapportionment within states, but since a series of Supreme Court decisions in the 1960s mandating that the votes of all citizens should count equally and that electoral districts should, as far as possible, have equal populations, the House has had remarkably low levels of malapportionment.

These Supreme Court rulings, which began in 1962 with *Baker v. Carr,* gave federal and state courts the authority to declare a state's redistricting plan null and void. This judicial review of districting plans dramatically altered the strategic situation facing politicians (state legislators and governors) involved in the reapportionment process. When the courts rejected a state's districting plan, they gave the legislature and the governor a deadline, and if the legislature and governor failed to reach a satisfactory agreement by the deadline, the court imposed its own plan. The threat of losing control of the reapportionment process to the courts gave politicians a powerful incentive to agree to a districting plan that conformed closely to the "one person, one vote" principle. In Germany, the High Court has played a similar oversight role since the early 1960s that has also helped keep lower-chamber malapportionment at low levels.

What are the implications of the U.S. and German cases for Latin American countries? First, it bears emphasizing that the strategy of reducing malapportionment via judicial oversight presupposes that the courts (whether local, state, or national) are insulated from partisan influence. Otherwise, the prospect of judicial review would not necessarily induce politicians to act to avoid the legally defined default outcome (a court-imposed districting plan). If the courts are exposed to political pressures and operate as reliable agents of partisan interests, then judicial oversight of the reapportionment process is unlikely to serve as an effective mechanism for reducing malapportionment. In such a scenario, court-imposed plans, like politically engineered plans, are likely to manipulate apportionment for partisan purposes. Moreover, the effectiveness of the judicial oversight strategy depends on the courts' capacity to make a credible threat either to redraw district boundaries themselves or to invalidate an election.

In Latin America, neither judicial autonomy nor capacity can be taken for granted. In many countries in the region, courts are notorious both for their politicization and for their weakness.[18] Consequently, most Latin American judiciaries probably lack the ability to define a credible legal default outcome that could induce politicians to implement districting plans conforming to the "one person, one vote" principle.

Since the judicial oversight strategy for reducing malapportionment does not seem especially feasible in contemporary Latin America, a more promising alternative would be to create a neutral, nonpartisan electoral commission that is legally obligated to reduce lower-chamber malapportionment. This strategy for reducing malapportionment has been employed effectively in Mexico, where, since 1996, the Federal Electoral Institute (IFE) has exercised full authority over redistricting decisions and has helped compensate for the weakness of the Mexican judiciary. In July 1996, IFE's top governing body, the General Council, unanimously approved a lower-chamber redistricting plan—designed by a committee of nonpartisan technical experts with impressive academic and professional credentials—that significantly reduced malapportionment in anticipation of the 1997 elections. Mexico's political parties also played a key role in designing the plan: Their representatives were invited to comment on drafts of the plan, and some of their suggestions were incorporated into the final version, contributing to the plan's undisputed acceptance.[19]

This approach to reducing malapportionment could work in other Latin American countries where the judiciary lacks the capacity to enforce the "one person, one vote" principle. In assessing the prospects for replicating the "IFE model" in other countries, it is important to highlight that IFE had its roots in the allegedly stolen presidential victory of Institutional Revolutionary Party candidate Carlos Salinas in 1988. In exchange for recognizing Salinas's legitimacy, the opposition National Action Party successfully demanded a package of electoral reforms, including the formation of an independent electoral commission.[20] This suggests that effective independent, nonpartisan electoral commissions emerge out of partisan competition and may require an interparty pact.

2) Electoral-law reform. Reforming the electoral laws is probably a more viable strategy than judicial oversight for reducing malapportionment in Latin America. We consider here three distinct types of electoral law reform: 1) reapportionment; 2) a single-district chamber; and 3) a mixed electoral system with tiers.

One method for reducing malapportionment involves reallocating seats across districts so that underrepresented districts receive a proportionally larger share of the total number of seats and overrepresented districts receive a proportionally smaller share. In the absence of nonpartisan judicial oversight, however, such reapportionment may be extremely difficult to achieve. Efforts to reallocate seats typically require complex negotiations in order to avoid a "winner-take-all" situation where losers would face permanent disenfranchisement and would therefore have compelling incentives to undermine any proposed agreement. Consequently, attempts to implement reapportionment are unlikely to succeed unless they are incorporated into a broader package of electoral and institutional reforms. For example, Britain's landmark reapportionment in 1885 was but one piece of the Third Reform Act, which included a major expansion of suffrage and resulted from a complex interparty pact. To our knowledge, reapportionment initiatives have not been linked to broader proposals for electoral and institutional reform in Latin America, but this could be a viable strategy for reducing malapportionment. Such reform proposals might even include provisions for creating the kind of nonpartisan electoral commission discussed above to manage the apportionment process in a neutral fashion. Because the problem of malapportionment in countries like Brazil seems so closely connected with other institutional flaws, such as a fragmented party system and overly decentralized federalism, correcting malapportionment could become part of a wider package of reforms that would significantly enhance the quality of democracy, economic efficiency, and socioeconomic justice.

A second method for reducing malapportionment in Latin America would be to abandon an electoral system with multiple districts by adopting a single nationwide district, as Israel and the Netherlands have done. In Latin America, only Peru has implemented a single-district format in its lower chamber. In 1993, President Alberto Fujimori abolished Peru's Senate and created a unicameral legislature with a single nationwide district, thereby eliminating malapportionment altogether. Three Latin American countries (Colombia, Paraguay, and Uruguay) have recently eliminated malapportionment in their upper houses by adopting a single-district format.

Although a single-district chamber eliminates malapportionment, this strategy has important disadvantages that outweigh the goal of perfect apportionment. Single-district chambers can weaken citizen control over their representatives by making it harder for voters to hold legislators responsible for their actions. The weakening of citizen control raises troubling issues about the accountability of elected officials in single-district chambers: Because citizens lose the sense that a particular legislator "belongs" to them, they may have weak incentives to monitor and punish the performance of individual legislators. Consequently, the ability of the "electoral connection" to serve as a mechanism of accountability may be severely attenuated in systems with single-district chambers. This would be especially unfortunate in countries where accountability is already a crucial problem.

Finally, several Latin American countries have recently adopted a "two-tiered" electoral system that combines elements of single-member-district (SMD) systems and proportional-representation (PR) systems. For example, Mexico now elects 300 deputies in a tier of SMDs and 200 additional deputies in a second tier of five 40-member PR districts. Venezuela and Bolivia have recently implemented similar systems, and a mixed system is often proposed as an alternative to Brazil's open-list PR framework.

Countries do not typically adopt such systems with the goal of reducing malapportionment. Rather, the objective is to guarantee the representation of minority parties that would fail to win a plurality in any single district because their base of support is geographically dispersed. Nevertheless, a mixed system could serve to reduce malapportionment, depending on the number of seats added to the second tier and whether or not the second-tier seats are allocated to a nationwide district.

Mixed systems significantly reduce malapportionment only if the number of seats in the upper tier is substantial. For example, adding a tier with 20 seats elected in a nationwide district to a malapportioned legislature with 300 seats would have only a slight effect on the overall level of malapportionment. Moreover, a mixed system will reduce malapportionment only if the upper tier allocates seats exclusively to a nationwide district (as in El Salvador and Nicaragua). By contrast, tiers that distribute seats to *subnational* (provincial, state, or regional) districts may actually *increase* overall malapportionment (as in Bolivia and Venezuela).[21]

The strategy of allocating a large number of seats to a nationwide district has several advantages. First, it can be implemented in the context of a chamber with multiple, territorially defined electoral districts. Consequently, a far greater degree of citizen control over legislators is possible than in the case of a single-district chamber. Second, a tier of new seats can easily be added to the legislature without taking away any existing seats. This possibility reduces the likelihood of opposition from incumbent legislators concerned about protecting their districts. In short, because courts generally lack the capacity to supervise the reapportionment process in a nonpartisan fashion, the strategy of adding a tier may offer the best solution to the problem of malapportionment in Latin America.

Revaluing the Vote

Our critique of malapportionment in contemporary Latin America is anchored in the view that elections should, first and foremost, represent the will of individual citizens. Of course, alternative conceptions of representation exist—for example, that legislators should represent corporate or territorial units. Although few instances of corporate representation remain in Latin America,[22] the constitutions of many Latin American countries do explicitly provide for representation of territorial units in the upper chamber. Such "territorial" chambers are intended to protect the interests of less-populated regions. A high degree of malapportionment may be necessary to achieve this objective, which is certainly a legitimate democratic goal.

Yet while malapportionment may be warranted in the upper chamber, there is no normative justification for unfairness in the lower chamber. The lower chamber should be based upon "one person, one vote," with citizens represented as political equals. Because many Latin American countries have high levels of malapportionment in both their upper and lower chambers, they essentially have *two* territorial chambers, and *none* in which citizens' votes count equally. As we have argued, this situation has had a negative effect on the quality of democracy in the region. Latin America's democracies should revalue the vote by solving the problem of malapportionment in their lower chambers.

NOTES

We appreciate helpful comments on earlier drafts from Alberto Diaz Cayeros, John Gerring, Edward Gibson, Juan Linz, Scott Mainwaring, N. Guillermo Molinelli, Gerardo Munck, Guillermo O'Donnell, Diego Reynoso, Andreas Schedler, and Steven Solnick.

1. Dahl writes that the "unimpaired opportunit[y]" of all full citizens to "have their preferences weighed equally" is a necessary condition for democracy. Robert Dahl, *Polyarchy: Participation and Opposition* (New Haven: Yale University Press, 1971), 2. Dahl also includes "voting equality" as one of his "five criteria for a democratic process." Robert Dahl, *Democracy and Its Critics* (New Haven: Yale University Press, 1989), 109–11.

2. The table on p. 170 above is based on David Samuels and Richard Snyder, "The Value of a Vote: Malapportionment in Comparative Perspective," *British Journal of Political Science* 31 (October 2001): 651–71. To calculate malapportionment, we used a modified version of the Loosemore-Hanby index of electoral disproportionality, taking the absolute value of the difference between each

district's seat and population shares, adding them, and then dividing by two. Wherever available, we used population rather than registered voters per district, as most countries apportion seats on the basis of population.

3. In fact, the only way to avoid malapportionment completely is to elect representatives in a single nationwide district, as a few countries do (such as Israel, Namibia, the Netherlands, Peru, and Sierra Leone).

4. Guillermo O'Donnell, "On the State, Democratization, and Some Conceptual Problems: A Latin American View with Glances at Some Post-Communist Countries," *World Development* 21 (August 1993): 1355–70; and Jonathan Fox, "The Difficult Transition from Clientelism to Citizenship: Lessons from Mexico," *World Politics* 46 (January 1994): 151–84.

5. Guillermo O'Donnell, "Illusions About Consolidation," *Journal of Democracy* 7 (April 1996): 34–52, 41.

6. In terms of comparative research on democracy, recognizing this formal flaw offers important advantages. Precisely because it is a formal component of electoral systems, malapportionment is amenable to systematic measurement and statistical analysis. By contrast, informal flaws, like "brown areas" and the (un)rule of law, while critical, often frustrate scholars because of the difficulty of gathering systematic data that go beyond fertile anecdotal evidence.

7. Alfred Stepan, "Brazil's Decentralized Federalism: Bringing Government Closer to the Citizens?" *Daedalus* 129 (Spring 2000): 145–69, 163. Part of the explanation for this omission surely involves the fact that solving the problem of malapportionment would require a constitutional amendment, and such an amendment would require the unlikely support of a supermajority of senators and deputies from the *over*represented states. For an insightful analysis of malapportionment in Brazil, see Jairo Nicolau, "As Distorções na Representação dos Estados na Câmara dos Deputados Brasileira," *Dados* 40 (1997): 441–64.

8. By contrast, *informal* practices such as clientelism and particularism may be less compatible with these rules and institutions.

9. Here, we follow Dahl's threefold distinction between the formulating, signifying, and weighing of citizens' preferences as necessary conditions for democracy. Robert Dahl, *Polyarchy*, 1–3.

10. See Richard Snyder and David Samuels, "Legislative Malapportionment in Latin America: Comparative and Historical Perspectives," in Edward L. Gibson, ed., *Federalism and Democracy in Latin America* (Baltimore: Johns Hopkins University Press, 2004).

11. See Edward L. Gibson, "The Populist Road to Market Reform: Policy and Electoral Coalitions in Mexico and Argentina," *World Politics* 49 (April 1997): 339–70; and Edward L. Gibson and Ernesto Calvo, "Federalism and Low-Maintenance Constituencies: Territorial Dimensions of Economic Reform in Argentina," *Studies in Comparative International Development* 35 (September 2000): 32–55.

12. Matthew Shugart and John Carey, *Presidents and Assemblies* (Cambridge: Cambridge University Press, 1992), 286.

13. David V. Fleischer, "Manipulações Casuísticas do Sistema Eleitoral Durante o Período Militar, ou Como Usualmente o Fetiço Voltava contra o Feitiçeiro," *Cadernos de Ciência Política* 10 (1994).

14. Peter Pyne, "The Politics of Instability in Ecuador: The Overthrow of the President, 1961," *Journal of Latin American Studies* 7 (May 1975): 109–33.

15. Barry Ames, *Political Survival: Politicians and Public Policy in Latin America* (Berkeley: University of California Press, 1987).

16. Edward L. Gibson, Ernesto Calvo, and Túlia Falleti, "Reallocative Federalism in the Western Hemisphere," paper presented at the Conference on Federalism, Democracy, and Public Policy, Centro de Investigación y Docencia Económica (CIDE), Mexico City, 14–15 June 1999.

17. Alfred Stepan, "Brazil's Decentralized Federalism," 165. Contemporary Mexico provides additional examples of persistent subnational authoritarian enclaves. See Richard Snyder, "After the State Withdraws: Neoliberalism and Subnational Authoritarian Regimes in Mexico," in Wayne A. Cornelius, Todd A. Eisenstadt, and Jane Hindley, eds., *Subnational Politics and Democratization in Mexico* (La Jolla, Calif.: Center for U.S.-Mexican Studies, University of California–San Diego, 1999), 295–341.

18. Juan E. Méndez, Guillermo O'Donnell, and Paulo Sérgio Pinheiro, eds., *The (Un)Rule of Law and the Underprivileged in Latin America* (Notre Dame: University of Notre Dame Press, 1999).

19. Alonso Lujambio and Horacio Vives, "Nota Sobre la Redistritación," unpubl. ms., September 2000. On IFE's important role in Mexico's transition to democracy, see Andreas Schedler, "Mexico's Victory: The Democratic Revelation," *Journal of Democracy* 11 (October 2000): 5–19.

20. Jorge Domínguez and James McCann, *Democratizing Mexico* (Baltimore: Johns Hopkins University Press, 1995), 118–19.

21. It should be noted, however, that in Venezuela, as in Germany, "extra" seats can be allocated to different states to make the party results more proportional.

22. One such instance is the automatic granting of a Senate seat to ex-presidents in some Latin American countries (Chile and Venezuela, for example).

16

WHY DIRECT ELECTION FAILED IN ISRAEL

Emanuele Ottolenghi

Emanuele Ottolenghi *is Leone Ginzburg Senior Fellow in Israeli Law, Politics and Society at the Oxford Centre for Hebrew and Jewish Studies and at St. Antony's College, Oxford University. He wishes particularly to thank the Middle East Centre and the British Academy for the financial support which made possible the research upon which this essay is based. The essay originally appeared in the October 2001 issue of the* Journal of Democracy.

Less than a decade ago, Israel became the world's first parliamentary democracy to adopt direct popular election as the method of choosing its prime minister. The passage of this controversial reform was spurred by a three-month-long government crisis in the spring of 1990, during which Israelis looked on in shock and dismay as members of their parliament (the 120-seat Knesset) indulged in an unprecedented public orgy of floor-crossing and unseemly bargaining, with parties and individual legislators scrambling for place, preferment, and political advantage. This episode—known ever after as "the stinking maneuver"—led Israelis to change their Basic Law in 1992 to require that a separate popular election of the prime minister (PM) be held concurrently with balloting for the Knesset, although the PM's mandate would continue to depend upon a parliamentary vote of confidence.

But the reform did not work as planned. After using it three times—in the 1996 and 1999 general elections and in the February 2001 by-election in which Ariel Sharon of Likud defeated Ehud Barak of Labor—Israel ended the experiment. In March 2001, the country reverted to a slightly modified version of the pre-1992 system for choosing its premier. It will use this system in its next general elections, which are currently scheduled for November 2003.

Israel turned to direct election to counteract the fragmentation, instability, and immobilism that came to a head in the crisis of 1990. These maladies are often associated with proportional representation

(PR), particularly the low-threshold Israeli variety, which allows parties winning as little as 1.5 percent of the vote to take Knesset seats.[1] Yet the very effort to secure the passage of reform introduced distortions that caused it to fall short and even backfire. Much to the chagrin of reform's supporters, the 1996 and 1999 elections each led to a troubled time of coalition building. Small parties, far from being sidelined, vied to play kingmaker. And each time the result was an awkwardly patched-together coalition government with little coherence or staying power.[2]

Perhaps the most disappointing thing about the reform was its failure to give either the Labor or the Likud leader "coattails" that his colleagues could ride to victory in the at-large, list-based contest for the Knesset's 120 seats. On the contrary, the system's use of two ballots per voter (one for prime minister and one for the Knesset) encouraged ticket splitting. Many voters rejected Labor and Likud Knesset candidates, opting instead for smaller parties with sharper issue profiles, leaving the two big parties with less bargaining power than ever and increasing the fragmentation that ultimately caused the system's undoing.

What lessons may we draw from Israel's attempt to introduce elements of presidentialism or quasi-presidentialism into its parliamentary form of government?

Direct election was premised on a number of conditions. Voting for both the PM and the Knesset was to take place on the same day, so as to maximize the prospects for prime-ministerial "coattails" and to minimize the risk of French-style "cohabitation," in which the PM would be from a party not included in the Knesset majority. Stability would be ensured by the fact that the Knesset and the PM each had the institutional means to oust the other, but in doing so would have to face new elections as well.

To be chosen PM, a candidate would need at least 50 percent of the popular vote, with a runoff between the top two vote-getters to be held two weeks later in the event of an inconclusive first round. In the three elections under this arrangement, only two candidates for the premiership ran each time, and there was never any need for a runoff. Otherwise—and crucially—Israel's PR system for electing Knesset members remained unchanged. It continued to be highly proportional, with a single nationwide constituency, a low threshold of 1.5 percent, and a rigid list system.

Once certified as the winner, the new PM would have 45 days to present a list of cabinet ministers and to outline the policy direction of the new government. The Knesset would then formally have to consent to both through the familiar parliamentary mechanism of a vote of confidence. Lacking that, the new government would have to step down, the Knesset would dissolve, and new elections would have to occur within another 45 (later changed to 90) days.

Among the other scenarios for an early PM election envisioned by the Basic Law as amended in 1992, the most important for present purposes was the one in which a sitting PM could resign his premiership or his Knesset seat, thereby forcing a fresh PM election but leaving the existing Knesset in place. The principle of twinning prime-ministerial and parliamentary elections, in other words, had loopholes.

It is also worth noting that the final wording of the 1992 reform opted decisively for parliamentarism by making the Knesset's vote of confidence—as opposed to the direct mandate of the voters—critical to the prime minister's ability both to take and to hold office. The wholly independent electoral legitimacy of the executive, a *sine qua non* of presidentialism, played no part in Israel's new system.[3] Thus the electoral system for parliament, and its interaction with the direct PM election, would be key. This aspect of the reform was paid too little attention, precisely because direct election was introduced as *an alternative to more basic electoral-system change.*

In order to explain why the reform took this shape, one must look at how it got passed. A study of the compromises that were needed to turn it into law sheds light on the causes of some of its worst faults, including the problem caused by the double ballot, making it possible to evaluate the system's performance and to draw lessons from Israel's experience for other democracies with similarly fragmented party systems.

Why Direct Election?

The adoption of direct election was part of a wider attempt to reform Israel's political system at the beginning of the 1990s, following the series of drawn-out, PR-induced stalemates that had followed Likud's first electoral triumph over the once-dominant Labor Party in 1977. While Labor and Likud vied for leadership, an array of smaller leftist, rightist, and religious parties began to chip away at both their voter bases. The role of these small parties as crucial makeweights in ruling coalitions grew so prominent that both Labor and Likud found themselves hard-pressed to form stable governments.

Both the 1984 and 1988 elections were basically ties between Labor and Likud, and in each instance a government of national unity resulted. But under these governments between 1984 and 1990, Labor and Likud tied themselves in knots over the Middle East peace process, even as neither managed to create an alternative coalition with junior parties.

Both Labor and Likud declared that they would try to moderate Israel's excruciatingly proportional electoral system (most obviously by raising the Knesset threshold and switching to constituency-based rather than nationwide PR), but the determination and growing leverage of the smaller parties doomed all such efforts. The search for alternative solutions was on. From some quarters came the suggestion that Israel should adopt a constructive vote of no confidence. This would mean that the Knesset would be able to bring down a government through a no-confidence vote only if the Knesset could, through the same vote, name a new prime minister and cabinet (hence the "constructive" qualifier). But this more modest reform proposal did not make headway, and with a boost from public disgust over "the stinking maneuver," the idea of direct voting for the prime minister became the centerpiece of reformist thinking, and eventually of the reform package that was passed in 1992.

Direct election came to the fore not as an aspect of fundamental electoral reform, but as an *alternative* to it—a second-best option to be pursued once the smaller parties had effectively vetoed any serious revision of PR. Reformers argued that injecting presidentialist elements into Israeli parliamentarism would dim the prospect of small-party blackmail. The big-party Knesset lists, they said, would get a boost from the popular balloting for PM, while the PM would enjoy a far larger zone of independence in the day-to-day running of government.

Under the reformers' original plan, the Knesset would have been able to oust the PM only by means of a no-confidence motion that would need the support of at least 70 of the 120 legislators, and which would also dissolve the Knesset to make way for new elections. The reformers calculated that by thus joining no-confidence to dissolution, they would tie the Knesset's hands. Israel's prime minister would then be free to act much like a president, making decisions without needing to keep a weather eye on the shifting moods and alliances in parliament. In particular, reformers hoped to 1) strengthen the PM's legitimacy with a direct voter mandate; 2) ensure that changes of government would come from popular voting; and 3) reduce the size, number, and overall influence of smaller parties.

In short, the reformers hoped that direct election of the PM would produce the same results as a *less proportional* electoral system.

Direct election was meant to reshape the relation between the executive and the legislature by giving the voters' a direct say in the government-formation process. In the original scheme, the PM was not supposed to need a parliamentary confidence vote in order to install his government, but such a provision was added in order to ease fears that PMs might turn populist or even authoritarian. Still, reform advocates hoped that PMs would be independent enough of the Knesset to be able to appoint and remove ministers without fear of frowns from parliament.

The Struggle for Electoral Reform

As the reinstitution of the preliminary confidence vote indicates, the reform that was proposed and the reform that got passed were two very different things. Indeed, some people argue that the changes that the reform's proponents accepted in order to secure its passage explain why the new system failed, though as we will see, the reform suffered from a more basic contradiction.

As we have seen, the serious push for direct election grew out of the crisis of 1990. Both support for and opposition to direct election cut across party lines: the three left-wing secular parties (Shinui, Mapam, and Ratz) tended to favor reform, although some of their members opposed it. The ultra-Orthodox parties, which viewed themselves as targets of the reform campaign, were united in opposition. The religious Zionist Mafdal party, however, supported the reform. Labor was in favor, but Likud was a mixed bag: The party officially was against it, though some members, including future prime minister Benyamin Netanyahu, defied party discipline to line up behind direct election. Small parties that later were generally to benefit from the reform (such as the communist Hadash on the extreme left and Techiyah and Moledet on the extreme right) were also among its foes.

The earliest proposals for direct election had their first reading in the Knesset in May 1990. Public debate, which included extensive media and grassroots campaigning for direct election, would continue for two years. Final passage came, after much parliamentary maneuvering, on 18 March 1992.

Under intense public pressure and aggressive lobbying on behalf of direct election, the law was brought before the full Knesset for a final reading in January 1992. After a stormy session featuring accusations of obstructionism against the Speaker, the voting ended in chaos and the bill was sent back to the Constitution Committee amid bitter recriminations. In the end, the amendment restoring the vote of confidence passed as part of the reform.

Likud took most of the blame for the outcome of the parliamentary debate as well as for the manner in which it was conducted. Then–prime minister Yitzhak Shamir strongly opposed direct election (apparently fearing that he would lose a head-to-head matchup against a Labor candidate). In view of this, Likud Knesset member Uriel Lynn, the reform's principal sponsor, agreed not only to keep the vote of confidence but also to drop the number of votes required for a no-confidence vote from 70 to 61 and to delay the application of the new law until the 1996 elections. With these changes allaying some of their worst fears, Likud's leaders allowed a free vote, and the amended reform package became law five days before the end of the spring session.

The political circumstances surrounding these amendments and the final passage of the law help to explain why it failed. Despite the lengthy debate, a critical element of the reform—namely, the requirement that the PM would have to obtain the Knesset's confidence—was introduced at the eleventh hour, with almost no discussion of its implications.[4] Reform backers hoped that the four-year delay in implementation would leave time to make further changes, and that the Knesset to be chosen in June 1992 would have more members committed to direct election. But these hopes never materialized. The Yitzhak Rabin–led Labor government that came out of the June 1992 elections had little interest in the issue, and efforts at further amendment went nowhere. The law that the

Knesset had approved in March 1992 would carry Israel through the 1996 and 1999 elections.

The Results of Reform

Adopted to counter the problems of fragmentation, small parties with outsized clout, and governmental paralysis, the new institutional setup backfired. The centrifugalism of voting patterns for the Knesset under the new system dashed hopes that the specters of coalition crises and early elections could be exorcised, and the executive remained hamstrung in its ability to forge ahead with coherent policies on controversial issues.

In addition, the stabilizing effect that reformers hoped would flow from the threat of early elections was limited to the early part of a PM's mandate. As the term wore on and scheduled elections drew closer, restless coalition partners would become more likely to leave and force an early vote.

And what of the other results that supporters of the 1992 reform hoped to achieve? Let us run through these one by one in order to see how the reforms actually fared, comparing the outcomes under direct election with what happened during the last election held under the old system, in June 1992.

1) The legitimacy of the prime minister. Direct election, it was said, would give Israel's prime minister the kind of legitimacy that the previous system simply did not provide, due to the fragmented nature of parliament. In 1996, Netanyahu won by the slimmest of margins, 50.4 to 49.6 percent. In 1999, however, Ehud Barak's direct legitimacy was indisputable: he beat Netanyahu by 12 points, 56 to 44 percent. Yet barely 21 months later, Barak was ousted by current prime minister Ariel Sharon, who won more than 63 percent in an election heavily conditioned by the ongoing al-Aqsa Intifadah and the lowest turnout in Israel's electoral history (59.9 percent). Three elections in five years (when the full tenure is four) hardly sounds like stability.

Being able to claim a direct popular mandate doubtless made the PM stronger, but party fragmentation continued to make this strength often more notional than real. The PM could easily appear, in Giovanni Sartori's phrase, "a general without an army," as he sought to impose coherence and discipline on small parties—or even individual members—armed with strong views, claims of their own to direct voter support, and the knowledge that their exit from the PM's coalition could bring his government down.

2) Popular voting as the only method of changing governments. In reaction against the notorious intraparliamentary horse trading of 1990, the 1992 reform enshrined the idea that a government must be always as much as possible a direct expression of popular will. Since low-threshold PR tends to fracture the legislative expression of that will, the reformers wanted to plant in basic law the rule that the legislative branch and the now-to-be-directly-elected executive branch would have to enter and leave office at the same time.

In other words, the new system required that any change of majority within the Knesset (something conceivable in the framework of a multi-party parliamentary system ruled by coalitions) be endorsed by popular vote. Moreover, the system transferred the power to choose a PM from the parties to the voting public, with parties relegated to the role of putting candidates forward to receive the popular verdict.

The 1992 reform no doubt achieved this goal, but at a price. Arranging matters such that any coalition crisis triggers elections can be a recipe for drift and paralysis as disparate coalition partners, united mainly by an urge to stay in power, settle on "not rocking the boat" as the best survival strategy. Thus direct election channeled power to the people and away from horse-trading elites, but at the cost of energy in the executive.

The irony in all this, as the record shows, is that inaction has actually not been a good survival strategy for Israeli governments. Differences of political allegiance aside, the coalitions put together by all three directly elected PMs—Netanyahu, Barak, and Sharon—all resemble one another. Each man had to contend with the same pair of tensions that cut across his coalition: the cleavages between secular and religious parties, and between hawks and doves on the peace process. It was hard for each of these PMs to act on matters touching these divisions without causing rifts within his own household.

Yet given the separate ballot for the Knesset and the low threshold, no PM could choose an alternate and more viable coalition. Instead, each was forced to work with an inherently unstable government that could not readily face up to tough decisions on thorny issues such as the state and religion or dealings with the Palestinians. In short, the system produced instability because it shaped a political landscape that prevented the PM from governing.

3) Fewer and weaker small parties. The reduction in the number of parties in parliament—especially the smaller ones—and the strengthening of the major parties was to have been ensured by the devoutly wished-for but chimerical "coattail effect." Reform advocates expected that Labor and Likud candidates for PM would act as vote-getters in Knesset races too, carrying members of their respective parties along with them on their electoral "coattails" much as U.S. presidential candidates are said to do in congressional races. In turn, a streamlined party system was expected to foster more coherent and hence stabler coalitions.

In fact, only a mechanism that forces upon the voter a consistent choice for both parliament and prime minister will prevent people from splitting their ticket. The introduction of a two-ballot system created no incentive for voters to select either Labor or Likud over some smaller (but perhaps to the voter ideologically more congenial) party in the voting for parliament. In the event, voters in both 1996 and 1999 did shy away from Labor and Likud on the parliamentary ballot, and a bevy of smaller parties picked up seats.

Reformers should have realized that a double ballot promotes ticket splitting, yet they downplayed or even ignored this strong possibility. In the wake of increased fragmentation and instability, supporters of reform defended it by suggesting that direct election was not the cause. On the contrary, they said, the weakening of Labor and Likud and the rise of small parties flowed from trends dating back to the 1980s. Had direct election not been adopted, they added, the system would have been even less stable.[5]

While flagging partisan loyalties and voter "dealignment" have indeed been facts of political life in Israel (as throughout the West) for the last several decades, a reform that aims at enhancing stability should be designed to encourage voters to choose parties closer to the center of the spectrum. But as political scientists Gideon Doron and Michael Harris explain:

> the reformers neglected to consider . . . [that] changing the rules may also change the way individuals think and act, which will then make results deviate from expectations. . . . The voters actually became more likely to vote for the smaller parties for Knesset, thereby continuing to limit the ability of the prime minister to govern.[6]

Direct election did in fact foster a centripetal trend, but *only* in voting for prime minister. In Israel's highly polarized, fragmented, and far from homogeneous system, no such trend in Knesset voting should ever have been taken for granted. Hence the odd spectacle of campaigns in which the two major parties and their standardbearers touted their centrism while voters with parliamentary ballots in hand looked for smaller and sharply ideological parties unafraid to take strong stands on controversial issues. Consequently, while the majoritarian principle underlying direct election of the PM impelled the electorate to choose between two seemingly moderate options, the proportional principle at work in the parliamentary elections pulled the very same voters in precisely the opposite direction.

While long-run structural factors certainly play a big role in the decline of Labor and Likud, the double ballot exacerbated this trend, as the 1996 and 1999 election results show. In 1992, under the old system, Labor won 34.6 percent of the vote and 44 seats (up from 39 in 1988), while Likud mustered just under 25 percent and dropped from 40 to 32 seats. In 1996, Likud's Netanyahu won the prime ministership directly with 50.4 percent while his party list, which included also the Gesher and Tsomet parties and controlled 40 seats going in, garnered just over 25 percent and lost 8 seats. In May 1999, Netanyahu lost the race for prime minister with just under 44 percent, while Likud posted an all-

TABLE—PARTIES AND SEATS IN KNESSET ELECTIONS, 1981–99

ELECTION	NO. OF KNESSET SEATS			NO. OF PARTIES IN
	LABOR	LIKUD	OTHERS	GOVERNING COALITION
1981	47	48	25	5
1984	44	41	35	6
1988	39	40	41	6
1992	44	32	44	3
1996	34	32*	54	6
1999	26†	19	75	7

* In 1996 Likud ran on a joint list with two other parties, Gesher and Tzomet, that controlled 10 of the 32 seats.
† In 1999 Labor ran under the name of One Israel, a joint listing including Meimad and Gesher. Labor controlled 23 seats.

time low of barely more than 14 percent and 19 seats. Throughout this period, smaller parties to Likud's right made steady gains.

Labor suffered similar setbacks under direct election. In 1996, Shimon Peres barely lost with 49.6 percent while Labor's Knesset share dropped to 26.8 percent and 34 seats. Thus neither side enjoyed a "coattail" effect in 1996. The gainers were the peripheral parties. Arab parties, for instance, went from three to nine seats between 1988 and 1996. The 1999 elections confirmed the trend of big-party decline. Ehud Barak won a hefty 56 percent, but his three-party "One Israel" coalition managed only 20 percent and 26 seats. Of these, Labor controlled 23, down 11 seats from 1996, *despite its victory in the prime minister's race.*

The "coattail" effect, if there was one, was the opposite of what the reformers had predicted. The number of parties in the Knesset grew, going from 10 in 1992 to 13 in 1996 and 15 in 1999.[7] And this growth occurred despite the 1991 raising of the Knesset threshold from 1 to 1.5 percent—a reform that had been enacted to keep "one-person lists" out after the number of parties in the Knesset had reached 15 in 1988. It is clear that by enabling voters to express two choices on election day, direct election cut the number of strategic votes cast for either Labor or Likud as a parliamentary party.

This development also explains why forming majority coalitions became harder. In 1992, Labor had 44 seats and needed an additional 17 to reach the magic number of 61. In 1996, Likud had 32 seats and needed 29 more. In 1999, Labor found itself with 26, and needed 35 more. When Ariel Sharon took over after his landslide by-election win in February 2001, he faced the same Knesset elected in 1999 and had to start building a coalition around a Likud bloc of just 19 seats. Obviously, a prime minister who needs the support of at least 42 more legislators in a 15-party parliament will have to "shop for votes" among a disparate array of parties, and will wind up with a wobbly, tension-ridden coalition. The structural shortcomings of such a system are plain.

From 1992 to 1999, the number of so-called center parties, which are ready to join any winner of the PM race, rose from three (with a total of

16 seats) to six (with 38 seats in all). Religious parties, seen by many as the ones making the heaviest demands in the coalition-formation process, increased their representation steadily from 16 seats in 1992, to 23 in 1996, and 27 in 1999.[8] Sectarian and ethnic lists also flourished, as did single-issue parties. As already mentioned, Arab parties went from an aggregate of 5 seats in 1992 to 9 in 1996 and 10 in 1999. A lone Russian-immigrant party won 7 seats in 1996. Three years later, a pair of such parties won 10 seats between them. The single-issue Third Way party (in favor of retaining the Golan Heights) won 4 seats in 1996. Though the party disappeared in 1999, its middle-of-the-road appeal was taken over by the Centre Party and the secular Shinui (6 seats each).

The fragmentation of the party system made it ever harder to build and maintain coalitions. Proponents of direct election had argued that the new system would prevent a repeat of the 1990 fiasco. Direct election would ensure that on election night there would be a clear winner with whom all parties would have to deal. There would be no shuttling back and forth between Labor and Likud, as in 1990, when parties and legislators played both sides in order to exact the highest political "price" for their support.

But the record of Israel's experience under direct election tells another story. In 1992, Rabin managed to present a three-party government 23 days after election day. Four years later, Netanyahu needed 21 days to forge an eight-party coalition. In 1999, Barak took 51 days to present a seven-party coalition. Sharon's seven-party national-unity government won a confidence vote 30 days after the 2001 elections. In short, the presence of a "clear winner" PM whose prospective cabinet was "the only game in town" did little or nothing to streamline coalition negotiations. Indeed, coalitions grew even bigger and more awkward.

The need to "pay off" more coalition partners with cabinet seats and funding for their pet programs or offices produced higher public spending and shifted more resources to these smaller parties, making them stronger than ever. Thus despite the PM's notional prominence, partisan dynamics and the stern arithmetic of coalition maintenance often forced him to dance to the smaller parties' tunes.

Coalitions can handle a degree of ideological distance among partners, all of whom must weigh the costs of compromise against the rewards of power. Direct election (as the annual budget marathons attest) stretched this feature of coalition government to its limits. The sheer cost—in time, trouble, and state funds—of holding disparate coalition governments together sapped the executive's ability to tackle pressing political issues. What makes the problem particularly difficult in Israel is the sheer fragmentation of the Knesset. In a parliament so riven, a stable coalition is essentially beyond the reach of even the cleverest and most energetic prime minister. Unworkable coalitions are literally all there is.

The reform had hoped to achieve the same results that a less proportional electoral system would have produced. Throughout Israel's entire history, political impediments—the sheer difficulty of changing the rules of the game from which so many players benefited—had blocked serious electoral reform. Reformers convinced themselves that the enhanced powers and legitimacy enjoyed by directly elected PMs would raise them above the clamor of narrow partisan pressures. The hoped-for streamlining of the party system was to have further bolstered the PM, adding effectual powers to the formal ones listed in the new law. A reduced party system was to have curtailed the blackmail potential of coalition partners. Israel would benefit from a stronger and steadier executive power, without having to dislodge the principle of proportionality enshrined in its constitution.

As we have seen, the results of the 1996 and 1999 elections dashed these hopes. By the middle of 2000, events under Labor prime minister Ehud Barak would catalyze opposition to direct elections and set the stage for its final repeal on 7 March 2001.

Barak's Tenure and the Demise of Direct Election

The plight of Barak's government mirrored reform's structural failure. Despite his convincing 12-point victory, Barak faced a Knesset under the control (albeit by a razor-thin margin) of the religious and right-of-center parties that had been members of Netanyahu's government. Barak had no choice but to woo some of those parties. As we have seen, it took him almost two months. In the end, he won the confidence vote with seven parties totaling 75 votes. The Arab parties and the secular Shinui were left out. The three religious parties—Shas (17 seats), United Torah Judaism (5), and the Mafdal (5)—as well as the immigrant-based Israel Be'aliyah (6), were included along with Meretz (10) and the Centre Party (6).

The coalition, said some at the time, was so broad that it would be extremely difficult to bring the new government down, especially given that no single party could topple the government by leaving on its own. (Barak did not include Shinui and the Arab parties in his coalition, but could count on their votes to maintain his government if defections occurred.) Yet this optimism proved unfounded. Barely 12 months after taking office, Barak left for the July 2000 Camp David talks with a 29-seat minority government made up of just Labor, One Israel, and the Centre Party. And the Knesset had grown more contentious than ever, with several individual legislators breaking all party bonds and demanding their share of the pie to join the government.

Why did Barak's coalition break down so quickly? Barak's personal leadership style did not help, but the main reason was the presence of deep divisions over two key sets of issues. The first set revolved around relations between religion and the state, while the second set hinged on the conduct of the already-faltering peace process.

Riven by friction and rancor, especially between the ultra-Orthodox,

Sephardic-dominated Shas and the secular-leftist Meretz, the doomed coalition limped along for another nine months. The heaviest blow fell on the very eve of Barak's departure to meet with Yasser Arafat and Bill Clinton at Camp David in early July 2000, when Shas, Mafdal, and Israel Be'aliyah left.

Thanks to his own skillful maneuvering and his foes' lack of concert, Barak managed to fend off no-confidence motions for several months. Supporters of direct election claimed that Barak's ability to hold out for so long despite lacking a Knesset majority was a direct consequence of the reformed system, and in that sense a sign that reform was helping the cause of stability.[9] Finally, in early December 2000, Barak decided to resign personally but not to dissolve the Knesset. With this move he aimed to ensure that Sharon rather than Netanyahu would become his opponent in the new election for prime minister: Having left parliament, Netanyahu would not be eligible to run unless the Knesset itself were dissolved.

With the outbreak of the al-Aqsa Intifadah in late September 2000, Barak's government appeared frighteningly feeble and hopelessly un-equal to the task of dealing with the diplomatic and security crisis that exploded after the Oslo process collapsed. Nor could Barak's cabinet handle such mundane but significant matters as the 2001 budget, which wound up having to wait until after the new election for prime minister.

The executive's inability to overcome the emergency was just the superficial manifestation of a deeper problem. Direct election had am-plified political fragmentation and created a system that condemned the PM to inaction and ineffectiveness, and the country to chronic political instability and frequent elections. The terrible demands of the security and diplomatic crisis shined a harsh light on the system's shortcomings. As the new Sharon government took office in the spring of 2001, Israel reverted to a slightly modified version of the old parliamentary arrange-ment. Direct election was abolished, a constructive vote of no confidence was introduced, and no-confidence motions required a 61-vote major-ity. In addition, the PM's power to dissolve the Knesset was preserved. Direct election had been tried, found wanting, and discarded.

The consensus in favor of repeal was broad. The bill to replace direct election passed the Knesset by a vote of 72 to 37, with 3 abstentions. Among those who favored the change were Labor, Likud, Meretz, the right-wing National Union and Herut, four legislators from the Centre Party, and four Arab legislators from different lists. The ultra-Orthodox United Torah Judaism voted in favor, in exchange for a promise by Likud to support religious legislation; Shas instead voted against, as did two out of the five Mafdal legislators. Among the opponents to the change were small parties, including the secular Shinui and the immigrant parties.

With a few individual exceptions, legislators from the more narrowly focused and "sectorial" parties opposed repeal, while members of the bigger or more ideological parties (the very ones that direct election was supposed to favor) endorsed it. Clearly, those most likely to lose from the return of the previous system tried to keep direct election alive. It was an eloquent testimony to the reality of direct election's unintended consequences.

Will the old-new system that was restored in March 2001 strengthen the executive? Time will tell. Meanwhile, what is most surprising about the last chapter of Israel's brief experience with direct election is that the law replacing it was so hastily discussed and approved. As if to attest to the failure of direct election, only three committee sessions were needed to reach an agreement on the new law, and very little public debate accompanied the legislative process.[10]

Israel's experience weighs strongly against adoption of this model in other parliamentary democracies characterized by a divided society and a similarly fragmented PR system. There is no doubt that Israel's failure to benefit from the reform derives from the fact that direct election became *an alternative to* fundamental electoral reform, rather than one element thereof.

If there is a key lesson to be learned from Israel's failed experiment, it is precisely that direct election of the PM can strengthen the executive only if the PM can govern without parliament. This of course adds to the risk of a populist or even a plebiscitarian-authoritarian turn, but it is a risk that will have to be run by any polity resolved on such a reform.

If direct election is to be coupled with parliamentary government, as Israel tried to do, the electoral system for parliament must also be adjusted in order to encourage a "coattail" effect for the parties to which candidates for prime minister belong. What would such an adjustment have to look like? Is it even possible?

These are difficult questions to answer in the abstract. One approach might be to force parties to form coalitions behind individual candidates *before* the elections. This would in turn require setting up the ballot so that voters could not split their tickets. But this system too has its complications, especially if more than two candidates run for prime minister. And what, moreover, is to guarantee that coalitions will stick together *after* the elections?

Other parliamentary democracies, including Japan, that have been considering the adoption of direct election should not necessarily view the Israeli experience as decisive evidence that it must fail. It was Israel's ballot system that doomed its version of direct election. The one clear lesson of the Israeli experiment is that direct election can succeed only if it is accompanied by an electoral system for parliament that ensures strong majorities for the elected prime minister.

NOTES

1. See Vernon Bogdanor, "The Electoral System, Government, and Democracy," in Ehud Sprinzak and Larry Diamond, eds., *Israeli Democracy Under Stress* (Boulder, Colo.: Westview, 1993), 83–106.

2. For a favorable view of the new system, see Bernard Susser, "The Direct Election of the PM: A Balance Sheet," in Daniel J. Elazar and Shmuel Sandler, eds., *Israel at the Polls 1996* (London: Frank Cass, 1998), 237–57.

3. The vote of confidence is the most obvious feature of a parliamentary system. Along with it, the 1992 reform also strengthened other parliamentary features, by framing practices in the new legislation. According to the Basic Law, the PM and at least half the ministers should be also members of parliament and, as if to further emphasize the parliamentary nature of the system, the PM's resignation of his Knesset seat was equated to resignation from office.

4. Uriel Lynn himself uttered prophetic words on this score. On 21 November 1990, in response to a fellow legislator who was insisting on a confidence vote for each new government, Lynn observed: "Anyone who wants to receive the Knesset's confidence is better off giving up on direct election and keeping the present system. It is not possible to do two things which contradict one another. It is not possible to legislate a law that tries to reach a central goal and afterwards to empty the law of this central purpose. The moment that one enables the Knesset, or that one says that the Knesset ought to express a vote of confidence in the Prime Minister, the meaning is that the Knesset is given the power to annul the mandate that the PM received from the people."

5. As late as 1997, Uriel Lynn was defending the reform package in interviews, calling it "an excellent law, without which complete anarchy would reign, even worse than the situation on the eve of the 'stinking maneuver.'" *Jerusalem Post,* 11 March 1997, 3.

6. Gideon Doron and Michael Harris, *Public Policy and Electoral Reform: The Case of Israel* (Boston: Lexington Books, 2000), 72.

7. Within a month after the elections, the number had already grown to 16, due to a split in the Israel Be'Aliyah party. This incidentally raised the prospects of that party leaving the coalition, only one week after the government won the confidence of the Knesset.

8. This is another indication of failure, since it may be argued that the reform was presented and marketed to the public as a way to reduce the religious parties' power. See Nehemiah Stressler, "Photo-op with whom?" *Ha'aretz* (Tel Aviv), 8 November 1991, 1B: "The proposed system of government will most of all hurt the blackmail powers of the ultra-religious parties and the power of the extreme right. This is why it is worthy of full support." See also Amnon Rubinstein, "Still Time for Electoral Reform," *Jerusalem Post International Edition,* 3 August 1991, 2: "Direct election would drastically slash the power vested in such minorities by the current system in 'tipping the balance.'"

9. See Iki Elner, *It's not the system,* in *Y-net, Yediot Aharonot* online, 18 December 2000, *www.ynet.co.il.* Elner fends off criticism of direct election by saying, "Without it, we would certainly be witnesses to an unending alternation of Prime Ministers, and this without going to an election and without asking the will of the people."

10. The sessions occurred on 20 December 2000 and 13 and 20 Febrary 2001. The record of these truncated deliberations can be found under Proceedings 2361, 2728, and 2761 of the Law, Constitution and Justice Committee, *www.knesset.gov.il.*

17

THE POLITICS OF REFORM IN JAPAN AND TAIWAN

Jih-wen Lin

Jih-wen Lin *is associate research fellow at the Institute of Political Science at Academia Sinica and associate professor at National Chengchi University and National Sun Yat-sen University in Taiwan. His articles have appeared in* Electoral Studies, China Quarterly, *the* Journal of East Asian Studies, *and* Issues and Studies. *This essay originally appeared in the April 2006 issue of the* Journal of Democracy.

Among the significant parallels in the political development of Japan and Taiwan is their longtime use of the unusual single nontransferable vote (SNTV) system for electing representatives to the legislature. Moreover, in the past dozen years both countries have undergone significant electoral reform, resulting in a switch to more majoritarian mixed systems. In each case reform had been long in the making before finally being implemented—in Japan in 1994 and in Taiwan in 2005. This should lead us to ask: What lies behind these fairly recent changes?

Japan and Taiwan were once the paragons of late-developer countries. Japan, leveled by World War II, maintained one of the world's highest economic-growth rates from the 1960s until the 1990 stock-market crash put a brake on its progress. Taiwan, also torn by war, kept up remarkable economic growth despite its diplomatic isolation. Many developmental theorists attribute these countries' phenomenal performance to the guidance of developmentalism; yet Japan and Taiwan differ from the stereotypical developmental state in that they have long held competitive elections, a critical condition of democracy.[1]

Elections have been an indispensable component of Japan's modern state-building, and in Taiwan, partial electoral competition existed even during the heyday of authoritarian rule. How did developmentalism coexist with electoral competition in these two countries? In other words, what kept economic planners from being disturbed by office-seeking politicians? The answer might be useful to countries struggling to pursue both economic development and political reform.

An important clue lies in how the elections were conducted. To achieve their economic goals, the helmsmen of a developmental state often seek to shape the role of the elected politicians so that this group serves to approve plans rather than debate policy. To this end, elections focus less on policy issues than on personal interests, and a stable ruling coalition keeps government turnover from upsetting the developmentalists' freedom to manage the economy. These needs are met by SNTV, the peculiar electoral system used for decades in Japan and Taiwan. This system is extremely rare; today only Jordan, Afghanistan, Vanuatu, and the Pitcairn Islands use it to elect their national legislators. In Japan and Taiwan, SNTV was used from the introduction of electoral competition until recent electoral reforms—in 1994 and 2005, respectively—introduced mixed systems. In light of the South Korean experience with the same system, SNTV is a defining feature of the East Asian model of democracy.[2]

Under SNTV, each voter casts one vote for a specific candidate in what are typically multimember districts; votes received by a candidate cannot be transferred to others; and seats are allocated by the plurality rule to the top vote-getters. The system is unique in that the threshold for victory decreases as the number of candidates to be elected from the district increases. This makes the system more proportional—as the distribution of seats among parties comes to match more closely their relative shares of the vote—but the vote goes to individual candidates rather than to parties. By contrast, in an open-list proportional representation (PR) system, votes for any of a party's candidates are a "public good" for that party, inasmuch as votes for a candidate in excess of the threshold for election are transferred to other party candidates. In this way, seats are allocated in accord with the party's overall vote share. Under SNTV, the vote won by a candidate is nontransferable, and whether one gets elected depends only on the rank of his or her own vote share. Their vote being restricted to one candidate, voters tend to select a candidate who serves their special interests.

Several results follow. First, SNTV gives those elected an incentive to cultivate patron-client networks, as this is the best way to secure the support of particular interest groups. Second, it generates factionalism and divisions within political parties, whose candidates must compete with each other over the ballots cast by the party faithful. Third, the system favors well-organized parties which can coordinate their nominations and distribute their supporters' votes in a way that maximizes the number of their candidates elected in each district. Fourth, under SNTV those whose election depends on patronage and other particularistic connections need the support of a stable coalition that can effectively manage the tasks of resource distribution and nomination coordination.

These features of SNTV explain why the leaders of Japan's and Taiwan's developmental states favored it. It allows for a strong govern-

ing coalition made up of state-builders, who plan economic development, and elected representatives, who legitimate the process. Moreover,
SNTV tends to cause internal disputes and fragmentation among opposition parties.[3] But these benefits come at a price for the ruling coalition.
Financing the particularistic politics created by an SNTV electoral system requires tremendous expenditure, which becomes a serious burden
when the economy no longer sustains rapid growth. Moreover, citizens
without access to patronage networks may launch calls for reform that
the government cannot always contain. In Japan and Taiwan, such social grievances were a major force behind electoral reform.

Intriguingly, in both countries the initiative for electoral change
came in large measure from within the dominant party. How could this
happen when the structure of party dominance was based largely on the
SNTV system? To answer this question, we must examine the strategic
choices that some major ruling-party politicians made in the face of
social protest. As the SNTV system came under fire, these politicians
sought to ensure their political survival by calling for reform. Indeed,
the cases of Japan and Taiwan show that the success of electoral reform
often hinges on power struggles among incumbents.

Public resentment of the status quo is often a driving force behind
electoral reform. In Japan, the reform debate gained momentum when
incessant scandals made the Japanese aware of the old system's entrenched corruption.[4] In Taiwan, the debate was triggered by public discontent with an inefficient and chaotic national legislature.[5] But the
citizenry's disgruntlement, while indispensable, does not fully explain
the success of electoral reform in Japan in the 1990s and in Taiwan in the
past half-decade. Another crucial factor was the belief among a few leading incumbent legislators that a new system would improve their odds of
reelection.[6] But because reform would make it harder for weaker members of parliament to win reelection, it was difficult for these reformers to
assemble the majority needed to adopt changes to the electoral system.
How did they pull together majority coalitions in Japan and Taiwan?

As argued above, maintaining the dominant-party system is very
costly, and economic downturns can trigger public protest against the
government. In both Japan and Taiwan, public disappointment eroded
the governing party's electoral strength and finally deprived the party
of its dominant status. In the face of this challenge, ruling-party politicians owing their electoral success to personal image rather than
particularistic connections began considering strategies for political
survival. They came up with similar solutions in both countries: By
pushing to replace SNTV with a first-past-the-post (FPTP) electoral system—in which the winner in each single-seat district is the candidate
who wins the most votes—they stood to lead a party based more on its
policy platform than on factions. But how could these politicians engineer the reform process, given their minority status?

Successful electoral reform in countries using SNTV depends on three conditions. First, the reformers themselves must benefit from the proposed new electoral system. With FPTP as the alternative to SNTV, politicians relying on personal popularity to win are most likely to promote reform. With only one candidate to select from a party, voters casting their ballot under FPTP are more susceptible to candidate image and partisan identification, while under SNTV they are encouraged to choose the providers of special interests. Second, electoral reform is much more viable when no single party controls a parliamentary majority. When there is a majority party, those of its members who are electorally insecure will resist electoral reform.[7] There is also little incentive for the center of a majority party to promote electoral reform as long as the party maintains its dominant position. This also implies that, when social pressure is so strong that some members of the governing party decide to form a reformist group, the party runs the risk of splitting up.

Third, in order to bring about a change away from SNTV there must be some incentives for a *majority* of legislators to pass the electoral-reform proposal. Small parties (or independents) who find their survival at risk under a system that includes an FPTP component might trade their endorsement of such a proposal for such benefits as cabinet posts, budgetary items, or policy concessions. Another reason for them to join a reform coalition could be the fear of losing votes in the next election precisely because of their opposition to electoral reform.

The legal requirements for electoral reform differ by country: In some countries the system may be changed by executive decree, while in others it requires a parliamentary majority or even a supermajority. If a country is already democratic, some form of legislative approval will be necessary, but the threshold varies. The higher the threshold, the greater the cost involved in bringing together a proreform majority. As we are about to see, Japan and Taiwan both met the above three conditions, and the relative speed with which each enacted reform can be explained by various institutional requirements.

Japan: Old Blueprint for a New Nation

The SNTV system had its longest run in Japan. Chosen by the state-builders of modern Japan,[8] it was used in most elections held from the onset of electoral competition in the late nineteenth century until 1994. The current form of SNTV was adopted in 1947 and coexisted with the perennial dominance of the Liberal Democratic Party (LDP) between 1955 and 1993.[9] Political scandals erupted from time to time under LDP governance, and each time the party responded to popular protest by finding fault with the electoral system. In 1956, Prime Minister Ichiro Hatoyama attempted unsuccessfully to replace SNTV with FPTP, hoping to boost the LDP's seat share in the bicameral Diet (Japan's parliament) so that the party could carry out a constitutional revision. After the 1960 lower-house election, the Diet established the Electoral Reform Advisory Council, which played the role of narrowing down the reform proposals to several alternatives—most of them combining SNTV and FPTP. Yet none of the Council's proposals were approved by the Diet until early 1994, when all three of the above conditions for electoral reform finally came into alignment.

During decades of LDP-majority rule, a succession of prime ministers advocated the use of FPTP, figuring that the ruling party's seat share would be amplified by the relatively low proportionality of the proposed systems. The reformist parties, comprising in large part LDP defectors, were led to push for electoral reform by the very logic of their claim to be reformists. But there were other reasons for them to support the FPTP-leaning proposals. For example, the LDP's support base, as an effect of its reliance on particularistic networks, was mainly rural; thus, the reformist parties saw prospects for electoral gain in urban districts.

In the 1993 parliamentary election, the two major reformist parties— the Japan New Party (JNP) and the Japan Renewal Party (JRP)—performed extraordinarily well, depriving the LDP of its majority status. This further motivated these parties to introduce a new electoral system that would make it harder for the LDP to regain its strength by utilizing its traditional patronage-intensive tactics.[10] Moreover, while 42.9 and 44.4 percent of the winning JNP and JRP candidates were the top vote-getters in their districts, among *all* successful candidates, only 25.3 percent ranked first in their districts. This suggested that the successful opposition candidates would have a good chance of being elected even under the FPTP system.

The splitting of the LDP, as well as other changes to the party system, supplied additional reasons why electoral reform finally succeeded in the early 1990s. In fact, one of the major causes of the LDP's 1993 electoral fiasco was the internal dispute over electoral reform—the LDP was seriously weakened when reformers within its ranks deserted to join or form opposition parties. It is also noteworthy that all reform proposals—in 1956, 1976, and in the late 1980s—were rejected as long as the LDP remained in power.[11] The result of the 1993 election clearly indicated the willingness of Japanese voters to punish antireformists. Particularly discredited were the Socialists and the Communists, as indicated by their poor electoral performances. This alarmed those members of the coalition government who supported political reform at large but were not confident of their fortunes under FPTP—it appeared that, were they to disapprove of the reform bill, voters would likely punish them.

After the 1993 reshuffle in the lower house, the electoral-reform debate gained momentum. The JRP and the Clean Government Party (CGP) favored a mixed system with an FPTP component, while the JNP and the New Party Harbinger (NPH) were insistent on a two-ballot system, under which voters cast one ballot for a party and another one for a candidate. The final version of the new election law proposed by the coalition government was a compromise, as indicated by the two-ballot format, yet the high percentage of FPTP seats still reflected the influence of politicians who were confident of their vote-getting abilities. The bill came out as it did because small-party leaders were sharing some of the cabinet portfolios—an opportunity that had been beyond their imagination when the LDP controlled the government. These parties also received additional benefits from other reform bills grouped together with the new election law, such as the restrictions on party and campaign financing.

While the reformist coalition controlled the majority in the lower house, it did not in the upper house. Japan's bicameral system gives the upper house the right to veto lower-house actions not related to the budget, the treasury, or prime-ministerial appointments. Only a two-thirds majority of the lower house can override such a veto. The coalition government did not have the support of a majority in the upper house, nor did it control two-thirds of the lower house. As expected, the upper house vetoed the reform bills passed by the lower house on 18 November 1993, forcing Prime Minister Morihiro Hosokawa to hold an emergency meeting with the LDP president. When these bills were eventually adopted by the upper house in January 1994, their content had been revised to satisfy the LDP's demands. In particular, the portion of FPTP seats was increased from 250 to 300, the same formula that had been proposed in two earlier LDP reform bills. For the minor parties, the only hope was the 200 closed-list PR seats (later reduced to 180) elected in 11 PR districts.

Taiwan: A Party Larger Than a Nation

The history of SNTV in Taiwan is also long. Although the authoritarian rule of the Kuomintang (KMT, the Nationalist Party) from 1949 until 1992 meant that not *all* members of the Legislative Yuan (LY) were elected, SNTV has been widely used in both legislative and local elections for almost seventy years. The system was introduced in 1935, under Japanese colonial rule, for the purpose of electing members of the local assembly. The Taiwanese electorate was thus quite familiar with SNTV, and the system had become an integral feature of Taiwan's electoral politics.

Retreating to Taiwan after losing the Chinese civil war in 1949, the KMT government maintained its authoritarian rule by insisting that delegates elected in mainland China before 1949 would not have to run for reelection until the government based in Taiwan recovered the mainland. As the KMT was an "immigrant" regime, facing constant local challenges to its claim rightfully to rule over Taiwan, the use of SNTV served the party's interest in many ways. First, local elections, held soon after the KMT arrived in Taiwan, helped to justify the party's rule by making Taiwanese politics partially competitive. While the KMT sometimes had problems winning local executive offices, SNTV helped the party to dominate the local assemblies. Moreover, by incorporating some members of the indigenous Taiwanese elite into its electoral machine, the KMT managed to blur its image as a rootless immigrant regime.

Second, as in the Japanese case, the electoral system played a very important role in nurturing clientelist relationships between Taiwanese elites and the KMT. Having inherited the state-controlled economic resources left by the Japanese colonial government, the KMT had the political and economic power to coordinate the party's contestants for political office at various levels. This enabled it to avoid one of the greatest dangers for a large party under SNTV: Nominating too many candidates in a district and fragmenting its total vote to a degree that would cost it seats. In exchange for benefiting from the party's strategic resources, local elites pledged their loyalty to the party-state.

Lastly, SNTV put a constraint on the growth of the non-KMT forces (originally known as *dangwai* or "outside the party"). In contrast to the KMT's one-China doctrine, the *dangwai* movement progressed by calling for Taiwanese sovereignty, making national identity and independence Taiwan's foremost political issue. But the movement did not enjoy the KMT's economic and political leverage, organizational discipline, or strategic resources. Thus, as it expanded and as its members began to run against one another in the elections, the movement suffered internal divisions.

Although only part of the LY was elected prior to the transition to democracy during the early 1990s, SNTV in Taiwan played a role similar to the one it had played in Japan. KMT premier Lien Chan first introduced the issue of electoral reform after the party almost lost its majority in the 1994 LY election. Despite this humiliating electoral setback, the ruling party had won all the single-seat districts, motivating Lien to propose a system in which the majority of seats would be filled through FPTP. The KMT soon began to promote a Japanese-style mixed system, even though many of its members opposed reform. The positions of other parties varied with their respective electoral fortunes: For instance, the opposition Democratic Progressive Party (DPP) insisted on a German-style mixed but fully proportional system[12] in late 1996, but after its presidential victories in 2000 and 2004, it shifted its position, favoring a Japanese-style partially proportional mixed system. The minor parties in Taiwan generally opposed the FPTP component of any formula, favoring instead a fully proportional system.

Nonetheless, it took a decade for Lien's vision of electoral reform to turn into reality. In August 2004, the LY voted to propose constitutional amendments that halved its size (from 225 to 113 seats) and implemented a mixed electoral system with each voter casting two ballots (one each for candidate and party). Under the new system, 73 seats were to be elected by FPTP; another 34 (half of them set aside for women) were to be allocated by closed-list PR in a nationwide district; and 6 were to be filled from the aboriginal districts. The National Assembly—a 334-seat marginally important legislative body scheduled for elimination by 2008—approved these amendments on 7 June 2005. Though the reform package was adopted only after the KMT had lost its majority in the LY—indeed at a time when there was no majority party—the changes to the electoral system are very similar to what Lien had proposed in 1994.

As in Japan, there are numerous reasons why the reform efforts succeeded when they did in Taiwan. Some politicians—mainly from the KMT and the DPP—calculated that they would benefit from the new electoral system. While these two major parties take opposite stands on the issue of Taiwanese independence, they shared a tacit interest in lowering the electoral system's proportionality so as to enhance their seat shares in competition with splinter parties. Under SNTV, if a party nominates too many candidates in a district, it fragments its votes and may lose seats, because votes for poorly performing candidates cannot be transferred to other party candidates. But if the party nominates too few candidates, it may also squander potential seats. The KMT in 2001, and the DPP in 2004, optimistic about their electoral fortunes, nominated too many candidates, reducing the average vote shares of their nominees and hence their party's seat share. Based on their respective miscalculations, the KMT and the DPP realized that under FPTP their chances of winning a majority would greatly improve and there would be no need for elaborate nomination strategies.

As in Japan, raising the support necessary for electoral reform required some persuasion. The smaller parties—in particular the People First Party (PFP) and the Taiwan Solidarity Union (TSU), a proindependence party flanking the DPP—were threatened by the proposed move to a majoritarian electoral system. Yet their opposition was mollified by the inclusion in the reform package of some other constitutional amendments that they favored. The TSU achieved its longstanding goal of halving the size of the Legislative Yuan. The PFP, by contrast, was compensated by the addition of an amendment requiring that future constitutional amendments win the approval of an absolute majority of the population in a referendum. This provision assured opponents of Taiwanese independence—the PFP in particular—that any future constitutional shift toward independence would be extremely difficult.

The Effects of Reform in Japan

If Japan's adoption of a new electoral system reflected the intention of some politicians to produce a more favorable political environment,

TABLE 1—THE EVOLUTION OF JAPAN'S PARTY SYSTEM

ELECTION YEAR	EFFECTIVE NUMBER OF LEGISLATIVE PARTIES	SEAT SHARE OF THE LARGEST PARTY*	TOTAL SEAT SHARES OF TWO LARGEST PARTIES
1980	2.66	0.57	0.78
1983	3.23	0.49	0.71
1986	2.57	0.59	0.75
1990	2.71	0.53	0.80
1993	4.26	0.43	0.56
1996	2.94	0.48	0.79
2000	3.18	0.49	0.75
2003	2.56	0.49	0.86
2005	2.23	0.62	0.85

*Always the LDP

we should expect elections held under the new rules to differ somehow from prereform ones. According to the reformers, electoral campaigns under the new system would focus more on policy debates than on resource redistribution, and bipartisan competition would replace factionalized one-party dominance. The minor parties would pay attention to their party images to win the PR seats rather than try to cultivate district-level connections that would turn out to be futile. Whether the new system produced these expected results can be seen from the outcomes of the lower-house elections held under the new electoral system in 1996, 2000, 2003, and 2005.

Japan has been traveling a path of party realignment since the LDP lost its majority in the 1993 election. The short-lived New Frontier Party (NFP) was founded in 1994 to unite the non-LDP politicians. Before the 1996 lower-house election, some politicians formed the Democratic Party, which changed into the Democratic Party of Japan (DPJ) in 1998 by incorporating some minor parties. The DPJ performed well in the 2000 election and merged with Ichiro Ozawa's Liberal Party in 2003, making it Japan's major opposition party. Since then, Japanese politics has been dominated by the competition between the LDP and the DPJ, with other parties playing subsidiary roles. The vicissitudes of Japan's postreform party system do not falsify the bipartism hypothesis; rather, they reflect the struggle among the opposition parties to fight for the anti-LDP leadership. If so, the long-term trend should be toward a two-party system.

A good indicator of the postreform evolution of Japan's party system is the number of legislative parties. The smaller this number, the more likely it is for two randomly chosen Diet members to be from the same party.[13] Table 1, showing the effective number of parties in Japan's lower house, exhibits an interesting twist in the past two decades. Until 1993, the party system was indeed becoming more fragmented, which was crucial to the success of electoral reform. The impact of the new electoral system is indicated by the decrease in the number of legislative parties since 1993, which now is indeed approaching two. Table 1 also displays the total seat shares of the two largest parties in the lower house, which are not only increasing, but are now higher than during the period of one-party dominance. A two-party system is clearly taking shape in Japan.

Another remarkable pattern is the shifting seat share of the LDP, which has always been Japan's largest party. Although the 1993 lower-house election deprived the party of its majority status, subsequent elections gradually saw the revival of its power. This confirms the hypothesis that Japan's electoral reform was engineered by some conservative politicians who wanted to extend their own political lives. Most of these elites started their careers in the LDP, though some left the party to attract voters alienated by the old regime. The LDP's resurgence is strongly related to the low proportionality of the new, more majoritarian electoral system. In the last four lower-house elections, the LDP's vote shares in the constituency-based seats were 38.6, 41.0, 43.9, and 48.0 percent. Its PR vote shares went down over the same period (there are two separate ballots). The new system has boosted the LDP's seat shares significantly—indeed, to a stunning 62 percent in 2005. Without the new electoral system, the LDP would have had a hard time sustaining its dominance.

Regarding the style of electoral campaigning, the reformers expected the new electoral system to increase the importance of party-oriented policy debate and bipartisan competition. But the legacy of the old system still affects electoral campaigning under the new rules. In the 1996 election, for example, the raising of the consumption tax was a salient issue that clearly divided the political lineup, yet most candidates relied heavily on personal support groups *(kōenkai)* to gather votes. The competition for the 180 seats filled by PR also took on personalistic overtones, as the new system allows for dual candidacy, whereby candidates can run for an FPTP seat while also being included on the party's PR list.[14] In the long term, however, as the two-party system takes shape, the mode of campaigning will likely come to focus more on policy issues and debate.

Will Taiwan Follow Japan's Lead?

Taiwan has experienced significant changes to its party system since its transition to democracy in the early 1990s. Unlike in Japan, however, the underlying fundamental partisan division remains unchanged: Most of the parties that have formed since 1992 are splinters of either the KMT (against independence) or the DPP (for independence). In August 1993, a group of urban-based politicians left the KMT and established the New Party (NP). In 2000, after losing the presidential

TABLE 2—THE EVOLUTION OF TAIWAN'S PARTY SYSTEM

ELECTION YEAR	EFFECTIVE NUMBER OF LEGISLATIVE PARTIES	SEAT SHARE OF THE LARGEST PARTY*
1992	2.55	0.59
1995	2.65	0.52
1998	3.24	0.55
2001	3.48	0.39
2004	3.26	0.40

*1992–98: KMT; 2001–2005: DPP

polling, former KMT secretary-general James Soong broke with the party and established the PFP. On the proindependence side, some affiliates of former president Lee Teng-hui created the TSU in late 2000 to attract proindependence loyalists. Despite this fragmentation, the vote shares of the two sides are actually quite stable, with the anti-independence ("pan-Blue") camp slightly outnumbering the proindependence ("pan-Green") one.

Table 2 illustrates the evolution of Taiwan's party system over the past ten years. Comparing it with prereform Japan, we find a striking similarity: The party system has become more fragmented, and the largest party no longer dominates the national legislature. If these conditions explain why Taiwan followed the Japanese model of electoral reform, Japan's postreform consequences should shed light on Taiwan's future. But there are two features of Taiwanese politics that must be kept in mind when making such a comparison: first, the rigidity of Taiwan's national-identity cleavage, and second, the system of presidential elections. When held under SNTV, Taiwan's legislative elections were relatively unaffected by these factors, as this system encouraged particularistic representation rather than policy debate, and as legislative and presidential elections took place nonconcurrently using different electoral formulas. With the 2004 electoral reforms, however, these factors are likely to begin influencing Taiwanese politics.

The revised constitution has extended the term of the LY members from three to four years, producing a very unusual electoral cycle, where the president and legislators serve the same four-year terms. Moreover, since the constitution requires the LY to convene in February and the president to serve a four-year term beginning on May 20 of the election year, legislative and presidential elections are likely to take place in December and March, respectively. Barring the unlikely event that the LY is dissolved after a vote of no confidence, the presidential and legislative elections will take place within a few months of each other, cycle after cycle. Due to this short interval, Taiwan will likely see an effect commonly experienced by systems that hold concurrent elections—namely, a higher probability that one and the same party will control both the executive and the legislative branches.

Moreover, the dynamics of the presidential election will likely have a strong impact on legislative campaigning. The short interval between the two elections means that parties will have to have already nominated their presidential candidates by the time the LY election takes place. Since Taiwan elects its president by FPTP, voters will tend to gravitate to the two leading presidential candidates. Such a two-person presidential race is likely to overshadow the legislative election and to make it hard for smaller parties to make their voices heard during the campaign. With little hope to win the presidency or the FPTP legislative seats, these parties will bet everything on winning the PR seats. Even so, unless the leading parties both stumble and fail to gain a legislative majority, Taiwan's minor parties will quickly lose their pivotal position as potential coalition partners. Thus, Taiwan may well be moving toward a two-party system at a quicker pace than Japan.

Although it is rarely used, SNTV satisfies the culture and demands of emerging democracies more easily than do its alternatives. As party systems in these countries often are either nonexistent or highly unstable, SNTV makes the election process simpler by requiring voters to choose a candidate rather than a party. It also makes vote counting simpler and cheaper than it would be under PR or any form of preferential voting. The system is also relatively proportional, so it serves well to ensure minority representation.

Moreover, SNTV tends to factionalize local interests, giving state-builders convenient leverage to enforce their commands from the center by offering their local agents particularistic benefits. From the experiences of Japan and Taiwan, these factors do seem to contribute to the growth of the developmental state. But the argument is not reversible: SNTV does not inherently nurture a dominant party, let alone a strong state. Young democracies should find other ways to develop their economies.

Once a dominant-party system evolves in tandem with SNTV, however, some citizens will be systematically disfavored. This state of affairs will eventually prompt some politicians to propose an electoral reform that increases their odds for survival. This dynamic explains not only the abandonment of SNTV, but also the subsequent outcomes. As can be seen from the premiership of Junichiro Koizumi (2001–present), the LDP revived under his reign by choosing a new winning strategy.[15] With Taiwan having adopted the same new electoral system, the KMT has a similar chance to rise again—if it can learn to play the electoral game in a different way.

NOTES

1. For a review of how the developmental-state theory explains East Asian development, see Meredith Woo-Cumings, ed., *The Developmental State* (Ithaca, N.Y.: Cornell University Press, 1999).

2. South Korea used SNTV in two-member districts between 1980 and 1987. SNTV has also seen some use in other places, such as Puerto Rico, Vanuatu, Thailand, and most recently in Afghanistan. Yet its effects are most visible in Japan and Taiwan, as only in these countries has SNTV been the exclusive electoral system over an extended period.

3. As a result, Japan and Taiwan both experienced a long period of one-party dominance. For the case of Japan, see J. Mark Ramseyer and Frances M. Rosenbluth, *Japan's Political Marketplace* (Cambridge: Harvard University Press, 1993) and T. J. Pempel, ed., *Uncommon Democracies: The One-Party Dominant Regimes* (Ithaca, N.Y.: Cornell University Press, 1990). For Taiwan, see Yun-han Chu, "SNTV and the Evolving Party System in Taiwan," *Chinese Political Science Review* 22 (June 1994): 33–51.

4. Raymond Christensen, "Electoral Reform in Japan: How It Was Enacted and Changes It May Bring," *Asian Survey* 34 (July 1994): 589–605; Rei Shiratori, "The Politics of Electoral Reform in Japan," *International Political Science Review* 16 (January 1995): 79–94.

5. "Amendment raises hope for a new constitution," *Taipei Times,* 24 August 2004.

6. Steven R. Reed and Michael F. Thies, "The Causes of Electoral Reform in Japan," in Matthew Soberg Shugart and Martin P. Wattenberg, eds., *Mixed-Member Electoral Systems* (New York: Oxford University Press, 2001), 153.

7. Under SNTV, a party usually maximizes its seat share by strategically allocating its vote equally among its candidates, which makes most members of a dominant party electorally insecure. See Gary W. Cox, *Making Votes Count: Strategic Coordination in the World's Electoral Systems* (Cambridge: Cambridge University Press, 1997), 242.

8. SNTV was drafted by the state-builders of the Meiji Restoration. See J. Mark Ramseyer and Frances M. Rosenbluth, *The Politics of Oligarchy: Institutional Choice in Imperial Japan* (Cambridge: Cambridge University Press, 1998), 37.

9. Brian Woodall, "The Politics of Reform in Japan's Lower House Electoral System," in Bernard Grofman, Sung-Chull Lee, Edwin A. Winckler, and Brian Woodall, eds., *Elections in Japan, Korea, and Taiwan Under the Single Non-Transferable Vote* (Ann Arbor: University of Michigan Press, 1999), 26–27.

10. Some saw NFP leader Ichiro Ozawa as the chief orchestrator of Japan's political reform. The new electoral system, he hoped, would unshackle Japan from the LDP's dominance and generate a dynamic bipartisan system. See Ichiro Ozawa, *Blueprint for a New Japan: The Rethinking of a Nation* (New York: Kodansha International, 1994), 62–75.

11. Other reform bills were proposed in 1967 and 1968 by Prime Minister Ezaku Sato, but the content was not directly related to electoral reform. See Brian Woodall, "The Politics of Reform in Japan's Lower House Electoral System," 36.

12. The German system is mixed in that half the seats are filled by FPTP and half from PR lists, but many observers do not realize that it is in essence a system of proportional representation, in that it draws from the party lists to achieve *overall* proportionality in the allocation of parliamentary seats (after imposing a five percent threshold for party representation). By contrast, the Japanese system achieves proportionality only in the distribution of the share of seats (about 40 percent of them) assigned to the PR rule. Therefore, the German system better represents smaller opposition parties if they clear the threshold.

13. The effective number of legislative parties is $1/SSi2$, where Si stands for the seat share of party i. See Rein Taagepera and Matthew Soberg Shugart, *Seats and Votes: The Effects and Determinants of Electoral Systems* (New Haven: Yale University Press, 1989), 77–81.

14. With dual candidacy, candidates can run for an FPTP constituency while also appearing on the party PR list, where they can be ranked individually or equally. In the latter case, the candidate whose FPTP vote ratio is closest to the FPTP winner receives the PR seat. This system, a safety net for senior politicians, reinforced the personalistic tendency of Japan's elections under the new rule. On the 1996 elections, see Albert L. Seligmann, "Japan's New Electoral System," *Asian Survey* 37 (May 1997): 409–28; and Margaret McKean and Ethan Scheiner, "Japan's New Electoral System: La Plus Ça Change," *Electoral Studies* 19 (December 2000): 447–77.

15. According to a survey conducted by the *Asahi Shimbun* newspaper, the proportion of Japanese citizens agreeing that the LDP has changed under Koizumi's leadership increased significantly in recent months. See *Asahi Shimbun* (Tokyo), 2 November 2005.

18

THE CURIOUS CASE OF AFGHANISTAN

Andrew Reynolds

Andrew Reynolds *is associate professor of political science at the University of North Carolina at Chapel Hill.* *He has consulted on issues of electoral and constitutional design for a wide array of countries.* *His latest book is* The Architecture of Democracy: Constitutional Design, Conflict Management, and Democracy *(2002).* *This essay originally appeared in the April 2006 issue of the* Journal of Democracy.

On 18 September 2005, nearly six and a half million Afghans voted in the freest and most competitive legislative elections they had ever experienced. Almost half of them were women, which had a significant impact on the power dynamics of the new legislature. Elections were held for the 249-seat Wolesi Jirga (Council of the People) and the indirectly elected 102-seat Meshrano Jirga (Council of the Elders), as well as for local councils. With the convening of the new parliament on 18 December 2005, the international community proclaimed that a substantial part of the 2001 Bonn Agreement had been fulfilled, namely "the establishment of a broad-based, gender sensitive, multiethnic and fully representative government through national elections."[1]

This election, as well as Afghanistan's October 2004 presidential polling, vividly demonstrated that vibrant and meaningful elections can be conducted even under the most unpromising circumstances. Moreover, the 2004 and 2005 ballotings showed that, when given the opportunity, women can make significant political progress even in highly patriarchal, conservative societies. Regardless of how the country began its transformation from dictatorship to democracy, its two elections have proven that the yearning to choose leaders freely and hold them accountable is the human condition. Indeed, the "ordinary citizen"—the man on the Kabul bus, the woman in the Herat library, the nomad shepherd in the mountains—will vote with confidence when given the chance.

But the Afghan legislative elections also illuminate some far less celebratory truisms about the transition to democracy. First, designing appropriate institutions tailored to the needs of an emerging democratic society remains the greatest challenge. Second, the electoral system is the most important of these democratic institutions; an inappropriate or flawed electoral system can retard democracy's progress as much as warlords, religious fundamentalists, and corrupt business leaders taken together. Third, if the choice of an electoral system is based on mistaken theory or a poor grasp of what election and party-system mechanics will mean "on the ground," the results are likely to be far from desirable. Indeed, if an electoral system is less chosen than haphazardly assembled by means of drift and accident, an ineffective legislature will be the upshot. Last, Afghanistan exemplifies the difficulty of promoting multiparty politics in an inchoate democracy, where leadership is heavily swayed by the need to incorporate and assuage corrupt and deeply undemocratic sectional interests.

The electoral system ultimately used in the September 2005 Wolesi Jirga elections featured the rarely used single nontransferable vote (SNTV), a system employed in Japan from 1948 to 1993, but today used only in Jordan, Vanuatu, the Pitcairn Islands, and partially in Taiwan (although there change is underway). Under the SNTV system, Afghan voters cast ballots for individual candidates rather than political parties. Each province elects a number of members, some of whom have to be women, but each voter can vote for one and only one candidate. Candidates are elected by simply winning the most votes: If a district has been allotted four seats, then the top four vote-getters are elected. Thus, if collectively a party wins a majority of the votes, it does not necessarily win a majority of the seats—the number of seats won depends on whether individual candidates whom the party has fielded have performed adequately. "Adequate" candidates need not be especially popular, however: In a notional four-seat district, for instance, one candidate could be elected with 90 percent of the votes while three others could be elected with 3 percent each.

The advantages of the SNTV system are that it is simple, both for voters and for those who administer the election; that it promotes representation of independents in a nascent party system; and that it boosts representation and accountability by giving the individual voter a sense of being "invested" in a known individual candidate rather than some faceless party-determined list. But the system is believed to lose its efficacy when the districts are too large in size, because the vote then becomes too fragmented. For that reason, the average district in Japan, Jordan, and Vanuatu had four seats. In Afghanistan, however, the districts ended up being based on provincial boundaries and ranged from 2 to 33 seats—a third of the districts had more than nine seats.

How Afghanistan Ended Up With SNTV

The process for designing Afghanistan's new constitution was laid out by the December 2001 Bonn Agreement. It was an efficient but closed process, whose product was ultimately rooted in the transitional government's own interests and presented to the public largely as a *fait accompli*. A nine-member committee appointed by interim president Hamid Karzai came up with an initial draft between October 2002 and March 2003. One of the most important constitutional issues with which these drafters had to grapple was the choice of an electoral system for the new legislature: Should they return to the first-past-the-post (FPTP) system inherited from British colonial rule and used in the brief period of competitive multiparty politics during the 1960s? Or should they adhere to the trend of list-based proportional representation (list PR), which has been the system of choice in the vast majority of postconflict situations since 1989? Or was there another system that would better fit Afghan circumstances?

The drafting committee received expert advice from, among others, the International Foundation for Election Systems, Princeton University's Liechtenstein Institute for Self Determination (LISD), and from the constitutional experts who authored "Afghanistan's Political and Constitutional Development: Summary and Key Recommendations."[2] All these advisors sought to steer the drafters away from the old FPTP system and toward a form of proportional representation that had some geographic basis and allowed space for independent candidates. According to the abovementioned report:

> The electoral system [needs] to allow for the representation of Afghanistan's diversity, and give all contenders for power enough of a stake in the system that they remain bound to democratic politics. Given the factionalized nature of Afghan politics, the primary goal should be to produce reasonable proportionality. In addition, most Afghans want an opportunity to vote for candidates from their own area, and the distrust of political parties means that voters should be given the chance to vote for individuals, rather than only parties. Voting procedure will also need to be simple and transparent; illiteracy and innumeracy limit the complexity of possible voting systems, and inexperience with voting also means that results must be easily explicable.[3]

Between April and November 2003, a 35-member all-Afghan constitutional commission selected by Karzai refined the earlier committee's draft, and produced a final document that was presented for ratification to the constitutional Loya Jirga in December 2003.[4] The new constitution, which provoked significant unhappiness and was ratified only with the help of strong political pressure,[5] did not make explicit the electoral system to be used for the legislative elections. A decision had been reached, however, that some form of list PR was to be used: This was spelled out in an appendix to the constitution. The Transitional Government assumed the task of working out the details of the system in cooperation with the Joint Election Management Body (JEMB) and the UN Assistance Mission in Afghanistan (UNAMA).

By early 2004, they had designed what they thought was the best alternative: a closed-list PR system using multimember districts based on Afghanistan's 34 historic provinces. Less complicated than open-list PR, such a system would allow party leaders to determine which candidates would appear on the ticket and in what order, meaning that voters would cast their ballots for a party, not a specific candidate. Enayat Qasimi, a young Afghan-émigré lawyer who had recently returned to act as legal advisor to President Karzai, was selected to present this system to the cabinet of the transitional government. By the accounts of some of those present—including cabinet ministers as well as UNAMA and JEMB representatives—Qasimi made an utter hash of presenting the system, demonstrating that he himself was confused about its workings.[6] This gave an opening to critics: If the president's own legal advisor could not make the system intelligible to the cabinet, the ministers argued, then how were ordinary Afghans supposed to understand the system?

In such a fragile and distrustful environment—the cabinet being a loose patchwork of feuding technocrats, returnees, jihadi leaders, and unreconstructed warlords—Qasimi's inept presentation of the system opened the door for some ministers to complain that it was a bad system for Afghanistan. This sentiment was fueled by the distrust of political parties common among Afghans due to the chaotic nature of multiparty politics in the 1960s and the subsequent Communist Party rule and Soviet occupation (1978–89). Leading the charge against PR was Minister for Rural Development Mohammad Haneef Atmar, with the backing of several other ministers from the Pushtun southeast.

In the face of this onslaught of objections, President Karzai decided to ask about alternatives to closed-list PR. He asked the international members of the JEMB to draw up a memorandum, detailing which electoral systems would allow Afghans to vote for individual candidates rather than parties, while retaining the province as the base constituency (he understood that for logistical and political reasons single-member districts were not an option). The SNTV system ultimately chosen was the "least bad" of the alternatives that fit these criteria. Thus Afghanistan ended up with SNTV not as a result of extensive deliberation and careful evaluation of its pros and cons, but rather by a fairly random process of elimination. SNTV was simply better than the other systems combining a single vote for a candidate with provincial multimember constituencies. It is important to note that Karzai did not choose SNTV with any understanding of its consequences or history.

How Was It *Supposed* to Work?

The received wisdom on SNTV—based on forty years of use in Japan and a decade in Jordan—is that the system can be manageable under specific circumstances, but that it is not generally desirable as a means of translating votes into seats in a democracy. In the case of Japan, the system had been part of the institutions "bestowed" upon the country after the Second World War, and in Jordan it was the product of the late King Hussein's 1993 manipulation of the former bloc-voting system.[7] The chief flaw of SNTV is the difficulty of strategic coordination that it creates for parties: How many candidates should a party field within a given constituency, and how can a party induce voters to share their votes equally across these candidates? The system's most undesirable consequences include a high disproportionality between votes and seats won, a tendency to exclude minority parties, the encouraging of clientelism and corruption among those elected, and ultimately the fragmentation of the ruling party.

In September 2004, I joined Andrew Wilder, the director of the Kabul-based Afghan Research and Evaluation Unit (AREU), in speculating as to how SNTV might work were it to be used under Afghan conditions.[8] We foresaw five negative consequences involving 1) the translation of votes into seats; 2) the party system; 3) the vote itself; 4) the ability of the elected bodies to govern; and 5) female representation.

1) The relationship between votes and seats won. Founding elections in fledgling postconflict democracies need to do a particularly good job of fairly translating votes cast into seats won for majorities, minorities, and independents. Election results are particularly susceptible to challenge if the losing candidates feel that the electoral system has discriminated against them or their core constituencies. Candidates should also be afforded the reasonable assumption that if they do relatively well in the vote they will get elected. We worried that in Afghanistan SNTV would be unable to live up to these expectations. Because it creates a capricious relationship between votes and seats, we reasoned that seat shares would depend on how many candidates stood in a province and how voters distributed their votes across those candidates. We predicted that in the larger districts STNV would create a lottery effect: It would be entirely random as to who among independents and minority candidates got elected.

2) The establishment of a stable party system. Experience shows that in postconflict environments democracy and stability require the promotion and encouragement of a stable party system. Even in systems that discourage or do not recognize parties, likeminded interests gravitate together to form party-like movements, blocs, lists, and alliances. Manipulating electoral systems in an effort to eliminate parties merely makes such blocs unaccountable, less democratic, and less able to respond to voters' interests.

The SNTV electoral system weakens the role of political parties, thereby working against the rise of a stable, dynamic, and accountable party system. While Afghanistan's electoral law did not bar political parties from fielding candidates, party affiliations were left off the ballot. We predicted that this would result in a fragmented legislature comprising a multitude of independents and small political factions—making government formation and legislative politics hard to manage—and that any parliamentary factions or alliances would likely be disjointed and personality-driven, beholden to regional bases or strongmen rather than national interests.

3) Ensuring a clear and effective vote. We argued that it was crucially important for the voting itself to be easy, so that Afghans could use their ballots to make their political preferences heard "loud and clear." Should the ballot itself prove too complex, voters would be alienated and unable to see the link between their votes and the newly formed government. We speculated that SNTV, particularly in the larger districts, would encourage a great number of candidates, making ballots long and confusing and causing illiterate voters to suffer most. There could be hundreds of names and symbols on the ballot (one for each candidate regardless of party affiliation), making it difficult for candidates to publicize their unique symbol. Furthermore, the vote-seat anomalies and vagaries of the SNTV system would result in a fragmented parliament and a lack of transparency in government formation, leaving many voters wondering what their ballot had had to do with the whole murky process.

4) Allowing the executive and legislature to govern. In emerging democracies where power is balanced between the legislature and a directly elected executive, it is important that the former is designed to work in harness with the president and not block his or her will at every turn. Considering the pressing need for effective legislation and policy making in democratizing countries, gridlock in government is particularly dangerous. We reasoned that if legislative elections had been held concurrently with the October 2004 presidential election, the SNTV system might have been more likely to produce a solid pro-Karzai bloc in the Wolesi Jirga. Instead, the year-long gap between the two elections was bound to weaken his legislative base. In a memorandum I wrote for President Karzai in January 2005, I argued:

> The system [SNTV] will advantage those parties/movements most able to mobilize and manipulate votes. While the President has broad multi-ethnic support he does not have the level of party "machines" that commanders and provincial power brokers have in the North, East and West. Thus if anti-Karzai forces are attuned to the winning strategy of SNTV they are likely to win many more seats than their vote share would suggest.[9]

5) Promoting dynamic women in parliament. Affirmative-action mechanisms, or electoral quotas, generally boost the advancement of women's interests when a) voters do not consider them overtly manipulative; b) they facilitate the election of women who are less dependent on traditional power structures; c) the women elected have an electoral base and enjoy some degree of legitimacy; and d) male-dominated parties find it in their interests to field progressive women candidates who will appeal to both male and female voters.

The Afghan electoral law set aside an average of two seats per province—a national total of 68 seats—to be filled by women candidates. We speculated that, in combination with the SNTV system, these quotas increased the likelihood of women winning such reserved seats with dramatically fewer votes than losing male candidates throughout the country. In an environment not known to be particularly open to women's involvement in political leadership, or even to women holding visible social or professional positions, we feared that this might breed concentrated resentment against women legislators.

Many international organizations, foreign diplomats, UNAMA, and emerging progressive Afghan political and civil society movements in Kabul shared some or all of our concerns regarding the malign consequences of SNTV. Though Karzai had signed the SNTV electoral law on 25 May 2004, intensive efforts to persuade him and his closest confidants to revert to list PR continued until early 2005. UN special representative Jean Arnault and EU representative Francisco Vendrell led the diplomatic lobbying effort, which notably did not enjoy the support of U.S. ambassador Zalmay Khalilizad—who was close to Karzai but was said to doubt the salience of the electoral-system issue. The AREU and the International Crisis Group both prepared reports on the potential problems of SNTV in an emerging democracy, while senior international members of the JEMB wrote confidential memoranda outlining how disastrous SNTV could prove to be for the nascent Afghan democracy.[10]

On 17 January 2005, 35 of Afghanistan's 40 registered political parties released a joint statement saying that they supported a list-PR system and wanted the electoral law revised along the lines of a draft law produced by UNAMA. To get over the general distaste for political parties, the UNAMA draft law talked of seats being awarded to "lists" rather than parties. In January 2005, the three main challengers to Karzai in the 2004 presidential election—opposition leaders Abdul Rashid Dostum (an Uzbek warlord), Yunous Qanooni (a Tajik from the Northern Alliance), and Haji Mohammad Mohaqiq (a Hazara)—stated that they supported list PR and not SNTV.

The momentum for change seemed overwhelming, and members of the JEMB believed that Karzai had decided to revert to a province-based, closed-list–PR system as had initially been envisaged.[11] By early February 2005, however, a new objection to closed lists had surfaced among Pushtun cabinet members close to Karzai, a Pushtun. They feared that the list system could benefit the charismatic non-Pushtuns Dostum, Qanooni, and Mohaqiq, as well as the opposition candidates riding their coattails. This would injure the strategy of Karzai and his confidants, who envisioned a legislature divided between Pushtun MPs—

most of whom, if push came to shove, would support the president—and a fragmented non-Pushtun opposition. Thus, without much theoretical basis, the president and his advisers determined that SNTV was the system that would best serve their interests.

In response to this decision, I drafted a memorandum suggesting an open-list version of PR that would allow voters to cast their ballots in support of individual candidates on the party lists. Solicited by Karzai's national security advisor Zalmay Rassoul (who later presented it to Karzai), this proposal was presented to the cabinet by Interior Minister Ali Jalali and garnered the support of some non-Pushtun ministers. But before the debate could be reenergized, the cabinet on February 15 confirmed the SNTV system—with only three cabinet members voting against it.

What Actually Happened

The final results of the September 2005 legislative elections, delayed by accusations of fraud, were eventually announced on November 12, and the new legislature convened on December 18. Considering the controversy that had surrounded Afghanistan's choice of electoral system, what kind of legislature did the SNTV system eventually produce?

1) The relationship between votes and seats won. Whether SNTV produced a legislature broadly representative of Afghan society's political cleavages is difficult to judge. The party system is so embryonic that one cannot simply compare political movements' vote shares with their seat shares in parliament. There are approximately 33 identifiable parties, factions, and alliances in the Wolesi Jirga, but few of them campaigned on any form of coherent ideological platform. Rather, these groups merely consist of independent MPs allied with regional and national strongmen.

One measure of balance is the degree of ethnic diversity in the new legislature. Indeed, there were concerns that partisan politics would produce a Tajik-Uzbek-Hazara opposition bloc pitted against a collection of Pushtun representatives presumed to support President Karzai. Andrew Wilder's recent analysis shows that the ethnic proportions in the new Wolesi Jirga largely adhere to the estimated ethnic proportions in the country as a whole (though these estimates are controversial, as there has not been a nationwide census for more than three decades).[12]

Though the new legislature is divided along ethnic lines, ethnicity is by no means the only cleavage in evidence. Only 40 percent of the Pushtun MPs can be categorized as pro-Karzai, while 14 percent are in the opposition camp, and nearly half are nonaligned—including many of the female representatives. Tajiks are split almost equally among pro-Karzai, opposition, and nonaligned camps; only the Hazara and Uzbek MPs sit overwhelmingly on the opposition benches.

TABLE 1—ETHNICITY AND ELECTED REPRESENTATION

ETHNICITY	NUMBER OF LEGISLATIVE SEATS	PERCENT OF LEGISLATIVE SEATS	ESTIMATED POPULATION SHARE
Pushtun	118	47	40–45
Tajik	53	21	20–25
Hazara	30	12	10–13
Uzbek	20	8	8–10
Others	28	12	n/a
Total	249	100	–

Source: Andrew Wilder, "A House Divided? Analysing the 2005 Afghan Elections," Afghanistan Research and Evaluation Unit, December 2005.

Both pro-Karzai and opposition factions are likely to push hard for legislation rooted in a conservative interpretation of Islam. Approximately 65 MPs are fundamentalist Muslims, with Abd al-Rabb al-Rasul Sayyaf's and Burhanuddin Rabbani's pro-Karzai factions and Qanooni's opposition faction in the vanguard. These groups may also come to enjoy the support of many of the 47 MPs in the more moderate traditionalist camp led by the Hazara Shi'ites. The smallest faction in the Wolesi Jirga comprises 43 more-progressive MPs, including the 13 liberal democrats and leftists as well as the 20 MPs affiliated with Dostum's secular National Islamic Movement.

Some remarkable facts about the members of the Wolesi Jirga, identified by a Kabul-based human rights group, indicate that they are not entirely representative of the greater population. Among the 249 legislators, there are 40 commanders still linked to militias, 24 who belong to criminal gangs, 17 drug traffickers, and 19 against whom there are serious war-crimes allegations. Moreover, nearly half of all MPs were *mujahideen* (holy warriors) against Soviet occupation during the 1980s.[13]

When judging the relationship between votes and seats in the Wolesi Jirga, it is important to stress that the candidates elected are not those for which a majority of Afghan voters cast their ballots. Just over two million of the more than six million votes (32 percent) were cast for winning candidates, and thus four million votes (68 percent) were cast for candidates who lost. The extent of this "wasted vote" is remarkably high; in comparison, only 5.3 percent of votes were wasted in the January 2005 Iraqi elections, and less than 1 percent in South Africa's first democratic election in 1994.

The reason for the high ratio of wasted votes was the abundance of competing candidates, which in turn was an expected effect of the SNTV system. With so many candidates in each province, the votes were spread very thin: The first seat in each region was won with an average of 11.5 percent of the vote, and the last seat was taken with an average of just 5.7 percent. In Kabul province, more than 400 candidates competed for 33 seats, and the last seat went to a candidate who received only 0.5 percent of the vote.

SNTV indeed caused the lottery effect that we had predicted, especially in the larger districts. On average, there were only 864 votes between the lowest-polling elected candidate and the highest-polling (male) runner up. Such tiny margins brought into dispute the results in areas tainted by vote fraud and campaign manipulation. They also make wild swings of legislative power likely from election to election: Despite incumbency—or perhaps because of it—most members of this Wolesi Jirga could very easily be ousted next time around.

2) The establishment of a stable party system. In the runup to the parliamentary elections, SNTV was expected to retard the development of a stable party system by causing political fragmentation, thereby making national legislation the business not of ideologically coherent political parties but of regional warlords and religious fundamentalists. The election outcome gave credence to each of these concerns. Only 16 percent of the more than 2,700 candidates were from registered political parties; these candidates won less than a third of the seats in the Wolesi Jirga.

As noted earlier, there are as many as 33 identifiable parties, factions, and alliances in the 249-seat legislature, the largest group being Qanooni's New Afghanistan party with 25 seats (10 percent of the total). Members of the National Democratic Front, a new alliance comprising 14 liberal-democratic parties, won only 7 seats, and candidates representing the old leftist parties won just 6. Supporting Karzai is a motley collection of small bands led by powerful individuals whose interests will need to be assuaged to guarantee a voting bloc for the president's legislative agenda.

3) Ensuring a clear and effective vote. There is substantial evidence that many voters found the SNTV system and the poster-sized ballots confusing. Because 49 percent of Afghan males and 79 percent of Afghan females are illiterate, the electoral commission had assigned each candidate an icon that was included on the ballot next to the candidate's name and picture. Because there were not enough different icons, some candidates had multiple icons as their symbol, which further added to the confusion.[14] Many candidates, especially those new on the political scene, found it immensely difficult to communicate to illiterate voters either their face or their assigned symbol.

According to an October 2005 opinion poll carried out by Charney Research, the main reason respondents gave for not voting was that they did not find a candidate whom they could support.[15] Craig Charney argued that this was compounded by the ballot itself, associating "the low turnout in Kabul [with] the electoral system there, where people, often of low literacy, were confronted with pages and pages of ballots."[16] Moreover, the extreme fragmentation of the vote also indicates that in the absence of parties—affiliation was not listed on the ballot even for those candidates backed by a party—it was difficult for voters to fathom which blocs were likely to be influential in the new parliament.

Further evidence regarding the level of confusion among voters comes from the high percentage of invalid or "spoiled" ballots: 2.9 percent of all ballots were rejected because they were marked in error or for disqualified candidates, and 2.1 percent because they were blank. The total of 5 percent compares to less than 1 percent in South Africa's 1994 elections, 1.1 percent in the January 2005 Iraqi elections, and 2.4 percent in Liberia's November 2005 election. Voter confusion was possibly one of the main reasons behind the low overall turnout, which dropped from 69 percent in the October 2004 presidential election to 50 percent in the September 2005 Wolesi Jirga elections (going as low as 29 percent in the south). In Iraq, by contrast, turnout *increased* from 58 percent in January 2005 to 70 percent in December 2005.

4) Allowing the executive and legislature to govern. The new legislature is likely to obstruct the passage of President Karzai's reform agenda. The plethora of vested interests and the extreme fragmentation caused by the SNTV system mean that Karzai will have to cobble together a majority for every executive bill by way of piecemeal promises and logrolling.

Karzai won 55 percent of the vote in the 2004 presidential election—more than three times the vote share of his closest rival—but the pro-Karzai bloc now makes up less than a third of the Wolesi Jirga (and is by no means monolithic). The opposition makes up slightly more than a third, and so do nonaligned legislators. The strength of the opposition to Karzai became clear when, as soon as the new legislature convened, Qanooni won the coveted Wolesi Jirga chairmanship by 122 to 117 votes over Sayyaf, Karzai's favored candidate. Qanooni subsequently resigned from his de facto position as opposition leader in favor of Rabbani, who previously had been seen as a member of the pro-Karzai camp.

5) Promoting dynamic women in parliament. Female representation was the only area in which SNTV actually proved to have a positive effect. The quota mechanism, which ensured that a total of 68 women were elected (on average two per province), remained largely unchallenged. The fragmenting effect of SNTV helped 19 women—8 percent of all MPs—get elected in their own right without the aid of the affirmative-action mechanisms. In the large Western province of Herat, for example, female candidate Fauzia Gailani outpolled all male candidates, including those backed by local warlords. In the province of Farah, female candidate Malalai Joya came in second; she had bravely denounced the warlords at the constitutional Loya Jirga, and her election may have been the result of protest votes cast by those alienated from traditional, corrupt, and warmongering male candidates.[17] It is also worth noting that in December, the new Wolesi Jirga chose as its second deputy chairperson Fawzia Kofi, who had been elected without the help of quotas in the eastern province of Badakhshan.

TABLE 2—AFGHAN ELECTION RESULTS

BLOC	2004 PRESIDENTIAL ELECTION (% VOTES)	2005 LEGISLATIVE ELECTION (% SEATS)
Pro-Karzai	55	32
Anti-Karzai	45	34
Yunous Qanooni	*16*	*10*
Abdul Rashid Dostum	*10*	*8*
Haji Mohammad Mohaqiq	*12*	*7*
Others	*7*	*9*
Nonaligned	–	34

Source: JEMB

Taken together, the 68 women MPs form a highly significant voting bloc, one that is for the most part unaligned with traditional interests. Yet their future influence in the legislature remains unclear. While our fear that many women would get elected with dramatically lower vote shares than unsuccessful male candidates was not borne out, 49 of the 68 female MPs still owe their election to the quota mechanism, having leaped over 422 male candidates who outpolled them (there was an average of twelve higher-polling males per district).

Even the 19 women elected without the aid of quotas received an average of only 3 percent of the vote; their election was as much a consequence of the lottery aspect of SNTV as of their popularity. Altogether, the 68 women elected polled an average of just 2.3 percent each—significantly lower than their male counterparts. The highest vote share for a woman was 9.2 percent in the Panshjir Valley—the heartland of the Northern Alliance—and the highest number of votes was 9,092 for a woman who came in third in Nangarhar province. In Zabul province, the woman who claimed the reserved seat had polled a total of only 751 votes, while the highest-polling defeated male candidate had received 1,816.

The advantages that women received from the quota system, however, should not diminish the amazing progress that they have made in the Afghan political arena. Their advancement is particularly remarkable considering the oppression that they endured under the Taliban just a few years ago.

What Next?

By and large, the SNTV electoral system based on large districts did just what experts had predicted that it would do: It decreased turnout by confusing voters, it created a fragmented legislature largely unrepresentative of the votes cast, and it diminished the prospects for legislative-executive cooperation. And it did not work in favor of President Karzai, as he and his advisors had hoped. Karzai and his clique had envisioned the emergence of a loyal Pushtun-majority bloc upon which the executive could rely for legislative support. While the SNTV system did to a degree serve to fragment the opposition and retard the emergence of new parties, it also fragmented the president's largely Pushtun base. Indeed, it transformed the absolute majority that he had won in the presidential election into a disjointed bloc comprising no more than a third of the Wolesi Jirga.

As predicted, the new legislature has already shown itself to be a place of wheeling and dealing, of clientelism and shifting alliances, where men with tainted pasts hold significant sway over the future of Afghan democracy. As the liberal-democratic and progressive parties faced high hurdles in getting their messages across and their candidates elected, most hopes for moderation and nonviolent reform are now pinned to the 68 women MPs, most of whom are nonaligned and independent of traditional power structures. If the reserved women's seats are ever abolished, the prospects for reform and democratic progress will be much bleaker than they are today.

The SNTV electoral system came about by a path of muddled missteps, and it was a disservice to the millions of Afghans who deserved a clear and transparent tool to craft their first democratic parliament. Not only did the system fail to provide such a tool, but it is destined to work in favor of those who seek to strongarm and bribe their way into office. If SNTV is used in subsequent elections, the fragmentation and parochialism of the legislature will increase, and politics in general will remain detached from the masses.

No electoral system can transform an illiberal polity into a representative democracy without a raft of supporting social, economic, and institutional transformations. But an appropriately crafted PR system—one that both is proportional and allows Afghans to vote for individual candidates—can do much to encourage the emergence of a stable party system, better translating votes cast into seats won, simplifying the vote, and promoting cooperation between the executive and the legislature. Only by adopting such a system will Afghanistan be able to avoid the great anomalies that were so apparent in the 2005 Wolesi Jirga elections.

NOTES

1. Preamble to the Bonn Agreement, officially called the Agreement on Provisional Arrangements in Afghanistan Pending the Re-establishment of Permanent Government Institutions, signed 5 December 2001. Available at *www.un.org/news/dh/latest/afghan/afghan-agree.htm.*

2. Chris Johnson, William Maley, Alexander Thier, and Ali Wardak, "Afghanistan's Political and Constitutional Development," report by the Overseas Development Institute and the UK Department for International Development, London, January 2003. Available at *www.odi.org.uk/hpg/papers/evaluations/afghandfid.pdf.* In the interests of full disclosure, I was a consultant to this study.

3. Chris Johnson, et al., "Afghanistan's Political and Constitutional Development," 7.

4. See Barnett Rubin, "Crafting the Afghan Constitution," *Journal of Democracy* 15 (July 2004): 5–19.

5. See Larry Goodson, "Afghanistan's Long Road to Reconstruction," *Journal of Democracy* 14 (January 2003): 82–99.

6. Author's private conversations with international members of the JEMB, an Afghan cabinet minister, and others close to the process.

7. King Hussein believed that limiting a voter to a single vote in a multimember constituency would reduce the capacity of the Muslim Brotherhood to win seats. Subsequent elections gave some credence to this notion. See Andrew Reynolds and Jorgen Elklit, "Jordan: Electoral System Design in the Arab World," in Andrew Reynolds and Ben Reilly, eds., *International IDEA Handbook of Electoral System Design* (Stockholm: International IDEA, 1997), 53–54.

8. Andrew Reynolds and Andrew Wilder, *Free, Fair or Flawed: Challenges for Legitimate Elections in Afghanistan* (Kabul: Afghanistan Research and Evaluation Unit, 2004).

9. The memo was solicited by Karzai's National Security Advisor, Zalmay Rassoul, and was discussed with Minister of Reconstruction Amin Farhang and Finance Minister Ashraf Ghani before reaching President Karzai.

10. See Andrew Reynolds, Lucy Jones, and Andrew Wilder, "A Guide to Parliamentary Elections in Afghanistan," Afghanistan Research and Evaluation Unit, August 2005, available at *www.areu.org.af*; and International Crisis Group, "Afghanistan: From Presidential to Parliamentary Elections," *Asia Report* 88, 23 November 2004.

11. Author's private conversations with international members of the JEMB, January 2005.

12. Andrew Wilder, "A House Divided? Analysing the 2005 Afghan Elections" Afghanistan Research and Evaluation Unit, December 2005, 8. Available at *www.areu.org.af*.

13. See "Let's Make A Deal: A Democracy Arrives, Afghan Style," *New York Times,* 4 December 2005, 14.

14. Candidates were given a choice of three symbols drawn at random. These included representations of animals, forms of transport, cell phones, oil rigs, and weather patterns. Thirty-five MPs were elected with animal symbols (with birds leading the way with 16); 32 won with planes, trains, or automobiles (plus four boats in this land-locked nation); and there were 14 fruit-and-vegetable MPs.

15. ABC News poll, "Despite Deep Challenges in Daily Life, Afghans Express a Positive Outlook," 7 December 2005. Available at *http://abcnews.go.com/images/Politics/998a1Afghanistan.pdf*.

16. Comment by Craig Charney at "Afghanistan at a Crossroads," a roundtable discussion hosted by the Century Foundation, 7 December 2005.

17. See Andrew Wilder, "A House Divided?"

19

IRAQ'S YEAR OF VOTING DANGEROUSLY

Adeed Dawisha and Larry Diamond

Adeed Dawisha is professor of political science at Miami University in Ohio and author of Arab Nationalism in the Twentieth Century: From Triumph to Despair *(2003). He has written extensively on competitive politics in Iraq during the first half of the twentieth century and in the recent postwar period.* Larry Diamond *is senior fellow at the Hoover Institution, coeditor of the* Journal of Democracy, *and author of* Squandered Victory: The American Occupation and the Bungled Effort to Bring Democracy to Iraq *(2005). This essay originally appeared in the April 2006 issue of the* Journal of Democracy.

The year 2005 may prove to have been one of the most politically consequential in the modern history of Iraq. In the space of less than eleven months, the country held three elections. Two of these, at the beginning and the end of the year, elected parliaments under a transitional and then a permanent constitution. Sandwiched between these, in October, was a referendum to approve the draft constitution. The elections took place successfully, with Iraqis voting in large numbers despite widespread logistical challenges, terrorist intimidation, and insurgent violence. But in their entrenchment of ethnic and sectarian fissures as the main organizing principle of politics, the three votes highlighted the role and limits of electoral-system design in the quest to manage and contain potentially polarizing divisions.

As the postwar reconstruction of Iraq began to move past the challenge of immediate stabilization into a phase of political reconstruction, one of the key challenges that had to be faced was the selection of a system to elect first the Transitional National Assembly, and then ultimately a permanent National Assembly.[1] Some months after its inception in May 2003, the Coalition Provisional Authority (CPA) commissioned experts from IFES (established as the International Foundation for Election Systems) and elsewhere to advise on how elections might be administered in Iraq. Meanwhile, Iraqi politicians and their advisors were also beginning to consider the question. In theory, all options were on the table: one or another form of proportional representation (PR); the single-member first-past-the-post system (FPTP); some kind of mixed system combining these two methods; the alternative vote (AV); the single transferable vote (STV); and the single nontransferable vote (SNTV).

Most of these options were eliminated early on because they were either impractical or unsuited to Iraq's political circumstances. FPTP was appealing in that it promised to limit the power of parties with autocratic tendencies and to encourage the election of independent and locally rooted representatives, diminishing the prospect of the election morphing into a polarizing referendum based on religious and ethnic identity. As a distinctly majoritarian system, however, FPTP in its pure form was clearly inappropriate for as deeply divided a country as Iraq, where it was important to ensure some degree of fairness in the representation of all major groups as well as smaller minorities.[2] AV was in theory more appealing, for the reason that Donald Horowitz describes: By requiring the voters in each single-member district to *rank* the candidates on the ballot, it forces candidates to compete for the lower-order preferences of voters and thus induces moderation.[3] But it quickly became apparent that neither of these systems would be practical, for the simple reason that a new Iraqi electoral administration—no matter how well assisted and advised it might be by the international community—was not going to have the time, the resources, the reliable census data, or the political credibility to draw the boundaries of some 275 individual districts (the size of parliament that the interim constitution established in March 2004).

One also had to consider the Iraqi voter. Although there were plans for an extensive program of civic education, it was still a priority to keep the ballot and the voting process as simple as possible. Requiring people who had not voted in a democratic election in fifty years to rank several choices on a ballot seemed to be asking too much. For the same reason, STV—which requires the voter to consider and rank even more candidates in multimember districts—was considered even more impractical. All of these systems thus fell by the wayside fairly early in the planning for elections in Iraq. So did any kind of mixed system that would rely in part on single-member districts. So did SNTV—in which the voter selects a single candidate in a multimember district, with no possibility for excess votes to be transferred to other candidates of the same party. Although SNTV is for the voter a very simple system, all the experts knew of its perverse practical implications, which require a considerable degree of planning and coordination among parties and between parties and their supporters to ensure reasonable degrees of proportionality and rationality in outcomes.

Both substantive and practical considerations therefore strongly inclined the outside experts as well as the Iraqi political leaders and their advisors toward some form of PR. In fact, PR was a compelling choice for Iraq for several reasons. First, it fit with the power-sharing or "consociational" logic of institutional design that Iraq was moving to embrace. Proportionality had become a basic principle of Iraqi political life with the July 2003 appointment of the Iraqi Governing Council—whose 25 members represented a delicate balance among Shi'ites, Sunnis, and Kurds in numbers approximating their shares of the population (it also included one member each from the Turkoman and Assyrian Christian minorities).[4] PR sustained the logic that each group should expect to have a share of power roughly proportional to its weight in society. This expectation—which quickly became an entitlement—was deeply worrisome to some Iraqis and foreign advisors, but once the logic was established it became inescapable.

Second, the leaders of the principal Shi'ite and Kurdish political parties were attracted to party-list PR because it promised to reinforce their weight in the political system and give them tighter control over who would run on their party label. PR also made it easier for the various Kurdish and Shi'ite parties to coalesce into common lists. Finally, advocates of a guaranteed quota for women's representation in parliament—such as the Iraqi Higher Women's Council—were drawn to PR because of its greater technical suitability to ensuring women's representation. International experts estimated, for example, that if parties were required to place women at no worse than every third interval on their ranked lists, it was quite likely that a 25 percent minimum quota of female representatives in parliament—the target written into the interim constitution and retained, at least for a transitional period, in the permanent one—could be achieved, even if PR were conducted in a series of multimember districts. Devising a mechanism to ensure a minimum percentage of women in parliament would be much more difficult and cumbersome in a system of single-member districts, or even in a mixed system.

What Kind of PR?

Before too long, then, discussions over electoral-system design turned to the question of what kind of PR would be most suitable for Iraq. In addition to selecting a formula for allocating seats to parties, there were two other issues: whether there should be a minimum threshold for entry into parliament, and the choice between a district-based or national-list system (or some combination of the two). Some CPA officials, including Administrator L. Paul Bremer, wanted to discourage the extreme fragmentation of parliament into an unwieldy body of many small parties while also ensuring representation for ethnic minorities and liberals whose support might be thinly spread across parts of the country. This suggested a modest electoral threshold of no more than 2 or 3 percent of the vote. But as the alarming implications of arbitrarily excluding small religious minorities and secular liberal forces became clear, both the logic of inclusion and the desire to have in parliament as many moderate and independent voices as possible pressed in the direction of no threshold at all.[5]

In early 2004, several Iraqi and international officials began to develop proposals for a two-tiered PR system, based mainly in electoral districts, but with enough seats filled from national lists to ensure overall proportionality between votes and seats. At roughly the same time, in March 2004, an Iraqi advisor to the Governing Council and a U.S. advisor to the CPA independently developed virtually identical proposals for a system in which 220 of the 275 seats would be apportioned among Iraq's 18 provinces—each serving as an electoral district—based on their shares of the population.[6] These district seats would be filled first, using the PR rule within each province, and then the remaining 55 seats (20 percent of the total) would be allocated to national party lists to ensure that each party's or coalition's overall seat share would match as closely as possible its national vote share. (IFES had estimated that if 20 percent of the seats were held back to be filled from national lists, the system could ensure a high degree of overall proportionality.)

There were compelling reasons for basing PR primarily in moderately sized districts coinciding with Iraq's provincial boundaries. First, the provinces were already established. Second, even if the population balance among provinces was in dispute, the second-tier distribution of seats to national lists would ensure overall proportionality. Third, a district-based system would allow some ties to emerge between elected representatives and geographical constituencies. And fourth, it would be easier for voters to judge the individual candidates on each list, making for greater local accountability.

In the end, the decision on an electoral system for Iraq was made principally by Carina Perelli, the chief of the United Nations Electoral Assistance Division (and the head of its mission to Iraq), then adopted by the Iraqi Governing Council and signed into law by Bremer on 15 June 2004 as one of his final acts as CPA administrator. Somewhat unexpectedly, Perelli did not opt for two-tiered PR, but rather for PR in a single nationwide district. She did so for several reasons. It was by far the easiest to administer. It avoided having to determine how to apportion seats to districts, which was a thorny issue given the absence of broadly accepted census data. It neutralized concerns over where people would vote—a problem for natives of one province who might be living in another (and a particular problem for Kirkuk, where the Kurdish parties were energetically trying to resettle Kurds to reverse a previous campaign of ethnic cleansing under the Ba'ath Party). And, as Perelli explained in a June 4 press conference, the single nationwide district would make it easier "for [ethnic and religious] communities that have been broken up and dispersed around Iraq . . . to be able to accumulate their votes and to vote with like-minded people."[7] Yet a district system with a national-list component would also have enabled dispersed communities to aggregate their scattered votes to elect one or more members of parliament even if they lacked the electoral weight to do so from any one province. Without question, however, the nationwide system was easiest.

In the end, there were two chief consequences of Perelli's choice of electoral system for Iraq. First, in the absence of districts, the January 2005 elections became almost purely a national-identity referendum, untempered by any local component or flavor. And second, the lack of any minimum floor of representation for geographical areas, along with a host of other grievances, led most Sunni political parties to boycott the elections.[8] Each of these consequences would have major implications for Iraqi politics.

The First Two Votes

The January 30 elections were to choose a Transitional National Assembly, whose charge was to write a permanent Iraqi constitution, hold a referendum to approve it, and prepare the country for general elections to be held no later than December of the same year. In the midst of endemic violence, January saw a heated election campaign featuring thousands of candidates belonging to more than a hundred parties and coalitions. Noticeable by their absence were the Iraqi Sunnis. A demographic minority constituting some 20 percent of Iraq's population, they had been the country's political and power elite for centuries, a position of dominance that had been cemented under the blatantly sectarian rule of Saddam Hussein. Fearful of losing political power, they tried to thwart and delegitimize the elections, publicly boycotting and belittling them as a U.S. imperialist endeavor, while giving a silent nod to the threats and intimidation employed by the Sunni insurgents.

Ranged against the Sunni rejectionists were the Shi'ites and Kurds, who constitute roughly 60 percent and 20 percent of the country's population, respectively. Both communities had suffered considerably under Saddam's rule and were now determined to seize the moment that would elevate them to political ascendancy. Senior Shi'ite clerics, especially the most venerated Grand Ayatollah Sayyid Ali al-Sistani, publicly urged the Shi'ite majority to go to the polls. The Kurds, on the other hand, needed no encouragement to vote in heavy numbers; they had a major stake in designing a constitution that would safeguard their cultural and political autonomy. In the end, even with an almost total Sunni boycott, a healthy 58 percent of registered voters nationwide went to the polls.

From a vast field of party lists, three blocs emerged to dominate the 275-seat Transitional National Assembly. The largest group, garnering 140 seats, was the United Iraqi Alliance (UIA), a collection of mostly

Shi'ite parties and individuals led by the Supreme Council for Islamic Revolution in Iraq (SCIRI) under the leadership of the cleric Abd al-Aziz al-Hakim and the al-Da'wah party led by Ibrahim al-Jaafari. The Kurdistan Alliance, a coalition of the two major Kurdish parties under the leadership of Masoud Barzani and Jalal Talabani, won 75 seats; and the Iraqi List, a secular group of politicians under the leadership of interim prime minister Iyad Allawi, won 40 seats. Nine small parties accounted for the remaining 20 seats. Given the breakdown of the vote, it was abundantly clear that Iraqis overwhelmingly voted in accord with their ethnic and sectarian identities. Almost all Kurds (probably more than 95 percent) voted for the Kurdistan Alliance, some 75 percent of Shi'ites voted for the UIA, and at least 75 percent of Sunnis opted for their sectarian choice—boycott. Consequently, only 17 of those elected were Sunnis, and most belonged to secular and nationalist lists.

The election outcome was a harsh wakeup call for the Sunnis. Having bet on its failure, they instead emerged as the real losers. Controlling barely 5 percent of the seats in parliament, the Sunnis were left out of the political bargaining through which the new permanent constitution was going to be designed. Very soon after the April 2005 formation of the transitional government, the Sunnis changed their tune and demanded to join the constitution-drafting committee. Realizing that Sunni political inclusion was essential to diminishing the insurgency, the Americans pressed hard for a deal to include the Sunnis, and an agreement was finally reached with Shi'ite and Kurdish political leaders to add 15 voting and 10 nonvoting Sunni delegates to the 55-member drafting committee.

All the horsetrading meant that the constitutional committee did not begin serious deliberations until early July. Faced with an August 15 deadline and a host of contentious yet far-reaching and consequential issues, the committee produced a compromise document that left no fewer than 53 articles to be resolved at some point in the future.[9] Even so, the Sunni committee members refused to validate the document. Their main fear was that Iraq would collapse into a loose federal structure with a Kurdish region in the north and one massive Shi'ite region in the south—together controlling all of Iraq's oil and gas wealth—thus leaving the Sunnis with a central region bereft of resources and power.

As the October 15 referendum approached, intense bargaining among the various groups continued, this time with heavy U.S. involvement. The goal was to reach some political compromise that would address Sunni concerns, particularly those relating to Iraq's envisioned federal structure. Three days prior to the referendum, the Shi'ite and Kurdish leaders consented to the demand of the largest Sunni party, the Iraqi Islamic Party (IIP), for an additional article that called for a new constitutional committee to be formed after the general elections, with the task of implementing within four months of its creation "necessary amendments to the constitution."[10] Its wish having been granted, the IIP urged its followers not only to participate in the referendum, but also to vote in favor of the constitutional document. The following day, insurgents bombed IIP headquarters in the radical Sunni city of Fallujah.

Bringing the IIP on board did not overcome Sunni opposition to the constitution, however. While Shi'ite and Kurdish areas voted overwhelmingly for the adoption of the constitution, two Sunni provinces voted heavily against it, and a third registered a 55 percent negative vote. In fact, the Sunnis narrowly missed defeating the constitution altogether, since Iraq's interim constitution stipulated that a two-thirds majority against the constitutional document in any three of Iraq's 18 provinces would result in its rejection. While the Sunnis failed again to achieve their goal, the feeling among their political leaders was that they made a much greater statement through participation in the referendum than they had by boycotting the January elections.

The December General Elections

As a result, there were hardly any calls among Sunnis for boycotting the December 2005 election of a four-year National Assembly that would put in place a Presidency Council (of a president and two deputies), a prime minister, and a cabinet. Another important factor in the Sunni decision to participate in the December election was a significant change in the electoral system. While retaining the general system of PR without any threshold for representation, the Transitional National Assembly opted this time to employ a two-tiered system very close in design to the one recommended in March 2004 by both Iraqi and international advisors. Slightly more than 80 percent of the seats (230 of 275) were allocated to the provinces as multimember districts, while the remaining 45 seats were to be filled as "compensatory seats" from national lists to achieve overall proportionality. Each province would have a share of the 230 seats proportional to its share of registered voters in the country. Thus, regardless of how many people actually went to the polls in their provinces, the Sunnis were effectively guaranteed a certain bloc of seats in the new Assembly.[11]

Under this system, the seats in parliament were filled in two steps. First, the number of votes cast in each province (formally called governorates) was divided by the number of allocated seats to produce the "governorate quota." Any party that achieved the quota was entitled to one seat, and additional seats were allocated in multiples of the quota. This process was repeated in every province to fill the 230 district-based Assembly seats. The remaining 45 seats were then distributed first among the parties and entities that did not win seats on the provincial level but were able to accumulate votes nationally equal to or higher than the "national electoral quota." This quota was arrived at by dividing the total number of votes in the country by the number of Assembly seats (275). Only one party was able to earn a seat through this compensatory process. The remaining 44 seats were then distributed among all participating parties in accord with their respective national vote shares. Expatriate voting, which took place in 15 countries, was designed to claim a portion of these seats.

The Independent Electoral Commission of Iraq (IECI) announced on October 29 that 228 political parties, coalitions, and other entities had registered to compete in the elections. It was obvious from the start, however, that five coalitions would claim the lion's share of Assembly seats. These were the UIA (having acquired stronger Islamist credentials with the withdrawal of some Shi'ite secularists such as Ahmad Chalabi's Congress party and the incorporation of a group loyal to firebrand Shi'ite cleric Muqtada al-Sadr), the Kurdistan Alliance, Allawi's secular Iraqi National List, and two Sunni lists—the Iraqi Accord Front and the Iraqi Front for National Dialogue.

The most noticeable aspect of the campaign was its seeming localization. The confluence of geographic and ethnosectarian lines in most areas of Iraq precluded serious competition between the various parties and coalitions within their respective provincial strongholds. Thus neither the UIA nor the Sunni fronts bothered to electioneer in the Kurdish areas, and there was hardly any Kurdish presence in Shi'ite and Sunni provinces. Even in the large multiethnic cities—such as Baghdad, Mosul, and Kirkuk—there was little crossing of ethnosectarian lines. Rather, each alliance focused its energy on cementing support among its own base, while doggedly obstructing intrusions by other alliances into its home area. The logic of electoral politics as an identity referendum became further entrenched.

Under such arrangements, the groups that stood to lose most were the secular nonethnic parties and coalitions, whose performance in the elections depended on conducting an effective national campaign. For example, Allawi's Iraqi National List, the most sophisticated and best financed of the secular parties, encountered staunch resistance in areas considered by the UIA to be its own exclusive domain. Allawi's party headquarters were attacked by gunmen in Basrah and Nasiriyah, bombed in Najaf, and burned to the ground in Karbala.[12] Such activities were not confined to the UIA, but involved also the Sunni coalitions and the Kurdistan Alliance. It seems that what one group considered legitimate campaigning, the other saw as unacceptable electoral trespassing.

More unsettling still was a wave of assassinations and armed attacks in Baghdad and other Iraqi cities. A number of these were aimed at Sunni politicians who advocated electoral participation and rejection of violence. Two days after declaring that "nonparticipation in the coming elections is tantamount to treason,"[13] a prominent leader of the Accord was gunned down in broad daylight just outside Baghdad. Indeed, the Front claimed that no fewer than ten of its members were killed, including the head of its organization in the Sunni city of Ramadi.

Workers for other parties and groups were also killed either in individual attacks or in more coordinated assaults on party headquarters.[14]

While such levels of electoral violence and intimidation are hardly unknown in emerging democracies, they did compound the difficulties already presented by the general lack of security in Iraq, and the resulting climate severely limited the party leaders' freedom of movement. They consequently seemed to settle on campaigning through the mass media, especially the electronic media. Satellite and television stations carried incessant commercials for the various parties; in this domain, the Iraqi National List was by far the slickest and had the deepest pockets. But this was balanced by a plethora of feature stories, interviews, and debates involving prominent members of most parties.

Concern over the lack of security, basic services, and economic opportunity dominated much of the campaign rhetoric. The most blistering verbal attacks came from Iyad Allawi and his fellow candidates, who accused the UIA-led transitional government of indecisiveness, incompetence, and corruption while relentlessly decrying the country's many ills—the decrepit sewage system, the paralyzing shortages of electricity, the dearth of jobs, inadequate health care, and above all the violence and chaos of everyday life. In a widely-reported speech shortly before the elections, Allawi declared that the government "has sunk into financial and administrative corruption . . . [and] has left Iraq a weak and divided country on the verge of civil war."[15] He also strongly implied that a UIA government would continue doing Iran's bidding in Iraq, and therefore was enshrining sectarianism in a manner that would lead to the disintegration of the country.

The two Sunni coalitions focused their campaigns on what could be construed as a reversal of the security issue: They attacked the transitional government and the Ministry of the Interior for allegedly unleashing, or at least encouraging, irregular Shi'ite militiamen to assassinate innocent Sunni men in retaliation for atrocities committed by Sunni insurgents. Echoing Allawi's accusation, Sunni politicians also invoked the ghost of bloody civil war, which they placed squarely on the shoulders of the transitional government and its allegedly sectarian and partisan posture.

The second major theme of the campaign was the debate over federalism. From the very beginning of the new political order, the Kurds had made it clear that the price for their willingness to be part of Iraq was an acceptance by the Shi'ites and Sunnis of a loose federal structure in which Kurdistan would be accorded substantial autonomy within Iraq. While debate initially raged over the issue, it was not long before Kurdistan's autonomy had become a *fait accompli* that even the Sunnis grudgingly accepted. But the federalism debate reappeared with renewed intensity when SCIRI chief and UIA leader Abd al-Aziz Hakim proposed the creation of a Shi'ite super-region uniting all nine southern provinces. Sunnis saw the move as a bid to assert control over the 80 percent of Iraq's oil and gas wealth that lay deep in the Shi'ite south, and even as a precursor to the dismantling of Iraq. Bitter denunciations of the plan became a staple of the Sunni campaign.

Another issue on which the parties clashed was the role of religion in politics. The secular Iraqi National List railed against any move to insert religion into politics, implicitly and at times directly criticizing the Shi'ite Islamist UIA. Interestingly, the Sunni electoral alliances—whose most powerful party, the IIP, was an offshoot of the Muslim Brotherhood—also advocated the separation of religion from politics. Obviously, an Islamic state of the Shi'ite variety was hardly palatable to the Sunni fundamentalists. Meanwhile, the UIA, visibly constrained in its defense of the inseparability of religion and politics, held that it sought to remain true to its Islamist essence while reassuring voters that religion would constitute only one of several factors shaping public policy.[16]

Hovering over the religion-in-politics debate was the figure of Grand Ayatollah Sistani, the most senior and revered Shi'ite cleric. While the reclusive ayatollah himself did not make public comments or statements during the campaign, his assistants and disciples spoke on his behalf, emphasizing his neutrality. This did not, however, stop the UIA and other Shi'ite groups from appropriating Sistani to their cause by invoking his name, declaring their fidelity to him, and putting his image on their posters—a practice bitterly denounced by other groups, particularly members of the Iraqi List.

Finally, the campaign saw many references to the "occupation" of Iraq by U.S. and other coalition forces. But this topic never lived up to expectations that it would be the one burning issue to dominate the campaign. No party supported open-ended occupation, and they all pledged to negotiate with the United States some kind of timetable for withdrawal, taking into consideration existing constraints. Naturally, the Sunni parties were the most insistent, but apart from the radical Council of Islamic Scholars—which had rejected participation in an election under occupation—no one advocated immediate withdrawal.

Despite the violence and disruption that infused the campaign, Iraqis went to the polls with a broad awareness of where the main coalitions stood on the dominant issues. The election debate had been generally absorbing and at times fairly sophisticated, suggesting that it would have an impact on voter behavior. Yet when the voters finally went to the polls, they ended up turning to their primordial loyalties very much as they had in the January 30 elections.

More than 12 million Iraqis—representing over 77 percent of registered voters—cast ballots on December 15.[17] The two Sunni provinces of Salah al-Din and Anbar, the three Kurdish provinces of Erbil, Duhok, and Sulaymaniya, and Kirkuk with its Kurdish majority had the highest turnouts (84 percent and above). The average turnout in the nine Shi'ite

TABLE 1—RESULTS OF THE DECEMBER 2005 IRAQI ELECTIONS

PARTY OR ALLIANCE	PERCENT OF NATIONAL VOTE	PERCENT OF NATIONAL SEATS	GOVERNORATE SEATS	NATIONAL SEATS	TOTAL
United Iraqi Alliance (Shiite)	41.2	46.5	109	19	128
Kurdistan Alliance	21.7	19.3	43	10	53
Accord Front (Sunni)	15.1	16.0	37	7	44
Iraqi List (secular)	8.0	9.1	21	4	25
National Dialogue Front (Sunni)	4.1	4.0	9	2	11
Kurdish Islamic Union	1.3	1.8	4	1	5
Liberation & Conciliation (Sunni)	1.1	1.1	3	0	3
Risaliyoon (Shi'ite Sadrists)	1.2	0.7	1	1	2
Turkomen Front	0.7	0.4	1	0	1
Iraqi Nation (secular)	0.3	0.4	1	0	1
Yezidi Front	0.2	0.4	1	0	1
Rafidayn List (Christian)	0.4	0.4	0	1†	1
Total	95.3*	100	230	45	275

* The remaining votes were won by more than 200 other lists that failed to qualify for a single seat.
† This was technically a compensatory seat. This was the lone list to qualify for a national compensatory seat after failing to win any governorate seats.

provinces fell below the national figure at 71 percent, while Baghdad had one of the lowest turnouts, yet still managed a respectable 70 percent.

To ensure the integrity of the elections, the IECI deployed 126,125 observers in all 18 provinces. In addition to 949 international monitors, the political parties and coalitions themselves spread another 272,295 agents across the 31,348 polling stations around the country. As the chief electoral officer remarked, "This election has been one of the most observed in the whole world."[18]

Still, when partial results were announced a few days after the election, showing a victory for the UIA, a deluge of complaints alleging widespread fraud erupted in Baghdad and Sunni areas. Thousands of demonstrators took to the streets denouncing the IECI and accusing it of doing the UIA's bidding. The pressure became so intense that the IECI refrained from publishing the full and final results until an international commission, which arrived in Baghdad in late December, looked into the 1,985 complaints received by the IECI. The international commission decided that while infractions had indeed occurred, they had been mostly minor and would not affect the final distribution of Assembly seats. Hence, the final and complete results were announced on 17 January 2006 and certified on February 10, confirming once again both the victory of the UIA and the heavily sectarian character of the voting (Table 1).

The results show a clear preponderance of ethnosectarian loyalties. Any hopes that the electorate would vote to separate religion from politics or to transcend ethnic fissures were completely frustrated. The wish, certainly harbored by the Bush administration, for a muscular showing by the secular Iraqi List that would cement Allawi's bargaining posi-

TABLE 2—ETHNOSECTARIAN PATTERNS OF DECEMBER 15 VOTING

GOVERNORATE	ETHNICITY	# OF SEATS	UIA & OTHER SHI'ITES	IRAQI LIST	SUNNI LISTS	KURDISH LISTS	OTHERS
Basrah	Shi'ite	16	13	2	1	–	–
DhiQar	Shi'ite	12	11	1	–	–	–
Babel	Shi'ite	11	9	1	1	–	–
Najaf	Shi'ite	8	7	1	–	–	–
Qaddisya	Shi'ite	8	7	1	–	–	–
Misan	Shi'ite	7	6	1	–	–	–
Wasit	Shi'ite	8	7	1	–	–	–
Karbala	Shi'ite	6	5	1	–	–	–
Muthana	Shi'ite	5	5	–	–	–	–
Anbar	Sunni	9	–	–	9	–	–
Salah al-Din	Sunni	8	1	1	6	–	–
Sulaymaniya	Kurdish	15	–	–	–	15	–
Irbil	Kurdish	13	–	–	–	13	–
Duhok	Kurdish	7	–	–	–	7	–
Baghdad	Mixed[1]	59	35	8	14	1	1
Nineveh	Mixed[2]	19	2	2	10	4	1
Diyala	Mixed[2]	10	2	1	5	2	–
Kirkuk	Mixed[3]	9	–	–	3	5	1

[1] Shi'ite majority; [2] Sunni majority; [3] Kurdish majority

tion—or even allow him to emerge as the central character in a secular coalition—was shattered when the party ended up obtaining only about 8 percent of the vote, losing almost half the seats that it had received in the January 2005 election. The extent of the ethnosectarian character of the vote is better observed when voting is broken down at the provincial level. As Table 2 shows, the UIA dominated the voting in the nine southern Shi'ite provinces, winning 70 of the 81 district seats.[19] The two Kurdish lists (secular and Islamic) together won all 35 seats in Kurdistan. And the Sunni lists won 15 of the 17 seats in the predominantly Sunni Anbar and Salah al-Din provinces.

Why did the change in electoral system have no apparent effect in diminishing the sectarian pattern of the voting? There are at least three possible explanations. First, the electoral terrain was strongly defined by the January 30 elections and the old electoral system. Compounding all that had transpired in the nature of governance and politics since the fall of Saddam's regime, the January elections created such momentum for identity politics that it would have been asking too much of the district-based voting system to effect much change. Second, one might have expected the district-based PR system to aid the election of local and independent candidates. In the climate of widespread violence, however, a great many candidates declined even to reveal their identities, putting the premium on identification with parties and alliances.

Third, the only list that transcended the country's deep ethnic and sectarian cleavages was led by a politician, Iyad Allawi, whose tenure as interim prime minister had suffered from most of the flaws of ineffective performance for which he later condemned the UIA-led transitional government, and who was easily stigmatized as a former Ba'athist and paid agent of the CIA. This underscores that, when the underlying pressures and constraints are powerful and entrenched, a change in the electoral system may in the near term do little to transcend them.

The New Policy-Making Institutions

Since no party achieved an overall majority, the elected members of the National Assembly will have to cross ethnosectarian lines to get things done. In fact, a two-thirds majority (184 of the 275 members) is required to pass some significant measures. To begin with, no government can be formed until two-thirds of the National Assembly agrees on a single slate of candidates for the Presidency Council. Moreover, in constructing a viable coalition, factors other than numbers have to be considered. The specter of the insurgency, for instance, makes Sunni demands far weightier than their 55 seats. While it was obvious to all parties that Sunnis had to be included in the government, the dilemma after the election was how to balance the distribution of cabinet portfolios among the prospective coalition partners. The debate showed clear disparities in the aspirations and positions of the various parties: While Sunnis talked of a national-unity government, implying a kind of equality among the coalition parties, the UIA emphasized a governmental balance based on the election results.[20] For the sake of successful governance and effective policy making, significant compromises on all sides will need to be made and adhered to, not just in the immediate period but throughout the four-year life of the Assembly.

One factor that might enhance the fluidity of alliance-making is that, while the various party lists seem to be fairly cohesive on matters of identity, they differ within themselves on other issues. The UIA is particularly noteworthy in this regard. While Islamist Shi'ism constitutes the raison d'être of its four main constituent groups—SCIRI, al-Da'wah, al-Fadhilah, and the Sadrists—personal tensions, historic rivalries, and policy differences permeate their relations with one another. In fact, al-Fadhilah announced its withdrawal from the UIA on November 1, citing unhappiness with some of Hakim's policies and his handling of Assembly-seat distribution. They ended up remaining part of the UIA only because the IECI would not accede to their request.[21]

Differences surfaced after the election when al-Fadhila talked about the possibility of negotiating with the Allawi group, breaking with a seeming UIA consensus and drawing a sharp rebuke from the Sadrists.[22] Neither, for that matter, are relations between SCIRI and the Sadrists consistently fraternal. The Sadrists, who resent Hakim's seeming demeanor as the acknowledged head of the UIA, censured him for negotiating with the Kurds after the election, calling it "a personal endeavor that did not enjoy the UIA's blessings."[23] The Sadrists seem to have a pronounced affinity with Sunni groups, and as such do not support Hakim's idea of a nine-province Shi'ite region. Moreover, the militias of SCIRI and Sadr have clashed bloodily in the recent past.

Divisions within the other groups may not be as well publicized, but they exist. It remains to be seen whether the alliance of the two Kurdish leaders, Barzani and Talabani, and their parties will stand the test of time, or whether the two Sunni blocs will consistently vote together and refrain from striking different political bargains and entering into new alliances. There is thus some possibility in the new Assembly of increasing fluidity in coalitional politics, as new issues surface and the benefits of power await distribution. With good fortune and artful political management, it is possible that Iraq could gradually edge away from the high degree of ethnic and sectarian polarization produced by the past "year of voting dangerously." The ability of the parties and politicians to manage and mitigate this polarization, through negotiation and compromise, will likely determine not only the scope for democratic development but even Iraq's ability to survive as one country.

NOTES

1. The transition plan announced by U.S. officials on 15 November 2003 provided for direct elections for a constitutional convention but only indirect elections for the Transitional National Assembly. This met with intense Iraqi protest and was abandoned after UN mediation in favor of direct elections for the National Assembly—which was to act as both a parliament and a constitutional convention—by 31 January 2005.

2. Although this was the widely shared view of international experts and most Iraqi political leaders, some Americans nevertheless continued strongly to advocate FPTP while condemning PR. See, for example, Michael Rubin, "The Wrong Elections for Iraq," *Washington Post,* 19 June 2004.

3. Donald L. Horowitz, "Electoral Systems: A Primer for Decision Makers," *Journal of Democracy* 14 (October 2003): 115–27.

4. Later, when Iraqi ministers were appointed under the CPA, the ethnic and sectarian balance in the Governing Council was replicated.

5. In the typical situation, an electoral threshold is often favored in part to keep small extremist parties out of parliament. In Iraq, however, it became apparent that radical movements and parties like Muqtada al-Sadr's probably had enough support to clear any electoral threshold, while some of the more liberal politicians and parties would likely have had to struggle to obtain the needed vote share.

6. The population shares could be estimated based on either the 1997 census or the food-ration data, but in fact they yielded similar percentages for each province. The U.S. advisor also suggested the possibility of breaking up the largest provinces, particularly Baghdad (which had almost a fourth of the 220 district seats),

into multiple districts.

7. Carina Perelli, Coalition Provisional Authority Briefing, Baghdad, 4 June 2004. Transcript available at *www.iraqcoalition.org/transcripts/20040604_Perelli_Prep.html*.

8. The Sunni parties feared that without guaranteed district representation, based on the provinces, the much greater degree of violence, intimidation, and resentment in their areas would result in a sharply lower voter turnout, leaving them underrepresented. Yet by boycotting, they left themselves virtually unrepresented. Larry Diamond, *Squandered Victory: The American Occupation and the Bungled Effort to Bring Democracy to Iraq* (New York: Times Books, 2005), 323.

9. There was in fact strong sentiment in the Transitional Assembly to vote for a six-month postponement of the deadline, as the interim constitution allowed on a one-time basis. But the United States was strongly opposed to it, and the Sunnis as well were not enthusiastic about remaining in the inferior status of unelected members.

10. *Al-Rafidayn* (Baghdad), 13 October 2005.

11. Specifically, all or at least most of the nine seats allocated to Anbar Province and the eight seats allocated to Salah Al-Din, plus a good share of the seats in the mixed provinces such as Nineveh, which has 19 seats.

12. For the above incidents, see *Al-Sharq al-Awsat* (London), 9 and 11 December 2005; *Al-Ahali* (Baghdad), 7 December 2005; and *Al-Rafidayn* (Baghdad), 29 November and 17 December 2005.

13. *Al-Sharq al-Awsat,* 30 November 2005.

14. *New York Times,* 11 December 2005.

15. *Al-Sharq al-Awsat,* 11 December 2006.

16. The gist of the UIA position was that political decisions are based on considerations of the national interest, but most Iraqis after all are devout Muslims who will not be comfortable with Western-type secularism.

17. Out of 15,568,702 registered voters, 11,895,756 valid votes, 139,656 invalid votes, and 62,836 blank votes were cast in all Iraqi governorates.

18. "Observers' reports tell of good conduct of elections," Independent Electoral Commission press release, 24 December 2005, available at *www.ieciraq.org.*

19. The disparity between the UIA's percentage of national votes and parliamentary seats is probably explained by the IECI's decision to use Hare's "Largest Remainder Method" to distribute seats.

20. *Al-Sabah* (Baghdad), 14 January 2006; *al-Arabiya* television station, 14 January 2006.

21. *Al-Rafidayn,* 2 December 2005.

22. *Al-Hayat* (London), 6 January 2006.

23. *Al-Ahali,* 4 January 2006.

INDEX

Afghanistan, 18*t*, 21*t;* democracy in,
  210–11, 216, 222; election
  results in, 221*t;* ethnic groups in,
  218*t;* parties in, 219; SNTV in,
  xxiv, 21, 23, 197, 210–23
Albania, 18*t*, 21
Alliance for Democracy (AFORD)
  (Malawi), 123, 141*t*, 151
Alternative vote (AV), xi-xiv, xxv,
  9–12, 17, 20, 29, 32–33, 122; in
  Australia, xiv, 9, 20, 32–33, 59,
  106; in Fiji, 9, 20, 34–35, 37, 39,
  44; in Iraq, 44, 225; in Papua
  New Guinea, 9, 20, 22, 35–37,
  38–40, 59–60
Angola, 18*t*, 123, 129, 133, 148*t*
Argentina, 18*t*, 64, 165, 169, 170;
  malapportionment in, 171–74
Australia, 18*t*, 62*t*, 79*t;* AV in, xiv,
  9, 20, 32–33, 59, 106; centripetal
  systems in, 33; constitutional
  crisis of, 51; federalism in, 61,
  64–66; parliamentary-plurality
  system in, 75, 78, 98; preferential voting in, xiii, 38; presidency
  in, 50; STV in, xiv, 32–33
Australian Labor Party, 33
Austria, 18*t*, 78, 79*t*, 98, 100, 148*t;*
  proportionality in, 64

Belgium, 18*t*, 28, 45, 62*t*, 64, 69,

79*t*, 98–100, 148*t;* minorities in,
  49, 51, 78, 88, 127; PR in, 113,
  127
Belize, 18*t*, 170*t*
Benin, 8, 18*t*, 148*t*
Block vote (BV), 17, 18*t*–19*t*, 20
Bolivia, xii, 18*t*, 21*t*, 170*t;* malap-
  portionment in, 169, 171–72,
  178; MMP in, 21, 22
Borda count, 18*t*–19*t*, 21
Bosnia, 18*t*, 30, 45
Botswana, 18*t*, 123, 148*t*
Brazil, xxi, 18*t*, 62*t*, 170*t;* federalism
  in, 61, 64, 65; malapportionment
  in, 169–75
Bulgaria, 18*t*, 22
Burke, Edmund, 93

Cameroon, 18*t*, 20
Canada, 18*t*, 62*t*, 79*t*, 141*t*, 148*t*,
  150*t;* federalism in, 61, 64–67;
  FPTP/SMP in, 8, 9, 20, 24, 68,
  69, 75, 98; power sharing in, 43
Centrifugal effects, 27, 93, 96, 122
Centripetal systems, xii, 30, 37, 38,
  40; in Australia, 33; in Fiji, 34;
  in Israel, 189; in Northern
  Ireland, 30–31, 37–39
Chad, 18*t*, 20
Chaudhry, Mahendra, 34–35
Chile, 18*t*, 170*t;* malapportionment

Chile *(continued)*
in, 169–173; presidentialism in, 83, 156, 181n.22
Colombia, 18*t*, 43, 45, 77, 170*t;* malapportionment in, 169, 177
Condorcet winners, x, 4, 6, 10, 11; in Lebanon, 10
Consensus model; xv, xvi, 74
Consociational model, xiii, 10, 28, 43, 56, 64, 125, 136, 138, 140, 143, 146, 148; in Iraq, 226. *See also* Power-sharing
Coombs rule, 6, 11, 14
Costa Rica, 18*t*, 77, 83, 148*t*, 170*t*
Cyprus, 18*t*, 43, 45
Czech Republic, 18*t*, 45, 110–11

Dahl, Robert A., 79*t*, 102, 168, 179n.1, 180n.9
Democracy, 74*t*, 79*t*, 80*t;* in Afghanistan, 210–11, 216, 222; character of, ix–x; commitment to, x; consensus model of, xv, 69, 74, 131; consociational, 10, 43, 125, 136, 138, 140, 143, 148; culture of, 26; developing countries and, 83; in divided societies, 27–28, 43, 47, 82–83, 103, 129, 150, 214; in East Asia, 197; economic development and, 80–83, 87, 177; and elections, 168, 196; impact of electoral systems on, 17, 27; failures of, 102; in Israel, 182; in Latin America, 77, 155, 169–71, 179; law and order and, 80, 85n.13; majoritarian model of, 73; in Papua New Guinea, 35, 37; and parties, 47–48, 214; power-sharing model of, xiii, 28, 43–45, 136; quality of, xv, xxi, 76, 171–72, 179; in South Africa, 91, 123, 137; success of, 26; sustainable, 16, 27, 131, 137;

threats to, x, 150; transitions to, xviii, 22, 90–91, 126, 133, 135, 137, 156, 170, 181n.19, 202, 205, 210; in Uruguay, xxi, 154–56, 162, 165; in Zimbabwe, 124
Denmark, 18*t*, 79*t*, 148*t;* PR in, xiv, 47, 54n.15, 78, 87, 98, 100, 114
Direct election, 89; in Israel, xxii, 182–95; in the United States, 64
Djibouti, 18*t*, 20
Dominican Republic, 18*t*, 170*t*
Double-simultaneous vote (DSV): in Uruguay, xx, xxi, 157–58

Ecuador, 18*t*, 170*t;* malapportionment in, 165, 169–74
El Salvador, 18*t*, 170*t;* malapportionment in, 178
Electoral systems: aims of, x, xi, 3–7, 93; changes to, ix, xi, 21–24, 156–157, 184; continuity of, 25, 26; design of, ix–x, 16–17, 121, 132, 211; inventory of, 18*t*–19*t*
Estonia, 18*t;* list-PR in, 22; preferential voting in, xiii; STV in, 30–32, 39
Ethnic groups: in Afghanistan, 218*t;* in Australia, 32–33; in Belgium, 49, 78, 88; in Benin, 8; conciliation among, xi, 6, 7, 27–40, 42–52; conflict management among, xii, xv, xvi; consociational model and, xiii, xvi, 28; in Fiji, xiii, 30, 34–35; in India, 40, 145n.16; in Iraq, xxv, 233–34, 235*t*, 236–37; in Kenya, 142; in Lebanon, xi, 6, 28; in Malawi, xix, 123; in Malaysia, 40, 43, 82; in Nigeria, xvi, 6, 7, 14, 28, 54n.8, 82; in Northern Ireland, 30–31, 39, 82; in Papua New Guinea, 30, 35–37; PR and, 16, 28, 46, 88, 104; in South Africa, xviii, 91. *See also* Minorities;

Religious groups
European Parliament, 58, 65, 66

Federalism, xiii–xv, 50–51, 56–70;
    in Australia, 61, 64–66; in
    Brazil, 61, 64–65; in Canada, 61,
    64–67; in Iraq, 232; in Latin
    America, 168–79; in the United
    States, 50, 61, 64
Fiji, 18*t*, 21*t*; AV in, 9, 20, 34–35,
    37, 39, 44; balloting in, 25;
    centripetal system in, 34; ethnic
    groups in, xiii, 30, 34–35;
    power-sharing in, 44; preferen-
    tial voting in, xiii
Finland, 18*t*, 78, 79*t*, 84n.4, 87, 90,
    98, 101, 148*t*
First-past-the-post (FPTP), xi–xii,
    xv, xviii–xix, xxiii–xxiv, 17,
    18*t*–19*t*, 20, 22, 112; in Africa,
    xix, 102–3; in English-speaking
    countries, 8, 20, 24, 148; in
    India, 9, 20, 24; in Iraq, xxiv,
    225; in Japan, 199–201, 204–5;
    in Malaysia, 8, 9; and political
    parties, 9; in Taiwan, 202–3,
    207; in the United States, xi, 8,
    20, 112. *See also* Plurality
    systems; Single-member
    plurality systems
France, 8, 18*t*, 105, 115; Fifth
    Republic in, 48–50, 89; Fourth
    Republic in, xvi, 89, 94–95, 102;
    mixed system in, 59, 75, 86,
    103; PR in, xvi, 88, 103, 108–9;
    TRS in, 20
Free Democratic Party (Germany),
    88, 110

Germany, xv, 18*t*, 49, 62*t*–63*t*, 64,
    66, 67, 74, 78, 79*t*, 81, 98-100,
    106, 148*t*; malapportionment in,
    175; mixed member proportional

(MMP) in, xii, xiii, 8, 21, 60, 86,
    90, 103–6, 115, 125; parties in,
    xviii, 109–10, 114; Weimar
    Republic, xvi, 95, 102
Greece, 18*t*, 88, 90, 109
Guatemala, 18*t*, 170*t*
Gurr, Ted Robert, 43

Hanson, Pauline, 33
Honduras, 18*t*, 170*t*
Hungary, 18*t*, 21, 22, 26, 111

India, xvii, 8, 18*t*, 43, 46, 51, 63*t*,
    64, 74*t*, 75; ethnic groups in, 40,
    145n.16; FPTP in, 9, 20, 24
Indonesia, 7, 18*t*, 30
Iraq, 18*t*, 21*t*; AV in, 44, 225;
    balloting in, 25, 220; consocia-
    tional model in, 226; elections in,
    224–37; electoral systems
    considered, xiv, xxiv, 224–25;
    ethnic groups in, xxv, 44, 235*t*;
    FPTP in, 225; power sharing in,
    43–44, 52; PR in, xxv, 22, 225–
    28
Ireland, 18*t*, 75, 78, 148*t*; STV in,
    8, 9, 20, 23–25, 38, 84n.4, 106
Israel, 18*t*, 78*t*, 148*t*; centripetal
    system in, 189; democracy in,
    182; direct election in, xxii, 182–
    95; Palestinian problem in, 88;
    parties in, 13, 183, 188–89,
    190*t*; PR in, x, xvii, 90, 101,
    177, 180, 182–83, 187–88
Italy, 18*t*, 21*t*, 79*t*, 148*t*; changes to
    electoral systems in, 22, 65;
    mixed system in, xii, 8, 21, 46,
    52, 65, 68–69, 78, 80–81;
    parties in, 67–69, 88, 95; prewar,
    xvi, 94; PR in, xvii, 90, 95, 98,
    100, 126; stability of, 80

Jamaica, 18*t;* 69, 74*t,* 75
Japan, 18*t,* 21*t,* 204*t;* changes to
    electoral system in, xxiv, 14, 22,
    65, 194, 196–201; FPTP in,
    199–201, 204–5; mixed-PR in,
    8, 46, 75, 201; parties in, 204–5;
    SNTV in, xxii, xxiii, 19, 22, 46,
    196–201
Justice and Development Party
    (Turkey), 13

Karzai, Hamid, xxiv, 23, 212–13,
    215–21, 223n.9
Kenya, 18*t,* 140, 141*t,* 148*t;* ethnic
    groups in, 142
Kyrgyzstan, 18*t,* 21

Lebanon, 18*t;* Condorcet winners
    in, 10; ethnic conciliation in, xi,
    6, 28; power sharing in, 43–46
Lesotho, 18*t,* 21*t,* 123, 148*t*
Lewis, W. Arthur, 53n.2, 102, 121–
    22
Limited vote (LV), 21, 46, 54n.13
Linz, Juan J., 47–48, 73, 77, 154,
    158
Lithuania, 18*t,* 22*t*

Malapportionment, 4, 5, 13; in
    Argentina, 171–74; in Bolivia,
    169, 171–72, 178; in Brazil,
    169–75; in Chile, 171–73; in
    Colombia, 169, 177; in Ecuador,
    165, 169–74; in El Salvador,
    178; in Germany, 175; in Latin
    America, xxi–xxii, 168–79; in
    Mexico, 176; in Nicaragua, 178;
    in Paraguay, 177; in Peru, 177;
    single-district chambers and,
    177–78; in the United Kingdom,
    177; in the United States, 175; in
    Uruguay, 177; in Venezuela, 178

Malawi, xix, 18*t,* 122–24, 128, 129,
    130–31, 141*t,* 143, 147, 149,
    151; PR in, xviii–xix, 123
Malawi Congress Party (MCP),
    123, 141*t*
Malaysia, 18*t,* 74*t,* 75, 82; ethnic
    groups in, 40, 43, 82; FPTP in,
    8, 9
Mandela, Nelson, 123, 131, 137,
Marshall Plan, 94–96
Mexico, 19*t,* 21*t,* 170*t;* IFE in, xxi,
    176; malapportionment in, xxi,
    176; mixed system in, xii, 21–
    23, 178; parties in, 90
Minorities, x, xi, xiv, 7, 22, 28, 29,
    52, 58, 152; in Afghanistan, 214;
    in Africa, 39–40; in Belgium, 49,
    51, 78, 88, 127; in Fiji, 34; in
    Iraq, 44, 225–27; in Northern
    Ireland, 44; PR and, 46, 75, 78,
    86–89, 122, 126; single-member
    districts and, 138–39; SMP and,
    69. *See also* Ethnic groups;
    Religious groups
Mixed electoral systems, xi, xii,
    xxv, 21–13, 46, 59–60, 65, 115;
    in France, 59, 75, 86, 103; in
    Germany, xii, xiii, 8, 21, 60, 86,
    90, 103–6, 115, 125; in Iraq,
    225; in Italy, xii, 8, 21, 46, 52,
    65, 68–69, 78, 80–81; in Japan
    and Taiwan, 196–205; in Latin
    America, 178; in Mexico, xii,
    21–23, 178; MMP (mixed-
    member proportional), 21, 22,
    66; in New Zealand, 9, 20, 34–
    35, 37, 39, 44; parallel system,
    21
Moldova, 19*t,* 21*t,* 22
Mozambique, 19*t,* 122–23, 133,
    148*t*

Namibia, 122-123, 125, 127, 129,
    130-131, 141*t* 143; power-

sharing in, 125; PR in, xviii,
137–38

National Front (FN) (France), 88,
109, 126

Nauru, 19*t*, 21

Netherlands, the, 19*t*, 79*t*, 148*t*;
power-sharing in, 28, 43, 51; PR
in, x, xvii, 22–23, 78, 81, 98–
100, 106–8, 112–14, 126, 177

New Zealand, 19*t*, 21*t*, 79*t*, 148*t*,
150*t*; changes to electoral
system, 22; mixed system in, 9,
20, 34–35, 37, 39, 44

Nicaragua, 19*t*, 170*t*; malapportionment in, 178

Nigeria, 19*t*, 129, 133; ethnic
conciliation in, xvi, 6, 7, 14, 28,
54n.8, 82

Nordic countries, 23, 78, 86–87,
98–100

Northern Ireland: centripetal
systems in, 30, 31, 37–39;
federalism in, 56, 58; power-
sharing in, 31, 45, 55n.21, 82;
STV in, 39, 64, 66–68

Northern League (Italy), 68–69

Norway, 19*t*, 78, 79*t*, 87, 98, 100,
112, 148*t*

Papua New Guinea, 19*t*; AV in, 9,
20, 22, 35–37, 39; cabinet
stability in, 49; centripetal
election rules in, 30; changes to
electoral system in, 22, 35–37;
democracy in, 35, 37; ethnic
groups in, 30, 35–37; preferential voting in, xiii, 35

Panama, 19*t*, 170*t*

Paraguay, 19*t*, 90, 165, 170*t*;
malapportionment in, 177

Parallel system, xii, 19*t*, 21, 22, 23

Parti Québécois (Canada), 68

Parties: in Afghanistan, 219; antisystem, 68; democracy and,

47–48, 214; electoral systems'
effects on, 9, 16, 79, 87, 108;
extremist, 88, 126–127; and
FPTP, 9; in France, 109; in
Germany, 109–10; in Iraq, 228–
37, 234*t*; in Israel, 183, 188–89,
190*t*; in Italy, 67–69, 88, 95; in
Japan, 204–5; in Mexico, 90; in
Namibia, 138; and plurality
systems, 70, 89; in Poland, 111–
12; in Portugal, 113; and PR, 13,
47–48, 68, 87, 88, 97, 147; in
South Africa, 125; in Taiwan,
203, 205–7; territorial subnational, 67; in Uruguay, 155–56

Party block vote (PBV), 17,18*t*, 19*t*,
20

Peru, xxi, 19*t*, 170*t*; malapportionment in, 177

Philippines, 19*t*, 21*t*, 74*t*, 75

Plurality systems, xvi–xvii, 9, 17,
65, 66, 73, 78, 79*t*, 80*t*, 89; in
Africa, 123–24, 127, 134–44,
141*t*, 146–53, 148*t*; in Canada,
68; and economic indicators, 80,
81; and parties, 89; and PR, 92–
97, 98–104, 105–15, 146–53; in
the United Kingdom, 75, 107,
127; in the United States, 75, 76,
78, 78, 81, 86, 103, 149; in
Zambia, 122–24, 127, 149, 151.
See also Alternative vote; Block
vote; First-past-the-post; Party
block vote; Single-member
plurality systems; Two-round
system

Poland, 19*t*, 22, 111–12, 114

Portugal, 19*t*, 86, 90, 103, 113, 106,
117n.21, 148*t*

Power-sharing, xiii–xv, xxi, 28, 42–
52, 129–32, 136; in Fiji, 34; in
Iraq, 226; in Namibia, 125; in the
Netherlands, 28, 43, 51; in
Northern Ireland, 31, 45, 55n.21,
82; in South Africa, 125,

Power-sharing *(continued)*
134n.12, 140
Preferential electoral systems, xii,
xiii, xvi, 11, 12, 17, 28, 29–40,
41n.9, 110, 207. *See also*
Alternative vote; Single transferable vote
Presidentialism, xv, 47–48, 82; in
Africa, 129–32; (with plurality)
in the United States, 75, 76, 78,
79, 81, 86, 103, 149
Proportionality, x, xii, xiv, xi–xxx,
4, 5, 7, 11–13, 22–23, 41n.9, 46,
47, 53n.1, 56, 58, 60, 64, 65, 67,
76, 104–6, 112–13, 115,
117n.20, 128, 142–44, 145n.15,
146–49, 151, 152, 179n.2, 192,
200, 203, 205, 208n.12, 212,
214, 225–27, 230
Proportional representation (PR), x,
xi, xiii–xviii, 22, 28, 58–59, 64–
66, 73, 74*t,* 75–83, 86–91,
92–97, 98–104, 105–15; in
Africa, xviii, xix, 121–33, 135–
45, 141*t,* 146–53, 148*t;* in
Belgium, 113, 127; in Benin, 8;
in Britain, 58, 65, 151; criticism
of, 92–97; in Denmark, xiv, 47,
54n.15, 78, 87, 98, 100, 114;
and economic indicators, 81; and
ethnic groups, 16, 28, 46, 88,
104; extreme vs. moderate, 74,
100; in France, xvi, 88, 103,
108–9; in Iraq, xxv, 22, 225–28;
in Israel, x, xvii, 90, 101, 177,
180, 182–83, 187–88, in Italy,
xvii, 90, 95, 98, 100, 126; in
Japan, 8, 46, 75, 201; list-
system, 9–10, 12–13, 20, 22, 28,
47, 81, 124, 128, 152-153, 165;
in Malawi, xviii, 123; in
Namibia, xviii, 137–38; in the
Netherlands, x, xvii, 22–23, 78,
81, 98–100, 106–8, 112–14,
126, 177; and parties, 13, 68, 74,

87, 88, 97, 147; in South Africa,
xvii–xx, 123–40, 147–48, 153;
strengths of, 83, 90, 103, 128; in
Uruguay, 157, 159; and voter
participation, 79, 86; in Zambia,
xviii, 123–24; in Zimbabwe,
xviii, 123–24. *See also*
Alternative vote; Single transferable vote
Puerto Rico, 75, 208n.2

Ramos, Fidel, 26
Religious groups: in Afghanistan,
xxiv; conciliation among, xii, 4,
6, 10, 14, 27, 46, 51; and
federalism, 64; and FPTP, 225;
in Iraq, 227–28, 235*t;* in Israel,
xxii, 184, 186, 188, 191–93; in
Northern Ireland, 58, 82; and
PR, 75, 78, 94, 127, 136. *See
also* Ethnic groups
Romania, 19*t,* 22
Russia, 19*t,* 21*t,* 22, 90

Sartori, Giovanni, 10, 15n.4, 17, 74,
Scotland, 68
Singapore, 19*t,* 20, 40, 91
Single-member plurality systems
(SMP), 57–70, 62*t,* 63*t;* in
Britain, 65; in Canada, 68, 69;
and minorities, 69; and parties,
70; in Scotland, 68. *See also*
First-past-the-post
Single non-transferable vote
(SNTV), xxi–ixxiv, xxvi, 18*t,*
19*t;* in Afghanistan, xxiv, 21,
23, 210–23; in Iraq, 225; in
Japan, xxii, xxiii, 19, 22, 46,
196–201; in South Korea, 197;
in Taiwan, xxii–xxiv, 196–99,
201–3, 206, 208n.2, 211
Single transferable vote (STV), xii,
xiv, xxv, 5, 12, 18*t,* 19*t,* 20, 29,

38–40, 59-60, 62*t*, 63*t*; in
  Australia, xiv, 32–33; in Estonia,
  31–32; in Iraq, 225; in Ireland, 8,
  9, 20, 23–25, 38, 84n.4, 106; in
  Northern Ireland, 30–31, 39, 64,
  66–68; in the United Kingdom,
  66
Sinn Fein (Northern Ireland), 31, 68
Social Democratic and Labour Party
  (SDLP) (Northern Ireland), 31,
  67
South Africa, 19*t*, 21*t*, 50, 91, 122,
  129, 131–32, 141*t*, 145n.16;
  democracy in, 91, 123, 137;
  ethnic groups in, xxviii, 91;
  power-sharing in, 49, 54n.9,
  140; PR in, xviii–xx, 123–40,
  147–48, 153
South Korea, xxii, 19*t*, 82, 91,
  208n.2; SNTV in, 197
Spain, 19*t*, 21, 49, 63*t*, 67, 86, 103
Sweden, 18, 19*t*, 66, 78, 79*t*, 81, 87,
  148*t*; PR in, xv, 98–100, 101,
  112, 125
Switzerland, 19*t*, 28, 43, 52, 61, 63*t*,
  64, 75, 78, 91, 148*t*, 155

Taiwan, 19*t*, 82, 91, 206*t*; FPTP in,
  202–3, 207; parties in, 205–7;
  SNTV in, xxii–xxiv, 196–99,
  201–3, 206, 208n.2, 211
Two-round system (TRS), 17, 18*t*,
  19*t*; in France, 20, 59

Ukraine, 19*t*, 21*t*, 22
United Democratic Front (UDF)
  (Malawi), 123, 141*t*, 149, 150*t*
United Kingdom (U.K.), 19*t*, 74*t*,
  79*t*, 141*t*, 148*t*, 150*t*; FPTP/SMP
  (plurality) in, xvii, 8, 20, 24, 30,
  57, 66, 67, 75, 78, 81, 83, 99,
  107, 110, 112–14, 126, 148,
  149; malapportionment in, 177;

PR in, 58, 65, 151; Westminster
  model in, 96. *See also* Nothern
  Ireland; Scotland
United States, 19*t*, 74*t*, 79*t*, 170*t*;
  electoral boundaries in, 24;
  federalism in, 50, 61, 64
  FPTP in, xi, 8, 20, 112;
  malapportionment in, 153, 175;
  minorities in, 7; preferential
  voting in, 30, 41n.9, 46;
  presidentialism and plurality, 75,
  76, 78–81, 86, 103, 149; SMP
  in, 57; voter turnout in, 79, 86,
  102; "yellow dog" candidates in,
  151
Uruguay, 19*t*, 154–67, 170*t*;
  democracy in, xxi, 154–56, 162,
  165; DSV in, xx, xxi, 157–58;
  malapportionment in, 177; PR in,
  157

Venezuela, 19*t*, 21*t*, 22, 77, 170*t*,
  181n.21; malapportionment in,
  178
Voting Rights Act, 7

Westminster system, xvi, 73, 82–83,
  89, 96, 149

Yeltsin, Boris, 90

Zaire, 123, 133
Zambia, xviii, 19*t*, 148*t*, 150*t*;
  plurality elections in, 122–24,
  127, 149, 151
Zimbabwe, 19*t*, 150*t*; democracy in,
  124; plurality system in, 123–24,
  127, 147, 149, 151; presidentialism in, 129, 130–31